Units

Acceleration $\rightarrow \frac{m}{s^2}$

Angular momentum $\rightarrow \frac{kg\,m^2}{s}$

Charge $\rightarrow C$

Coefficient kinetic friction $\rightarrow$ *no units*

Coefficient static friction $\rightarrow$ *no units*

Current $\rightarrow A = \frac{C}{s}$

Electric field $\rightarrow \frac{N}{C}$

Electric potential difference $\rightarrow V = \frac{J}{C}$

Energy $\rightarrow J = N\,m$

Force $\rightarrow N = \frac{kg\,m}{s^2}$

Frequency $\rightarrow H_z = \frac{1}{s}$

Heat $\rightarrow J = N\,m$

Intensity $\rightarrow \frac{W}{m^2}$

Internal energy $\rightarrow J = N\,m$

Kinetic Energy $\rightarrow J = N\,m$

Magnetic Field $\rightarrow T = \frac{N}{A\,m}$

Mass $\rightarrow kg$

Momentum $\rightarrow \frac{kg\,m}{s}$

Period $\rightarrow s$

Permeability $\rightarrow \frac{N}{A^2}$

Permittivity $\rightarrow \frac{C^2}{N\,m^2}$

Planck's constant $\rightarrow J \cdot s$

Power $\rightarrow W = \frac{J}{s}$

Pressure $\rightarrow Pa = \frac{N}{m^2}$

Radian frequency $\rightarrow \frac{rad}{s}$

Resistance $\rightarrow \Omega = \frac{V}{A}$

Spacetime interval $\rightarrow m$

Specific heat $\rightarrow \frac{J}{kg\,K}$

Speed $\rightarrow \frac{m}{s}$

Temperature $\rightarrow K$

Tension $\rightarrow N$

Torque $\rightarrow m\,N$

Universal Gravitation Constant $\rightarrow \frac{N\,m^2}{kg^2}$

Velocity $\rightarrow \frac{m}{s}$

Voltage $\rightarrow V = \frac{J}{C}$

Weight $\rightarrow N$

Work $\rightarrow J$

Work function $\rightarrow J$

Clear Cut
Physics

Hugh V. Hickman

P.O. Box 13165
Tampa, FL 33681-3165

www.ccwallis.com
physics@ccwallis.com

ISBN 978-0-9815853-0-7

Verification by experiment is the most credible way to validate any scientific calculation. To the best of the author's knowledge, none of the calculations in this book have ever been verified by experiment.

Clear Cut Physics

HOW TO USE THIS BOOK

1. Read through the text, including the examples, until you get to a quiz.
2. Attempt the quiz on a seperate sheet of paper. (You may refer to the text if necessary.) Then compare your quiz solution to the quiz solution in the back of the book.
3. Repeat 1. and 2. until you reach the end of the chapter.
4. Work the odd numbered Homework Problems at the end of the chapter, and compare your answers to the answers in the back of the book.
5. Pretend that the even numbered Homework Problems are a test, and work through them keeping track of the time.

Please Note: **The timelines are not complete.** They were included for historal perspective, but they do not cover everything, and they are certainly not intended to be a complete history of Physics. **The timelines are not complete.**

Table of Contents

Chapter 1 - Math

Timeline

3000 BC Egyptians develop a base 10 number system.

1900 BC Babylonians are using the Pythagorean Theorem more than 1000 years before Pythagoras proves that it is true.

510 BC Pythagoras and his followers use mathematics to analyze the music of vibrating strings during the golden dawn of ancient Greek science.

360 BC The Greek philosopher Plato further 'mathematizes' science by describing nature in terms of geometric solids.

280 BC Students of Aristotle's Lyceum school in Athens establish a foundation for what would later become the parallogram law of vector addition.

250 BC Matrices appear in the Chinese text *Nine Chapters on Mathematical Art.*

240 BC Archimedes of Syracuse calculates π to be between $3\,\frac{10}{71}$ and $3\,\frac{1}{7}$.

150 AD Ptolemy of Alexandria includes tables of a kind of sine function in his comprehensive astronomical text the *Almagest.*

630 AD A Hindu mathematician named Brahmagupta describes a technique very similar to the modern quadratic formula.

825 Muhammad Al-Khwarizmi, a scholar at the House of Wisdom in Baghdad, writes a math text called *Hisab al-jabr w'al-mugabala.* The second word in the title becomes the modern word algebra.

1570 The Italian mathematician Raffael Bombelli develops a 30 year old idea by Cardano into the moden concept of an imaginary number.

1637 French mathematician and philosopher Rene Descartes developes the rectangular (or Cartesian) xy co-ordinate system.

1843 Sir William Hamilton, Royal Astronomer of Ireland, introduces $\hat{\imath}$, $\hat{\jmath}$, $\hat{k}$ notation as a part of his system of vector-like quaternions.

1880 Professor J. Willard Gibbs begins teaching modern vector analysis in his physics classes at Yale. The dot product and cross product are included.

TEXT

Math is the language of physics. Without math a beginning physics student has absolutely no chance to really understand what is going on. Fortunately, a surprising number of physics concepts can be described reasonably well, just by using very basic mathematics. This book presupposes that the reader already knows Algebra I.

But Algebra I alone is not quite enough. It is also necessary to introduce some mathematical techniques that were developed with physics in mind. They are easy, but essential. If you can 'get' the math in this 1st chapter, then you should be able to 'get' the physics in the rest of the book.

Vectors

Many quantities in physics can be described by a single number (plus units). Time is an example. If someone tells you that a process took 7 seconds, that's all that needs to be said. You don't need any more numbers to know what 7 seconds means. The kinds of quantities that can be described by a single number are called *scalars.* In this case, the number 7 is called the *magnitude* of the scalar.

Many other quantities however, have both a *magnitude* and a *direction.* Those kinds of quantities are called *vectors.* Force is a classic example. If you are sitting ringside at WrestleMania XXI, and Hulk Hogan is about to throw Macho Man Randy Savage out of the ring, it suddenly becomes very important to you **which way** he's going to throw him. (You probably couldn't care less about how hard he throws him, as long as he's not being thrown at you!) So force needs both a magnitude (how hard), and a direction (which way).

Unit vectors are any vectors whose magnitude is 1. Physicists tend to think of vectors as being little arrows. In that picture a unit vector would be a little arrow that is 1 long (Figure 1.1, page 18).

Co-ordinate vectors are unit vectors that point in the directions of the co-ordinate system. In Cartesian or rectangular co-ordinates, $(+\hat{\imath})$ is the co-ordinate vector that points in the $+x$ direction and $(-\hat{\imath})$ is the co-ordinate vector that points in the $-x$ direction. In the $+y$ direction the co-ordinate vector is $(+\hat{\jmath})$, while the $-y$ direction is $(-\hat{\jmath})$. Figure 1.2 shows a picture.

Co-ordinate vectors enable us to express more general vectors in what is called 'component form'. For example,

$$\vec{F} = 3(+\hat{\imath}) + 2(+\hat{\jmath}) \ . \qquad (101)$$

On the left side of equation (101), **the $\vec{}$ over the F means that $\vec{F}$ is a vector.** On the right side, 3 is the magnitude of the x component, and $(+\hat{\imath})$ points to the right. 2 is the magnitude of the y component, and $(+\hat{\jmath})$ points up.

In order to draw a picture of $\vec{F}$, we start at the origin, then go 3 to the right, and up 2. The tail of the vector is located where we started (0,0), and the arrowhead is where we wind up (3,2). Figure 1.3 shows how to do it.

For another example, let's sketch

$$\vec{B} = 4(-\hat{\imath}) + 3(+\hat{\jmath}) \; . \tag{102}$$

This time the 'road map' for $\vec{B}$ says go 4 to the left, then up 3. Figure 1.4 shows the picture.

Vectors are added by adding components.

Example 1.1

$\vec{F} = 3(+\hat{\imath}) + 2(+\hat{\jmath})$ and $\vec{B} = 4(-\hat{\imath}) + 3(+\hat{\jmath})$. Find $\vec{F}+\vec{B}$ and sketch a picture that shows $\vec{F}$, $\vec{B}$, $\vec{F}+\vec{B}$, and the 2 dotted lines. Make your picture big, and make sure that you label everything, including enough axis ticks so that the reader doesn't have to count.

<u>Solution 1.1</u>

In order to find $\vec{F}+\vec{B}$, the components of $\vec{F}$ are added to the components of $\vec{B}$.

$$\begin{aligned} \vec{F} &= 3(+\hat{\imath}) + 2(+\hat{\jmath}) \\ \vec{B} &= \underline{4(-\hat{\imath}) + 3(+\hat{\jmath})} \\ \\ \vec{F}+\vec{B} &= 1(-\hat{\imath}) + 5(+\hat{\jmath}) \end{aligned} \tag{103}$$

The $\hat{\jmath}$ components in equation (103) are no problem because they both go up and $2+3=5$. The $\hat{\imath}$ components need a little thought. The 1st one says go 3 to the right. The 2nd one says go 4 to the left. If you go 3 to the right, then come back 4 to the left, you will be 1 to the left. Or you could think of it as $(+3)+(-4) = -1$.

When you draw the picture it is important to estimate the spacing of the axis ticks as accurately as you can. They should all be close to the same size because the final picture will be distorted if the spaces are too much bigger on one axis than the other. The smart thing to do is use the lines that are already on your notebook paper for the y axis ticks. That way the y axis ticks will all be the same size for sure. Then draw in the x axis ticks by eye, and try to make them have the same separation as the ones on the y axis.

The 2 dotted lines are drawn from the arrowheads of $\vec{F}$ and $\vec{B}$ to the arrowhead of $\vec{F}+\vec{B}$. If everything is right, then $\vec{F}$, $\vec{B}$, and the 2 dotted lines will form a parallelogram. That fact is called *the parallelogram rule of vector addition*, and it is always true. (In other words, if it doesn't happen on your picture then you did something wrong.)

Finally, it is very important to label everything- all of the vectors, both axes, and enough axis ticks so that the reader doesn't have to count. Figure 1.5 shows the final picture.

Quiz 1.1 $\vec{A} = 1(-\hat{\imath}) + 2(-\hat{\jmath})$. $\vec{B} = 3(+\hat{\imath}) + 1(-\hat{\jmath})$. Find $\vec{A} + \vec{B}$ and sketch $\vec{A}$, $\vec{B}$, $\vec{A} + \vec{B}$, and the 2 dotted lines. Make your picture big, and label everything.

Sometimes it is necessary to find a vector that stretches from one specific point to another specific point. Here the key thing to remember is

$$(\; to \;) \; - \; (\; from \;) \; . \tag{104}$$

Example 1.2

Find the vector that stretches from $(2, -1)$ to $(-3, 2)$. Draw a picture, count to check, then express your answer in magnitude unit-vector form.

<u>Solution 1.2</u>

Remembering $(to) - (from)$,

$$\underbrace{(-3, 2)}_{to} - \underbrace{(2, -1)}_{from} \Longrightarrow (-5, 3) \tag{105}$$

The position vector, which we'll call $\vec{r}$, goes 5 to the left, then up 3, so that

$$\vec{r} = 5(-\hat{\imath}) + 3(+\hat{\jmath}) \; . \tag{106}$$

Figure 1.6 shows the picture. Notice that the tail of $\vec{r}$ goes on the $(from)$ point, and the arrowhead of $\vec{r}$ goes on the (to) point.

The counting check is easy. Vector $\vec{r}$ is supposed to be $\vec{r} = 5(-\hat{\imath}) + 3(+\hat{\jmath})$. So if we start at the $(2, -1)$ *from* point, then count 5 to the left, and 3 up, we should arrive at the $(-3, 2)$ *to* point. Figure 1.7 shows that we do.

The last part of Example 1.2 asks us to express $\vec{r}$ in magnitude unit-vector form. The magnitude of $\vec{r}$ is symbolized by

$$|\vec{r}| \;\; \equiv \;\; \text{the magnitude of } \vec{r} \, .$$

It can be calculated using the Pythagorean Theorem, $c^2 = a^2 + b^2$. (Notice that the $| \;\; |$ magnitude symbol looks just like the $| \;\; |$ absolute value symbol from Algebra I. It's fine if you want to think of it that way, because *a magnitude can never be negative.*)

The Pythagorean Theorem has to be applied to a triangle, and Figure 1.8 shows the triangle for $|\vec{r}|$. In this case

$$c^2 = a^2 + b^2 \qquad \text{becomes} \qquad |\vec{r}|^2 = |\vec{r}_x|^2 + |\vec{r}_y|^2 \, ,$$

so that

$$\begin{aligned}
|\vec{r}| &= +\sqrt{|\vec{r}_x|^2 + |\vec{r}_y|^2} \\
&= +\sqrt{(5)^2 + (3)^2} \\
&= \sqrt{25+9} \\
|\vec{r}| &= \sqrt{34}
\end{aligned} \tag{107}$$

A magnitude can never be negative, which is why the positive square root is emphasized at the beginning of equation (107). It is not customary however to write the final answer as $|\vec{r}| = +\sqrt{34}$. Instead it is just written as $|\vec{r}| = \sqrt{34}$, and everybody knows $\sqrt{34}$ is positive because the left side of the equation says that $\sqrt{34}$ is a magnitude.

Multiplication of a scalar times a vector is easy. You just distribute it through, and make sure to keep track of the signs. If $\vec{F} = 4(+\hat{\imath}) + 3(-\hat{\jmath})$, then $-2\vec{F}$ would be

$$\begin{aligned}
-2\vec{F} &= -2\left[4(+\hat{\imath}) + 3(-\hat{\jmath})\right] \\
-2\vec{F} &= 8(-\hat{\imath}) + 6(+\hat{\jmath})\ .
\end{aligned} \tag{108}$$

Here the $-$ sign in front of the 2 has changed the directions of both of the co-ordinate vectors.

It is also possible to factor a constant multiplier out of a vector. For example,

$$\begin{aligned}
\vec{E} &= 6(-\hat{\imath}) + 2(-\hat{\jmath}) \\
&= 3\left[\frac{6}{3}(-\hat{\imath}) + \frac{2}{3}(-\hat{\jmath})\right] = 3\left[\frac{6(-\hat{\imath}) + 2(-\hat{\jmath})}{3}\right] \\
\vec{E} &= 3\left[\frac{\vec{E}}{3}\right]\ .
\end{aligned} \tag{109}$$

In order to convert a vector from component form to magnitude unit-vector form, you 1st find the magnitude, and then factor it out. In symbols

$$\vec{r} = |\vec{r}|\left[\frac{\vec{r}}{|\vec{r}|}\right]\ , \tag{110}$$

where $|\vec{r}|$ represents the magnitude of $\vec{r}$, and

$$\frac{\vec{r}}{|\vec{r}|} \equiv \text{a unit vector that points in the direction of } \vec{r}\ .$$

For Example 1.2, $\vec{r} = 5(-\hat{\imath}) + 3(+\hat{\jmath})$ and $|\vec{r}| = \sqrt{34}$, so the magnitude unit-vector form of $\vec{r}$ would look like

$$\vec{r} = \overbrace{\sqrt{34}}^{\text{magnitude}}\ \underbrace{\left[\frac{5}{\sqrt{34}}(-\hat{\imath}) + \frac{3}{\sqrt{34}}(+\hat{\jmath})\right]}_{\text{unit vector}} = |\vec{r}|\left[\frac{\vec{r}}{|\vec{r}|}\right] \tag{111}$$

If $\frac{\vec{r}}{|\vec{r}|}$ is really a unit vector, then $\frac{\vec{r}}{|\vec{r}|}$ must have a magnitude of 1. In symbols,

$$\left|\frac{\vec{r}}{|\vec{r}|}\right| = 1\,. \tag{112}$$

Let's check to make sure that the unit vector in equation (111) really does have a magnitude of 1.

$$\begin{aligned}
\frac{\vec{r}}{|\vec{r}|} &= \frac{5}{\sqrt{34}}(-\hat{\imath}) + \frac{3}{\sqrt{34}}(+\hat{\jmath}) \\
\left|\frac{\vec{r}}{|\vec{r}|}\right| &= \sqrt{\left(\frac{5}{\sqrt{34}}\right)^2 + \left(\frac{3}{\sqrt{34}}\right)^2} \\
&= \sqrt{\frac{(5)^2}{(\sqrt{34})^2} + \frac{(3)^2}{(\sqrt{34})^2}} = \sqrt{\frac{25}{34} + \frac{9}{34}} \\
\left|\frac{\vec{r}}{|\vec{r}|}\right| &= \sqrt{\frac{34}{34}} = 1\,. \qquad (113)
\end{aligned}$$

Everything looks OK, so the answer to the last part of Example 1.2 is

$$\vec{r} = \sqrt{34}\left[\frac{5}{\sqrt{34}}(-\hat{\imath}) + \frac{3}{\sqrt{34}}(+\hat{\jmath})\right]\,. \tag{114}$$

Figure 1.9 shows a picture of $\frac{\vec{r}}{|\vec{r}|}$. placed next to $\vec{r}$. Notice that they both point in the same direction, but while $\vec{r}$ *is the full vector* with a length of $\sqrt{34}$, $\frac{\vec{r}}{|\vec{r}|}$ *is the unit vector* with a length of 1. Which brings us to the interpretation of magnitude. If the vector in question is a distance, position, or radius vector, then the magnitude represents its length. If the vector in question is a force or a field vector, then the magnitude represents its strength. If it is a velocity vector, then the magnitude represents its speed. So the magnitude of a vector means different things for different vectors. Soon we will see that the science of Physics utilizes a system of units to keep track of the different kinds of vectors and scalars, but for now -

Quiz 1.2 Find the vector that stretches from $(-1, 3)$ to $(2, -1)$. Draw a picture, count to check, then express your answer in magnitude unit-vector form.

Dot Product

There are two different types of frequently encountered vector-vector multiplication. One of them is called the *cross product*, and we'll look at that one later. The other is called the *dot product*, and we'll look at it now.

The dot product gets its name from the fact that a big dot is placed between the 2 vectors. The symbols $\vec{A} \bullet \vec{B}$, for example, indicate the dot product of $\vec{A}$ with $\vec{B}$. In words they would read, "$\vec{A}$ dot $\vec{B}$".

Finding the dot product is easy in Cartesian co-ordinates. You just multiply the 2 x-components together, keeping the co-ordinate vector sign with each component. Then do the same with the two y-components, again keeping the signs. After that, you add the two products.

Example 1.3

$\vec{K} = 2.5(-\hat{\imath}) + 3(+\hat{\jmath})$, and $\vec{D} = 4(+\hat{\imath}) + 2(+\hat{\jmath})$. Find $\vec{K} \bullet \vec{D}$, $\vec{D} \bullet \vec{K}$, and $+\sqrt{\vec{K} \bullet \vec{K}}$.

Solution 1.3

It's easier to do it than it is to talk about it.

$$\begin{aligned}
\vec{K} \bullet \vec{D} &= \left[2.5(-\hat{\imath}) + 3(+\hat{\jmath})\right] \bullet \left[4(+\hat{\imath}) + 2(+\hat{\jmath})\right] \\
&= (-2.5)(+4) + (+3)(+2) \\
&= -10 + 6 \\
\vec{K} \bullet \vec{D} &= -4 \qquad (115)
\end{aligned}$$

$$\begin{aligned}
\vec{D} \bullet \vec{K} &= \left[4(+\hat{\imath}) + 2(+\hat{\jmath})\right] \bullet \left[2.5(-\hat{\imath}) + 3(+\hat{\jmath})\right] \\
&= (+4)(-2.5) + (+2)(+3) \\
&= -10 + 6 \\
\vec{D} \bullet \vec{K} &= -4 \qquad (116)
\end{aligned}$$

Equations (115) and (116) point out a couple of important facts. 1). The dot product does not give you back a vector. Instead it results in a scalar. 2). $\vec{K} \bullet \vec{D} = \vec{D} \bullet \vec{K}$. That will happen with any two vectors because the dot product is commutative.

For the last part,

$$\begin{aligned}
\vec{K} \bullet \vec{K} &= \left[2.5(-\hat{\imath}) + 3(+\hat{\jmath})\right] \bullet \left[2.5(-\hat{\imath}) + 3(+\hat{\jmath})\right] \\
&= (-2.5)(-2.5) + (+3)(+3) \\
&= 6.25 + 9 \\
&= 15.25 \\
+\sqrt{\vec{K} \bullet \vec{K}} &= +\sqrt{15.25} \qquad (117)
\end{aligned}$$

Dropping the + signs, $\sqrt{\vec{K} \bullet \vec{K}} = \sqrt{15.25}$. Suppose we were trying to find the magnitude of $\vec{K}$. From the Pythagorean Theorem,

$$\begin{aligned}
|\vec{K}| &= \sqrt{|\vec{K}_x|^2 + |\vec{K}_y|^2} \\
&= \sqrt{(2.5)^2 + (3)^2} = \sqrt{6.25 + 9} \\
|\vec{K}| &= \sqrt{15.25} \qquad (118)
\end{aligned}$$

Equations (117) and (118) indicate that the magnitude of $\vec{K}$ and the square root of $\vec{K} \bullet \vec{K}$ are the same thing. That will always be true in Cartesian co-ordinates, so that in general

$$|\vec{A}| = \sqrt{\vec{A} \bullet \vec{A}}\,. \tag{119}$$

Quiz 1.3 $\vec{L} = 1.4(-\hat{\imath}) + 2(+\hat{\jmath})$, $\vec{C} = .5(-\hat{\imath}) + 3(+\hat{\jmath})$. Find $\vec{L} \bullet \vec{C}$. Then use the dot product to find $|\vec{L}|$, and check your answer by using the Pythagorean Theorem.

Quadratic Formula

A quadratic equation of the form

$$ax^2 + bx + c = 0 \tag{120}$$

has two solutions, x_1 and x_2. They can both be found by using the *quadratic formula,*

$$x = \frac{-b \pm \sqrt{b^2 - 4ac}}{2a}\,. \tag{121}$$

Example 1.4

Use the quadratic formula to find the solutions of $\Psi^2 - 2\Psi + 10 = 0$. If the solutions are complex, find $|\Psi_1|$. (Ψ is the Greek letter Psi.)

Solution 1.4

Comparing the Ψ equation to equation (120), $a = 1$, $b = -2$, and $c = 10$. Substituting those values into the quadratic formula leads to

$$\begin{aligned}
x &= \frac{-b \pm \sqrt{b^2 - 4ac}}{2a} \\
\Psi &= \frac{-(-2) \pm \sqrt{(-2)^2 - 4(1)(10)}}{2(1)} \\
&= \frac{2 \pm \sqrt{4 - 40}}{2} = \frac{2 \pm \sqrt{-36}}{2} = \frac{2 \pm \sqrt{36(-1)}}{2} = \frac{2 \pm 6\sqrt{-1}}{2} \\
\Psi &= \frac{2}{2} \pm \frac{6\sqrt{-1}}{2} = 1 \pm 3\sqrt{-1}\,.
\end{aligned} \tag{122}$$

The square root of -1 in equation (122) seems to be an impossible quanity. After all, $(+1)^2 = +1$ and $(-1)^2$ also $= +1$, so there is no number that you can square to get -1. For that reason $\sqrt{-1}$ is said to be an imaginary number, and it is symbolized by

$$i = \sqrt{-1}\,. \tag{123}$$

(Note that the i in equation (123) is not an $\hat{\imath}$ unit vector. It is just a lower case i.)

Substituting i into equation (122) results in

$$\begin{aligned} \Psi_1 &= 1+3i \\ \Psi_2 &= 1-3i\ . \end{aligned} \tag{124}$$

The two Ψ's from equation (124) are *complex numbers* of the form $a+bi$. They have a real part a, and an imaginary part b.

Complex numbers also have a magnitude. In order to find $|\Psi|$, you 1st find $\Psi^\star$, the *complex conjugate* of Ψ, then use

$$|\Psi| = \sqrt{\Psi^\star \Psi}\ . \tag{125}$$

(In words, $\Psi^\star\Psi$ reads "Psi star Psi".)

The complex conjugate of Ψ can be found by replacing all of the i's in Ψ by $-i$'s. For Ψ_1,

$$\begin{aligned} \Psi_1 &= 1+3i \\ \Psi_1^\star &= 1+3(-i) = 1-3i\ . \end{aligned} \tag{126}$$

Next multiply out $\Psi_1^\star\Psi_1$.

$$\begin{array}{rllll} \Psi_1^\star = & 1 & -3i & & \\ \Psi_1 = & 1 & +3i & & \\ \hline & 1 & -3i & & \\ & & +3i & +3i(-3i) & \\ \hline & 1 & +0 & -9i^2 & \end{array}$$

$$\Psi_1^\star\Psi_1 = 1 - 9(\sqrt{-1})^2 = 1 - 9(-1) = 1 + 9 = 10 \tag{127}$$

Finally,

$$|\Psi_1| = \sqrt{\Psi_1^\star\Psi_1} = \sqrt{10}\ . \tag{128}$$

Quiz 1.4 $\Phi^2 - 4\Phi + 20 = 0$. Use the quadratic formula to find Φ_1 and Φ_2. If the answer turns out to be complex, also find $|\Phi_2|$.

Matricies

From Algebra I, a typical system of 2 equations in 2 unknowns might look like

$$\begin{aligned} -2x + y &= -3 \\ 4x + 5y &= 18\ . \end{aligned} \tag{129}$$

It is also possible to write that same system as

$$\begin{bmatrix} -2 & 1 \\ 4 & 5 \end{bmatrix} \begin{bmatrix} x \\ y \end{bmatrix} = -3 \begin{bmatrix} 1 \\ -6 \end{bmatrix}, \tag{130}$$

where the 2×2 array of numbers is called a *matrix*, the two 2×1 arrays are called *column vectors*, and -3 is a scalar multiplier.

$$\underbrace{\begin{bmatrix} -2 & 1 \\ 4 & 5 \end{bmatrix}}_{2 \times 2 \ \textit{matrix}} \overbrace{\begin{bmatrix} x \\ y \end{bmatrix}}^{\substack{\textit{column} \\ \textit{vector}}} = \underbrace{-3}_{\substack{\textit{scalar} \\ \textit{multiplier}}} \overbrace{\begin{bmatrix} 1 \\ -6 \end{bmatrix}}^{\substack{\textit{column} \\ \textit{vector}}} . \tag{131}$$

In order to get from equation (131) back to system (129), we need rules for multiplying out the left and right sides of equation (131). The scalar multiplier on the right side is pretty apparent

$$k \begin{bmatrix} a \\ b \end{bmatrix} = \begin{bmatrix} k(a) \\ k(b) \end{bmatrix} , \tag{132}$$

and the matrix multiplication on the left side is also fairly easy

$$\begin{bmatrix} a & b \\ c & d \end{bmatrix} \begin{bmatrix} q \\ r \end{bmatrix} = \begin{bmatrix} a(q) + b(r) \\ c(q) + d(r) \end{bmatrix} . \tag{133}$$

Starting with equation (131), and using the rules given by equations (132) and (133),

$$\begin{aligned} \begin{bmatrix} -2 & 1 \\ 4 & 5 \end{bmatrix} \begin{bmatrix} x \\ y \end{bmatrix} &= -3 \begin{bmatrix} 1 \\ -6 \end{bmatrix} \\ \begin{bmatrix} -2(x) + 1(y) \\ 4(x) + 5(y) \end{bmatrix} &= \begin{bmatrix} -3(1) \\ -3(-6) \end{bmatrix} \end{aligned}$$

or just

$$\begin{aligned} -2x + y &= -3 \\ 4x + 5y &= 18 \end{aligned} , \tag{134}$$

and we are back to where we started at system (129).

Please note that we are not concerned with *why* anyone would want to write system (129) in the form of eqution (131). Right now we are only looking at math terminology and technique. Applications will come later.

Example 1.5

Multiply out both sides of equation (135), and see whether or not the left side really does equal the right side. (Don't forget to answer 'yes' or 'no'!)

$$\begin{bmatrix} 3 & -4 \\ -2 & 7 \end{bmatrix} \begin{bmatrix} 2 \\ 1 \end{bmatrix} = -\frac{1}{2} \begin{bmatrix} -2 \\ -6 \end{bmatrix} \tag{135}$$

Solution 1.5

$$\begin{aligned}
\begin{bmatrix} 3 & -4 \\ -2 & 7 \end{bmatrix}\begin{bmatrix} 2 \\ 1 \end{bmatrix} &= -\frac{1}{2}\begin{bmatrix} -2 \\ -6 \end{bmatrix} \\
\begin{bmatrix} 3(2)+(-4)(1) \\ (-2)(2)+7(1) \end{bmatrix} &= \begin{bmatrix} \left(-\frac{1}{2}\right)(-2) \\ \left(-\frac{1}{2}\right)(-6) \end{bmatrix} \\
\begin{bmatrix} 6-4 \\ -4+7 \end{bmatrix} &= \begin{bmatrix} 1 \\ 3 \end{bmatrix} \\
\begin{bmatrix} 2 \\ 3 \end{bmatrix} &\neq \begin{bmatrix} 1 \\ 3 \end{bmatrix} .
\end{aligned} \tag{136}$$

No. The left side does not equal the right side.

Quiz 1.5 $\begin{bmatrix} 2 & -3 \\ 4 & 1 \end{bmatrix}\begin{bmatrix} \frac{1}{2} \\ 3 \end{bmatrix} = 4\begin{bmatrix} -2 \\ \frac{5}{4} \end{bmatrix}$. Multiply out both sides to see whether or not they are equal. Don't forget to answer 'yes' or 'no'.

Two more points about matricies: 1.) The rule for multiplying a 1×2 matrix (sometimes called a *row vector*) by a 2×1 matrix (sometimes called a *column vector*) is given by

$$[a \quad b]\begin{bmatrix} d \\ e \end{bmatrix} = (a)(d) + (b)(e) . \tag{137}$$

And, 2.) the *determinate* of a 2×2 matrix is defined as

$$\det \begin{bmatrix} a & b \\ c & d \end{bmatrix} = (a)(d) - (b)(c) . \tag{138}$$

Example 1.6

Find x such that the product of $[-2 \quad 1]$ and $\begin{bmatrix} x \\ 3 \end{bmatrix}$ will equal the determinant of $\begin{bmatrix} 4 & -6 \\ 2 & -1 \end{bmatrix}$. Then substitute x back in and check your answer.

Solution 1.6

Here we just need to set the product equal to the determinant and solve for x.

$$\begin{aligned}
[-2 \quad 1]\begin{bmatrix} x \\ 3 \end{bmatrix} &= \det \begin{bmatrix} 4 & -6 \\ 2 & -1 \end{bmatrix} \\
-2(x)+1(3) &= 4(-1)-(-6)(2) \\
-2x+3 &= -4+12 \\
-2x &= 5 \\
x &= -\frac{5}{2}
\end{aligned} \tag{139}$$

For the check, plug in $-\frac{5}{2}$ for x and see if the right side really does equal the left side.

$$\begin{aligned}
[-2 \;\; 1] \begin{bmatrix} -\frac{5}{2} \\ 3 \end{bmatrix} &= \det \begin{bmatrix} 4 & -6 \\ 2 & -1 \end{bmatrix} \\
-2\left(-\frac{5}{2}\right) + 1(3) &= 4(-1) - (-6)(2) \\
5 + 3 &= -4 + 12 \\
8 &= 8 \qquad (140)
\end{aligned}$$

Both sides equal 8, so everything looks OK.

Quiz 1.6 $\det \begin{bmatrix} 2 & 3 \\ x & 5 \end{bmatrix} = [6 \;\; 2] \begin{bmatrix} 1 \\ -4 \end{bmatrix}$. Sove for x and check the answer.

Conversion of Units

Students are eternally frustrated by the fact that *all physics answers have units.* The bad news is: You cannot be sloppy with the units. (NASA crashed a 125 million dollar Mars probe in 1999 because of confusion between English and metric units.) The good news is: Handled properly, units can actually help with the solution of a problem, and will sometimes double check your work.

This book uses *Standard International* (SI) metric units. The basic unit of mass is a *kilogram* (kg). The unit of length is a *meter* (m). And the unit of time is a *second* (s). Sometimes however, it is necessary to convert from one type of unit to another. All of our permissible conversions are shown in Table 1. (Other conversions exist, but these are the only ones that we are going to use here.)

Table 1. Conversions

1 inch (in) = 2.54 centimeters (cm)
100 cm = 1 meter (m)
10 millimeters (mm) = 1 cm
$360\,^o = 2\,\pi$ radians (rad)
12 in = 1 foot (ft)
5280 ft = 1 mile (mi)

The ^{o} symbol in Table 1 stands for degrees, and π (pronounced 'pie') is defined as the circumference of a circle divided by its diameter.

Unit conversions are accomplished by multiplying the original quantity by the number 1. For example, suppose we wanted to convert 15 cm into inches. First we would write the 15 cm as a fraction.

$$15\; cm = \frac{15\; cm}{1}\;. \qquad (141)$$

Then we look in Table 1 for the appropriate conversion.

$$1\ in = 2.54\ cm\ . \tag{142}$$

The right side of equation (141) indicates that *cm* are in the numerator of our original quantity. We know that we don't want *cm* in our final answer. In order to cancel them out, we will need *cm* in the denominator of our conversion factor. So divide both sides of equation (142) by 2.54 *cm*.

$$\begin{aligned} 1\ in &= 2.54\ cm \\ \frac{1\ in}{2.54\ cm} &= \frac{2.54\ cm}{2.54\ cm}\ . \end{aligned} \tag{143}$$

The right side of equation (143) is equal to 1.

$$\frac{1\ in}{2.54\ cm} = 1\ . \tag{144}$$

That means the left side of equation (143) is also equal to 1. Multiplication by 1 cannot change the value of our original quantity, so the conversion process looks like

$$\begin{aligned} 15\ cm &= \frac{15\ cm}{1} = \frac{15\ cm}{1}(1) = \frac{15\ cm}{1}\left(\frac{1\ in}{2.54\ cm}\right) \\ &= \left(\frac{15}{2.54}\right)\ in \\ 15\ cm &\approx 5.906\ in\ . \end{aligned} \tag{145}$$

The final number was obtained via calculator, and the $\approx$ symbol means "approximately equal to". (Here the final answer has been rounded to 3 decimal places.)

Of course things will not usually be so simple that the conversion only takes one step. Most of the time you need to multiply by a series of 1's.

Example 1.7

Convert 92 *mm* into feet. Show all cancellations of intermediate units.

<u>Solution 1.7</u>

Looking at Table 1, there is no direct conversion from *mm* to *ft*. There is however, *mm* to *cm*. Then *cm* to *in*. And finally *in* to *ft*. So

$$\begin{aligned} 92\ mm &= \frac{92\ mm}{1}\left(\frac{1\ cm}{10\ mm}\right)\left(\frac{1\ in}{2.54\ cm}\right)\left(\frac{1\ ft}{12\ in}\right) \\ &= \frac{(92)(1)(1)(1)}{(1)(10)(2.54)(12)}\ ft \\ 92\ mm &\approx .302\ ft\ . \end{aligned} \tag{146}$$

Notice how each conversion factor is carefully crafted so that the units in the conversion factor denominator will cancel out the left over units in the numerator of the previous conversion factor.

Quiz 1.7 Convert 3 ft into m and show all intermediate cancellations.

The Sine Function

Consider the two right triangles shown in Figure 1.10. Both of them have the same length hypotenuse. But angle β is bigger than angle α, and the side opposite angle β is longer than the side opposite angle α. It looks like there must be some kind of a relationship between the size of the angle and the length of the opposite side. That relationship is called the *sine* function, and it is defined by

$$\sin(\theta) = \frac{\text{opposite}}{\text{hypotenuse}}\,, \tag{147}$$

where θ is an angle that could either be measured in *radians* or *degrees.*

Most people are familiar with the idea that the circumference of a circle can be divided into 360°. Less familiar is the idea that the same circumference can be divided into 2π radians. The symbol π is the Greek letter *pi* (pronounced pie), and it represents a never ending number. The first few digits of π are given by

$$\pi = 3.141592\ \cdot\ \cdot\ \cdot\ \cdot \tag{148}$$

For a circle, the distance around (or circumference) is equal to the radius multiplied by 2π. So 2π is considered to be the total angle, measured in radians, through which a circle would sweep (2π radians $= 360^o$).

The number π is fascinating and mysterious. Entire books have been devoted to the study of π. But for our purposes π is just going to be a key on the calculator. The same goes for the sine function. If this was a math course, we would spend a lot of time studying the properties of the sine function. It's not necessary for us to do that here, so we won't. For now we just need to know how to calculate $\sin(\theta)$, and to see what the graph looks like.

Example 1.8

Use your calculator to fill in the values for $\sin(\theta)$ indicated below. Make sure that you are in *radian mode*, and round the answers to 2 decimal places. Then use the completed table to prepare a point graph of $\sin(\theta)$ vs. θ.

$$\theta = \frac{3\pi}{8} \qquad \sin(\theta) =$$

$$\theta = \frac{6\pi}{8} \qquad \sin(\theta) =$$

$$\theta = \frac{9\pi}{8} \qquad \sin(\theta) =$$

$$\theta = \frac{16\pi}{8} \qquad \sin(\theta) =$$

Solution 1.8

Here you need to read the instructions for your calculator, then place it in radian mode. Use the π key for pi instead of entering an approximate number like 3.14. After a little practice you should be able to obtain:

$$
\begin{array}{ll}
\theta = \dfrac{3\pi}{8} & \sin\left(\dfrac{3\pi}{8}\right) \approx .9238795\cdots \Rightarrow .92 \\
\theta = \dfrac{6\pi}{8} & \sin\left(\dfrac{6\pi}{8}\right) \approx .7071068\cdots \Rightarrow .71 \\
\theta = \dfrac{9\pi}{8} & \sin\left(\dfrac{9\pi}{8}\right) \approx -.3826834\cdots \Rightarrow -.38 \\
\theta = \dfrac{16\pi}{8} & \sin\left(\dfrac{16\pi}{8}\right) = 0 \Rightarrow 0
\end{array}
$$

Figure 1.11 shows the point graph. Notice that θ is plotted on the horizontal (x) axis and $\sin(\theta)$ is plotted on the vertical (y) axis. The increments on the θ axis are $\frac{\pi}{8}$ going from 0 to 2π, and the increments on the $\sin(\theta)$ axis are .1 going from -1.0 to $+1.0$.

Quiz 1.8 Use a small single piece of scotch tape to tack down a sheet of notebook paper over Figure 1.11 so that you can see the figure through the notebook paper. Trace the two main axes, but do not try to trace the entire grid. Now use your calculator to make a table of values for $\sin(\theta)$ from 0 to 2π in increments of $\frac{\pi}{8}$ (i.e. - $\frac{\pi}{8}$, $\frac{2\pi}{8}$, $\frac{3\pi}{8}$, etc.). Round the values of $\sin(\theta)$ to two decimal places. Next, looking through your notebook paper to the grid below, plot the 16 points of $\sin(\theta)$ vs. θ on your sheet of notebook paper. Finally remove the notebook paper from Figure 1.11, and draw a smooth line "best fit" curve through all 16 points.

Another important aspect of the sine function is that it repeats itself when θ gets bigger than 2π. Specifically,

$$\sin(\theta + 2\pi) = \sin(\theta)\ . \tag{149}$$

Those endless repetitions give the sine function a "wavelike" appearance. Figure 1.12 shows 3 cycles of $\sin(\theta)$ vs. θ.

Homework Problems Chapter 1

1.1 $\vec{H} = 1(-\hat{\imath}) + 3(+\hat{\jmath})$. $\vec{K} = 2(+\hat{\imath}) + 1(-\hat{\jmath})$. Find $\vec{H} + \vec{K}$, then sketch $\vec{H}$, $\vec{K}$, $\vec{H} + \vec{K}$, and the 2 dotted lines.

1.2 $\vec{P} = 3(-\hat{\imath}) + 1(+\hat{\jmath})$. $\vec{R} = 1(-\hat{\imath}) + 3(-\hat{\jmath})$. Find $\vec{P} + \vec{R}$, then sketch $\vec{P}$, $\vec{R}$, $\vec{P} + \vec{R}$, and the 2 dotted lines.

1.3 Find a unit vector that points from $(-6, -2)$ towards $(+3, -4)$.

1.4 Find the vector that stretches from $(-2, -3)$ to $(+3, +1)$ and sketch a picture.

1.5 $\vec{A} = 2(+\hat{\imath}) + 5(-\hat{\jmath})$. $\vec{B} = 1(-\hat{\imath}) + 2(+\hat{\jmath})$. Find $\vec{B} \bullet \vec{A}$, $\vec{A} \bullet \vec{B}$, and $|\vec{B}|^2$.

1.6 If two vectors are perpendicular then their dot product equals zero. Determine whether or not $\vec{H}$ and $\vec{K}$ are perpendicular if $\vec{K} = [3(-\hat{\imath}) + 6(+\hat{\jmath})]$ and $\vec{H} = [4(+\hat{\imath}) + 2(+\jmath)]$. (Don't forget to answer 'yes' or 'no'.)

1.7 $\Psi^2 - 6\Psi + 10 = 0$. Use the quadratic formula to find Ψ_1 and Ψ_2. If the Ψ's turn out to be complex, also find $|\Psi_1|$.

1.8 $\Phi^2 + 2\Phi - 8 = 0$. Find Φ_1, Φ_2, and $|\Phi_2|$ if the Φ's turn out to be complex.

1.9 $\begin{bmatrix} -4 & 2 \\ -2 & -5 \end{bmatrix} \begin{bmatrix} 3 \\ -2 \end{bmatrix} = -2 \begin{bmatrix} x \\ -2 \end{bmatrix}$ Find x so that both sides of the equation are equal.

1.10 $\begin{bmatrix} 1 & -1 \\ 1 & 2 \end{bmatrix} \begin{bmatrix} 4 \\ 6 \end{bmatrix} = \begin{bmatrix} 1 & 4 \\ 1 & 6 \end{bmatrix} \begin{bmatrix} -1 \\ 2 \end{bmatrix}$. Multiply out both sides to determine whether or not they are equal. (Don't forget to answer 'yes' or 'no'.)

1.11 Determine whether or not $\begin{bmatrix} 2 & -4 \end{bmatrix} \begin{bmatrix} 3 \\ -1 \end{bmatrix} = \det \begin{bmatrix} 6 & -2 \\ -4 & 3 \end{bmatrix}$ is a true statement. (Don't forget to answer 'yes' or 'no'.)

1.12 $\begin{bmatrix} x & 3 \end{bmatrix} \begin{bmatrix} -1 \\ 2 \end{bmatrix} = \det \begin{bmatrix} 4 & x \\ -1 & 2 \end{bmatrix}$. Find x and check your answer.

1.13 Convert 1000 meters into miles.

1.14 Convert .621 miles into meters.

1.15 Convert 1 radian into degrees. Round the answer to 2 decimal places then find the sine of the angle 2 different ways - 1st in degrees, next in radians. Explain why the answers are different.

1.16 Does $\sin\left(\frac{\pi}{6}\right) = \sin(750^o)$? If so, why? Since $\frac{\pi}{6}\ rad \neq 750^o$.

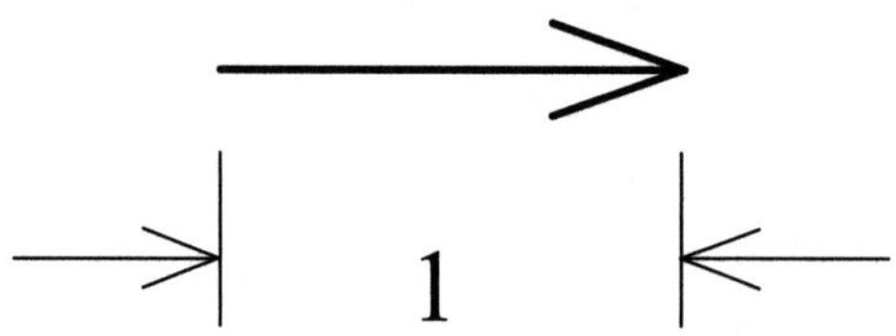

Figure 1.1 Unit vector

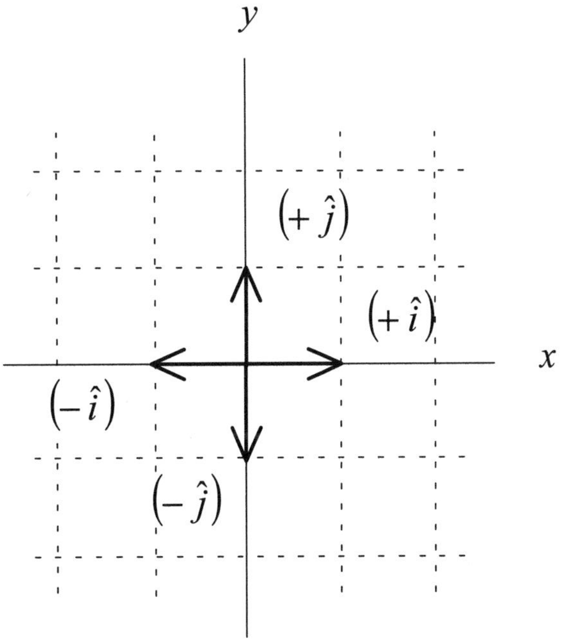

Figure 1.2   Co-ordinate vectors in the 2-dimensional Cartesian co-ordinate system

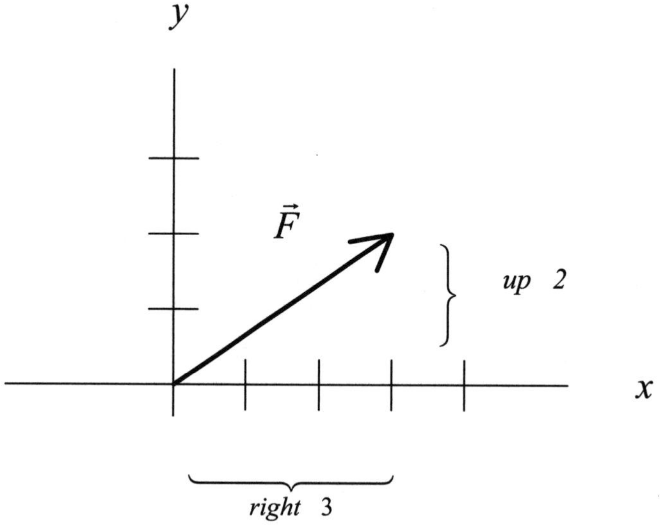

Figure 1.3 $\vec{F} = 3(+\hat{\imath}) + 2(+\hat{\jmath})$

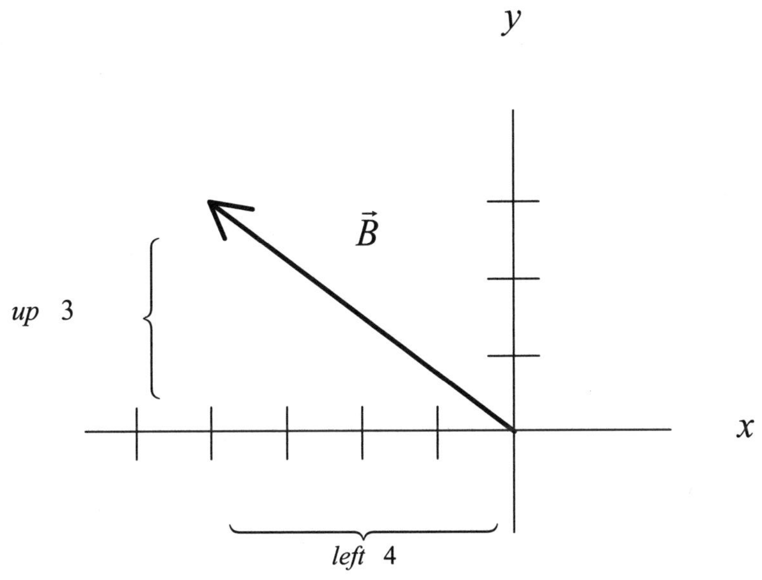

Figure 1.4 $\vec{B} = 4(-\hat{i}) + 3(+\hat{j})$

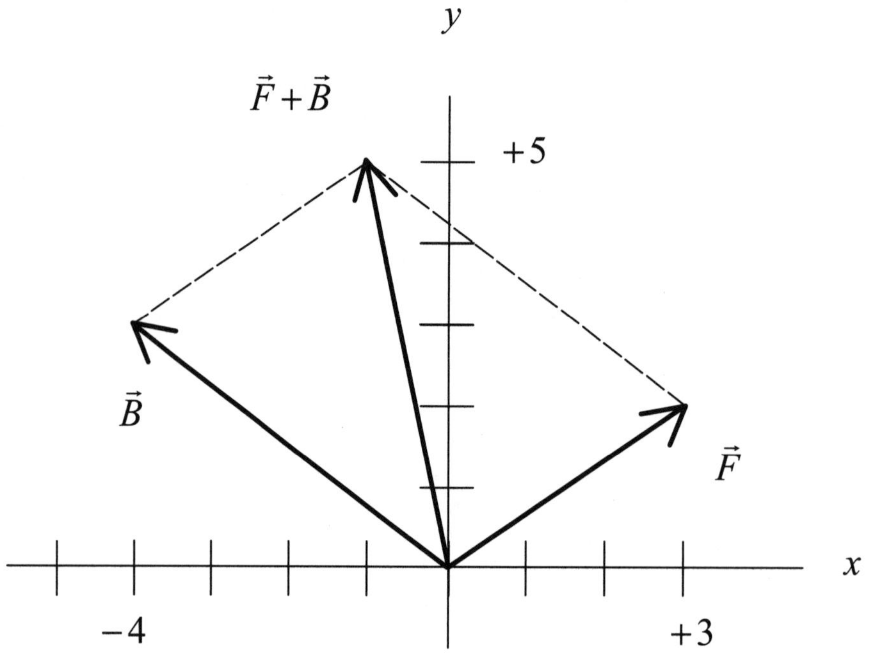

Figure 1.5 $\vec{F}+\vec{B}$ from Example 1.1. Notice that both axes, the 3 vectors and the 3 extreme axis ticks are all labeled.

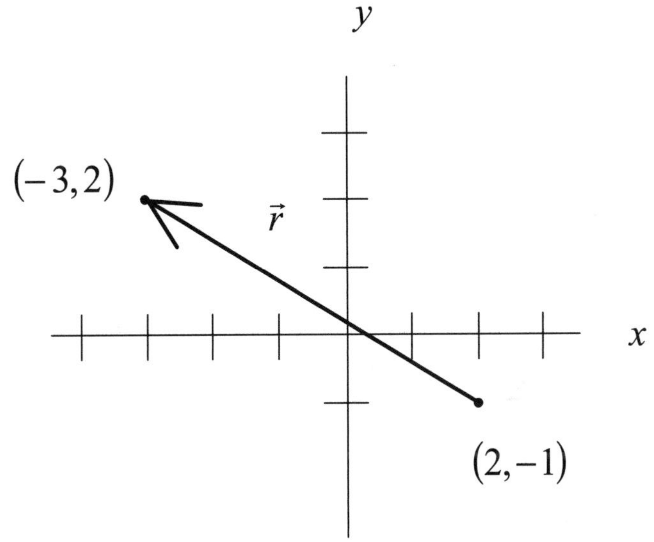

Figure 1.6 $\vec{r} = 5(-\hat{i}) + 3(+\hat{j})$ from Example 1.2

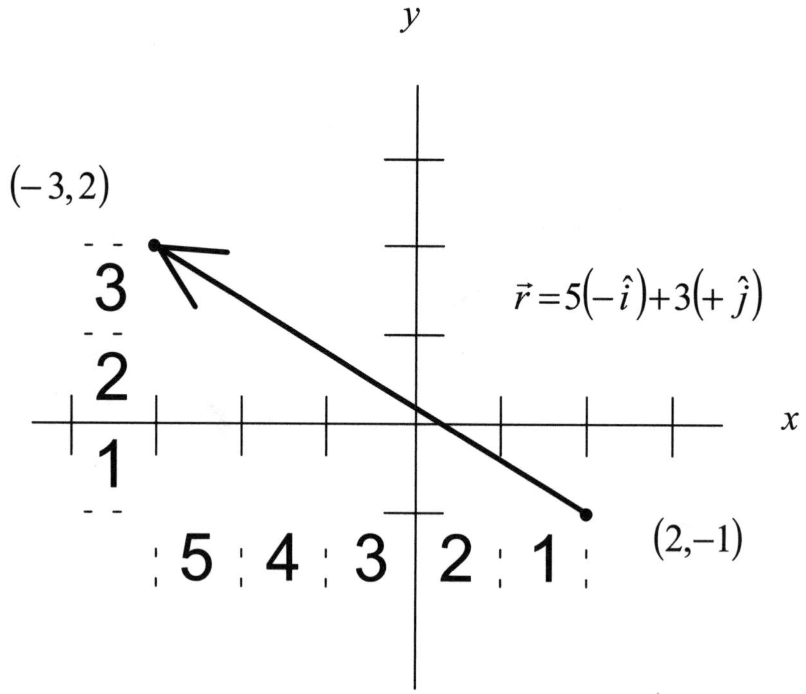

Figure 1.7 Count check for $\vec{r}$ from Example 1.2

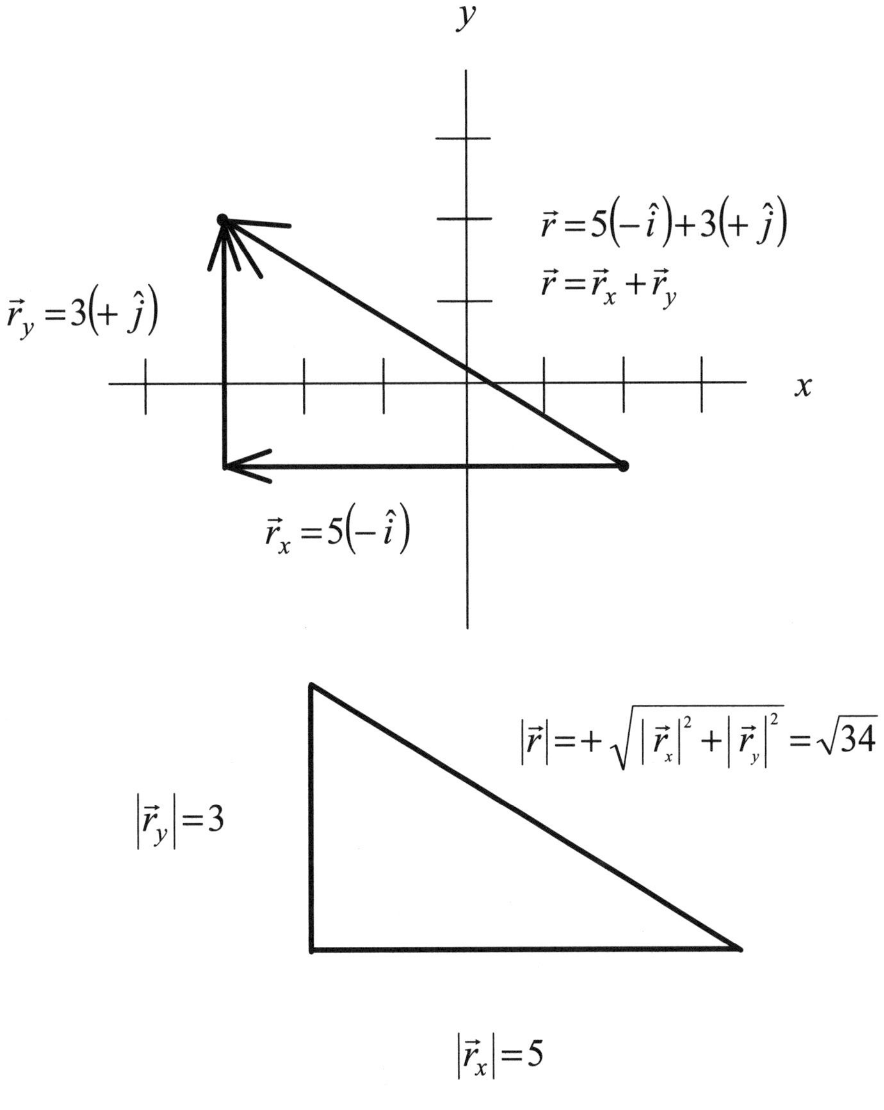

y
x
$\vec{r} = 5(-\hat{i}) + 3(+\hat{j})$
$\vec{r} = \vec{r}_x + \vec{r}_y$
$\vec{r}_y = 3(+\hat{j})$
$\vec{r}_x = 5(-\hat{i})$
$|\vec{r}| = +\sqrt{|\vec{r}_x|^2 + |\vec{r}_y|^2} = \sqrt{34}$
$|\vec{r}_y| = 3$
$|\vec{r}_x| = 5$

Figure 1.8 Pythagorean Theorem for Example 1.2

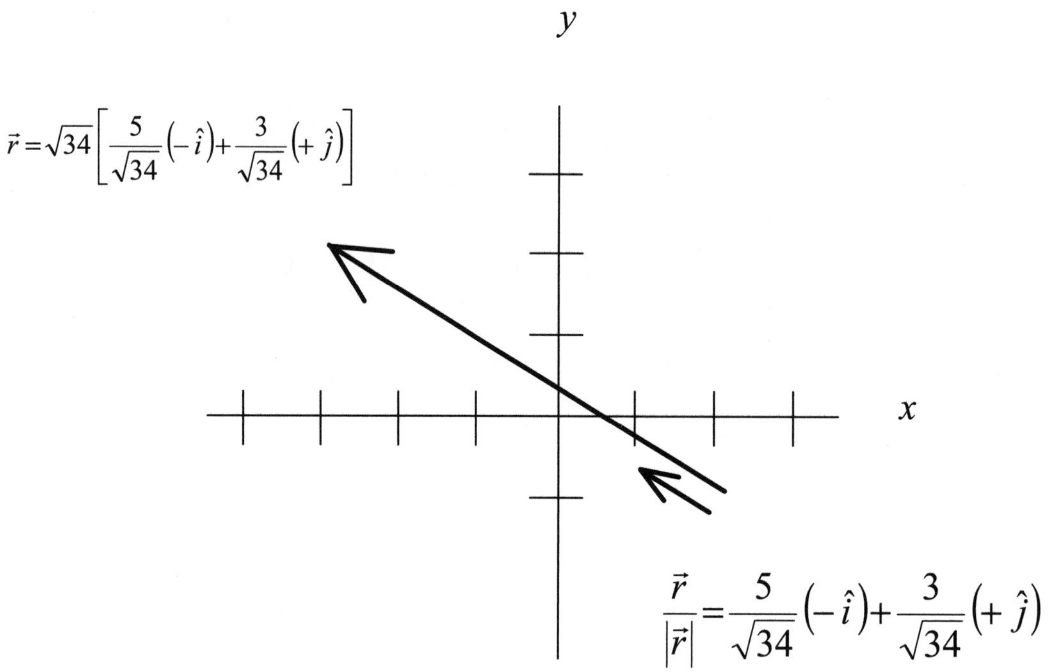

Figure 1.9 The unit vector $\frac{\vec{r}}{|\vec{r}|}$, placed next to the entire vector $\vec{r}$

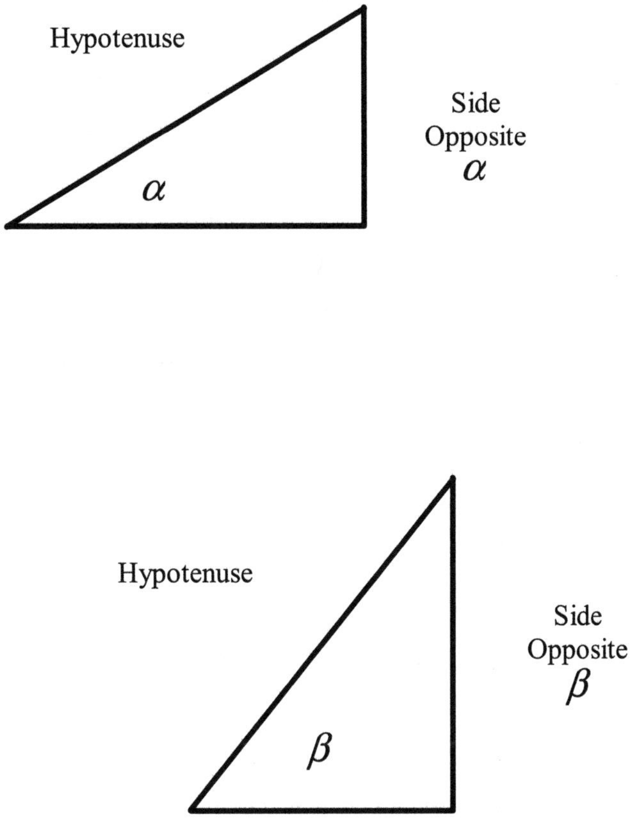

Figure 1.10 Two right triangles with the same length hypotenuse

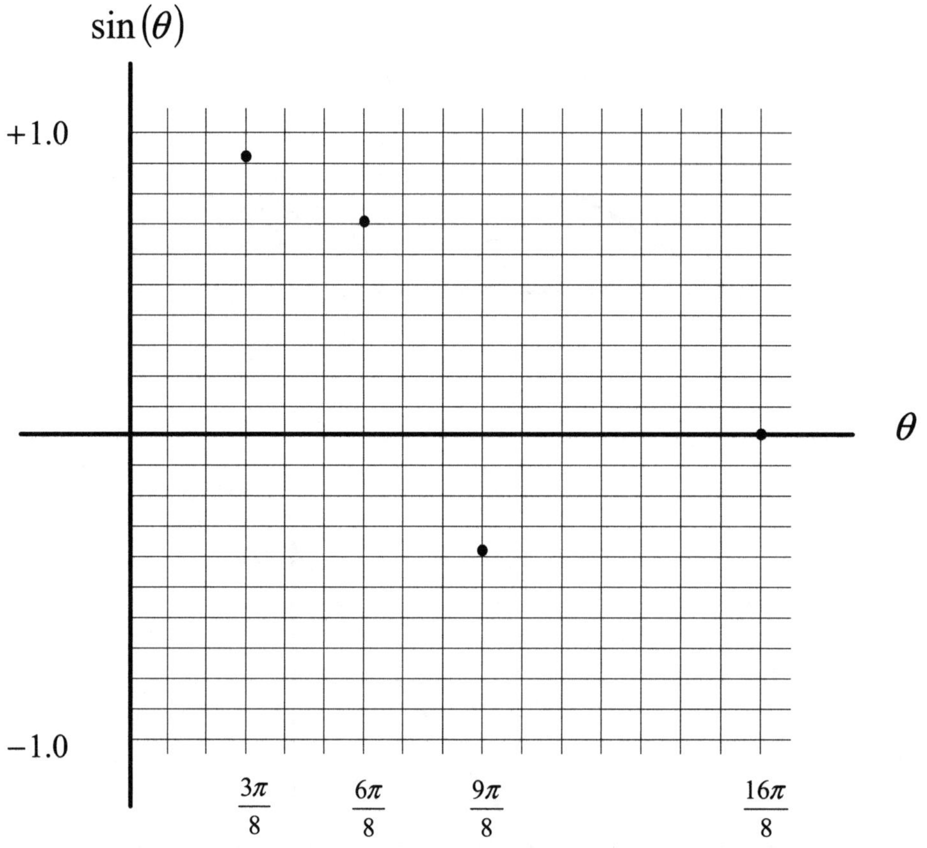

Figure 1.11 Graph of $\sin(\theta)$ vs. θ for Example 1.8

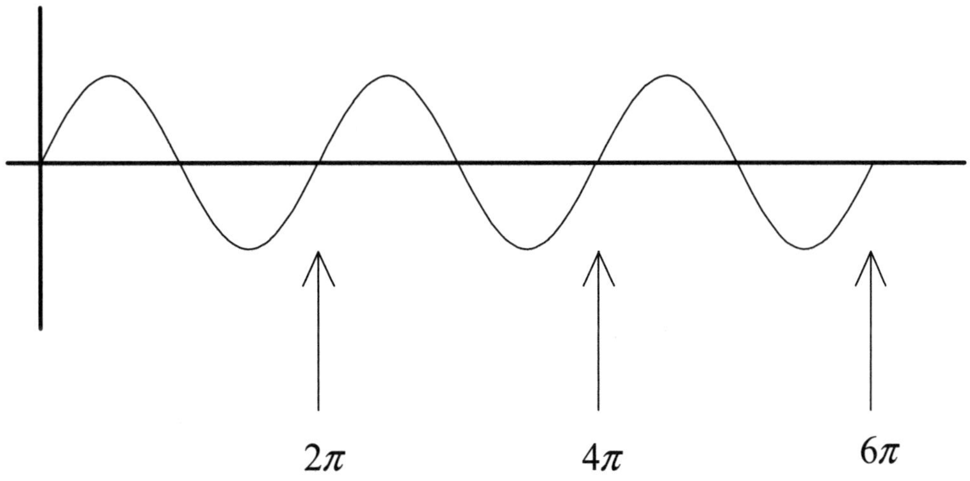

Figure 1.12 Three cycles of the sine function

Chapter 2 - Force

Timeline

1250 BC 19th dynasty Egyptians write about forces descending from the gods.

450 BC Greek philosopher Empedocles suggests that motion is caused by attractive and repulsive forces.

285 BC Euclid of Alexandria defines a solid as matter that has length, breadth, and depth.

75 AD Superstitious Romans like Pliny the Elder believe in magic forces.

360 AD Themistius, a Byzantine philosopher and commentator on the works of Aristotle, writes about the effects of what would today be called friction.

600 AD The Byzantine scholar John Philoponus proposes that a thrown object takes with it an impetus force, imparted by the arm of the thrower.

850 AD An Arabian philosopher called Al-Kindi concieves of force as an entity propogated by rays.

1325 John Buridan at the University of Paris refines the impetus theory, and also anticipates Newton's 1st law.

1490's The notebooks of Leonardo da Vinci contain studies of friction and include the discovery that friction does not depend on the surface area of contact.

1618 German astronomer Johannes Kepler initiates the modern concept of mass by associating matter, with resistance to motion.

1638 The Italian scientist Galileo Galilei disproves the impetus theory.

1659 Dutch scientist Christiaan Huygens measures the acceleration due to gravity and gets a number close to 9.8 $\frac{m}{s^2}$.

1666 In the countryside of England, Issac Newton begins work on his 3 laws of motion while hiding from the black plague.

1699 French physicist Guillaume Amontons discovers that friction is proportional to weight.

1748 Swiss mathematician Leonhard Euler differentiates between static and kinetic friction.

1894 Beginning with Professor Föppl in Germany, a new generation of physics textbooks worldwide are written to include vector analysis.

TEXT

Before we start, please note that this chapter could have been called "Learning to Write Vector Equations", because that's what is really being taught here. The problems are all about how you set them up. They are not about writing down the actual numerical answer. In fact, some of them are so easy numerically, that you can get the number in your head. But that's not the point. The point is how to draw the picture, label the forces, write the vector equation, then manipulate the units and unit vectors into the correct final form of the solution.

TEXT (again)

Mankind has always struggled to discover the rules of Nature. Aristotle in ancient Greece put together a huge book that attempted to explain how the world works. But much of it was wrong, and the study of physics didn't really crystallize until Issac Newton published his famous "3 Laws" in the late 1600's.

1. Objects moving in a straight line want to keep moving in a straight line.
2. $\vec{F} = m\vec{a}$.
3. When you push on an object, it pushes back just as hard.

The first law did not originate with Newton. It can be traced back to John Buridan in the 1300's, and it was actually demonstrated (sort of) by Galileo, before Newton was even born. (See page 327.)

It is however, very counterintuitive. The ancient Greeks thought that moving objects wanted to stop. Everything that they put into motion- a rolling ball, an arrow shot into the air, a stone skipping across a pond - always came to rest. So for many centuries most people believed that the natural state of an object was to be at rest. Then Galileo came along and conducted a brilliant set of experiments using balls and ramps. His conclusion: Moving bodies want to keep moving.

Of course Galileo's conclusion would only be true in the absence of friction. Friction, air resistance, fluid drag. Those are the forces that cause moving objects to come to rest, and caused the ancient Greeks to get the wrong idea.

Newton's second law was entirely due to Newton. Dividing both sides of the equation by m, we get

$$\vec{a} = \frac{\vec{F}}{m}, \qquad (201)$$

where $\vec{F}$ is the pushing force, m is the mass of the object being pushed, and $\vec{a}$ is the acceleration of the object. The 2nd law says that the acceleration of a pushed object will be equal to the pushing force divided by the object's mass.

Technically, acceleration is defined as the change in velocity divided by the change in time,

$$\vec{a} = \frac{\vec{v_2} - \vec{v_1}}{t_2 - t_1} \, , \tag{202}$$

where $\vec{v_2}$ is the velocity at time t_2 and $\vec{v_1}$ is the velocity at time t_1. Intuitively, we already know about acceleration. You are sitting in a car at a red light. Your speed is 0 miles per hour. The light turns green. You step on a pedal and give the car some gas. A little while later you are going 30 miles per hour. To get from 0 to 30, you had to accelerate. The pedal you stepped on is called the accelerator pedal.

Later we will come back to the technical definition of acceleration. For now we can think about it intuitively. But we need to be aware of two things. 1. Acceleration is a vector. It has both magnitude and direction. 2. Acceleration has units. The velocities in the numerator of equation (202) are expressed in meters/second. The times in the denominator are expressed in seconds.

$$\frac{\frac{m}{s}}{s} \longrightarrow \frac{\frac{m}{s}}{\frac{s}{1}} \longrightarrow \left(\frac{m}{s}\right)\left(\frac{1}{s}\right) \longrightarrow \frac{m}{s^2} \, .$$

So acceleration has units of meters per second squared.

The other quantity in Newton's 2nd law is mass. Mass can be thought of as the "quantity of matter". In other words, how much stuff is there. It units are kilograms (kg). From $\vec{F} = m\vec{a}$, the units of force then, are kilograms times meters per second squared. That unit comes up often enough to be given its own name. Appropriately it is named after Newton, so that

$$1 \; \frac{kg \; m}{s^2} \equiv 1 \; N \, .$$

The units of force are Newtons.

It is easier to feel Newton's 3rd law than it is to think about it. Right now while you're reading this, take the pointing finger of your right hand and push down - not too hard - on the top of the table. Do you feel the table pushing back on your finger? Now push down a little harder. The table pushes back a little harder. The harder you push down, the harder the table pushes back, until one of two things happens. Either you poke a hole through the table top, or your finger breaks. Newton's 3rd law: When you push on an object, it pushes back on you.

Most of this chapter is devoted to situations involving Newton's 2nd law. We will consider examples with and without friction. But before we begin, we need to extend the 2nd law to include cases where there is more that one force acting on the object's center of mass. Fortunately it's easy to do. If there is more than one force, you just add them together. If there were 3 forces, then

$$\vec{F_1} + \vec{F_2} + \vec{F_3} = m\vec{a} \, . \tag{203}$$

If there were n forces, then

$$\vec{F_1} + \vec{F_2} + ... + \vec{F_n} = m\vec{a} \, . \tag{204}$$

The left side of equation (204) is kind of long, so it is usually abbreviated by $\Sigma\vec{F}$ where

$$\Sigma\vec{F} = \vec{F_1} + \vec{F_2} + ... + \vec{F_n} \; . \tag{205}$$

The symbol Σ means "the sum of" , so Newton's 2nd law becomes,

$$\Sigma\vec{F} = m\vec{a} \; , \tag{206}$$

The sum of the forces equals $m\vec{a}$.

Forces in Outer Space

Example 2.1

Find $\vec{F_1}$ so that the space ball shown in Figure 2.1 will not move.

Solution 2.1

The term "space ball" indicates that the ball is in outer space so there are no hidden forces such as gravity. Also, there is no air resistance or friction. The only forces in play are the ones shown in the picture. We will always assume that all forces act in the same plane, and that all of them are applied along straight lines that go through the center of mass. That way we can avoid any twisting effect.

Newton's second law says that the sum of the forces equals $m\vec{a}$. But if the object doesn't move then,

$$\Sigma\vec{F} = m(0) = 0 \; . \tag{207}$$

There are 3 forces in this case, so that

$$\vec{F_1} + \vec{F_2} + \vec{F_3} = 0 \; . \tag{208}$$

The two that we know can be substituted into equation (208).

$$\vec{F_1} + \overbrace{[2(+\hat{\imath}) + 4(-\hat{\jmath})]N}^{\vec{F_2}} + \overbrace{[1(+\hat{\imath}) + 6(+\hat{\jmath})]N}^{\vec{F_3}} = 0 \; . \tag{209}$$

Adding those two together

$$\vec{F_1} + \overbrace{[3(+\hat{\imath}) + 2(+\hat{\jmath})]N}^{\vec{F_2}+\vec{F_3}} = 0 \; , \tag{210}$$

and subtracting the result from both sides of the equation

$$\begin{aligned} \vec{F_1} + [3(+\hat{\imath}) + 2(+\hat{\jmath})]N &= 0 \\ -[3(+\hat{\imath}) + 2(+\hat{\jmath})]N \qquad & \quad -[3(+\hat{\imath}) + 2(+\hat{\jmath})]N \end{aligned} \tag{211}$$

leads to

$$\vec{F_1} = -[3(+\hat{\imath}) + 2(+\hat{\jmath})]N \; . \tag{212}$$

Equation (212) is the right answer, but it is in bad form. We need to distribute the minus sign so that

$$\vec{F_1} = [3(-\hat{\imath}) + 2(-\hat{\jmath})]N \; . \tag{213}$$

This problem is very easy to check. We started with

$$\vec{F_1} + \vec{F_2} + \vec{F_3} = 0 \; . \tag{214}$$

Now that we know all 3 forces, we can just add them up and see if the total force really does equals zero.

$$\begin{array}{c} [3(-\hat{\imath}) + 2(-\hat{\jmath})]N \\ +[2(+\hat{\imath}) + 4(-\hat{\jmath})]N \\ \underline{+[1(+\hat{\imath}) + 6(+\hat{\jmath})]N} \\ [\;\; 0 \;\;\; + \;\;\; 0 \;\;]N \end{array} \tag{215}$$

$\Sigma\vec{F} = 0$ and the answer is right.

Quiz 2.1 Find $\vec{F_2}$ so that the space ball shown in Figure 2.2 will not accelerate, and check your answer.

Example 2.2

Find the acceleration of the space ball shown in Figure 2.3 and express your answer in magnitude unit vector form.

Solution 2.2

This time the applied forces do not cancel each other out, so we expect the ball to move. From $\Sigma\vec{F} = m\vec{a}$ we have,

$$\begin{aligned} m\vec{a} &= \Sigma\vec{F} \\ m\vec{a} &= \vec{F_1} + \vec{F_2} \\ &= [1(-\hat{\imath}) + 5(+\hat{\jmath})]N + [2(-\hat{\imath}) + 3(-\hat{\jmath})]N \\ m\vec{a} &= [3(-\hat{\imath}) + 2(+\hat{\jmath})]N \end{aligned} \tag{216}$$

At some point we have to convert the answer to magnitude unit vector form. The easiest way is to convert $\Sigma\vec{F}$ on the right side of the equation first, then divide by the mass later.

$$|\Sigma\vec{F}| = \sqrt{(3)^2 + (2)^2}\; N = \sqrt{9+4}\; N = \sqrt{13}\; N \; , \tag{217}$$

and

$$\frac{\Sigma\vec{F}}{|\Sigma\vec{F}|} = \frac{[3(-\hat{\imath}) + 2(+\hat{\jmath})]\ N}{\sqrt{13}\ N} = \frac{3}{\sqrt{13}}(-\hat{\imath}) + \frac{2}{\sqrt{13}}(+\hat{\jmath})\ . \tag{218}$$

So that in magnitude unit vector form,

$$\Sigma\vec{F} = \sqrt{13}\ N \left[\frac{3}{\sqrt{13}}(-\hat{\imath}) + \frac{2}{\sqrt{13}}(+\hat{\jmath})\right]\ . \tag{219}$$

Note that the Newtons in the numerator of equation (218) cancel with the Newtons in the denominator, leaving us with the interesting fact that a unit vector has no units !

Our equation now looks like

$$m\vec{a} = \sqrt{13}\ N \left[\frac{3}{\sqrt{13}}(-\hat{\imath}) + \frac{2}{\sqrt{13}}(+\hat{\jmath})\right]\ . \tag{220}$$

We just need to put in the number for m and divide both sides by that number. But first we have to express the N on the right side in terms of its basic components, so we can see what is going on with the units. An accceleration should have units of meters per second squared, and we have to show how that happens.

$$\begin{aligned}(2.5\ kg)\vec{a} &= \sqrt{13}\ \frac{kg\ m}{s^2}\left[\frac{3}{\sqrt{13}}(-\hat{\imath}) + \frac{2}{\sqrt{13}}(+\hat{\jmath})\right] \\ \vec{a} &= \frac{\sqrt{13}\ \frac{kg\ m}{s^2}}{2.5\ kg}\left[\frac{3}{\sqrt{13}}(-\hat{\imath}) + \frac{2}{\sqrt{13}}(+\hat{\jmath})\right]\end{aligned} \tag{221}$$

The kilograms cancel, and we finally wind up with

$$\vec{a} \approx 1.44\ \frac{m}{s^2}\left[\frac{3}{\sqrt{13}}(-\hat{\imath}) + \frac{2}{\sqrt{13}}(+\hat{\jmath})\right] \tag{222}$$

Note that only the magnitude of $\Sigma\vec{F}$ gets divided by the mass. The unit vector is not affected. That makes sense because the ball is going to move in the direction that you push it. Something would be wrong if $\vec{a}$ was in a different direction from $\Sigma\vec{F}$.

In equation (222), the $1.44\ \frac{m}{s^2}$ part of the answer tells us how much the ball will accelerate. The $\left[\frac{3}{\sqrt{13}}(-\hat{\imath}) + \frac{2}{\sqrt{13}}(+\hat{\jmath})\right]$ part of the answer tells us which way it will accelerate.

Quiz 2.2 Find the acceleration of the space ball shown in Figure 2.4 and express your answer in magnitude unit vector form.

Gravity and Tension

Objects that are brought close to a strong source of gravity such as a planet or a star, act as though they are being attracted to the center of that source's mass. A ball dropped from a tower on Earth for example, falls straight down as though it wants to go to the center of the Earth. Issac Newton believed that happened because objects with mass exert a gravitational force on each other in accordance with his own 2nd law. In 1915, Albert Einstein published a theory of gravity that was more like Newton's 1st law. In Einstein's theory, objects want to go in a straight line, but the "straight lines" bend in towards the center of the planet. There is no such thing as a gravitational force. Einstein's theory makes several predictions about gravity that Newton's theory does not make, and some of those predictions have already been confirmed. So we now believe Einstein to be more accurate. Unfortunately it is very difficult to calculate using Einstein's theory. Newton style calculations are much easier, and are still used for most purposes.

According to Newton's 2nd law, $\vec{F} = m\vec{a}$. So the force on an object due to gravity would equal the object's mass times the acceleration caused by gravity,

$$\vec{F}_{grav} = m\vec{a}_{grav} \, . \tag{223}$$

The acceleration caused by gravity comes up often enough to have its own name, $\vec{a}_{grav} = \vec{g}$. Galileo had observed that close to the surface of the Earth, the magnitude of the acceleration due to gravity seemed to be constant. Later on Christiaan Huygens found the actual number to be about 9.8 $\frac{m}{s^2}$.

$$\vec{a}_{grav} = \vec{g} = |\vec{g}|(-\hat{\jmath}) \approx 9.8 \, \frac{m}{s^2} \, (-\hat{\jmath}) \, , \tag{224}$$

where $-\hat{\jmath}$ is taken to be the direction of down.

Sometimes the gravitational force on an object needs to be included when you do $\Sigma\vec{F} = m\vec{a}$.

Example 2.3

Find the tension in the string that supports the hanging mass shown in Figure 2.5.

Solution 2.3

Tension, T, is the name that we give to the magnitude of the force exerted by a string. Note that tension is a magnitude, so it is not a vector. Tension is a scalar.

We start by drawing in all of the forces acting on the hanging mass. As shown in Figure 2.6, there are only two. The force due to gravity pulls the mass down. But the mass is not falling, so there must be an equal force going up, due to the tension in the string. (Remember that the forces actually act through the center of mass. They are drawn slightly to the right in Figure 2.6 simply because the string is in the way.)

The mass doesn't move in this problem, which means that its acceleration has to equal zero. Starting with $\Sigma\vec{F} = m\vec{a}$,

$$\Sigma\vec{F} = m\vec{a} = m(0) = 0$$

$$\begin{aligned}
\vec{F}_{up} + \vec{F}_{down} &= 0 \\
T(+\hat{\jmath}) + m|\vec{g}|(-\hat{\jmath}) &= 0 \\
T(+\hat{\jmath}) &= m|\vec{g}|(+\hat{\jmath}) \qquad (225)
\end{aligned}$$

Note that the $-\hat{\jmath}$ on the left becomes $+\hat{\jmath}$ when you move it to the other side of the equation. The $\hat{\jmath}$'s divide out, and

$$\begin{aligned}
\frac{T(+\hat{\jmath})}{(+\hat{\jmath})} &= \frac{m|\vec{g}|(+\hat{\jmath})}{(+\hat{\jmath})} \\
T &= m|\vec{g}| \\
&= (6\ kg)(9.8\ \frac{m}{s^2}) \\
&= 58.8\ \frac{kg\ m}{s^2} \\
T &= 58.8\ N \qquad (226)
\end{aligned}$$

We expected the tension to be a scalar, and it is.

Quiz 2.3 Find the mass shown in Figure 2.7 if the tension in the string is 49 N.

Example 2.4

A 1100 lb elevator has a tension of 3140 N in its cable. Find the acceleration of the elevator.

<u>Solution 2.4</u>

Here we are given the weight of the elevator, in units of pounds. Weight is the magnitude of the force due to gravity

$$Weight = |\vec{F}_{grav}| = m|\vec{g}|\ , \qquad (227)$$

and its SI units are Newtons. We need a way to convert pounds to Newtons. Fortunately the conversion is straightfoward,

$$2.2\ lbs = 9.8\ N\ , \qquad (228)$$

so that the weight in Newtons is

$$Weight = \left(\frac{1100\ lbs}{1}\right)\left(\frac{9.8\ N}{2.2\ lbs}\right) = 4900\ N\ . \qquad (229)$$

Because $\Sigma\vec{F} = m\vec{a}$, at some point we will need to find the mass of the elevator. We can find it right now from equation (227),

$$m = \frac{Weight}{|\vec{g}|} = \frac{4900\ \frac{kg\ m}{s^2}}{9.8\ \frac{m}{s^2}} = 500\ kg\ . \qquad (230)$$

Note that the $\frac{m}{s^2}$ in the numerator cancels the $\frac{m}{s^2}$ in the denominator leaving just kg for the units of mass.

In order to keep track of what is going on, we need to draw a picture like Figure 2.8. The picture should show the elevator and all of the forces acting on the elevator. In this case, there are two forces, a force going up due to the tension in the cable, $\vec{F}_{up} = T(+\hat{j})$, and a force going down due to gravity, $\vec{F}_{down} = \vec{F}_{grav} = m|\vec{g}|(-\hat{j})$.

$$\begin{aligned}
\Sigma\vec{F} &= m\vec{a} \\
m\vec{a} &= \vec{F}_{up} + \vec{F}_{down} \\
&= T(+\hat{j}) + m|\vec{g}|(-\hat{j}) \\
&= 3140(+\hat{j})\ N + (500\ kg)\left(9.8\ \frac{m}{s^2}\right)(-\hat{j}) \\
&= 3140(+\hat{j})\ \frac{kg\ m}{s^2} + 4900(-\hat{j})\ \frac{kg\ m}{s^2} \\
(500\ kg)\vec{a} &= 1760(-\hat{j})\ \frac{kg\ m}{s^2} \\
\vec{a} &= \frac{1760(-\hat{j})\ \frac{kg\ m}{s^2}}{500\ kg} \\
\vec{a} &= 3.52(-\hat{j})\ \frac{m}{s^2} \qquad (231)
\end{aligned}$$

The elevator is accelerating down, at 3.52 meters per second squared.

Quiz 2.4 A 770 lb elevator is accelerating up at 2.4 $\frac{m}{s^2}$. Find the tension in its cable.

Friction

Friction is the force that opposes us when we try to slide a stationary object across the floor. Probably everyone knows two facts from their own attempts to slide things: 1. The heavier the object, the harder it is to slide. 2. It is harder to start the object sliding than it is to keep it sliding.

From the 1st fact, we get the idea that friction depends on the weight of the object. From the 2nd fact, we conclude that there must be two different frictions, a stationary or *static* friction, and a moving or *kinetic* friction.

If the object is placed on a flat surface, then the strength of the static friction force is given by

$$\begin{aligned}
|\vec{F}_{fr}|_{static} &\leq \mu_s(Weight) \\
&\leq \mu_s m|\vec{g}|\ , \qquad (232)
\end{aligned}$$

and the strength of the kinetic friction force is given by

$$|\vec{F}_{fr}|_{kinetic} = \mu_k(Weight) = \mu_k m|\vec{g}|\ . \qquad (233)$$

The μ symbol is from the Greek letter "mu", and μ_s is called the coefficient of static friction, while μ_k is the coefficient of kinetic friction. The values of both μ's depend on several factors, including what kind of surface you have and what kind of material makes up the object. Also, neither μ has any units. The left sides of equations (232) and (233), are forces, with units of Newtons. The right sides are μ's multiplied by weights. But weight is already in Newtons, so for both sides of the equations to have the same units, there must not be any units on μ.

The static friction force in equation (232) has a less than or equal to sign because it can take on any value up to

$$|\vec{F}_{fr}|_{\,static\,max} = \mu_s m|\vec{g}| \,. \tag{234}$$

If you do not push a heavy object hard enough, it will not slide. Instead the friction force pushes back just as hard as you are pushing so that $\Sigma\vec{F} = 0$. You push a little, the static friction forces pushes back a little. You push a little harder, it pushes back a little harder. And so on, until you reach the maximum force that static friction can sustain. At that point the object breaks free and starts to slide. Once it is sliding, the static friction force disappears and the weaker kinetic friction force takes over. So it is easier to keep the object sliding than it was to start it sliding, and μ_k is always less than μ_s. The kinetic friction force doesn't click in until the object is already moving, and the kinetic friction force only has one single value. There is no less than sign in equation (233).

Note that equations (232) and (233) just specify the strength of the friction force. They do not specify the direction. But friction always works against you. The direction of the friction force is always opposite to the direction of the total applied force.

Example 2.5

Find the acceleration (if any) of the block shown in Figure 2.9.

<u>Solution 2.5</u>

This problem has 2 parts. First we use the static friction force to find out whether or not the block is being pushed hard enough to make it slide. If it's not, then $\vec{a} = 0$, and the problem is over. If it is, then we throw away the static friction force, and use the kinetic friction force to find $\vec{a}$. (Here was are only considering x directed forces. The y forces are there. Gravity pulls down on the block, and the surface pushes back up. But the y forces do not enter into the problem because they cancel each other out.)

Part 1

To determine whether or not the block is being pushed hard enough to make it slide, we have to answer the question

$$Is\ \ |\vec{F}_{applied}| > |\vec{F}_{fr}|_{\,static\,max}\ \ ? \tag{235}$$

From Figure 2.9

$$\begin{aligned} \vec{F}_{applied} &= 164(+\hat{\imath})\ N + 256(-\hat{\imath})\ N \\ &= 92(-\hat{\imath})\ N\,, \end{aligned} \tag{236}$$

and

$$
\begin{aligned}
|\vec{F}_{fr}|_{\ static\ max} &= \mu_s m|\vec{g}| \\
&= (.45)(16\ kg)\left(9.8\ \frac{m}{s^2}\right) \\
&= 70.56\ \frac{kg\ m}{s^2} = 70.56\ N\ . \qquad (237)
\end{aligned}
$$

$92\ N > 70.56\ N$, therefore the block is being pushed hard enough to make it accelerate, and we go on to Part 2.

Part 2

Here we are trying to find the acceleration vector, and we need to be careful about directions. It is best to draw a picture like Figure 2.10 using the information from Part 1. Note two things. The direction of the kinetic friction force is opposite to $\vec{F}_{applied}$, and it is no longer necessary to show μ_s in the picture.

$$
\begin{aligned}
\vec{F}_{fr\ kinetic} &= \mu_k m|\vec{g}| \quad \overbrace{(+\hat{\imath})}^{from\ picture} \\
&= (.40)(16\ kg)\left(9.8\ \frac{m}{s^2}\right)(+\hat{\imath}) \\
&= 62.72\ \frac{kg\ m}{s^2}(+\hat{\imath}) = 62.72(+\hat{\imath})\ N\ . \qquad (238)
\end{aligned}
$$

Now that we know $\vec{F}_{fr\ kinetic}$, we can finally add up the forces.

$$
\begin{aligned}
\Sigma\vec{F} &= m\vec{a} \\
m\vec{a} &= \vec{F}_{applied} + \vec{F}_{fr\ kinetic} \\
&= 92(-\hat{\imath})\ N + 62.72(+\hat{\imath})\ N \\
(16\ kg)\vec{a} &= 29.28(-\hat{\imath})\ N \\
\vec{a} &= \frac{29.28(-\hat{\imath})\ \frac{kg\ m}{s^2}}{16\ kg} = 1.83(-\hat{\imath})\ \frac{m}{s^2} \qquad (239)
\end{aligned}
$$

The block moves to the left, which is the direction of the total applied force, and $|\vec{a}| = 1.83\ \frac{m}{s^2}$.

Quiz 2.5 Find $\vec{a}$ for the block shown in Figure 2.11.

Things to Remember

Relationships

$$\vec{a} = \frac{\vec{v}_2 - \vec{v}_1}{t_2 - t_1}$$

$$\Sigma\vec{F} = m\vec{a}$$

$$\vec{F}_{grav} = m\vec{g}$$

$$Weight = |\vec{F}_{grav}| = |m\vec{g}| = m|\vec{g}|$$

$$|\vec{F}_{fr}|_{\,static} \leq \mu_s m|\vec{g}|$$

$$|\vec{F}_{fr}|_{\,kinetic} = \mu_k m|\vec{g}|$$

Units

$$\vec{v} \rightarrow \frac{m}{s} \qquad t \rightarrow s \qquad \vec{a} \rightarrow \frac{m}{s^2}$$

$$m \rightarrow kg \qquad \vec{F} \rightarrow \frac{kg\ m}{s^2} = N$$

$$Weight \rightarrow N \qquad T \rightarrow N \qquad \mu \rightarrow no\ units$$

Constants and Conversions

$$\vec{g} = 9.8\,\frac{m}{s^2}\,(-\hat{j}) \qquad 2.2\ lbs = 9.8\ N$$

Homework Problems Chapter 2

2.1

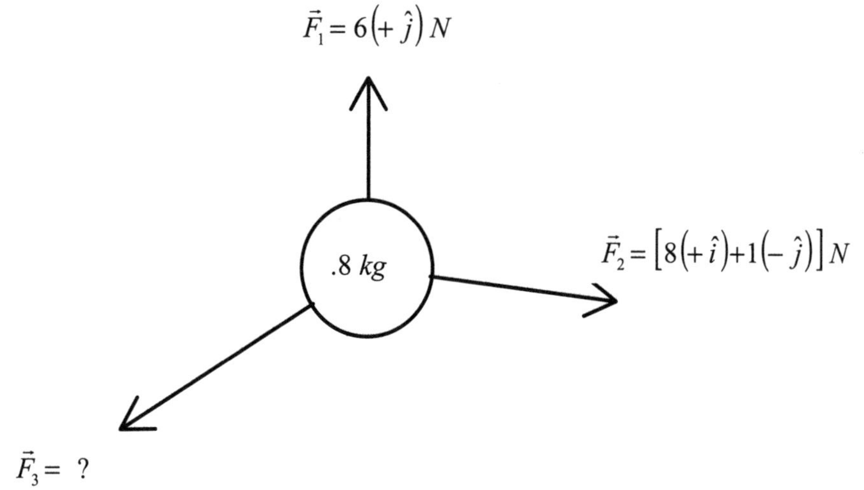

Find $\vec{F}_3$ so that the spaceball will not accelerate.

2.2

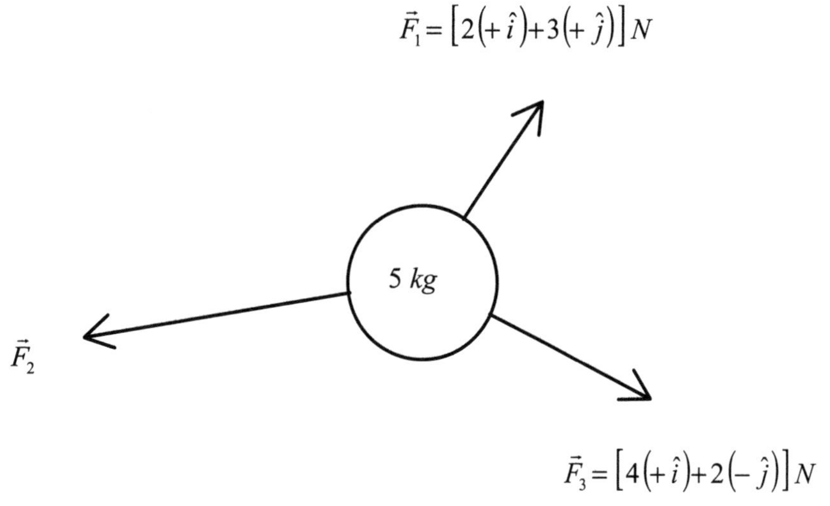

Find $\vec{F}_2$ so that the spaceball will not accelerate, and check your answer.

2.3

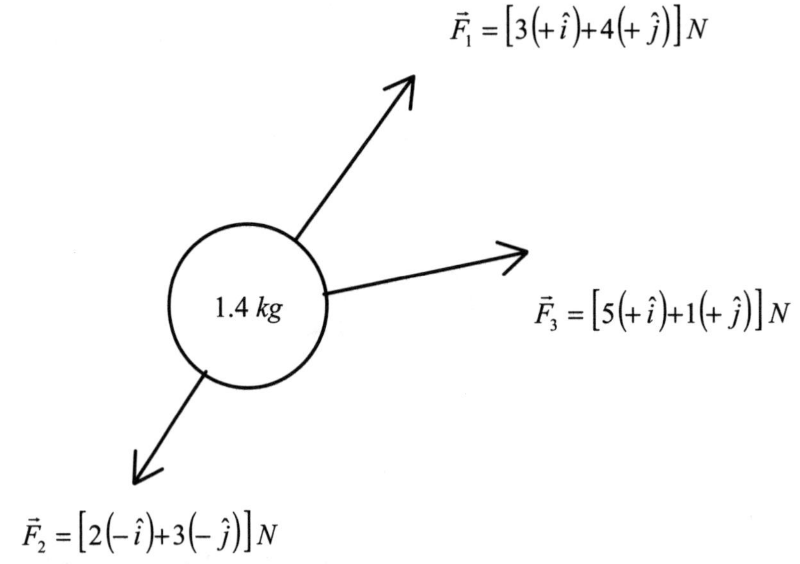

Find the spaceball's acceleration and express your answer in magnitude unit vector form.

2.4

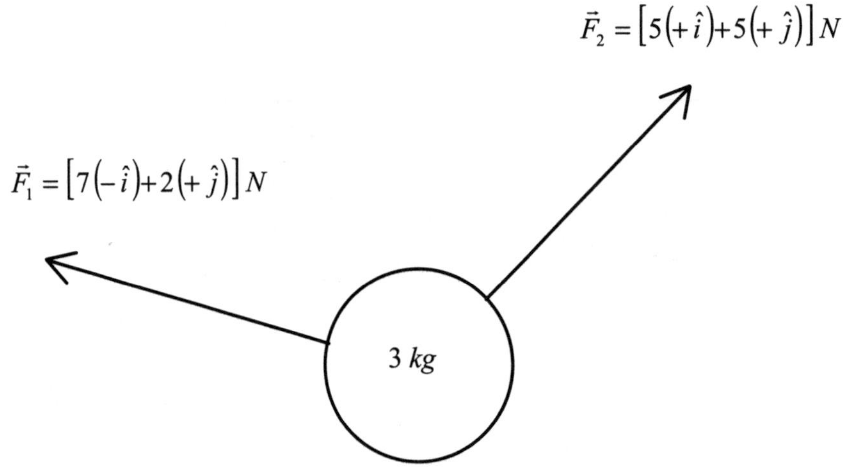

Find the spaceball's acceleration and express your answer in magnitude unit vector form.

2.5 An 8 kg hanging mass has a tension of 70.4 N in its string. Given that

$$|\vec{g}|_{Earth} \approx 9.8\ \frac{m}{s^2}$$

$$|\vec{g}|_{Venus} \approx 8.8\ \frac{m}{s^2}$$

$$|\vec{g}|_{Mars} \approx 3.7\ \frac{m}{s^2}$$

on which planet is the mass located? (Draw a picture, label forces, write a vector equation, etc.)

2.6 How much tension would be in the string of a 9.4 kg mass hanging near the surface of Mars? (Draw a picture, label forces, write a vector equation, etc.)

2.7 A 495 lb elevator is accelerating down at 1.2 $\frac{m}{s^2}$. Find the tension in its cable.

2.8 A 572 lb elevator has a tension of 1742 N in its cable. Find the acceleration of the elevator.

2.9

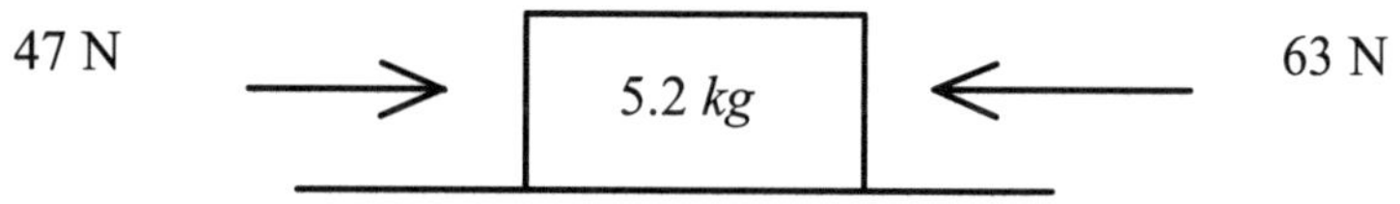

$\mu_s = .29 \qquad \mu_k = .25$

Find $\vec{a}$.

2.10

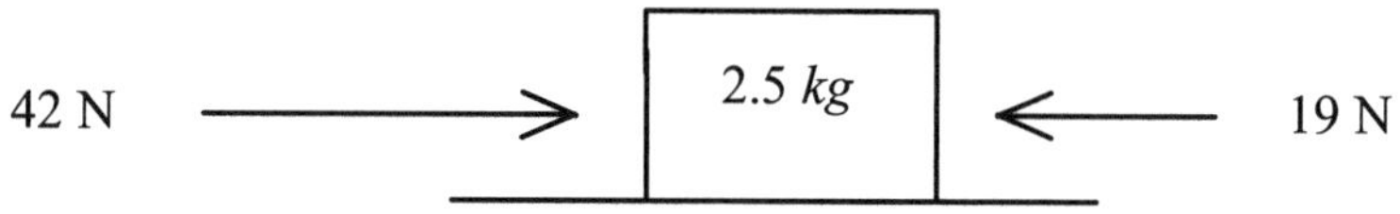

$\mu_s = .40 \qquad \mu_k = .34$

Find $\vec{a}$.

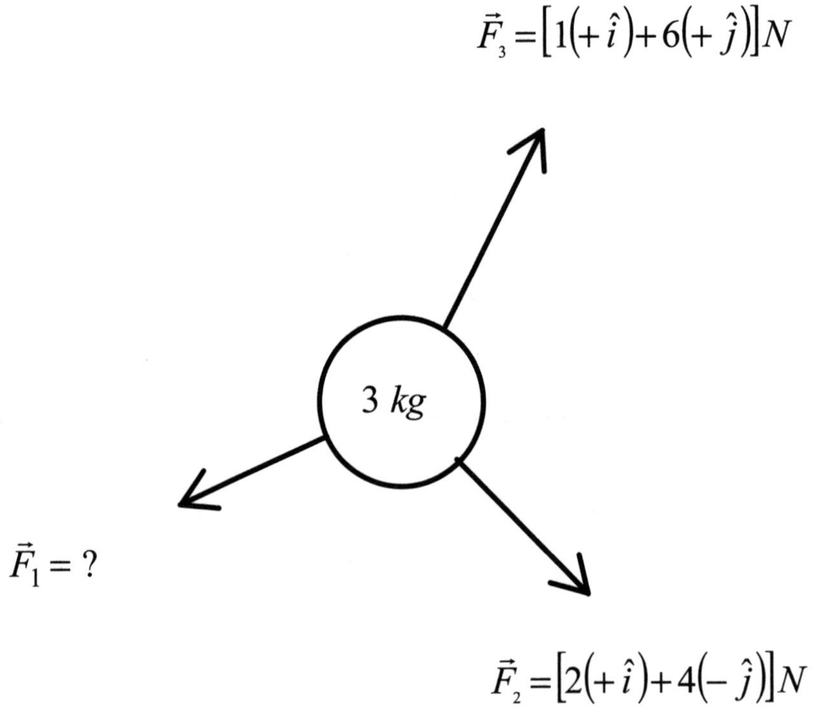

Figure 2.1 Space ball for Example 2.1

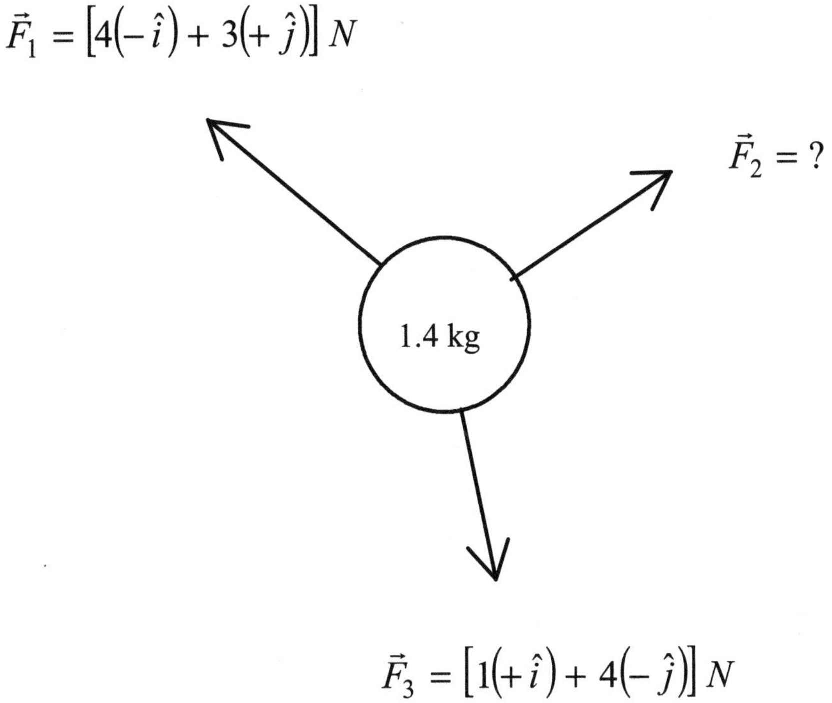

Figure 2.2 Space ball for Quiz 2.1

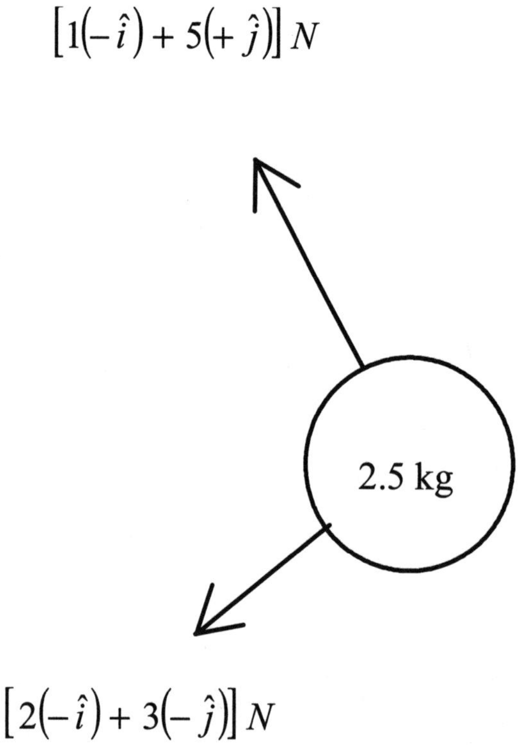

Figure 2.3 Space ball for Example 2.2

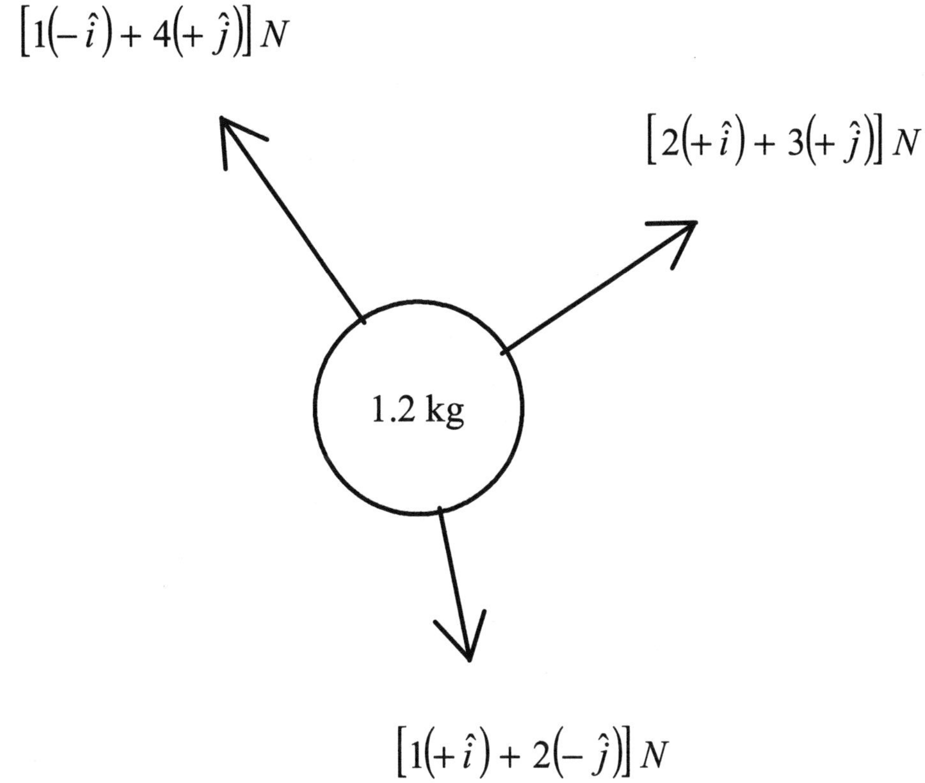

Figure 2.4 Space ball for Quiz 2.2

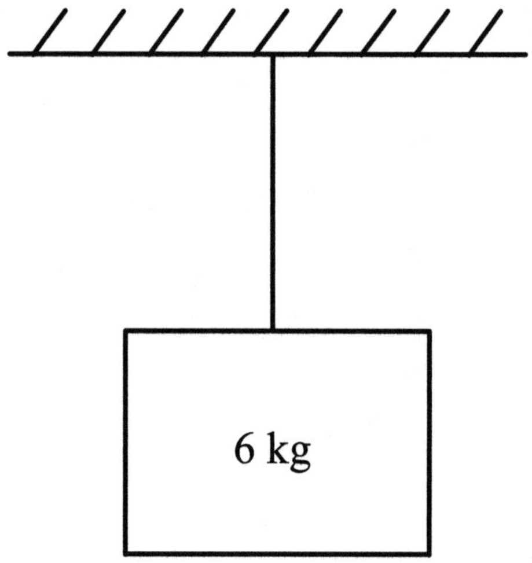

Figure 2.5 Hanging mass for Example 2.3

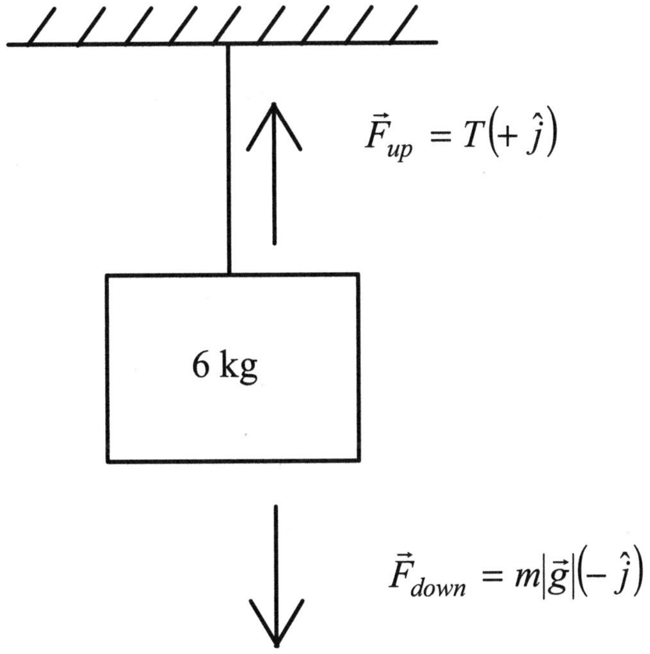

Figure 2.6 Hanging mass with forces for Example 2.3

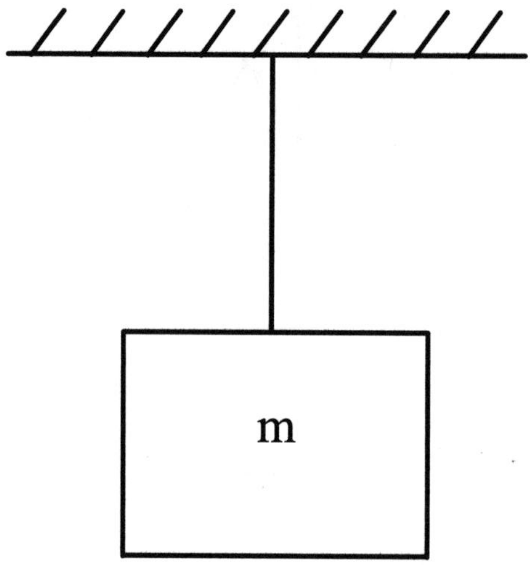

Figure 2.7 Hanging mass for Quiz 2.3

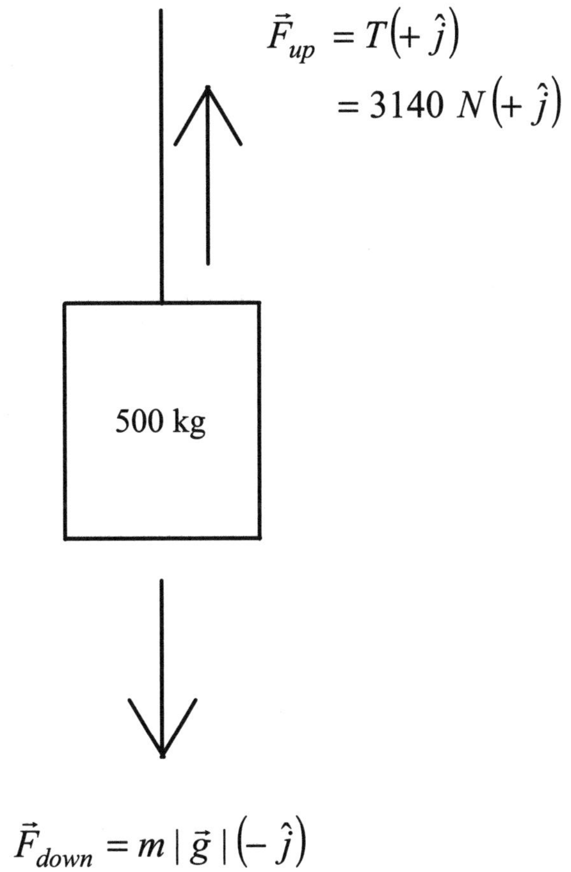

Figure 2.8 Elevator for Example 2.4

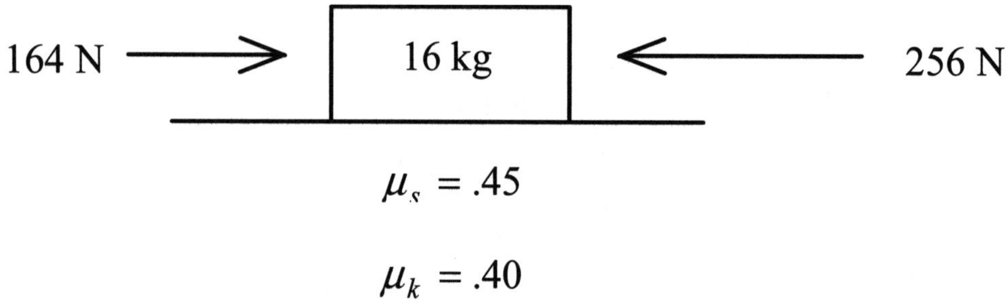

Figure 2.9 Block for Example 2.5

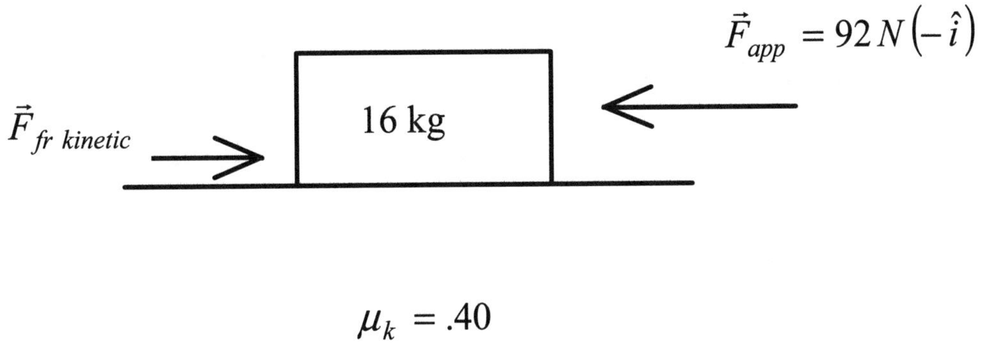

Figure 2.10 Redrawn block from Example 2.5

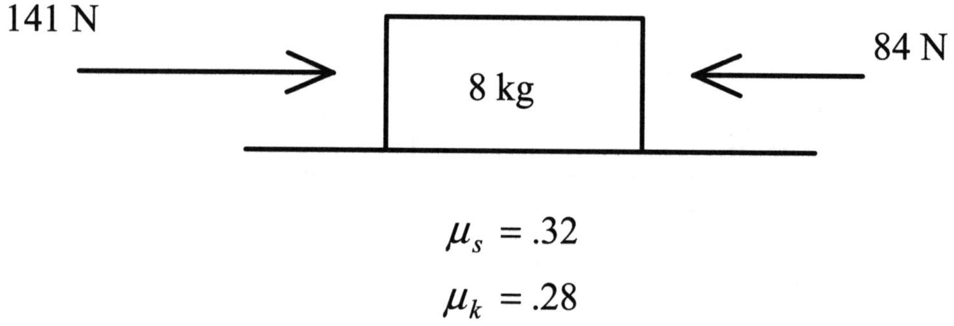

Figure 2.11 Block for Quiz 2.5

Chapter 3 - Conservation Laws

Timeline

420 BC The ancient Greek philosopher Hippocrates suggests that things posses "power" or *dynamis* - a capacity of acting or being acted upon. That idea sounds a lot like the modern concept of energy.

1638 French philosopher and mathematical scientist Rene Descartes uses the quanity that we now call *Work*. Some confusion occurs because he inappropriately names it *Force*.

1644 Rene Descartes concieves of a universe in which the *quanity of motion* $= mv$ would always be conserved. But mv doesn't work in every case.

1669 John Wallis, Christiaan Huygens, and Christopher Wren formulate a more correct Conservation Law by modifying Descartes scalar definition of *quanity of motion* $= mv$ into what would eventually become the vector definition of momentum, $\vec{p} = m\vec{v}$.

1686 A German mathematician and scientist Gottfried von Leibniz argues that *vis visa* $= mv^2$ is the quanity that is conserved, not Descartes' *quanity of motion* $= mv$.

1699 The Dutch scientist Christiaan Huygens shows that Leibniz's *vis viva* would be conserved in an elastic collision.

1829 The French physicist Gustave de Coriolis modifies von Leibniz's concept of *vis viva* $= mv^2$ into what is now called *Kinetic Energy* $= \frac{1}{2}mv^2$.

1831 An early version of what would today be called the Work-Energy Theorem appears in a paper by Coriolis.

1847 German physiologist Hermann von Helmholtz provides a mathematical formulation of the principle of Conservation of Energy. Helmholtz's terms 'living force' and 'tensional force' correspond to the modern concepts of 'kinetic energy' and 'potential energy'.

1852 Irish physcist Lord Kelvin asserts that mechanical energy can neither be created nor destroyed, only transformed.

TEXT

The history of mankind is a history of change. Nothing seems to stays the same. Governments come and go. Political ideas change. Entire civilizations rise and fall. Technology marches foward. Families are uprooted. Individuals get old and die. Even the weather, with its storms and earthquakes, droughts and floods, confronts us with continuous change.

Science is our attempt to understand the patterns of change, and to introduce an element of predictability whenever we can. The different branches of science are always searching for some aspect of a system that will stay the same, even though the system itself may change dramatically. That search reaches a high point in the conservation laws of physics.

Velocity

Imagine you are driving your car down a long stretch of empty highway. You look at the speedometer and it says 54 $\frac{miles}{hour}$. If you don't speed up, and you don't slow down, after 10 minutes you will have gone

$$\overbrace{\left(54\ \frac{miles}{hour}\right)}^{constant\ speed} \underbrace{\left(\frac{1}{6}\ hour\right)}_{travel\ time} = \overbrace{9\ miles}^{distance\ traveled} \quad . \tag{301}$$

Actually, even if you had been going 55 $\frac{miles}{hour}$ for 5 minutes, and 53 $\frac{miles}{hour}$ for 5 minutes, your distance traveled would still be

$$\overbrace{\left(54\ \frac{miles}{hour}\right)}^{average\ speed} \left(\frac{1}{6}\ hour\right) = 9\ miles\ , \tag{302}$$

because your *average speed* for the 10 minutes is still 54 $\frac{miles}{hour}$. In fact, we could define average speed as

$$average\ speed \quad = \quad \frac{distance\ traveled}{travel\ time} \quad .$$

But speed, either average or constant, by itself is not a very usuful quantity. It tells you how fast an object is going, but it does not tell you which way it is going. Fortunately we can convert speed into *velocity* by giving it a direction.

$$\vec{v} = |\vec{v}|\ (direction\ unit\ vector)\ , \tag{303}$$

where $\vec{v}$ is velocity, $|\vec{v}|$ is the magnitude of velocity (or speed), and the *direction unit vector* indicates which way the object is moving.

The distinction between speed and velocity, scalar and vector, is important enough to emphasize. Here it is.

$$\vec{v} = \text{velocity} \longrightarrow \text{a vector.}$$
$$|\vec{v}| = v = \text{speed} \longrightarrow \text{a scalar.}$$

Speed is the magnitude of velocity, and it can either be written $|\vec{v}|$ or v. (The author prefers $|\vec{v}|$ since that notation makes it very clear that speed is part of a vector.)

Conservation of Momentum

Look at the two inelastic balls shown in Figure 3.1. They start by moving towards each other, then they collide and move away from each other. Each ball has a incoming velocity before the collision, and each ball has a outgoing velocity after the collision. Note that velocity is a vector quantity. The speed part of velocity is its magnitude. It tells you how many meters the object will travel in one second. The direction part of velocity is its unit vector. It tells you which way the object is going.

During the collision, Newton's 3rd law states that the force exerted on ball 2 by ball 1 has to be equal and opposite to the force exerted on ball 1 by ball 2.

$$\vec{F}_{12} = -\vec{F}_{21} \ . \tag{304}$$

Starting with equation (304), and substituting Newton's 2nd law for $\vec{F}$, it is pretty easy to show that

$$m_1\vec{v}_{1\,b} + m_2\vec{v}_{2\,b} = m_1\vec{v}_{1\,a} + m_2\vec{v}_{2\,a} \ , \tag{305}$$

where

m_1 is the mass of ball 1,
m_2 is the mass of ball 2,
$\vec{v}_{1\,b}$ is the velocity of m_1 before the collision,
$\vec{v}_{1\,a}$ is the velocity of m_1 after the collision,
$\vec{v}_{2\,b}$ is the velocity of m_2 before the collision,
and
$\vec{v}_{2\,a}$ is the velocity of m_2 after the collision.

(See page 327.)

Equation (305) is a statement of Conservation of linear Momentum. The quantity $m\vec{v}$ is called linear momentum, and its units are $\frac{kg\,m}{s}$. Conservation of Momentum says that the total linear momentum of the balls before the collision has to equal the total linear momentum of the balls after the collision.

The units of linear momentum are $\dfrac{kg\,m}{s}$.

Example 3.1

A 3 kg mass moving to the left at 1 $\frac{m}{s}$ collides head on with a 2 kg mass moving to the right at 4 $\frac{m}{s}$. After the collision, the 2 kg mass changes direction and moves off to the left at 1.5 $\frac{m}{s}$. What is the new velocity of the 3 kg mass?

Solution 3.1

The 1st step is to draw a set of before and after pictures like the ones in Figure 3.2. You need a picture showing the masses and their velocities before the collision, and a picture showing the masses and their velocities after the collision.

Start with Conservation of Momentum,

$$m_1\vec{v}_{1\,b} + m_2\vec{v}_{2\,b} = m_1\vec{v}_{1\,a} + m_2\vec{v}_{2\,a}\ . \tag{306}$$

Now look at your picture, and plug the appropriate quantities into the equation.

$$(3\ kg)\left(1\ \frac{m}{s}\right)(-\hat{\imath}) + (2\ kg)\left(4\ \frac{m}{s}\right)(+\hat{\imath}) = (3\ kg)\vec{v}_{1\,a} + (2\ kg)\left(1.5\ \frac{m}{s}\right)(-\hat{\imath}). \tag{307}$$

Then solve for the unknown quanity.

$$\begin{aligned}
3\ \frac{kg\ m}{s}(-\hat{\imath}) + 8\ \frac{kg\ m}{s}(+\hat{\imath}) &= (3\ kg)\vec{v}_{1\,a} + 3\ \frac{kg\ m}{s}(-\hat{\imath}) \\
5\ \frac{kg\ m}{s}(+\hat{\imath}) + 3\ \frac{kg\ m}{s}(+\hat{\imath}) &= (3\ kg)\vec{v}_{1\,a} \\
\vec{v}_{1\,a} &= \frac{8\ \frac{kg\ m}{s}(+\hat{\imath})}{3\ kg} \\
\vec{v}_{1\,a} &= \frac{8}{3}\ \frac{m}{s}(+\hat{\imath})
\end{aligned} \tag{308}$$

It looks like the 3 kg mass also reverses direction and moves off to the right at about 2.66 $\frac{m}{s}$.

Quiz 3.1 A 5 kg mass moving to the right at 4 $\frac{m}{s}$ collides head on with a 2 kg mass moving to the left at 3 $\frac{m}{s}$. After the collision the 2 kg mass changes direction and moves off to the right at 4.5 $\frac{m}{s}$. What is the new velocity of the 5 kg mass ?

Conservation of Energy

Suppose you bend over, pick up a rock that is lying on the ground, then slowly lift it straight up to a height h. The force needed to lift the rock would be

$$\begin{aligned}
\vec{F}_{against\ gravity} &= m(-\vec{a}_{grav}) + \vec{F}_{extra} \\
&= mg(+\hat{\jmath}) + ma_{extra}(+\hat{\jmath})\ ,
\end{aligned} \tag{309}$$

where the $mg(+\hat{\jmath})$ force is necessary to overcome gravity, and $\vec{F}_{extra}$ is whatever extra force that you apply. If the rock is lifted very slowly so that a_{extra} is almost zero then

$$\vec{F}_{against\ gravity} \approx mg(+\hat{\jmath})\ . \tag{310}$$

So in the limit as

$$\vec{a}_{extra} \to 0 \quad \vec{F}_{against\ gravity} \to mg(+\hat{\jmath})\ . \tag{311}$$

With respect to the ground, the rock is lifted through a distance

$$\vec{d} = h(+\hat{j}) \ . \tag{312}$$

If we dot the distance into the force,

$$\vec{F}_{against\ gravity} \bullet \vec{d} = \left[mg(+\hat{j})\right] \bullet \left[h(+\hat{j})\right] = mgh \ . \tag{313}$$

The mgh in equation (313) is called *gravitational potential energy,* and it represents the work done against gravity to lift a mass m up to a height h (neglecting air resistance). Usually the word "gravitational" is dropped, so that

$$PE = mgh \ , \tag{314}$$

where PE represents potential energy (due to gravity in this case). Let's look at the units.

$$mgh \rightarrow kg\left(\frac{m}{s^2}\right) m \rightarrow \left(\frac{kg\ m}{s^2}\right) m \rightarrow N\ m \ .$$

The unit $N\ m$ comes up often enough to have its own name. It is called a Joule, after James Joule, who was the 1st person to demonstrate the equivalence of mechanical energy and heat energy. So

$$1\ N\ m \equiv 1\ J \ .$$

Potential energy has units of Joules (J).

Suppose now the rock is released. It falls, and as it falls it picks up speed. That kind of energy, the energy due to speed, is called *Kinetic Energy.*

$$KE = \frac{1}{2}mv^2 \ , \tag{315}$$

where m is the mass of the rock and v is its speed. Let's look at those units.

$$\frac{1}{2}mv^2 \rightarrow kg\left(\frac{m}{s}\right)^2 \rightarrow \left(\frac{kg\ m}{s^2}\right) m \rightarrow N\ m \rightarrow J \ .$$

So kinetic energy also has units of Joules (J).

The units of energy are Joules (J).

The rock starts out stationary, with a potential energy of $PE = mgh$, and a kinetic energy of $KE = \frac{1}{2}mv^2 = \frac{1}{2}m(0)^2 = 0$. As it falls, the rock goes faster and faster, but it gets closer and closer to the ground. In other words, h decreases but v increaes. By the time it hits, $PE = mgh = mg(0) = 0$ and $KE = \frac{1}{2}mv^2_{maximum}$. All of its potential energy has been converted into kinetic energy.

That conversion takes place in such a way that for any two points along the fall.

$$KE_1 + PE_1 = KE_2 + PE_2 + loss \tag{316}$$

where 1 represents point one, 2 represents point 2, and the *loss* term needs to be included if there is air resistance, friction, or some other source of loss (See page 328.)

Equation (316) is a statement of Conservation of Energy, and it is believed to apply to any mechanical situation (not just to a falling ball).

Conservation of Energy has been interpreted to mean, "Energy can neither be created nor destroyed, but only changed into other forms." We can see that change take place in the fall of a dropped ball. The ball starts out stationary at some height above the ground, h. It has a lot of potential energy, $PE = mgh$, but no kinetic energy, $KE = \frac{1}{2}m(0)^2 = 0$. As the ball falls, it gets closer and closer to the ground so that h is always decreasing. It is losing potential energy. At the same time the ball is going faster and faster so that v is always increasing. It is gaining kinetic energy. By the time it reaches the ground, $PE = mg(0) = 0$, and $KE = \frac{1}{2}mv^2_{max}$. All of its original potential energy has been transformed into kinetic energy. According to equation (316), that transformation takes place in such a way that the total $KE+PE$ at any point during the fall equals the total $KE + PE$ at any other point during the fall (neglecting air resistance).

Example 3.2

A .015 kg golf ball is dropped from a height of 3.2 m. How fast is the ball going when it hits the ground ?

Solution 3.2

Conservation of Energy problems always involve two different positions of the object being analyzed. The first step is to draw a picture like Figure 3.3 that shows the object in each position, then label the two KE's and the two PE's. For this particular problem the ball starts out stationary so that $KE_1 = 0$, and it winds up on the ground so that $PE_2 = 0$. **Note that the beginning position always has the 1 subscript and the final position always has the 2 subscript.**

Once the picture has been labeled, we can write the energy balance equation and sub in the labels from the picture. Ignoring loss,

$$\begin{aligned} KE_1 + PE_1 &= KE_2 + PE_2 + \overbrace{loss}^{\approx 0} \\ 0 + mgh_1 &= \frac{1}{2}mv_2^2 + 0 \end{aligned} \tag{317}$$

The next step is to algebraically solve for the variable of interest,

$$\begin{aligned} \frac{1}{2}mv_2^2 &= mgh_1 \\ v_2^2 &= \frac{mgh_1}{\frac{1}{2}m} \\ &= 2gh_1 \\ v &= \sqrt{2gh_1} \end{aligned} \tag{318}$$

Before we plug the numbers into equation (318), we need to do a unit analysis to make sure that our units are going to come out right. The speed v on the left side of the equation has units of $\frac{m}{s}$. On the right side,

$$\begin{aligned}\sqrt{2gh_1} &\rightarrow \sqrt{\left(\frac{m}{s^2}\right)m}\\ &\rightarrow \sqrt{\frac{m^2}{s^2}} \rightarrow \frac{m}{s}\,.\end{aligned}$$

The right side also has $\frac{m}{s}$, so the units look OK. Note that the number 2 in front of the gh_1 is not included in the unit analysis. A unit analysis just shows units. It does does not show numbers.

The last step is to plug in the numbers,

$$\begin{aligned}v &= \left[\sqrt{(2)(9.8)(3.2)}\right]\frac{m}{s}\\ &= \left[\sqrt{62.72}\right]\frac{m}{s}\\ v &\approx 7.92\,\frac{m}{s}\,. \qquad (319)\end{aligned}$$

Here we do not need to attach units to every term, because we have already done the units in a separate analysis. We do need to show the final units of $\frac{m}{s}$ as we go along.

It is very important to recognize that energy is a scalar quantity. The energy balance equation is a scalar equation. There are no directions associated with energy. Momentum on the other hand, is a vector quantity. The Conservation of Momentum equation is a vector equantion, and every term has to have a direction.

Quiz 3.2 A .02 kg rock is thrown straight up at 7.92 $\frac{m}{s}$. How high does it go? (Note that the ball goes up, stops, then comes back down, so that $v_{at\ top} = 0$.)

Example 3.3

A .025 kg ball is thrown straight up at 12 $\frac{m}{s}$. How high is it when it is going 5 $\frac{m}{s}$?

Solution 3.3

We start with a picture like Figure 3.4, showing the two positions and their respective energies. This time, only $PE_1 = 0$. Again ignoring loss,

$$\begin{aligned}KE_1 + PE_1 &= KE_2 + PE_2 + \overbrace{loss}^{\approx 0}\\ \frac{1}{2}mv_1^2 + 0 &= \frac{1}{2}mv_2^2 + mgh_2\end{aligned}$$

$$
\begin{aligned}
mgh_2 &= \frac{1}{2}mv_1^2 - \frac{1}{2}mv_2^2 \\
h_2 &= \frac{\frac{1}{2}mv_1^2 - \frac{1}{2}mv_2^2}{mg} = \frac{m\left(\frac{1}{2}v_1^2 - \frac{1}{2}v_2^2\right)}{mg} \\
h_2 &= \frac{1}{2}\left(\frac{v_1^2 - v_2^2}{g}\right) \qquad (320)
\end{aligned}
$$

We are ready to put in the numbers, but 1st we need to do a unit analysis. On the right hand side,

$$
\frac{\left(\frac{m}{s}\right)^2 - \left(\frac{m}{s}\right)^2}{\left(\frac{m}{s^2}\right)} \rightarrow \frac{\frac{m^2}{s^2}}{\frac{m}{s^2}} \rightarrow \left(\frac{m^2}{s^2}\right)\left(\frac{s^2}{m}\right) \rightarrow m \; .
$$

The right side has units of meters. The h on the left side also has units of m, so the units look OK. Note that the two $\left(\frac{m}{s}\right)^2$ terms in the numerator do not subtract away to zero. That's because our unit analysis does not contain any numbers. If the numbers in front of the $\left(\frac{m}{s}\right)^2$ terms were included, those two terms would definitely not subtract away to zero. Instead the difference of the terms would have a new number out in front, but it would still have the same units. In a unit analysis the numbers are not shown, so any string of identical units separated by a + or - sign just collapses to one term having those same units.

Continuing on,

$$
\begin{aligned}
h_2 &= \left\{\frac{1}{2}\left[\frac{(12)^2 - (5)^2}{9.8}\right]\right\} m \\
h_2 &\approx 6.07\, m \qquad (321)
\end{aligned}
$$

The ball is about 6 m high when it is going 5 $\frac{m}{s}$.

Quiz 3.3 A .04 kg rock is dropped from the top of a 20 m tower. How high is the rock when it is going 14 $\frac{m}{s}$?

Example 3.4

A 30 kg child climbs to the top of a 3 m high playground slide, and then slides down. How much energy was consumed by friction if she reaches the ground going 2 $\frac{m}{s}$?

Solution 3.4

Figure 3.5 shows the picture. This time $KE_1 = 0$ and $PE_2 = 0$.

The problem is asking for the loss of energy due to friction, so we need to include the loss term in our energy balance equation.

$$
\begin{aligned}
KE_1 + PE_1 &= KE_2 + PE_2 + loss \\
0 + mgh_1 &= \frac{1}{2}mv_2^2 + 0 + loss \\
loss &= mgh_1 - \frac{1}{2}mv_2^2 \qquad (322)
\end{aligned}
$$

Before we put in the numbers, we should check the units.

$$kg\left(\frac{m}{s^2}\right)m - kg\left(\frac{m}{s}\right)^2 \to \left(\frac{kg\ m}{s^2}\right)m \to N\ m \to J\ .$$

The units are OK, so

$$\begin{aligned} loss &= \left[(30)(9.8)(3) - \frac{1}{2}(30)(2)^2\right]\ J \\ &= [882 - 60]\ J \\ loss &= 822\ J \end{aligned} \qquad (323)$$

Most of the original energy in this problem was used up by friction, and that is why the child is going so slow by the time she reaches the bottom of the slide.

Conservation of Energy is believed to be true in any physical situation. So it is OK to apply the energy balance equation to the playground slide in Example 3.4, even though we derived the equation for a ball being thrown up into the air. (See page 328.)

Quiz 3.4 A .02 kg hockey puck slides across the ice with an initial speed of 18 $\frac{m}{s}$. How fast is it going by the time it has lost 2.1 Joules of energy ?

The Concept of Work

Equation (A-14) from page 329,

$$\vec{F} \bullet \vec{d} = \frac{1}{2}mv_2^2 - \frac{1}{2}mv_1^2\ , \qquad (324)$$

is a famous physics equation in its own right. It is called the constant force work-energy theorem. The right hand side of the equation is the energy part. It consists of the final KE minus the original KE. The left hand side is the work part. The work done on an object by a constant force is defined as

$$Work_{\,by\ cf} = \vec{F} \bullet \vec{d}\ , \qquad (325)$$

where $\vec{F}$ is the constant net force (after friction or any other opposition) that causes the object to move, and $\vec{d}$ is the vector distance traveled by the object.

We already know that the units on the energy side of the work-energy theorem are Joules. On the work side,

$$\vec{F} \bullet \vec{d} \to N\ m \to J\ ,$$

the units are also Joules.

The units of $Work$ are Joules (J).

Example 3.5

How much work is done by moving the Figure 3.6 wagon 4 m to the right ?

Solution 3.5

From the picture

$$\begin{aligned}
Work &= \vec{F} \bullet \vec{d} \\
&= 150\ N \left[\frac{1.8}{\sqrt{4.24}}(+\hat{\imath}) + \frac{1}{\sqrt{4.24}}(+\hat{\jmath}) \right] \bullet [4(+\hat{\imath}) + 0(+\hat{\jmath})]m \\
&= \left[(150)\left(\frac{1.8}{\sqrt{4.24}} \right)(4) \right]\ N\ m \\
Work &\approx 524.49\ J
\end{aligned} \tag{326}$$

Nothing to it, but there are a couple of things to note. The force is being applied to the wagon through the handle. Only the $+\hat{\imath}$ part of the force goes into moving the wagon to the right. The $+\hat{\jmath}$ part is directed up, trying to lift the wagon off the ground. The dot product in equation (326) makes sure that the only part of the force included in the work, is the part that causes the object to move. The other thing to note is that the mass of the wagon is not included in the work calculation.

Quiz 3.5 How much work is done on the Figure 3.7 piston if it moves 12 cm straight up?

Things to Remember

Relationships

$$\vec{p} = m\vec{v}$$

$$m_1\vec{v}_{1\,b} + m_2\vec{v}_{2\,b} = m_1\vec{v}_{1\,a} + m_2\vec{v}_{2\,a}$$

$$KE = \frac{1}{2}mv^2$$

$$PE = mgh$$

$$KE_1 + PE_1 = KE_2 + PE_2 + loss$$

$$Work_{\,done\ by\ a\ constant\ force} = \vec{F} \bullet \vec{d}$$

$$\vec{F} \bullet \vec{d} = \frac{1}{2}mv_2^2 - \frac{1}{2}mv_1^2$$

Units

$$\vec{p} \rightarrow \frac{kg\ m}{s} \qquad KE \text{ and } PE \rightarrow kg\left(\frac{m}{s^2}\right)m \rightarrow N\ m \rightarrow J$$

$$Work \rightarrow N\ m \rightarrow J$$

Homework Problems Chapter 3

3.1 A 1.4 *kg* mass traveling to the right at $5\frac{m}{s}$ collides head on with an unknown mass traveling to the left at $4\frac{m}{s}$. After the collision both masses travel to the left. The 1.4 *kg* mass moves at $2.2\frac{m}{s}$, and the unknown mass moves at $1.76\frac{m}{s}$. How many kilograms is the unknown mass?

3.2 A 3.6 *kg* mass moving to the right at $6\frac{m}{s}$ strikes a stationary 2 *kg* mass. After the collision the 2 *kg* mass moves off to the right at $7.2\frac{m}{s}$. What is the new velocity of the 3.6 *kg* mass?

3.3 On the Moon, a .2 *kg* ball thrown straight up at $3.6\frac{m}{s}$ goes 4 *m* high. What is the acceleration due to gravity on the Moon?

3.4 If a golf ball is dropped from the top of a 10 *m* tower (on Earth), how fast will it be going when it hits the ground?

3.5 Suppose instead of being dropped, that same golf ball is thrown straight down at $20\frac{m}{s}$ from the top of the 10 *m* tower. Now how fast will it be going when it hits the ground?

3.6 A .4 *kg* mass is dropped from a height of 8 *m*. How much kinetic energy does it have when it is 2 *m* high?

3.7 A .1 *kg* rubber ball is dropped from a height of 2 *m*. How high will it bounce back up if it loses .49 *J* of energy due to air resistance, the collision with the floor, etc.?

3.8 A .75 *kg* box slides across the floor and comes to rest after losing 13.5 *J* of energy. How fast was it going when it started to slide?

3.9 How much work is done by a net force of $\left[64(+\hat{i})+32(-\hat{j})\right]N$ that causes an object to move from $(-2,3)m$ to $(5,1)m$?

3.10 A shopper pushes on the handle of a 9 *kg* grocery cart delivering a net force of 55 *N* $\left[\frac{4}{5}(-\hat{i})+\frac{3}{5}(-\hat{j})\right]$. a) How much work is done when the cart moves 2 *m* to the left? b) Could the cart have moved to the right?

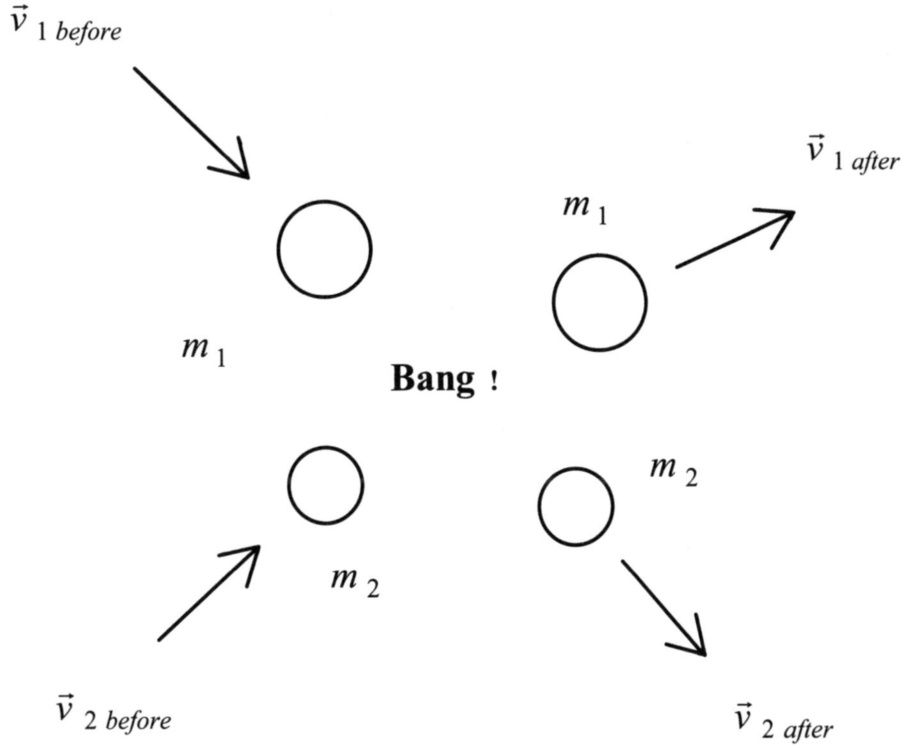

Figure 3.1 Colliding Masses

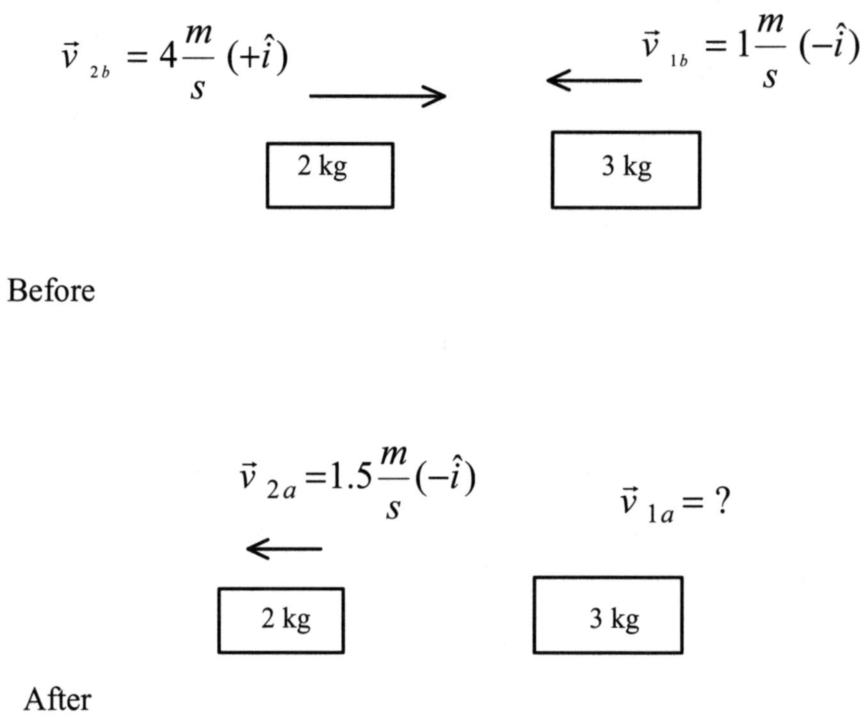

Figure 3.2 Collision for Example 3.1

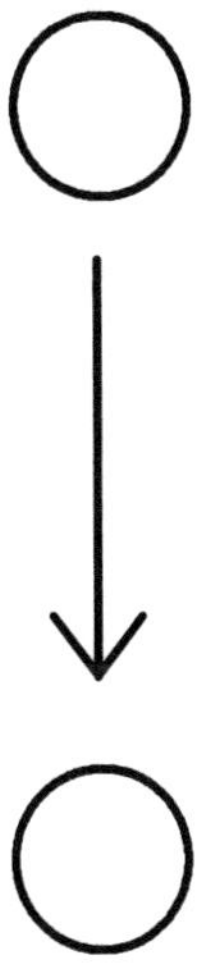

$$PE_1 = mgh_1$$

$$KE_1 = \frac{1}{2}mv_1^2 = \frac{1}{2}m(0)^2 = 0$$

$$PE_2 = mgh_2 = mg(0) = 0$$

$$KE_2 = \frac{1}{2}mv_2^2$$

Figure 3.3 Golf ball for Example 3.2

$$PE_2 = mgh_2$$

$$KE_2 = \frac{1}{2}mv_2^2$$

$$PE_1 = mgh_1 = mg(0) = 0$$

$$KE_1 = \frac{1}{2}mv_1^2$$

Figure 3.4 Ball for Example 3.3

$$PE_1 = mgh_1$$

$$KE_1 = \frac{1}{2}mv_1^2 = \frac{1}{2}m(0)^2 = 0$$

$$PE_2 = mgh_2 = mg(0) = 0$$

$$KE_2 = \frac{1}{2}mv_2^2$$

Figure 3.5   Slide for Example 3.4

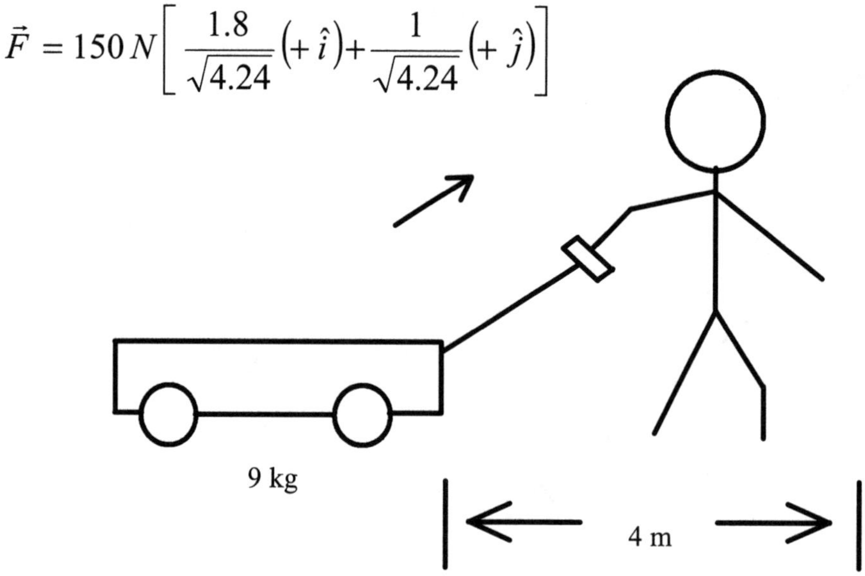

Figure 3.6 Wagon for Example 3.5

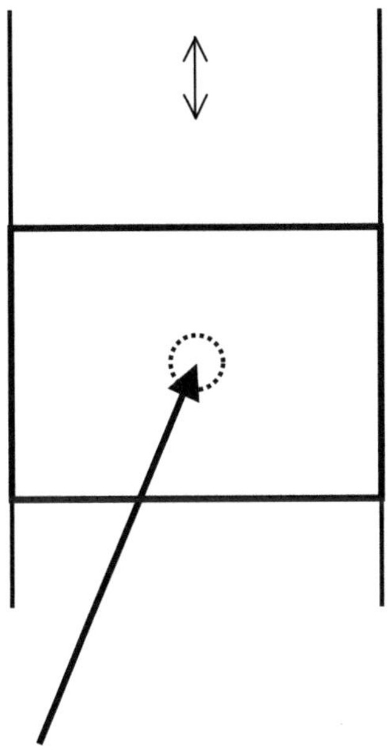

$$\vec{F}_{net} = m\vec{g} + \vec{F}_{friction} + \vec{F}_{applied}$$

$$= 420\,N\left[\frac{2}{\sqrt{20}}\left(+\hat{i}\right) + \frac{4}{\sqrt{20}}\left(+j\right)\right]$$

Figure 3.7 Sliding piston for Quiz 3.5

Chapter 4 - Thermodynamics

Timeline

1800 BC An ancient Egyptian document, known today as the Moscow Papyrus, includes a formula for calculating the volume of a truncated pyramid.

440 BC The early Greek philosopher Empedocles writes about air pushing water out of a bronze container.

70 AD Hero of Alexandria invents the world's 1st steam engine.

170 AD The Greek physician Galen attempts to set up a temperature scale and measure temperature.

1653 French mathematician and physicist Blaise Pascal clarifies the concept of pressure into $P = |\vec{F}| \div Area$

1712 English blacksmith Thomas Newcomen invents the 1st steam engine to use a piston.

1760 Scottish chemistry professor Joseph Black pioneers the concept of specific heat, which was later incorporated into $Q = mC(T_f - T_o)$.

1824 Sadi Carnot, a French engineer and mathematician, proposes a model for the ideal heat engine.

1834 French engineer Emile Clapeyron uses a pressure-volume diagram to analyze Carnot's heat engine. He also combines Boyle's Law and Charles' Law into the ideal gas law.

1843 British physicist James Prescott Joule demonstrates that mechanical work can be converted into heat energy.

1850 Rudolf Clausius, a German professor of physics and mathematics, proposes the 1st two laws of thermodynamics.

1851 William Thomson, the Irish scientist who became Lord Kelvin, publishes the idea that heat originates in the energy of motion of the unobservable particles (molecules) of a substance.

TEXT

Thermodynamics is the science of converting heat into work. Usually some kind of gas is confined inside a closed cylinder. The cylinder has a sliding top called a piston. The gas is heated and it expands. The piston gets pushed up, producing work. Thermodynamics drove the steam engines of the Industrial Revolution, and the same principles are still widely used today. Automobile engines, jet engines, and the turbines used to generate electricity, are a just few of the many modern applications of thermodynamics.

PVT and the Ideal Gas Law

In the thermodynamic picture, gasses are thought to be loose collections of individual molecules that are bouncing around all over the place like a swarm of angry bees inside a screen cage. The gas is described in terms of 3 internal quantities or "states":

Pressure is said to be the strength of the force pushing on a surface, divided by the surface area.

$$P = \frac{|\vec{F}|}{A} \ . \tag{401}$$

The force in this case would come from the molecules knocking up against the walls of the container. The units of pressure are $\frac{N}{m^2}$. That unit comes up often enough to have its own name. It is called a Pascal, after the French scientist Blaise Pascal, who did a lot of work with fluids.

$$1 \ \frac{N}{m^2} \equiv 1 \ Pa \ .$$

The units of pressure are Pascals (Pa).

Temperature is known to everyone as the number associated with warmth. We probably also know that it has something to do with molecular motion. The temperature at which all molecular motion stops for example, is called absolute zero. Inside a gas, the temperature is directly related to the kinetic energy of the gas molecules.

Unfortunately the measurement of temperature is complicated by the fact that many different temperature scales exist. Three of them you hear about all the time. Fahrenheit, symbolized by ^oF, is the scale commonly used in the United States. When the weatherman says its 87 ^{o} outside, he's talking about 87 ^oF. Centigrade, symbolized by ^oC, is the scale commonly used in Europe, where the weatherman might say its 26 ^oC outside. The scale used by scientists is called Kelvin, symbolized by a K with no ^{o} sign. When a scientist talks about absolute zero, she's talking about 0 K.

All these different temperature scales mean that we have to learn how to convert back and forth. Even though there are 3 scales, the conversions can be accomplished by just 2 equations:

$$T_{^oF} = \frac{9}{5} T_{^oC} + 32 \ , \tag{402}$$

and

$$T_K = T_{^oC} + 273.15 \ . \tag{403}$$

Any other conversion can be obtained from those two by algebraic manipulation.

Example 4.1

Liquid nitrogen boils at 77 K. What is that temperature in degrees Farenheit ?

Solution 4.1

We don't have a direct conversion from K to ^oF. But we can get $T_{^oC}$ from equation (403), and then substitute the result into equation (402).

$$\begin{aligned} T_K &= T_{^oC} + 273.15 \\ T_{^oC} &= T_K - 273.15 \end{aligned} \tag{404}$$

and

$$\begin{aligned} T_{^oF} &= \frac{9}{5} T_{^oC} + 32 \\ &= \frac{9}{5}(T_K - 273.15) + 32 \\ &= \frac{9}{5}(77 - 273.15) + 32 \\ &= \frac{9}{5}(-196.15) + 32 \\ T &= -321.07 \ ^oF \end{aligned} \tag{405}$$

Quiz 4.1 How many Kelvins is -74 ^oF ?

Volume is just the familar volume from solid geometry. The volume of a box for example is $V = lwh$, where l, w, and h are the length, width, and height. The volume of a sphere is $V = \frac{4}{3}\pi r^3$, where r is the radius. The volume of a cylinder is $V = Ah$, where A is the area of the base and h is the height.

The units of volume are cubic meters (m^3).

Volume, temperature, and pressure are the three states of a gas.

The pioneering work on gasses was done in the 17th and 18th centuries by a distinguished British chemist named Robert Boyle, and a wild French adventurer named Jacques Charles. Today the discoveries of those two men are combined into a single relationship called the ideal gas law.

$$\frac{P_1 V_1}{T_1} = \frac{P_2 V_2}{T_2} \ , \tag{406}$$

where P, is the pressure in Pa, V is the volume in m^3, and T is the temperature in K. The ideal gas law says that the pressure times the volume divided by the temperature at any one time, is equal to the pressure times the volume divided by the temperature at any other time.

A true ideal gas would follow the ideal gas law at all pressures and temperatures. Real gasses are not ideal. But most of them still follow the ideal gas law as long as the pressure is low and the temperature is high.

Example 4.2

An ideal gas is confined inside an expandable container. If the pressure of the gas is tripled and the volume is cut in half, what will be the new temperature in terms of the old temperature?

Solution 4.2

This kind of problem is called a "ratio problem", and it is a favorite of people who make up standardized exams. Step 1 in a ratio problem is to write the governing equation in terms of "old" and "new" variables.

$$\frac{P_{new}V_{new}}{T_{new}} = \frac{P_{old}V_{old}}{T_{old}} . \tag{407}$$

Next you list the relationships between the old and new variables that are given in the problem.

$$\begin{aligned} P_{new} &= 3\,P_{old} \\ V_{new} &= \frac{1}{2}\,V_{old} . \end{aligned} \tag{408}$$

Now substitute those relationships into your governing equation

$$\frac{(3P_{old})\left(\frac{1}{2}V_{old}\right)}{T_{new}} = \frac{P_{old}V_{old}}{T_{old}} , \tag{409}$$

and factor all numbers out front

$$\frac{3}{2}\left(\frac{P_{old}V_{old}}{T_{new}}\right) = \frac{P_{old}V_{old}}{T_{old}} . \tag{410}$$

You should get a bunch of cancellations enabling you to solve for the variable of interest.

$$\begin{aligned} \frac{3}{2}\left(\frac{1}{T_{new}}\right) &= \frac{1}{T_{old}} \\ \frac{3}{2}T_{old} &= T_{new} \\ T_{new} &= \frac{3}{2}T_{old} \end{aligned} \tag{411}$$

The answer is easy to check:

$$\begin{aligned}\frac{P_1V_1}{T_1} &= \frac{P_2V_2}{T_2}\\ \frac{P_1V_1}{T_1} &= \frac{3P_1\frac{1}{2}V_1}{\frac{3}{2}T_1}\\ \frac{P_1V_1}{T_1} &= \frac{\frac{3}{2}P_1V_1}{\frac{3}{2}T_1}\\ \frac{P_1V_1}{T_1} &= \frac{P_1V_1}{T_1}\end{aligned} \tag{412}$$

Note that the classic ratio problem does not involve numbers. Here you are never given the value of T_{old}, and you do not find the value of T_{new}. Instead you find the relationship or ratio between the two T's, so that if you did know one you could just plug in to find the other.

Quiz 4.2 An ideal gas at 300 K and 101300 Pa occupies .001 m^3. What will be the temperature if its pressure is increased to 303900 Pa and the volume is decreased to .0005 m^3 ? (This is not a ratio problem.)

Big Q and the Transfer of Heat

Look at the two objects shown in Figure 4.1a. The object on the left is hot, so its tepmerature T_H is high. The object on the right is cold, and its temperature T_C is low. They start out separated from each other so that there is no transfer of heat. Then in Figure 4.1b, they are brought together. As soon as they touch, heat begins to flow from the hot object on the left to the cold object on the right. T_H starts to come down, and T_C starts to go up. After a while, $T_H = T_C$, the flow of heat is complete, and the two objects are said to be in thermal equilibrium.

The Figure 4.1 transfer of heat scenario usually doesn't surprise anyone. We all seem to realize from experience that heat flows from hot to cold. Less widely known is the fact that heat is not temperature. Heat is not temperature, but it is related to temperature by an equation. For a liquid or a solid,

$$Q = mC(T_f - T_o) \ , \tag{413}$$

where big Q is the amount of heat gained or lost during the temperature change, m is the mass of the substance, C is a quantity called specific heat, T_f is the final temperature, and T_o is the original temperature.

The specific heat, C, is defined as the amount of heat required to raise 1 kilogram of a substance, 1 Kelvin in temperature. Different substances have different specific heats, so specific heat is a number that you look up somewhere in a table. Our specific heats are listed in Table 4A.

Table 4A. Specific Heat (in $\frac{J}{kg\,K}$)

Alcohol (ethyl)	2440
Aluminum	910
Silver	234
Water	4190

The question arises, if heat is not temperature, what is it ? Let's look at the units of equation (413). Mass is in kg, specific heat is in $\frac{J}{kg\,K}$, and the temperatures are in K.

$$kg\left(\frac{J}{kg\,K}\right)(K-K) \rightarrow \left(\frac{J}{K}\right)K \rightarrow J\ ,$$

Big Q has units of Joules, so it must be energy. Heat is energy.

The units of Heat are Joules (J).

Example 4.3

A 140 g ball of Aluminium at 82 ^oC is dropped into a styrofoam cup containing 400 g of water at 16 ^oC. What is the final temperature inside the cup in ^oC ?

Solution 4.3

The styrofoam cup has negligible mass, so its effect on the heat transfer can be ignored. Styrofoam is also a great insulator, and it will pretty much keep the contents of the cup from losing any heat to the environment. Any heat lost by the Aluminium in this problem is going to go into the water.

Heat is energy, and Conservation of Energy demands that

$$Q_{\,lost\ by\ hot\ material} + Q_{\,gained\ by\ cold\ material} = 0\ . \tag{414}$$

(There is no other place for the energy to go.) Note that the sum equals zero because $Q_{\,lost}$ will be a negative number and $Q_{\,gained}$ will be a positive number.

We know the expression for Q, so

$$\begin{aligned} Q_{\,lost\ by\ Al} &+ Q_{\,gained\ by\ water} = 0 \\ m_{\,Al}C_{\,Al}(T_{f\ Al} - T_{o\ Al}) &+ m_{\,water}C_{\,water}(T_{f\ water} - T_{o\ water}) = 0 \end{aligned} \tag{415}$$

Of course $T_{f\ Al} = T_{f\ water} =$ just $T_{\,f}$ since everything comes to the same temperature.

We need to convert the masses to kg and the temperatures to K.

$$\begin{aligned} m_{Al} &= \left(\frac{140\ g}{1}\right)\left(\frac{1\ kg}{1000\ g}\right) = .14\ kg \\ m_{water} &= \left(\frac{400\ g}{1}\right)\left(\frac{1\ kg}{1000\ g}\right) = .40\ kg \end{aligned}$$

$$\begin{aligned} T_{o\ Al\ K} &= T_{o\ Al\ ^oC} + 273.15 = 82 + 273.15 \\ T_{o\ Al} &= 355.15\ K \end{aligned}$$

$$\begin{aligned} T_{o\ water\ K} &= T_{o\ water\ ^oC} + 273.15 = 16 + 273.15 \\ T_{o\ water} &= 289.15\ K \end{aligned}$$

Table 4A gives us the specific heats, so we just need to plug everything into equation (415) and solve for T_f.

$$\begin{aligned} m_{Al}C_{Al}(T_f - T_{o\ Al}) &+ m_{water}C_{water}(T_f - T_{o\ water}) = 0 \\ .14\ kg\left(910\ \frac{J}{kg\ K}\right)(T_f - 355.15\ K) &+ .4\ kg\left(4190\ \frac{J}{kg\ K}\right)(T_f - 289.15\ K) = 0 \\ 127.4\ \frac{J}{K}(T_f - 355.15\ K) &+ 1676\ \frac{J}{K}(T_f - 289.15\ K) = 0 \\ 127.4\ T_f\ \frac{J}{K} - 45246.11\ J &+ 1676\ T_f\ \frac{J}{K} - 484615.4\ J = 0 \\ 1803.4\ T_f\ \frac{J}{K} &= 529861.51\ J \\ T_f &= \left(\frac{529861.51}{1803.4}\right)\left(\frac{J}{1}\right)\left(\frac{K}{J}\right) \\ T_f &\approx 293.81\ K \end{aligned} \tag{416}$$

The question asked for ^0C, so

$$\begin{aligned} T_K &= T_{^oC} + 273.15 \\ T_{^oC} &= T_K - 273.15 \\ &\approx 293.81 - 273.15 \\ T &\approx 20.66\ ^oC \end{aligned} \tag{417}$$

Note that the final temperature should be somewhere inbetween the two original temperatures, and it is. Also, when the equation is long like equation (416), and does not have much algebraic manipulation, it is sometimes more convenient to keep the units in the equation as you go along, instead of doing a separate unit analysis on the side.

Quiz 4.3 230 g of water at 68 ^oC are mixed with 360 g of alcohol at 32 ^oC inside a styrofoam cup. What temperature in ^oC will the mixture eventually reach ?

Thermodynamic Work

The thin piston in Figure 4.2 is being pushed up a distance $\Delta h = h_2 - h_1$ by expanding gas inside the cylinder. That process produces an amount of work given by

$$\begin{aligned} W &= \vec{F} \bullet \vec{d} \\ &= |\vec{F}|(+\hat{\jmath}) \bullet \Delta h(+\hat{\jmath}) \\ W &= |\vec{F}|\Delta h \,. \end{aligned} \tag{418}$$

If we multiply the right side of equation (418) by 1, we would not change its value because 1 times any number just gives you back that same number. The 1 that we want to use here is $1 = \frac{A}{A}$ where A is the area of the base of the cylinder.

$$\begin{aligned} W &= |\vec{F}|\Delta h \\ &= |\vec{F}|\Delta h \left(\frac{A}{A}\right) \,. \end{aligned} \tag{419}$$

Rearranging a little bit,

$$W = \left(\frac{|\vec{F}|}{A}\right)(A\Delta h) \,. \tag{420}$$

Pressure is defined by $P = \frac{|\vec{F}|}{A}$, and the volume of a cylinder is given by $V = Ah$. So $A\Delta h$ would represent a change in volume, ΔV. Making those substitutions into equation (420) leads to

$$\begin{aligned} W &= \left(\frac{|\vec{F}|}{A}\right)(A\Delta h) \\ W &= P\Delta V \end{aligned} \tag{421}$$

Equation (421) says that the amount of work done by the expanding gas is equal to the pressure inside the cylinder times the change in cylinder volume.

That change in cylinder volume could either be positive or negative. During one complete cycle, the volume increases when the piston goes up and decreases when it comes back down. Figure 4.3 shows an idealized cycle. In Figure 4.3a the gas is being heated which causes the pressure to increase. In Figure 4.3b the increased pressure causes the piston to go up. In Figure 4.3c the gas cools off causing the pressure to decrease. And in Figure 4.3d the decrease in pressure allows the piston to come back down to where it started, completing one cycle.

The total work done in one cycle can be analyzed using something called a Pressure-Volume Diagram.

Example 4.4

How much work is done by one cycle on the PV diagram shown in Figure 4.4 ?

Solution 4.4

The total work can be found by adding up the work done during each leg of the cycle.

$$W = W_{12} + W_{23} + W_{34} + W_{41} \ . \qquad (422)$$

Work is equal to $P\Delta V$. So the volume must change in order to produce work. Looking at Figure 4.4, there is no change in volume from 1 to 2, and there is no change in volume from 3 to 4.

$$\begin{aligned} W &= 0 + W_{23} + 0 + W_{41} \\ W &= W_{23} + W_{41} \end{aligned} \qquad (423)$$

Substituting $P\Delta V$, and then the numbers,

$$\begin{aligned} W &= P_{23}(V_3 - V_2) + P_{41}(V_1 - V_4) \\ &= 350,000\ Pa\ (.0014\ m^3 - .001\ m^3) + 200,000\ Pa\ (.001\ m^3 - .0014\ m^3) \\ &= 350,000\ \frac{N}{m^2}\ (.0004\ m^3) + 200,000\ \frac{N}{m^2}\ (-.0004\ m^3) \\ &= 140\ Nm - 80\ Nm \\ W &= 60\ J \end{aligned} \qquad (424)$$

Note that you have to follow the arrows when you find ΔV. From 2 to 3 for example, the arrow says that you wind up at 3. So ΔV for the top leg is $V_3 - V_2$, final volume minus original volume.

Quiz 4.4 Find V_2 in Figure 4.5 so that the total work around 1 cycle is 120.4 J.

The 3 Laws of Thermodynamics

The study of thermodynamics has produced 3 broad statements or "laws" regarding heat flow and the generation of work. The 1st law of thermodynamics says

$$\Delta U = Q - W \ . \qquad (425)$$

Big U is called the total internal energy of a gas, and it includes the sum of the kinetic and potential energies of all the individual gas molecules. ΔU represents a change in the internal energy of the gas. Q is the amount of heat added to the gas, and W is the amount of work done by the gas.

Figure 4.6 shows a process described by the 1st law. In Figure 4.6a, a piston rests on top of a cylinder filled with gas. The gas molecules have internal energy U represented by short momentum arrows, but nothing is happening so there is no change in the internal energy, $\Delta U = 0$. In Figure 4.6b, heat comes into the gas from outside. The increase in heat causes the gas molecules to move around more energetically, resulting in longer momentum arrows. The internal energy goes up, and the change is $\Delta U = Q$. But the longer momentum arrows mean that the gas molecules are going the hit the work-producing piston with more force. Some of the extra gas molecule momentum is transferred to the piston and the piston gets pushed up producing W, as shown in Figure 4.6c. Having lost momentum to the piston, the momentum arrows of the gas molecules go back to being short, and the internal energy of the gas goes back down according to $\Delta U = Q - W$.

Of course the gas could lose heat instead of gaining heat, and work could be done on the gas by ouside forces pushing the piston down, instead of the gas doing work by pushing the piston up. In order to account for all the possibilities,

$$\Delta U = (\pm Q) - (\pm W) \ , \tag{426}$$

where

$Q \rightarrow +Q$ if the gas gains heat.
$Q \rightarrow -Q$ if the gas loses heat.
$W \rightarrow +W$ if work is done by the gas pushing the piston up.
$W \rightarrow -W$ if work is done on the gas by something else pushing the piston down.

Example 4.5

The gas in a heat engine cylinder absorbs 120 J of heat and then does 300 J of work. Find the change in the internal energy of the gas.

Solution 4.5

$$\begin{aligned} \Delta U &= (\pm Q) - (\pm W) \\ &= (+Q) - (+W) \\ &= (+120\ J) - (+300\ J) \\ \Delta U &= -180\ J\ . \end{aligned} \tag{427}$$

Quiz 4.5 400 J of work are done on a system at the same time that it loses 240 J of heat. Find the change in internal energy.

There are two more laws of thermodynamics. The easiest way to look at the 2nd and 3rd law is to state them in words:

2nd law - Left alone, heat naturally flows from hot to cold.

3rd law - It is impossible to cool anything all the way down to absolute zero.

The heat transfer process pictured in Figure 4.1 is an example of the 2nd law in action. That type of thing happens all the time. Absolute zero on the other hand is -459.67 ^oF or -273.15 ^oC. We do not usually encounter temperatures that low, and testing of the 3rd law is something that would take place in a specialized laboratory.

Things to Remember

Relationships

$$P = \frac{|\vec{F}|}{A}$$

$$T_{^oF} = \frac{9}{5} T_{^oC} + 32$$

$$T_K = T_{^oC} + 273.15$$

$$\frac{P_1 V_1}{T_1} = \frac{P_2 V_2}{T_2}$$

$$Q = mC\left(T_f - T_o\right)$$

$$Q_{lost\ by\ hot\ material} + Q_{gained\ by\ cold\ material} = 0$$

$$W = P\Delta V$$

$$\Delta U = (\pm Q) - (\pm W)$$

Units

$$P \rightarrow \frac{N}{m^2} \rightarrow Pa \qquad V \rightarrow m^3 \qquad T \rightarrow \text{must be in K}$$

$$C \rightarrow \frac{J}{kg\ K} \qquad Q \rightarrow J$$

$$\Delta U \rightarrow J \qquad W \rightarrow J$$

Constants and Conversions

$$1\ kg = 1000\ g$$

Homework Problems Chapter 4

4.1 How many degrees Fahrenheit is absolute zero ?

4.2 Water boils at 100 ^oC. What is that same temperature in ^oF ?

4.3 If the temperature of an idea gas is increased by 25 %, and the volume is cut in half, what will the new pressure be in terms of the old pressure ?

4.4 If the pressure of an idea gas is increased by 2 1/2 times, and the volume is cut in half, what will the new temperature be in terms of the old temperature ?

4.5 A styrofoam cup contains 500 grams of water at $77\ ^oF$. A ball of silver at $320\ ^oF$ is dropped into the water. Eventually the temperature inside the cup reaches $86\ ^oF$. What is the mass of the silver ball?

4.6 A styrofoam cup contains 350 grams of water at $305.15\ K$. The addition of 600 grams of water causes the temperature inside the cup to reach $325.15\ K$ after thorough mixing. What was the original temperature of the 600 grams of water ?

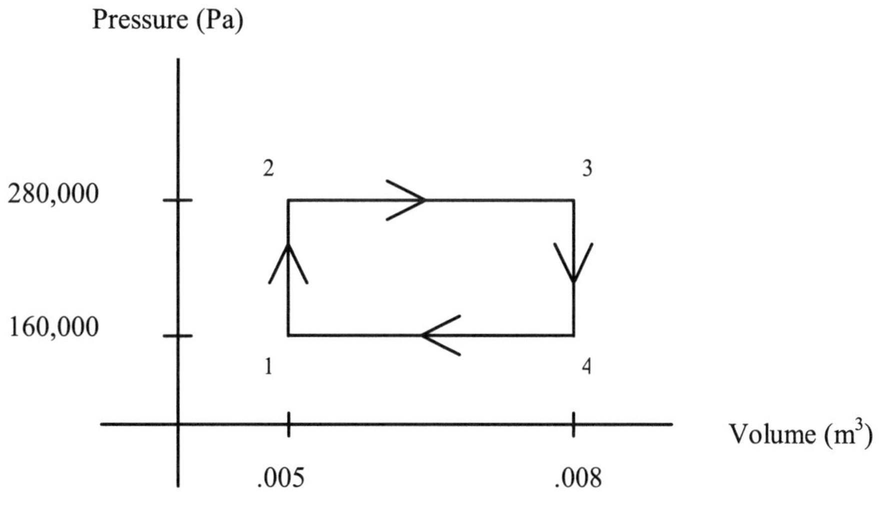

4.7 How much work is done around two cycles of the PV diagram shown above?

4.8

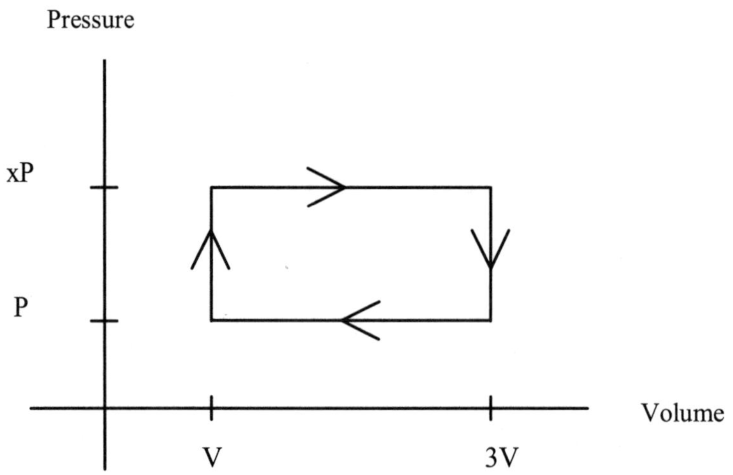

Find x so that the total work around one cycle will be PV.

4.9 A system gains 750 J of heat while it does 800 J of work. Does the internal energy of the system go up or down ? (Show work to justify your answer.)

4.10 A system loses 300 J of heat while it is doing 200 J of work. What is the change in the internal energy of the system ?

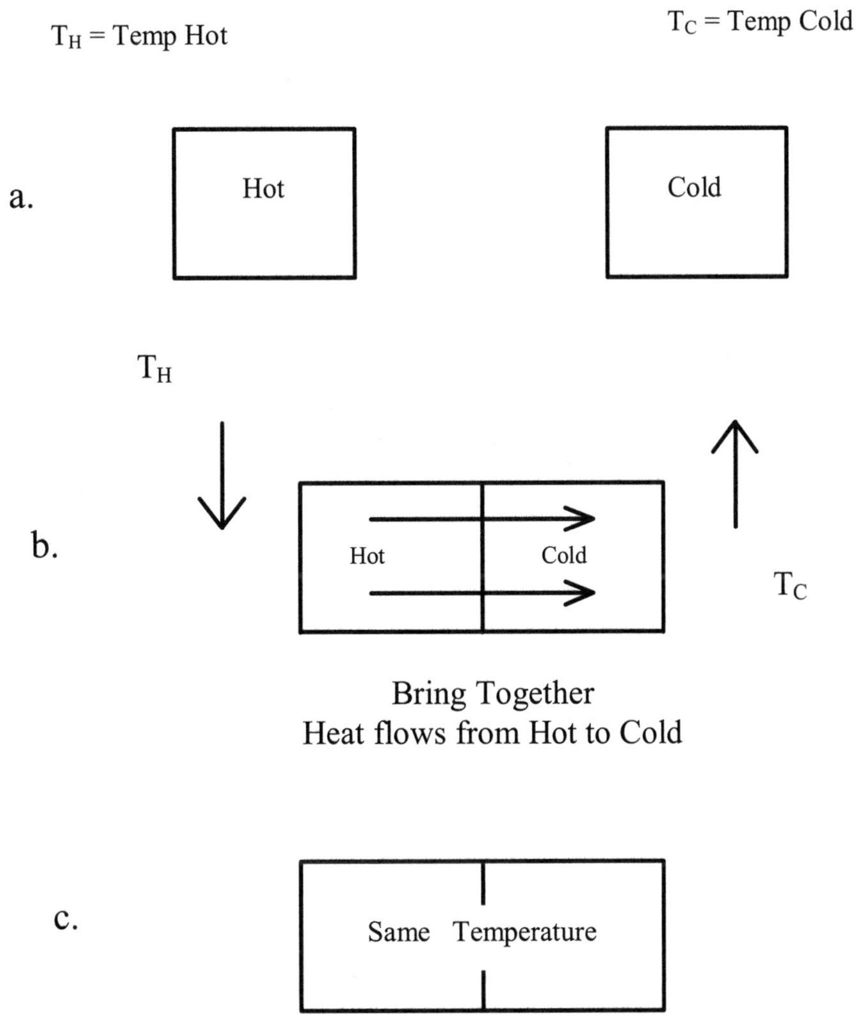

Figure 4.1 Transfer of Heat

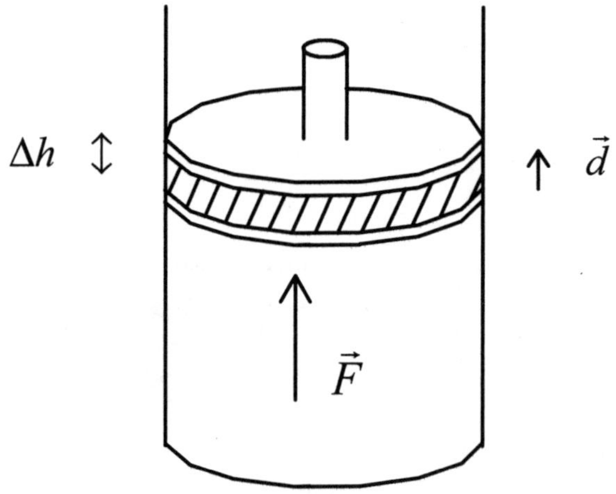

Figure 4.2   Expanding Gas Pushes Piston Up

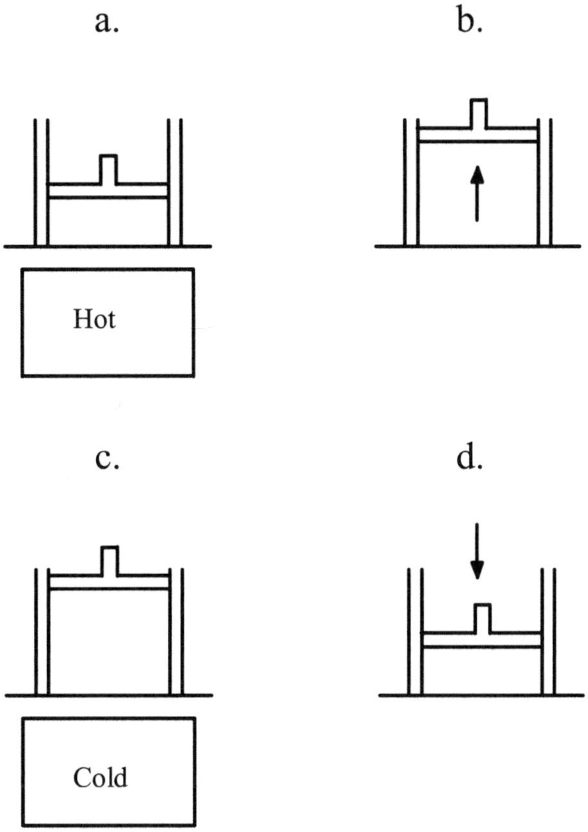

Figure 4.3 Idealized Heat Engine Cycle

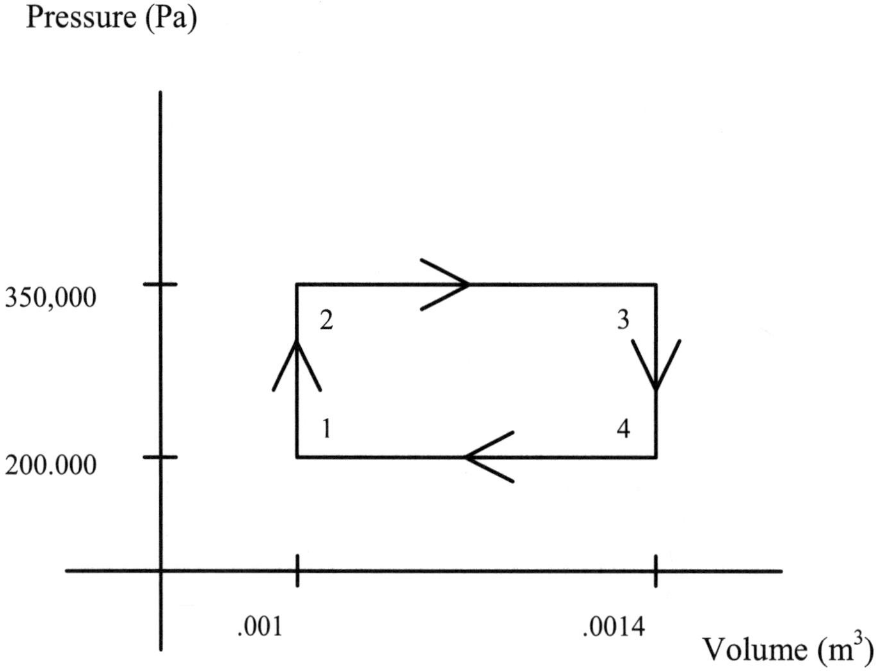

Figure 4.4 PV Diagram for Example 4.4

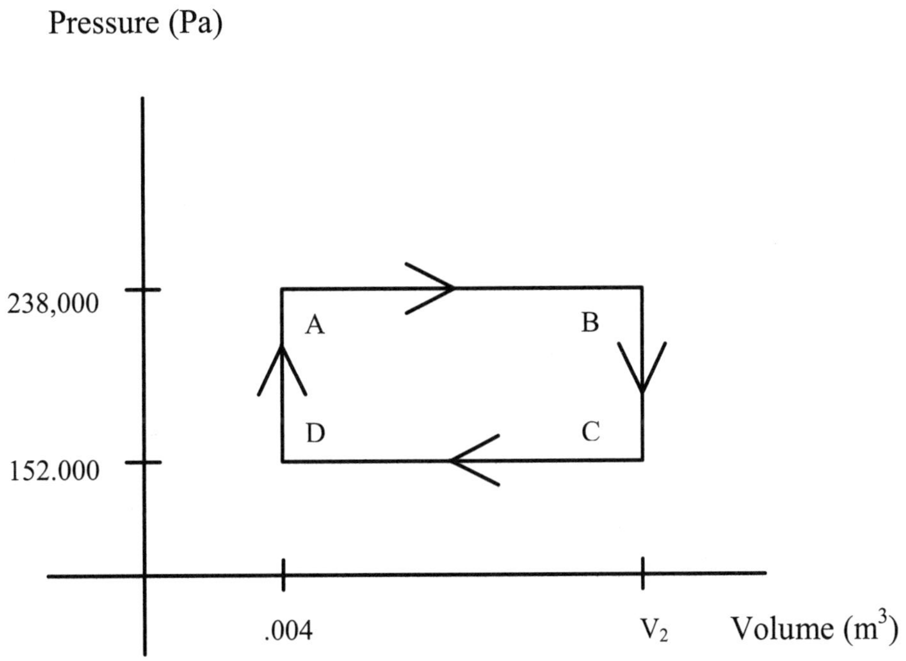

Figure 4.5 PV Diagram for Quiz 4.4

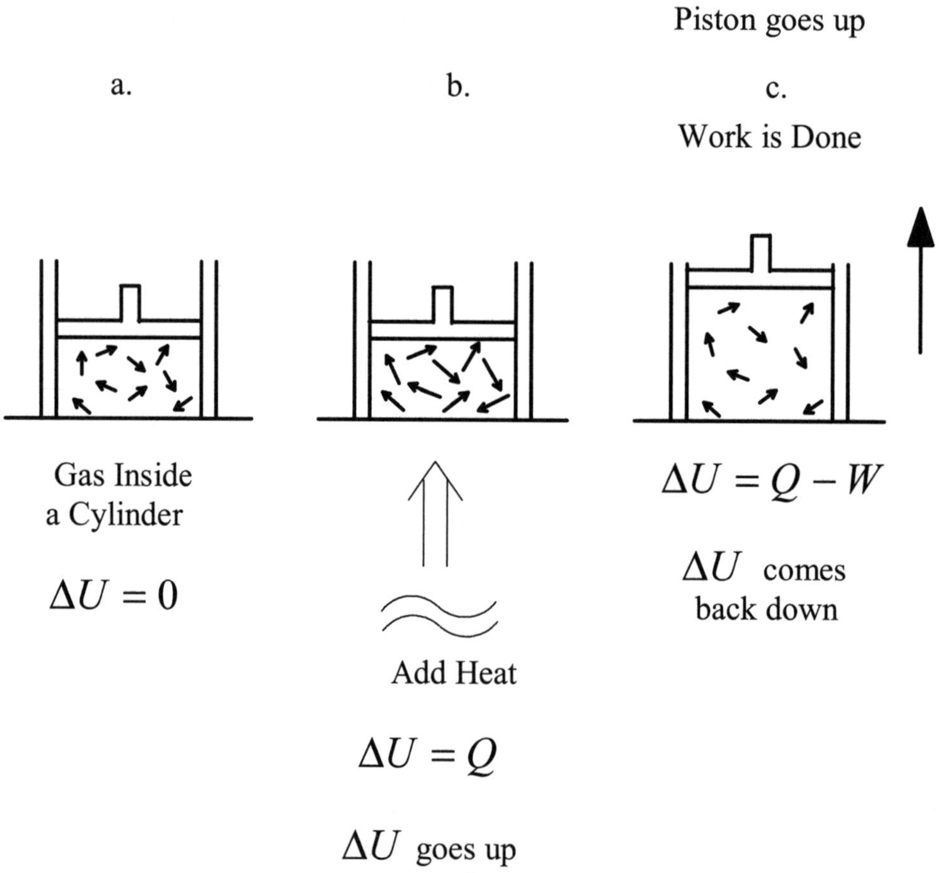

Figure 4.6   1st Law of Thermodynamics

Chapter 5 - Equations of Motion

Timeline

350 BC The Greek philosopher Aristotle describes motion in terms of distance and time, but does not incorporate mathematics into his descriptions.

1340 AD Four professors at Merton College in England investigate the concepts of velocity and acceleration. The professors are called the "Oxford Calculators", even though their approach still does not involve mathematics.

1357 Nicole Oresme at the University of Paris finally applies math to motion by expanding Giovanni di Casali's geometric approach into a graph-like system capable of proving theorems.

1659 Dutch physicist Christiaan Huygens works out the law of centrifugal force for an object in uniform circular motion.

1746 Swiss mathematician Leonhard Euler expresses velocity and acceleration as vector quantities.

1747 The wave equation is discovered (and solved) by Jean d'Alembert, a French mathematician who was studying the vibration of strings.

TEXT

Everything moves. The idea that objects change position as time goes by, is hard-wired in to our picture of reality. It would be difficult even to imagine a universe without any kind of motion.

Physics attempts to describe the characteristics of motion in mathematical terms.

Going Straight There

Look at the two points shown in Figure 5.1, (1,3) m and (3,-2) m. The distance vector $\vec{d}$ that stretches from (1,3) m to (3,-2) m is given by

$$\begin{aligned} &(to) - (from) \\ &(3,-2) - (1,3) \;\rightarrow\; (2,-5) \\ &\vec{d} \;=\; [2(+\hat{\imath}) + 5(-\hat{\jmath})]\, m \end{aligned} \tag{501}$$

That same distance vector can be expressed in magnitude unit vector form, where

$$\begin{aligned} |\vec{d}| &= \sqrt{(2)^2 + (5)^2}\, m \\ &= \sqrt{4+25}\, m \\ |\vec{d}| &= \sqrt{29}\, m \approx 5.4\, m \end{aligned} \tag{502}$$

so that

$$\vec{d} = |\vec{d}| \left[\frac{\vec{d}}{|\vec{d}|}\right] = \sqrt{29}\ m \left[\frac{2}{\sqrt{29}}(+\hat{\imath}) + \frac{5}{\sqrt{29}}(-\hat{\jmath})\right] . \tag{503}$$

The magnitude of $\vec{d}$ tells us how far it is from (1,3) m to (3,-2) m. The unit vector tells us which way to go.

Actually, there are many different ways to get from (1,3) m to (3,-2) m. But if we wanted to go straight there, we would follow $\vec{d}$. If we wanted to go straight there in some fixed amount of time, the straight line velocity that we would need is defined as

$$\vec{v} = \frac{\vec{d}}{\Delta t} . \tag{504}$$

In this case to go straight there in 3 seconds,

$$\begin{aligned} \vec{v} &= \frac{\vec{d}}{\Delta t} = \frac{\sqrt{29}\ m}{3\ s}\left[\frac{2}{\sqrt{29}}(+\hat{\imath}) + \frac{5}{\sqrt{29}}(-\hat{\jmath})\right] \\ \vec{v} &\approx 1.80\ \frac{m}{s}\left[\frac{2}{\sqrt{29}}(+\hat{\imath}) + \frac{5}{\sqrt{29}}(-\hat{\jmath})\right] . \end{aligned} \tag{505}$$

Note that only the magnitude gets divided by the number of seconds. The unit vector is not affected. According to equation (505), if you pass (1,3) m going at a constant speed of about 1.8 $\frac{m}{s}$, and you head in the direction given by the unit vector, 3 seconds later you will arrive at (3,-2) m.

It is important to understand that velocity $\vec{v}$ is a vector. It consists of two parts, a magnitude and a direction. Speed is the magnitude of velocity, v = speed = $|\vec{v}|$. Speed tells you how fast you are going, but it does not tell you which way you are going. In order to convert speed into velocity, you have to include the direction, which means you have to multiply the speed by the unit vector.

Example 5.1

How fast must you travel to go straight from (-1,2) m to (3,-4) m in 2.5 seconds?

Solution 5.1

Here the problem is asking for speed instead of velocity. (How fast means speed.) First we need to find $\vec{d}$.

$$\begin{aligned} (to)\ &-\ (from) \\ (3,-4) - (-1,2) &\rightarrow (4,-6) \\ \vec{d} &= [4(+\hat{\imath}) + 6(-\hat{\jmath})]\ m \end{aligned} \tag{506}$$

Speed is the magnitude of velocity,

$$v = |\vec{v}| = \left|\frac{\vec{d}}{\Delta t}\right| = \frac{|\vec{d}|}{\Delta t} \ . \tag{507}$$

Note that the difference in time is a positive scalar quantity, which means $|\Delta t| = \Delta t$, and it doesn't matter whether or not Δt is inside the absolute value signs.

$$\begin{aligned} v &= \frac{|\vec{d}|}{\Delta t} = \frac{\sqrt{(4)^2 + (6)^2}\ m}{2.5\ s} \\ &= \frac{\sqrt{16+36}}{2.5}\ \frac{m}{s} = \frac{\sqrt{52}}{2.5}\ \frac{m}{s} \\ v &\approx 2.88\ \frac{m}{s} \ . \end{aligned} \tag{508}$$

Quiz 5.1 What is the straight line velocity to get from (2,-5) m to (-2,3) m in 3.4 seconds?

The velocity of an object could certainly change. Acceleration is defined as the change in velocity divided by the amount of time necessary to make that change. If the acceleration is constant, then

$$\vec{a} = \frac{\vec{v_2} - \vec{v_1}}{\Delta t} \ , \tag{509}$$

where $\vec{v_2}$ is the new velocity, and $\vec{v_1}$ is the old velocity.

Example 5.2

An object originally moving with $\vec{v} = 4\ \frac{m}{s}(+\hat{j})$ experiences an acceleration $\vec{a} = \sqrt{13}\ \frac{m}{s^2}\left[\frac{3}{\sqrt{13}}(+\hat{\imath}) + \frac{2}{\sqrt{13}}(-\hat{\jmath})\right]$ for 2 seconds. What is its velocity at the end of the 2 seconds ?

<u>Solution 5.2</u>

The acceleration is constant, so we start with equation (509) and solve for $\vec{v_2}$.

$$\begin{aligned} \vec{a} &= \frac{\vec{v_2} - \vec{v_1}}{\Delta t} \\ \vec{a}(\Delta t) &= \vec{v_2} - \vec{v_1} \\ \vec{v_2} &= \vec{a}(\Delta t) + \vec{v_1} \ . \end{aligned} \tag{510}$$

Then just plug in the numbers.

$$\begin{aligned} \vec{v_2} &= \vec{a}(\Delta t) + \vec{v_1} \\ &= \left\{\sqrt{13}\ \frac{m}{s^2}\left[\frac{3}{\sqrt{13}}(+\hat{\imath}) + \frac{2}{\sqrt{13}}(-\hat{\jmath})\right]\right\}(2\ s) + 4(+\hat{\jmath})\ \frac{m}{s} \\ &= (2\ s)[3(+\hat{\imath}) + 2(-\hat{\jmath})]\ \frac{m}{s^2} + 4(+\hat{\jmath})\ \frac{m}{s} \\ &= [6(+\hat{\imath}) + 4(-\hat{\jmath})]\ \frac{m}{s} + 4(+\hat{\jmath})\ \frac{m}{s} \\ \vec{v_2} &= 6(+\hat{\imath})\ \frac{m}{s} \ . \end{aligned} \tag{511}$$

Note that $\vec{a}(\Delta t)$ had to be expressed in component form before it could be added to $\vec{v_1}$. You cannot add or subtract vectors when they are in magnitude unit vector form.

Figure 5.2 shows a parallelogram rule picture of $\vec{v_2}$ resulting from $\vec{v_1} + \vec{a}(\Delta t)$.

Quiz 5.2 An object originally moving with $\vec{v} = 10\ \frac{m}{s}\left[\frac{4}{5}(-\hat{\imath}) + \frac{3}{5}(-\hat{\jmath})\right]$ experiences a constant acceleration for 3 seconds. At the end of the 3 seconds the object is moving with $\vec{v} = \sqrt{82}\ \frac{m}{s}\left[\frac{1}{\sqrt{82}}(+\hat{\imath}) + \frac{9}{\sqrt{82}}(+\hat{\jmath})\right]$. Find $\vec{a}$ and express your answer in magnitude unit vector form.

Moving in Circles

Newton's 1st law states that an object moving in a straight line wants to keep moving in a straight line. In order to make it turn, it has to be given a push or a pull.

Look at the outer space rock being whirled around at the end of the string in Figure 5.3a. The rock goes around in a circle. It could be moving with constant speed. But it could not be moving with constant velocity. That's because the rock continuously changes direction as it goes around. So the magnitude of velocity could always be the same, but the direction of velocity has to change from point to point. We know what happens if the string is cut. The rock flies off in a straight line. The direction of that straight line coincides with the velocity vector of the rock, which is tangent to the circle at every point. Figure 5.3b shows a picture.

Of course the speed of the rock could change too. But we are not going to consider that case. All of our rocks will be moving with "uniform circular motion", which means the magnitude of velocity doesn't change as the rock goes around. The $\vec{v}$ vectors are all the same length. They just all point in different directions.

Newton's 1st law says that the rock wants to go in a straight line. That means you have to force it to go in a circle. The force on the rock is exerted through the string. One end of the string is tied to the rock. The other end is at the center of the circle. Strings cannot push. They can only pull. So the string must be pulling the rock around in a circle. The force on the rock comes through the string. The string goes to the center of the circle. So the force always has to point towards the center of the circle. That kind of force is called centripetal force, $\vec{F_c}$. It is the centripetal force that keeps the rock going around. If $\vec{F_c}$ disappears, the rock flies off in a straight line.

The acceleration caused by $\vec{F_c}$ is called centripetal acceleration. From Newton's 2nd law,

$$\vec{F_c} = m\vec{a_c}\ , \tag{512}$$

and

$$\vec{a_c} = \frac{\vec{F_c}}{m}\ . \tag{513}$$

Equation (513) indicates that $\vec{a_c}$ points in the same direction as $\vec{F_c}$, towards the center of the circle. Figure 5.4 shows a picture.

The direction of $\vec{a_c}$ is easy to figure out. It has to point the same way the force points. The magnitude of $\vec{a_c}$ takes a little more work. But starting on page 331 in the Appendix we eventually obtain

$$|\vec{a_c}| = \frac{v^2}{r} \, . \tag{514}$$

The magnitude of centripetal acceleration is equal to the speed of the rock squared, divided by the length of the string. The direction of $\vec{a_c}$ is down the string, towards the center of the circle.

Looking at the units,

$$\frac{v^2}{r} \rightarrow \frac{\left(\frac{m}{s}\right)^2}{m} \rightarrow \left(\frac{m^2}{s^2}\right)\left(\frac{1}{m}\right) \rightarrow \frac{m}{s^2} \, .$$

An acceleration should have units of meters per second squared, and this one does, so the units look OK.

Example 5.3

A .35 kg space rock is being whirled around at the end of a .5 m string. What is the speed of the rock if the tension in the string is 275 N?

Solution 5.3

Here the tension in the string has to be $|\vec{F_c}|$. So we start with $\vec{F_c} = m\vec{a_c}$. $\vec{F_c}$ and $\vec{a_c}$ always point in the same direction, so

$$\begin{aligned}
\vec{F_c} &= m\vec{a_c} \\
|\vec{F_c}|(unit\ vector) &= m|\vec{a_c}|(unit\ vector) \\
\frac{|\vec{F_c}|(unit\ vector)}{(unit\ vector)} &= \frac{m|\vec{a_c}|(unit\ vector)}{(unit\ vector)} \\
|\vec{F_c}| &= m|\vec{a_c}| \, .
\end{aligned} \tag{515}$$

Note that we do not need to know the value of the unit vector. Whatever it is, it's the same on both sides of the equation, so it will always divide out.

The next step is to substitute equation (514) for $|\vec{a_c}|$, and then solve for v.

$$|\vec{F_c}| = m|\vec{a_c}|$$

$$
\begin{aligned}
|\vec{F}_c| &= m\left(\frac{v^2}{r}\right) \\
|\vec{F}_c|r &= mv^2 \\
v^2 &= \frac{|\vec{F}_c|r}{m} \\
v &= \sqrt{\frac{|\vec{F}_c|r}{m}}\ .
\end{aligned} \tag{516}
$$

There was plenty of algebraic manipulation involved in equation (516), so we need to look at the units to make sure that they are going to come out right.

$$
\sqrt{\frac{|\vec{F}_c|r}{m}} \rightarrow \sqrt{\frac{N\ m}{kg}} \rightarrow \sqrt{\left(\frac{kg\ m}{s^2}\right)\left(\frac{m}{kg}\right)}
$$

$$
\rightarrow \sqrt{\frac{m^2}{s^2}} \rightarrow \frac{m}{s}\ .
$$

Speed should be in $\frac{m}{s}$, and that's what we have, so the units look OK.

Plugging in the numbers,

$$
\begin{aligned}
v &= \sqrt{\frac{|\vec{F}_c|r}{m}} = \left[\sqrt{\frac{(275)(.5)}{.35}}\right]\frac{m}{s} \\
v &\approx 19.82\,\frac{m}{s}\ .
\end{aligned} \tag{517}
$$

Quiz 5.3 A space rock at the end of a .4 m string is being whirled around at 26 $\frac{m}{s}$. What is the mass of the rock if the tension in the string is 312 N?

Waves

Suppose you tied a long piece of string to a wall, then began shaking the free end up and down as shown in Figure 5.5. The string will undergo a wavelike motion, with the wave starting at the end that you are shaking, then traveling down towards the wall. That type of motion is often modeled as a sine wave with two terms where the angle should be.

To see how it works, let's first look at the equation $y = x^2$. When $x = -1$, $y = +1$. When $x = 0$, $y = 0$. And when $x = +1$, $y = +1$ again. Figure 5.6a shows a picture.

Now look at $y = (x-1)^2$. Here, when $x = 0$, $y = +1$. When $x = 1$, $y = 0$. And when $x = 2$, $y = +1$ again, as shown in Figure 5.6b.

Finally let's try $y = (x-2)^2$. This time $y = 1$ when $x =$ either 1 or 3, and $y = 0$ when $x = 2$. Figure 5.6c.

The graph shown in Figure 5.6 is a parabola, and it could be expressed as $y = (x - A)^2$, with $A = 0$ in 5.6a, $A = 1$ in 5.6b, and $A = 2$ in 5.6c. As A gets bigger, the parabola moves to the right. So if we wanted to, we could call the Figure 5.6 graph a "traveling parabola".

Let's try the same thing again, except this time we'll use the equation $y = \sin(x - t)$. When $t = 0$, $y = \sin(x)$. From Chapter 1, if $x = 0$, $sin(x) = 0$, and the graph looks like Figure 5.7a.

When $t = 1$, $y = \sin(x - 1)$. Now in order to make the argument in parentheses equal zero, x has to equal one. Then $y = \sin(1 - 1) = \sin(0) = 0$, and the graph looks like Figure 5.7b.

One more time. When $t = 2$, $y = \sin(x - 2)$. This time y equals zero when $x = 2$, and we get Figure 5.7c.

The Figure 5.7 graph is a sine wave that moves to the right as t gets big, so we could call it a "traveling sine wave". The word "sine" is usually dropped though, and Figure 5.7 is just called a *traveling wave.*

There is a big problem however, with the physics part of the equation

$$y = \sin(x - t) . \tag{518}$$

The quantity x represents a distance, with units of meters. The quantity t represents a time with units of seconds. Not only do those units not match, neither x nor t has the units of radians that you need for the argument of a sine function. So equation (518) is just not right. Fixing it brings us to the standard form for a one-dimensional traveling wave.

$$y = y_o \sin(kx - \omega t) . \tag{519}$$

In equation (519), y_o is called the amplitude of the wave. The sine function remember, only goes up and down between $\pm$ 1. The purpose of y_o is to scale the sine function so that it goes up and down between the actual maximum and minimum of the wave. Figure 5.8 shows a picture.

The k in equation (519) is called the wave number. It is defined as

$$k = \frac{2\pi}{\lambda} , \tag{520}$$

where λ is the wave length in meters. If you took a photograph of the wave as it went by, and you measured the length of one cycle of the wave in the photograph, then that length would be λ. Figure 5.9 shows a picture. The λ in the denominator of k has units of meters. The 2π in the numerator has units of radians. So overall, k has units of radians per meter.

The wave number k has units of radians per meter $\left(\frac{rad}{m}\right)$.

The ω in equation (519) is called the radian frequency. (It's a small Greek letter omega. It is not a w.) Omega is defined as

$$\omega = 2\pi f \ , \tag{521}$$

where f is the regular (non-radian) frequency. The regular frequency, f, is the inverse of the period T.

$$f = \frac{1}{T} \ , \tag{522}$$

where the period T is the amount of time for one cycle of the wave. So f has units of 1/seconds, and it represents how many cycles of the wave go by in one second. For example, suppose you were out fishing, and you had a bobber on your line to tell you when you were getting a bite. Let's say the bobber is bobbing, not because there are any fish around, but because its floating on the water, and the water waves make it go up and down as they pass by. You could tell the frequency f of the water waves by counting how many times the bobber goes down and comes back up in one second. Figure 5.10 shows a picture. Suppose the bobber went all the way down and came all the way back up 4 times in one second. The frequency of the water wave would be $f = 4\,\frac{1}{s}$ and the period would be $T = \frac{1}{4}\ s$.

The 2π in equation (521) has units of radians. f has units of 1/seconds. So ω has units of radians per second.

The radian frequency ω has units of radians per second $\left(\frac{rad}{s}\right)$.

Now let's look at the units in the sine function argument of equation (519).

$$\begin{aligned} y &= y_o \sin(kx - \omega t) \\ &\rightarrow y_o \sin\left[\left(\frac{radians}{meter}\right)(meters) - \left(\frac{radians}{second}\right)(seconds)\right] \\ &\rightarrow y_o \sin(radians \ - \ radians) \\ &\rightarrow y_o \sin(radians) \end{aligned}$$

Radians are the proper units for the argument of a sine function, so that part looks OK. Please note however, that after you take the sine of some number of radians, your answer has no units. In other words

$$\sin(radians) \ \rightarrow \ no\ \ units \ .$$

That means that the units of the wave, y, are the same as the units on y_o. If the wave is traveling down a string for example, y represents the vertical displacement of the string in meters, and y_o represents the maximum possible vertical displacement of the string, also in meters.

Different kinds of waves travel through different kinds of "mediums". A sound wave might be traveling through air for example. A light wave could travel through glass. A wave on a string is traveling down the string. The speed of the wave through the medium is given by

$$v = \lambda f \ . \tag{523}$$

where λ is the wavelength in meters, and f is the frequency in 1/seconds, so that v has units of meters per second.

(The frequency f of a wave is the inverse of its period T. Period is in seconds, so frequency has to be in 1/seconds. That unit comes up enough to have its own name. It is named after Heinrich Hertz, who was the 1st person to verify the existence of electromagnetic waves. So 1/seconds = Hz.)

Frequency f has units of $\frac{1}{s}$ or Hertz (Hz).

Example 5.4

A certain traveling wave on a string, is specified by

$$y = .046 \sin\left[(6.4\pi)x - (160\pi)t\right]\ m\ .$$

Find a) the amplitude
b) the wavelength
c) the frequency
d) the period
e) the speed.

Solution 5.4

a) The equation is for the displacement of a string, and the maximum displacement, or amplitude, is the 1st number on the right side. You can write it down by inspection. But you have to remember to include the units.

$$y_o = .046\ m\ . \tag{524}$$

b) For the wavelength, from equation (520), $k = \frac{2\pi}{\lambda}$. Solving for λ,

$$\begin{aligned} k &= \frac{2\pi}{\lambda} \\ k\lambda &= 2\pi \\ \lambda &= \frac{2\pi}{k} \end{aligned} \tag{525}$$

Let's look at the units on the right hand side

$$\begin{aligned} \frac{2\pi}{k} &\rightarrow \frac{rad}{\frac{rad}{m}} \\ &\rightarrow \left(\frac{rad}{1}\right)\left(\frac{m}{rad}\right) = m \end{aligned}$$

The units look OK. Comparing the problem to equation (519), $k = 20$, so

$$\begin{aligned} \lambda &= \frac{2\pi}{k} = \left(\frac{2\pi}{6.4\pi}\right)\ m \\ \lambda &= .3125\ m \end{aligned} \tag{526}$$

c) For the frequency, from equation (521), $\omega = 2\pi f$. So

$$\begin{aligned} \omega &= 2\pi f \\ f &= \frac{\omega}{2\pi} \end{aligned} \tag{527}$$

The right side units are

$$\frac{\omega}{2\pi} \rightarrow \frac{\frac{rad}{s}}{rad} = \left(\frac{rad}{s}\right)\left(\frac{1}{rad}\right) = \frac{1}{s}$$

The units are all right. Comparing the problem to equation (519), $\omega = 160\pi$, which means

$$\begin{aligned} f &= \frac{\omega}{2\pi} = \left(\frac{160\pi}{2\pi}\right)\frac{1}{s} \\ f &= 80\ Hz \end{aligned} \tag{528}$$

d) The frequency is the inverse of the period. From equation (522)

$$\begin{aligned} f &= \frac{1}{T} \\ fT &= 1 \\ T &= \frac{1}{f} \end{aligned} \tag{529}$$

So

$$\begin{aligned} T &= \frac{1}{80\ \frac{1}{s}} \\ T &= .0125\ s \end{aligned} \tag{530}$$

e) Finally, for the speed of the wave, equation (523) says

$$\begin{aligned} v &= \lambda f \\ v &= (.3125\ m)\left(80\ \frac{1}{s}\right) \\ v &= 25\ \frac{m}{s} \end{aligned} \tag{531}$$

Quiz 5.4 A certain traveling wave is specified by

$$y = .038 \sin\left[(8\pi)x - (260\pi)t\right]\ m.$$

Find the speed of the wave.

Example 5.5

A wave with f close to $\frac{168}{\pi} Hz$ travels down a string at $28\ \frac{m}{s}$. What is the displacement of the string at $x = 2.4\ m$ and $t = 1.2\ s$ if the maximum displacement is $.05\ m$?

Solution 5.5

Here we need to assemble the expression for the wave, then plug in the values for x and t in order to find y. From equation (521)

$$\begin{aligned} \omega &= 2\pi f \\ &= (2\pi\ rad)\left(\frac{168}{\pi}\ \frac{1}{s}\right) \\ \omega &= 336\ \frac{rad}{s}\ . \end{aligned} \tag{532}$$

From equation (523)

$$\begin{aligned} v &= \lambda f \\ \lambda &= \frac{v}{f} = \frac{28\ \frac{m}{s}}{\frac{168}{\pi}\ \frac{1}{s}} \\ &= \left(28\ \frac{m}{s}\right)\left(\frac{\pi}{168}\ \frac{s}{1}\right) \\ \lambda &= \frac{\pi}{6}\ m\ . \end{aligned} \tag{533}$$

And from equation (520)

$$\begin{aligned} k &= \frac{2\pi}{\lambda} \\ &= \frac{2\pi\ rad}{\frac{\pi}{6}\ m} = (2\pi\ rad)\left(\frac{6}{\pi}\ \frac{1}{m}\right) \\ k &= 12\ \frac{rad}{m}\ . \end{aligned} \tag{534}$$

y_o is given in the problem, and we just found ω and k.. We need to plug those 3 values into the standard form for a traveling wave. Equation (519) says that

$$y = y_o \sin(kx - \omega t)\ .$$

So this particular wave becomes

$$y = .05 \sin(12x - 336t)\ m \tag{535}$$

At $x = 2.4\ m$ and $t = 1.2\ s$

$$\begin{aligned} y &= .05 \sin(12x - 336t)\ m \\ &= .05 \sin\left[(12)(2.4) - (336)(1.2)\right]\ m \\ &= .05 \sin(28.8 - 403.2)\ m \\ &= .05 \sin(-374.4)\ m \end{aligned} \tag{536}$$

Notice that we are not keeping the units with the numbers that go inside the sine argument. That's because we have already "fixed" things so that the argument of the sine function will come out in radians. That fix is not going to change, so it is not necessary to keep showing it over and over. Of course you have to remember that the argument is in radians, and *you have to put your calculator in radian mode.* Continuing on

$$\begin{aligned} y &= .05\sin(-374.4)\ m \\ &\approx (.05)(.5230915)\ m = .0261546\ m \\ y &\approx .026\ m \end{aligned} \tag{537}$$

This answer means that a snapshot of the wave taken right at $t = 1.2\ s$ would show that the y position of the string is about $+.026\ m$ when the x position is $2.4\ m$. Figure 5.11 shows the snapshot.

Quiz 5.5 A $\frac{250}{\pi}\ Hz$ wave traveling down a string has a wavelength of $\frac{\pi}{8}\ m$. Find the displacement of the string at $x = 16\ m$ and $t = .7\ s$ if the maximum displacement is $.035\ m$.

Things to Remember

Relationships

$$\vec{v} = \frac{\vec{d}}{\Delta t}$$

$$\vec{a} = \frac{\vec{v}_2 - \vec{v}_1}{\Delta t}$$

$$|\vec{F_c}| = m|\vec{a_c}|$$

$$|\vec{a_c}| = \frac{v^2}{r}$$

$$y = y_o\ \sin(kx - \omega t)$$

$$k = \frac{2\pi}{\lambda} \qquad \omega = 2\pi f$$

$$v = \lambda f \qquad f = \frac{1}{T}$$

Units

$$\lambda \rightarrow m \qquad f \rightarrow \frac{1}{sec} = H_z \qquad T \rightarrow sec$$

$$k \rightarrow \frac{rad}{m} \qquad \omega \rightarrow \frac{rad}{s}$$

Homework Problems Chapter 5

5.1 How long will it take to get from $(2,-6)\,m$ to $(-5,3)\,m$ if you go straight there at $5.7\,\frac{m}{s}$?

5.2 What is the straight line velocity to get from $(-1,-2)\,m$ to $(3,1)\,m$ in $\frac{1}{2}$ second ?

5.3 An object originally moving with $\vec{v} = 6\frac{m}{s}\left(-\hat{j}\right)$ suddenly experiences an acceleration of $\sqrt{5}\,\frac{m}{s^2}\left[\frac{3}{\sqrt{45}}\left(+\hat{i}\right) + \frac{6}{\sqrt{45}}\left(+\hat{j}\right)\right]$. A little while later the object is moving with $\vec{v} = 3\,\frac{m}{s}\left(+\hat{i}\right)$. For how long did the acceleration act ?

5.4 After experiencing an acceleration of $13\,\frac{m}{s^2}\left[\frac{12}{13}\left(-\hat{i}\right) + \frac{5}{13}\left(+\hat{j}\right)\right]$ for $\frac{1}{2}$ second, a certain object is moving with $\vec{v} = 2.5\,\frac{m}{s}\left(+\hat{j}\right)$. What was its original velocity ?

5.5 A .3 kg space rock is being whirled around at $31\,\frac{m}{s}$. How long is the string if it has a tension of $1153.2\,N$?

5.6 A .25 kg space rock at the end of a .64 m string is being whirled around at $28\,\frac{m}{s}$. How much tension is in the string ?

5.7 A 60 Hz wave travels to the right along a string at $12\,\frac{m}{s}$. Write down the equation for the wave, if the maximum string displacement is 4 cm.

5.8 What is the period of a wave traveling at $100\,\frac{m}{s}$ if its wave number is $20\pi\,\frac{rad}{m}$?

5.9 One cycle of a string wave is .25 m long and takes .04 sec to complete. Find the displacement of the string at $x = 4.6\ m$ and $t = 24$ sec if the maximum displacement is 3 cm.

5.10 Start with equation (523), then plug in values from equations (520) and (521) to algebraically show that the speed of a traveling wave equals the radian frequency divided by the wave number.

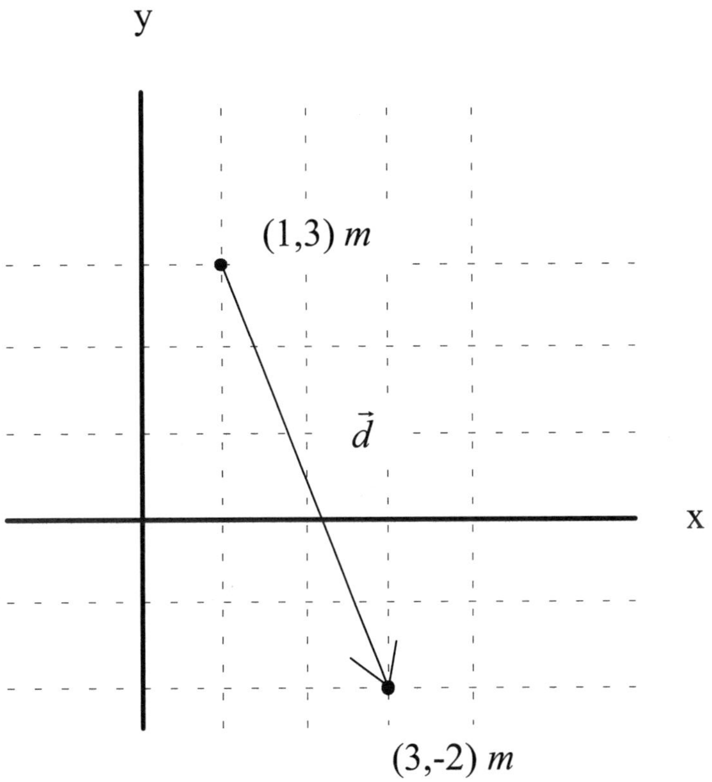

Figure 5.1 Distance vector stretches from (1,3) *m* to (3,-2) *m*

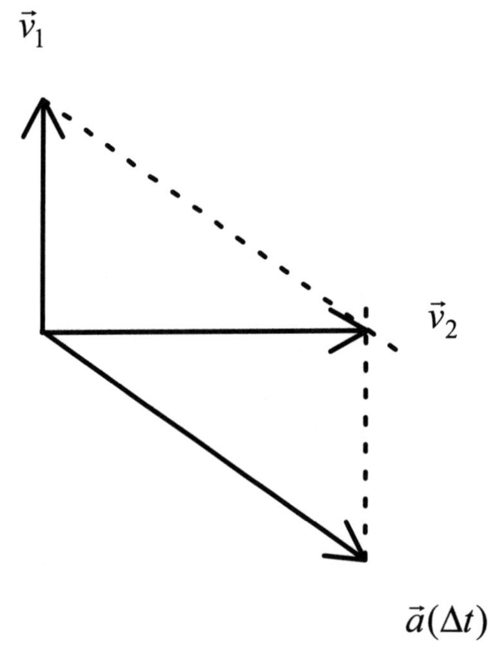

Figure 5.2 $\vec{v}_2 = \vec{v}_1 + \vec{a}(\Delta t)$

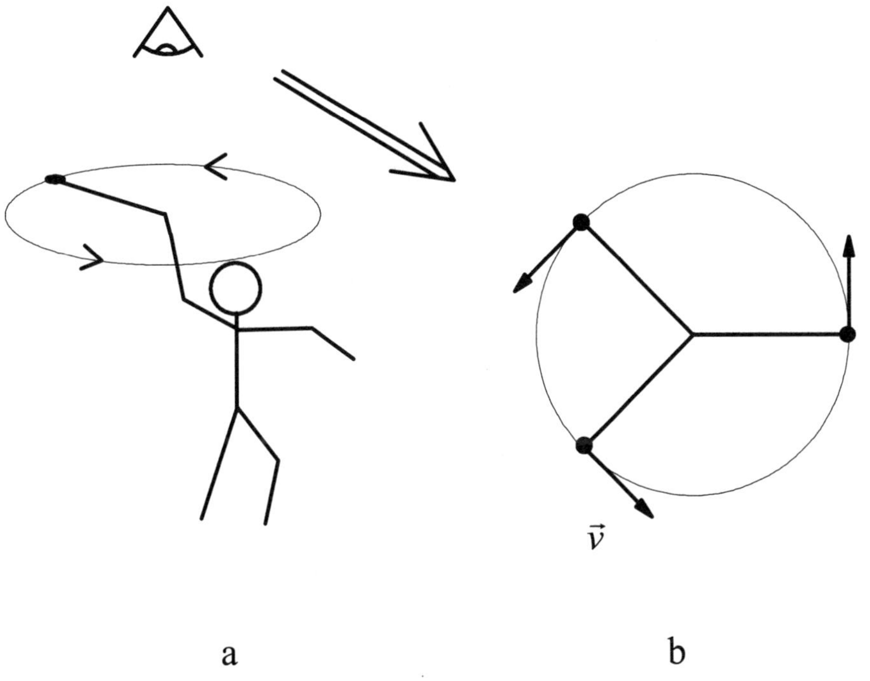

Figure 5.3 a.) Rock being whirled around at the end of a string
b.) Velocity vector is always tangent to the circle

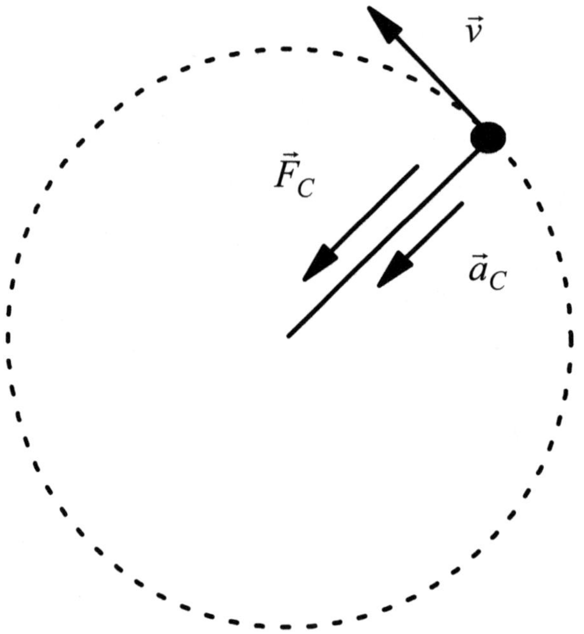

Figure 5.4 Centripetal Force and Centripetal Acceleration

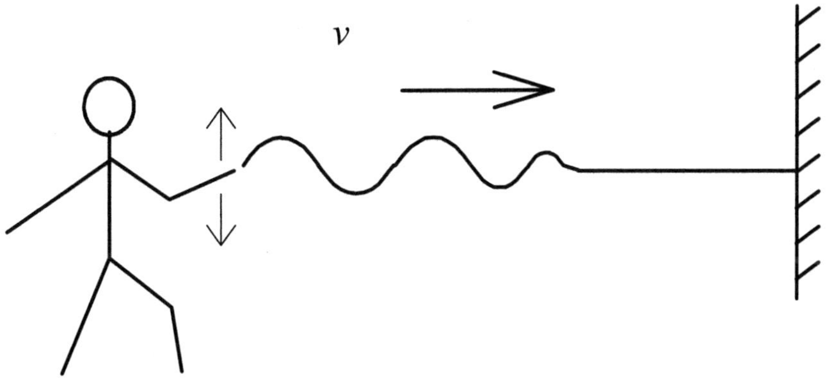

Figure 5.5 Wave on a string

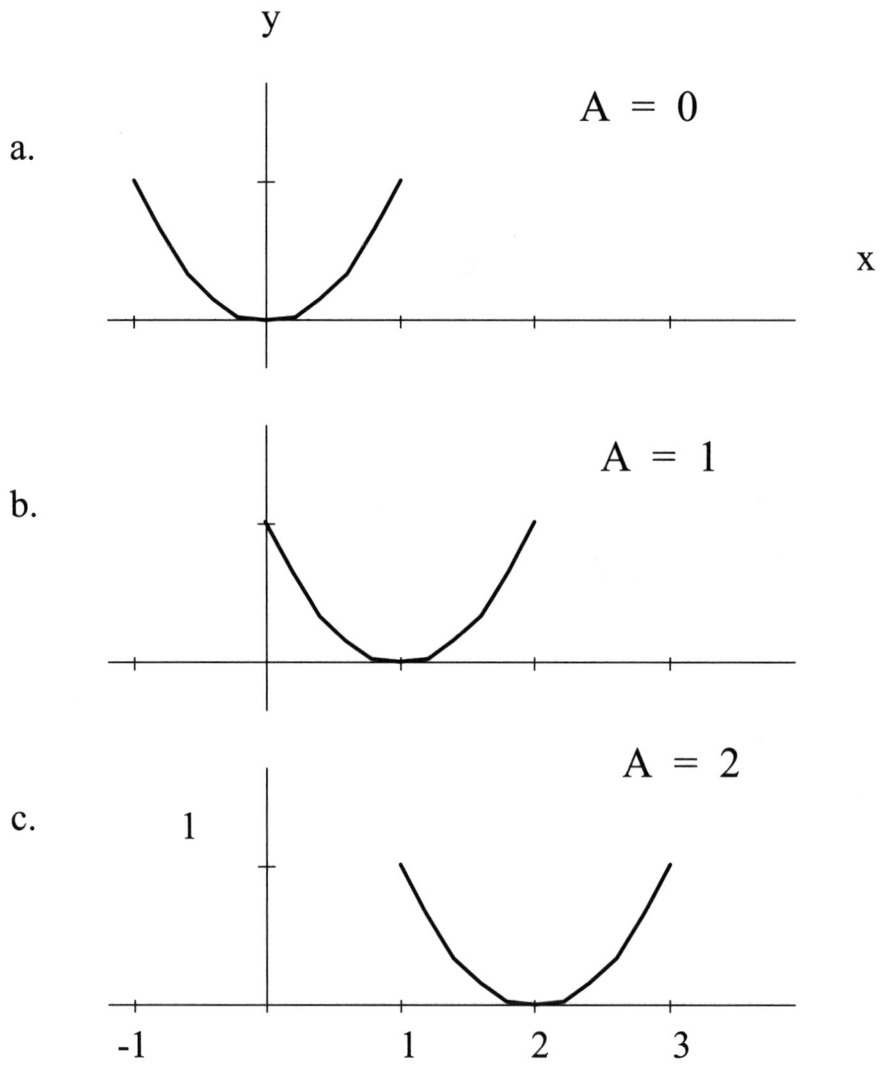

Figure 5.6 The equation $y = (x - A)^2$ produces a "Traveling Parabola" as A gets bigger

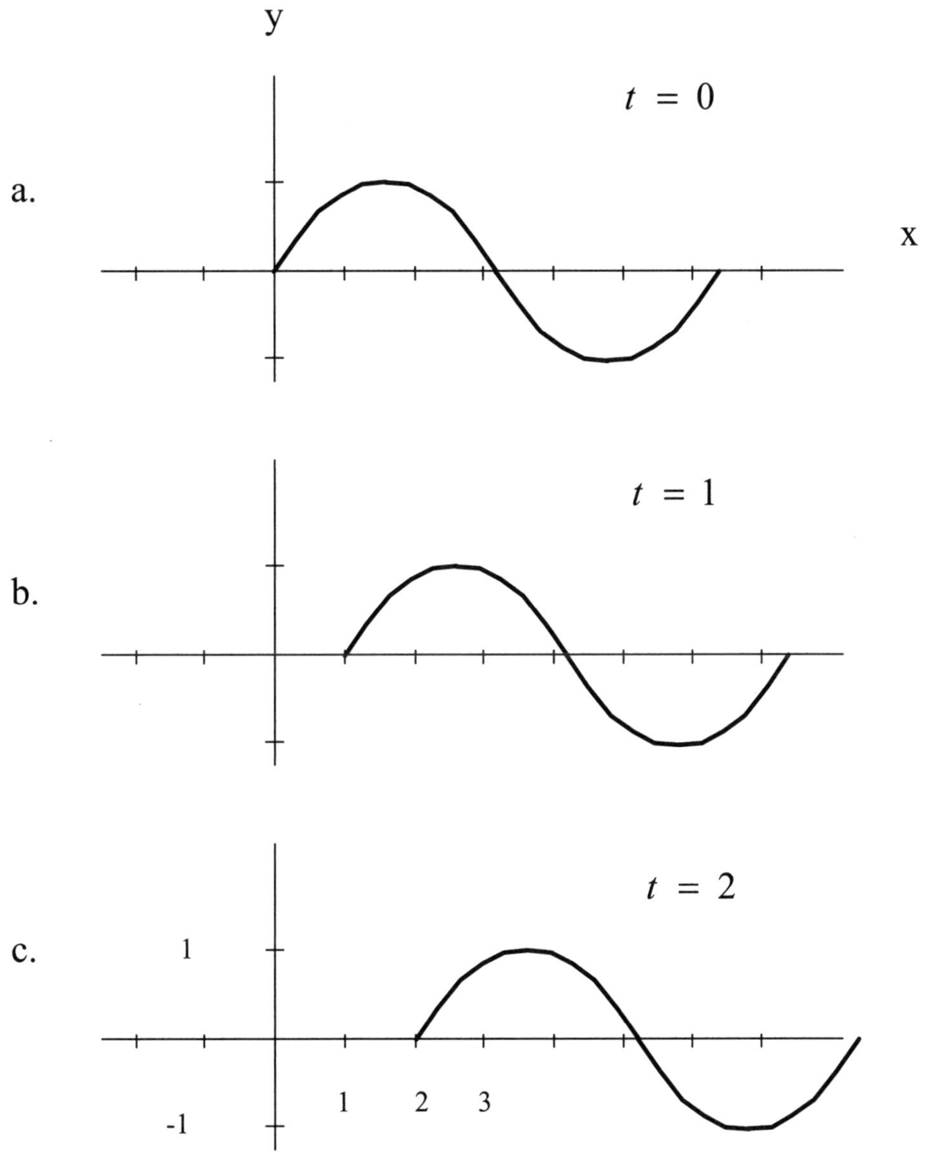

Figure 5.7 Traveling Wave

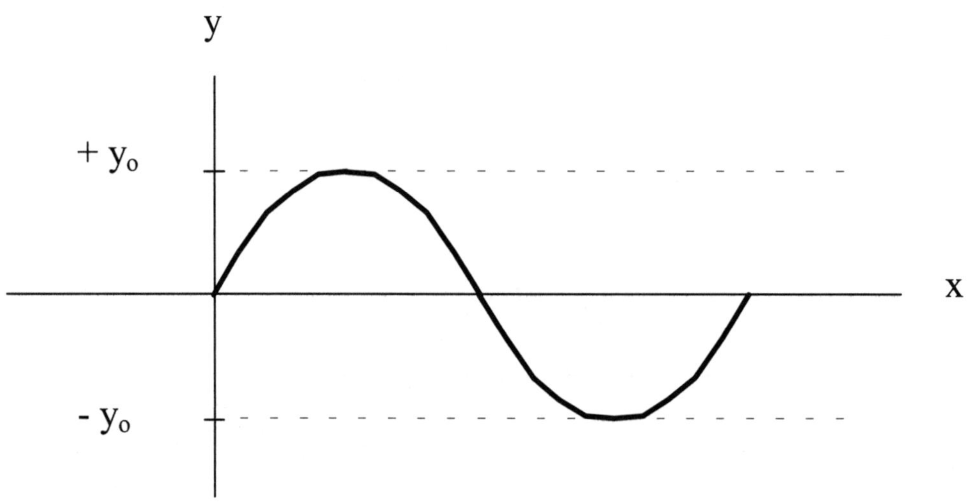

Figure 5.8 Wave goes up and down between $\pm\ y_o$

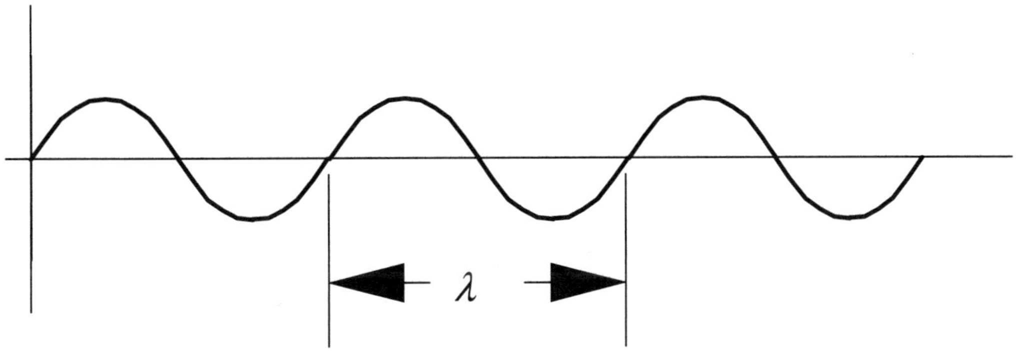

Figure 5.9 The wavelength λ is the number of meters in one cycle

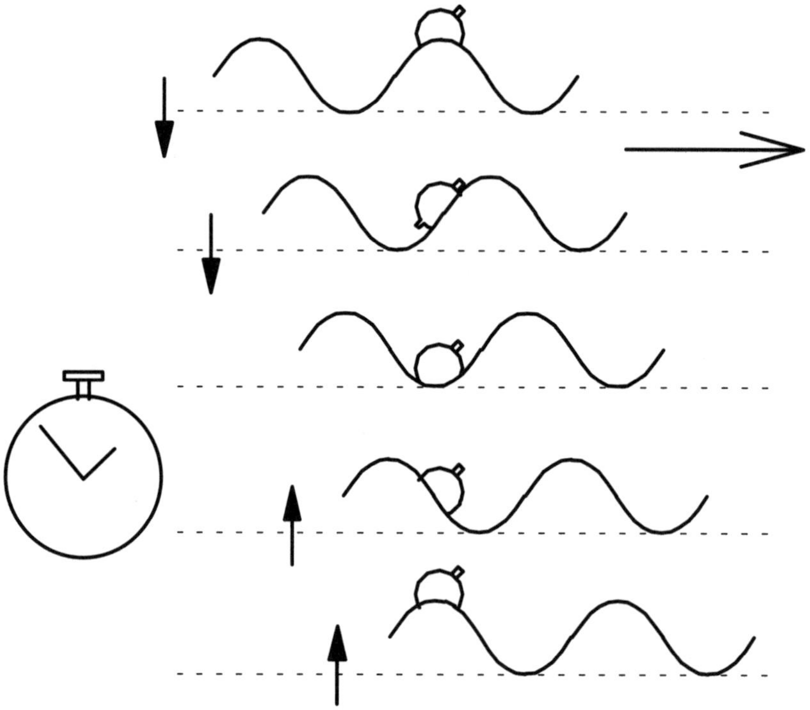

Figure 5.10 The amount of time that the fishing bobber takes to go all the way down and come all the way back up is the period of the passing water wave.

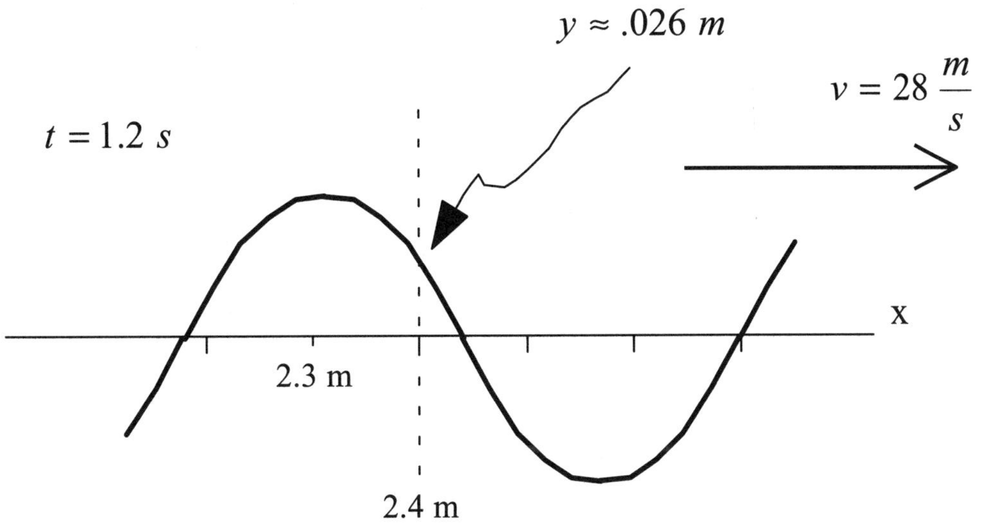

Figure 5.11 String displacement at $x = 2.4\ m$ and $t = 1.2\ s$ from Example 5.5

Chapter 6 - The Electric Field

Timeline

580 BC Thales of Miletos, one of the earliest Greek philosopher-scientists, notices that amber (*elektron* in Greek) will attract small objects after it has been rubbed. Not realizing that he has discovered static electricity, Thales attributes the effect to a living presence inside the amber.

100 AD Plutarch, a priest at the Oracle of Delphi in Greece, attempts to explain the amber effect in terms of air displacement.

1330 The French professor Jean Buridan anticipates the notion of a field of forces permeating space.

1620 Niccolo Cabeo, an Italian mathematics teacher and Jesuit priest, observes that the force due to electricity can be both repulsive and attractive.

1706 By dangling pieces of thread close to a charged cylinder, British experimenter Francis Hauksbee observes what would today be called an electric field pattern.

1733 The French chemist Charles du Fay discovers that there are two kinds of electricity. He calls one resinous($-$), and the other vitreous($+$).

1760 Daniel Bernoulli, a Swiss physicist, measures the electric force between two charged metal disks and concludes that it varies as $1/r^2$, where r is the distance between the discs.

1765-80 British scientists Joseph Priestly, John Robinson, and Henry Cavendish all independently conclude that the electric force between charges varies as $1/r^2$.

1787 French engineer and physicist Charles de Coulomb publishes measurements indicating that the force bewteen two charges is proportional to $1/r^2$. He also asserts that the force should be proportional to the product of the 'electrical masses' (charges in today's terms).

1811 French mathematician and physicist Simeon Poisson introduces the idea of electric potential difference (later called voltage).

1830's Michael Faraday, an English physicist and chemist, imagines the space around electrified matter to be filled with lines of electric force.

1865 Scottish physicist James Clerk Maxwell refines Faraday's lines of force into the modern concept of an electric field.

TEXT

By the 2nd half of the 20th century, physical scientists had come to believe that there were actually 4 different kinds of force:

The force due to Gravity

The Electromagnetic force

The Strong Nuclear force

The Weak nuclear force.

Today the trend in physics research is an attempt to unify all of those forces, so that each one would emerge as a different aspect of a single equation. Whether or not that attempt will ever be successful remains to be seen. For the moment, it is useful to talk about the forces separately.

The Electromagnetic force has two parts,

$$\vec{F}_{electromagnetic} = \vec{F}_{electric} + \vec{F}_{magnetic} \, . \tag{601}$$

The electric part is the subject of this chapter. The magnetic part is the subject of the chapter after next.

The Force between two Charges

As far as we know, there is just one kind of mass. The force between masses is called gravity, and it is always attractive. There are however, two kinds of electric charge - positive and negative. The force between electric charges is sometimes attractive and sometimes repulsive. "Like" charges repel, and "unlike" charges attract. Figure 6.1 shows a picture.

In 1686, Issac Newton published his Universal Law of Gravitation to describe the magnitude (or strength) of the gravitational force between two masses,

$$|\vec{F}|_{gravity} = G\left(\frac{m_1 m_2}{r^2}\right) \, . \tag{602}$$

In 1915 Albert Einstein was able to show that Newton's Gravity Law was only a special case of a more general theory. The key point for right now however, involves the r^2 that appears in the denominator of Newton's equation. Newton's law predicts that the gravitational force between two masses gets weaker as $\frac{1}{r^2}$, where r is the distance between the centers of mass.

The appearance of a $\frac{1}{r^2}$ factor in $|\vec{F}|_{gravity}$ means that the strength of the force due to gravity decreases very quickly as the two masses get further apart. For example, rewriting equation (602),

$$|\vec{F}|_{gravity} = G m_1 m_2 \left(\frac{1}{r^2}\right) \, ,$$

and looking at just the number values (not the units),

$$\text{for r} = 2, \qquad |\vec{F}|_{grav} = Gm_1m_2\left(\frac{1}{4}\right)$$

$$\text{for r} = 5, \qquad |\vec{F}|_{grav} = Gm_1m_2\left(\frac{1}{25}\right)$$

$$\text{for r} = 10, \qquad |\vec{F}|_{grav} = Gm_1m_2\left(\frac{1}{100}\right)$$

etc.

By the last half of the 1700's, several scientists had hypothesized that the force between electric charges should also fall off as $\frac{1}{r^2}$. Then in 1785, an experimenter named August Coulomb built a device to demonstrate just that. Coulomb further stated that the force should depend on the product of the two charges, and a modern vector version of Coulomb's Law would look like

$$\vec{F}_{12} = \frac{1}{4\pi\epsilon}\left[\frac{q_1q_2}{|\vec{r}_{12}|^2}\right]\frac{\vec{r}_{12}}{|\vec{r}_{12}|} \ . \tag{603}$$

Here $\vec{F}_{12}$ is the force on point charge 2 due to point charge 1. q_1 is charge 1. q_2 is charge 2. $|\vec{r}_{12}|^2$ is the square of the distance bewteen q_1 and q_2. And $\frac{\vec{r}_{12}}{|\vec{r}_{12}|}$ is a unit vector that points from charge 1 towards charge 2.

The quantity ϵ that appears in the denominator of Coulonb's Law is called permittivity. Permittivity characterizes how much the medium between the two charges affects the strength of the force. Suppose you hold your arms out in front of you, and you have a positive charge in one hand and a negative charge in the other hand. You can feel your hands trying to pull together because of the attractive force between the charges. Now you walk over to an aquarium, and put both hands under water. The question is: Will the strength of the force change because there is water between the charges instead of air? In general the answer is Yes. The medium between the charges can affect the strength of the force, and ϵ is the quantity in Coulomb's Law that accounts for the medium.

If there is just air between the charges, ϵ becomes ϵ_o. Epsilon nought is called the permittivity of free space. (The term "free space" really means "charge free space".)

Let's look at the units of ϵ. The unit vector on the right side of equation (603) has units of meters in the numerator, and meters in the denominator. In other words

$$\frac{\vec{r}_{12}}{|\vec{r}_{12}|} \rightarrow \frac{meters}{meters} = 1 \rightarrow no\ units\ .$$

Here we are faced with the curious fact that a unit vector has no units. Continuing on, the q's in the numerator of equation (603) represent charges. Charge is considered to be a fundamental quantity like mass or time, and

The unit of electric charge is called a Coulomb (C).

In the denominator of equation (603), $|\vec{r}_{12}|^2$ has units of meters squared, and the 4π is a pure number with no units. The left side of Coulomb's Law is a force, which has to be in Newtons. So if we just look at the equation in terms of its units,

$$N \rightleftharpoons \frac{1}{\epsilon}\left[\frac{(C)(C)}{m^2}\right] .$$

And then solve for the units on epsilon,

$$\epsilon \longrightarrow \frac{C^2}{Nm^2} .$$

In order to make Coulomb's Law come out in Newtons, ϵ has to have units of Coulombs squared divided by Newtons times meters squared.

For free space $\epsilon \longrightarrow \epsilon_o$ and

$$\epsilon_o \approx 8.85 \times 10^{-12} \, \frac{C^2}{Nm^2} . \tag{604}$$

Example 6.1

What is the force on a $-6\ \mu C$ charge located at $(-1,-2)\ m$ due to a $+16\ \mu C$ charge located at $(3,1)\ m$? (Note: $-4\ \mu C$ = -4 micro Coulombs = $-4\ \times\ 10^{-6}\ C$.)

Solution 6.1

The first step is to draw a picture like Figure 6.2, showing the location of both charges. A critical decision comes up right away. We have to determine which is charge 1 and which is charge 2. From Coulomb's Law, $\vec{F}_{12}$ gives you the force on charge 2. From the words of the problem, we are looking for the force on the $-6\ \mu C$ charge. So charge 2 must be the $-6\ \mu C$ charge, and we need to label the picture accordingly.

Notice that we already know the direction of the force on the $-6\ \mu C$ charge. Unlike charges attract, so the $-6\ \mu C$ charge will be drawn towards the $+16\ \mu C$ charge as shown in Figure 6.3. This advance knowledge gives us a way to test the 'reasonableness' of our final answer.

The solution to the problem really has two parts. For the 1st part, we need to find $\frac{\vec{r}_{12}}{|\vec{r}_{12}|}$. $\vec{r}_{12}$ stretches from (3,1) m to $(-1,-2)$ m so that

$$\begin{aligned} &(to) - (from) \\ (-1,-2) - (3,1) \;&\rightarrow\; (-4,-3) \\ \vec{r}_{12} \;&=\; [4(-\hat{\imath}) + 3(-\hat{\jmath})]\ m . \end{aligned} \tag{605}$$

For the magnitude of $\vec{r}_{12}$

$$\begin{aligned} |\vec{r}_{12}| &= \sqrt{(4)^2 + (3)^2}\; m \\ &= \sqrt{16+9}\; m = \sqrt{25}\; m \\ |\vec{r}_{12}| &= 5\; m\;. \end{aligned} \tag{606}$$

Putting the two together,

$$\begin{aligned} \frac{\vec{r}_{12}}{|\vec{r}_{12}|} &= \frac{[4(-\hat{\imath}) + 3(-\hat{\jmath})]\; m}{5\; m} \\ &= \frac{4}{5}(-\hat{\imath}) + \frac{3}{5}(-\hat{\jmath})\;. \end{aligned} \tag{607}$$

For the 2nd part, we need to find $|\vec{F}_{12}|$. There is no mention of any medium except air between the charges, so $\epsilon = \epsilon_o$ and Coulomb's Law becomes

$$\vec{F}_{12} = \frac{1}{4\pi\epsilon_o}\left[\frac{q_1 q_2}{|\vec{r}_{12}|^2}\right]\frac{\vec{r}_{12}}{|\vec{r}_{12}|}\;. \tag{608}$$

Plugging in the numbers

$$\begin{aligned} \vec{F}_{12} &= \frac{1}{(4\pi)(8.85\times 10^{-12})}\left[\frac{(+16\times 10^{-6})(-6\times 10^{-6})}{(5)^2}\right] N\,\frac{\vec{r}_{12}}{|\vec{r}_{12}|} \\ &\approx -.035\; N\left[\frac{4}{5}(-\hat{\imath}) + \frac{3}{5}(-\hat{\jmath})\right]\;. \end{aligned} \tag{609}$$

Equation (609) is not in magnitude unit vector form because there is a negative sign in front of the .035 N, and magnitudes can never be negative. Fortunately that problem is easy to fix. We just distribute the negative sign onto the unit vector to obtain our final answer,

$$\vec{F}_{12} \approx .035\; N\left[\frac{4}{5}(+\hat{\imath}) + \frac{3}{5}(+\hat{\jmath})\right]\;. \tag{610}$$

Notice that the final unit vector does point in the direction shown in Figure 6.3, which is what we expected it to do.

Also notice that we did not carry units along with the numbers in equation (609). Nor did we go out to the side and do a separate unit analysis. Instead we just put units of Newtons after the calculation for the magnitude. That's because we have already fixed the units on ϵ so that Coulomb's Law will always come out in Newtons. It is not necessary to keep showing that same analysis over and over again.

Quiz 6.1 What force does a $-4\mu C$ charge located at $(-2, 3)$ m exert on a $-5\mu C$ charge located at (1,1) m ?

The Electric Field

Issac Newton was often bothered by the fact that one mass could exert a gravitational force on another mass without touching it. Newton didn't like the idea of "action at a distance". Almost 200 years later, Michael Faraday sort of side-stepped Newton's objection by visualizing the space around an electric charge as being filled with "lines of force". As time went on, Faraday's force lines evolved into something we now call the electric field.

Suppose we take away one of the charges in Coulomb's Law. Mathematically the process of taking away a charge would correspond to dividing both sides of equation (603) by one of the q's. Let's divide by q_2.

$$\begin{aligned}\frac{\vec{F}_{12}}{q_2} &= \frac{1}{q_2}\left\{\frac{1}{4\pi\epsilon}\left[\frac{q_1 q_2}{|\vec{r}_{12}|^2}\right]\frac{\vec{r}_{12}}{|\vec{r}_{12}|}\right\} \\ &= \frac{1}{4\pi\epsilon}\left[\frac{q_1}{|\vec{r}_{12}|^2}\right]\frac{\vec{r}_{12}}{|\vec{r}_{12}|}\,. \end{aligned} \tag{611}$$

Coulomb's Law had both q's on the right hand side of the equation. That's why it was necessary to show all the 1 and 2 subscripts - so you could keep track of which q was where. Equation (611) only has one q on each side. The subscripts are no longer necessary, and we should write

$$\frac{\vec{F}}{q} = \frac{1}{4\pi\epsilon}\left[\frac{q}{|\vec{r}|^2}\right]\frac{\vec{r}}{|\vec{r}|}\,. \tag{612}$$

The quantity $\frac{\vec{F}}{q}$ is called the electric field, $\vec{E}$, and equation (612) is the expression for the electric field around a single point charge.

$$\vec{E}_{point\ charge} = \frac{1}{4\pi\epsilon}\left[\frac{q}{|\vec{r}|^2}\right]\frac{\vec{r}}{|\vec{r}|}\,, \tag{613}$$

where the single q on the right hand side is the point charge that is causing the field, and $\vec{r}$ is the distance vector from that charge to the point of interest.

Physicists think of a 'field' as being a region of space where forces <u>can</u> act. The forces do not have to be acting. They just have to be able to act. For example, suppose you drop a rock close to the surface of the Earth. The rock experiences a force due to gravity, and it falls down. This happens all around the Earth. No matter where you drop the rock it still falls 'down' toward the center of the Earth. You could then imagine that the Earth is surrounded by a gravitational field. When you release the rock somewhere near the Earth, the gravitational field causes it to fall. The main idea is that the gravitational field will still be there whether or not you actually drop a rock. The same thing goes for an electric field. You can envision a region of space being filled with an electric field. If you placed a 'test' charge in the electric field it would experience a force. But the electric field is still there even if you do not put in a test charge.

Equation (613) describes the electric field around a single isolated point charge. If there were many point charges together, then the electric field would have an expression different from equation (613). It would still be true however that

$$\vec{E} = \frac{\vec{F}}{q} , \tag{614}$$

because the electric field is defined as force divided by charge, which means that

The units for the electric field are $\frac{N}{C}$.

Example 6.2

A +70 nC charge is located at $(0, 0)$ m. Find the electric field at

a) $(0, 3)$ m

b) $(2.683, -1.342)$ m

c) $(-.5, -2.958)$ m.

(Note: $+70\ nC$ = +70 nano Coulombs = $+70 \times 10^{-9}\ C$.)

Solution 6.2

In this case, there is only one charge. So you do not have the question of which is the (to) point and which is the $(from)$ point. In $\vec{E}$ field problems the charge is always located at $(from)$. Like before there are two parts to the solution, finding the unit vector, and finding the magnitude.

For a)

$$\begin{aligned} &(to) - (from) \\ &(0,3) - (0,0) \quad \rightarrow \quad (0,3) \\ &\vec{r} \quad = \quad [0(+\hat{\imath}) + 3(+\hat{\jmath})]\ m = 3(+\hat{\jmath})\ m\ . \end{aligned} \tag{615}$$

From inspection, $|\vec{r}| = 3\ m$, or, if you do it the long way,

$$\begin{aligned} |\vec{r}| &= \sqrt{(0)^2 + (3)^2}\ m \\ &= \sqrt{0 + 9m} = \sqrt{9}\ m \\ |\vec{r}| &= 3\ m\ . \end{aligned} \tag{616}$$

So the unit vector looks like

$$\frac{\vec{r}}{|\vec{r}|} = \frac{3(+\hat{\jmath})\ m}{3\ m} = (+\jmath)\ . \tag{617}$$

$|\vec{E}|$ is the magnitude (or strength) of the electric field, and

$$\vec{E} = |\vec{E}| \frac{\vec{r}}{|\vec{r}|}$$

$$\vec{E} = \frac{1}{4\pi\epsilon_o}\left[\frac{q}{|\vec{r}|^2}\right]\frac{\vec{r}}{|\vec{r}|}$$

$$= \frac{1}{(4\pi)(8.85\times 10^{-12})}\left[\frac{70\times 10^{-9}}{(3)^2}\right]\frac{N}{C}\frac{\vec{r}}{|\vec{r}|}$$

$$\vec{E} \approx 69.94\,\frac{N}{C}\,(+\hat{\jmath})\,. \tag{618}$$

(Note that unless we are told differently, $\epsilon = \epsilon_o$.)

For b)

$$(to) - (from)$$

$$(2.683, -1.342) - (0,0) \rightarrow (2.683, -1.342)$$

$$\vec{r} = [2.683(+\hat{\imath}) + 1.342(-\hat{\jmath})]\ m$$

$$|\vec{r}| = \sqrt{(2.683)^2 + (1.342)^2}\ m \approx 3\ m$$

$$\frac{\vec{r}}{|\vec{r}|} \approx \frac{[2.683(+\hat{\imath}) + 1.342(-\hat{\jmath})]\ m}{3\ m}$$

$$\frac{\vec{r}}{|\vec{r}|} \approx .89(+\hat{\imath}) + .45(-\hat{\jmath})\,. \tag{619}$$

Since the magnitude (or length) of $\vec{r}$ is again 3 m, the calculation for the magnitude (or strength) of $\vec{E}$ is again

$$|\vec{E}| = \frac{1}{4\pi\epsilon_o}\left[\frac{q}{|\vec{r}|^2}\right]$$

$$= \frac{1}{(4\pi)(8.85\times 10^{-12})}\left[\frac{70\times 10^{-9}}{(3)^2}\right]\frac{N}{C}$$

$$\approx 69.94\,\frac{N}{C}\,. \tag{620}$$

So that

$$\vec{E} = |\vec{E}|\,\frac{\vec{r}}{|\vec{r}|}$$

$$\vec{E} \approx 69.94\,\frac{N}{C}\,[.89(+\hat{\imath}) + .45(-\hat{\jmath})] \tag{621}$$

Finally we get to c)

$$(to) - (from)$$

$$(-.5, -2.958) - (0,0) \rightarrow (-.5, -2.958)$$

$$\vec{r} = [.5(-\hat{\imath}) + 2.958(-\hat{\jmath})]\ m$$

$$|\vec{r}| = \sqrt{(.5)^2 + (2.958)^2}\ m \approx 3\ m$$

$$\frac{\vec{r}}{|\vec{r}|} \approx \frac{[.5(-\hat{\imath}) + 2.958(-\hat{\jmath})]\ m}{3\ m}$$

$$\frac{\vec{r}}{|\vec{r}|} \approx .17(-\hat{\imath}) + .99(-\hat{\jmath})\,. \tag{622}$$

Once more $|\vec{r}| = 3\ m$, so the $|\vec{E}|$ calculation is the same as in equations (618) and (620). This time

$$\vec{E} = |\vec{E}|\ \frac{\vec{r}}{|\vec{r}|} \approx 69.94\ \frac{N}{C}\ [.17(-\hat{\imath}) + .99(-\hat{\jmath})]\ . \tag{623}$$

To summarize the 3 results:

$$\vec{E}_{at\ (0,3)\ m} \approx 69.94\ \frac{N}{C}\ (+\hat{\jmath})$$

$$\vec{E}_{at\ (2.683,-1.342)\ m} \approx 69.94\ \frac{N}{C}\ [.89(+\hat{\imath}) + .45(-\hat{\jmath})]$$

$$\vec{E}_{at\ (-.5,-2.958)\ m} \approx 69.94\ \frac{N}{C}\ [.17(-\hat{\imath}) + .99(-\hat{\jmath})]$$

Notice that all 3 $\vec{E}$ fields have the same strength, but they point in 3 different directions. Figure 6.4 shows a picture. They all have the same strength because they are all the same distance from the charge. The $\vec{E}$ field falls off as $\frac{1}{|\vec{r}^2|}$, so if the $|\vec{r}|$'s are all the same, then the $|\vec{E}|$'s will all be the same. Each $\vec{E}$ lies on a 3 m radius circle centered around the charge, so each $|\vec{E}|$ is the same. If we had extended the example to 3 dimensions instead of 2, then any $\vec{E}$ lying on a sphere of radius $= 3\ m$ would have that same magnitude. Around a point charge, $|\vec{E}|$ is *spherically symmetric.*

Quiz 6.2 Find $\vec{E}$ at $(2, -1)\ m$ due to a $-64\ nC$ charge located at $(3, 2)\ m$.

One way to visualize the electric field is to think of a bunch of vectors sticking out around the charge(s). Electric fields are defined to begin on positive charges and end on negative charges. So the electric field vectors around a positive point charge would stick out in all directions sort of like the quills on a porcupine. Figure 6.5 attempts a picture. If the charge in Figure 6.5 had been negative instead of positive, the picture would look the same, but all of the arrowheads would be on the other ends of the $\vec{E}$ field vectors, pointing in towards the charge.

The $\vec{E}$ field vectors are sometimes called *electric field lines.* Electric field lines begin on positive charges and end on negative charges.

Line of Charge

Suppose you placed a lot of positive point charges next to each other in order to form a straight line of charge. In the interior of the line, away from the ends, the side-to-side components of $\vec{E}$ would cancel, while the components perpendicular to the line would add, as shown in Figure 6.6. If the line has a fair amount of length, then the $\vec{E}$ field near the center of the line would stick out radially, like the spokes of a wagon wheel. Figure 6.7 shows a segment near the center of the line. Notice that the electric field lines are parallel to each other along the length of the line, but diverging from each other around the circumference of the line. The parallel part keeps the field stronger than the field from a point charge. So instead of falling off as $\frac{1}{r^2}$, the $\vec{E}$ field around an infinite line charge falls off as $\frac{1}{r}$.

Flat Surface of Charge

We can carry this side-to-side cancellation argument one step further, and imagine that we have a flat 2-dimensional square surface, completely covered by a uniform layer of positive charge. Now each interior charge is surrounded by other charges, and all the interior side-to-side components of $\vec{E}$ cancel. Again the perpendicular components add, and the net effect is an $\vec{E}$ that sticks out from the surface like a bed of nails, as shown in Figure 6.8. (A real bed of nails only has nails sticking out on one side. Our charged surface would have $\vec{E}$ sticking out on both sides.) If the 2-dimensional surface extends into an infinite plane, then all of the $\vec{E}$ field lines are parallel. There is no divergence of field lines. That means $\vec{E}$ above and below the plane is constant. It does not fall off as $\frac{1}{r^2}$ or as $\frac{1}{r}$, but keeps the same value no matter how far away you are from the plane.

For the 3 different configurations of charge,

$$\begin{aligned} |\vec{E}|_{\,point\ charge} &= C_1 \left(\frac{1}{|\vec{r}|^2} \right) \\ |\vec{E}|_{\,\infty\ line\ charge} &= C_2 \left(\frac{1}{|\vec{r}|} \right) \\ |\vec{E}|_{\,\infty\ plane} &= C_3\,(1) = C_3\ , \end{aligned} \tag{624}$$

where C_1, C_2, and C_3 are 3 different constants that would depend on the amount of charge and whether or not the charge configuration is placed in free space.

(Of course many other charge configurations are possible, and each different configuration would have a different $\vec{E}$ field.)

Superposition of $\vec{E}$

Superposition is a serious-sounding word with a simple meaning. Superposition of $\vec{E}$ simply means that

$$\begin{aligned} \vec{E}_{\,total} &= \vec{E}_{\,from\ 1st\ source} + \vec{E}_{\,from\ 2nd\ source} + \vec{E}_{\,from\ 3rd\ source} + \cdots \\ &= \sum \vec{E}_{\,individual}\ . \end{aligned} \tag{625}$$

The total $\vec{E}$ field at some point in space consists of the sum of all the individual $\vec{E}$ fields that go through that point.

Example 6.3

A $-.8\ \mu C$ point charge is located at $(4,3)\ m$, and an infinite line charge is placed co-incident with the x axis. Find $\vec{E}_{total}$ at $(1,2)\ m$ if $\vec{E}_{line\ charge} = \frac{1079}{y}\ \frac{N}{C}\ (+\hat{\jmath})$, and express the answer in magnitude unit-vector form.

Solution 6.3

Here we need to find $\vec{E}_{line\ charge\ at\ (1,2)\ m}$ and $\vec{E}_{point\ charge\ at\ (1,2)\ m}$, then add the two $\vec{E}$'s together to find $\vec{E}_{total}$.

$$\begin{aligned}
\vec{E}_{line\ charge} &= \frac{1079}{y}\frac{N}{C}(+\hat{\jmath}) \\
\vec{E}_{line\ charge\ at\ (1,2)\ m} &= \frac{1079}{2}\frac{N}{C}(+\hat{\jmath}) \\
&= 539.5\ \frac{N}{C}(+\hat{\jmath}) \qquad (626)
\end{aligned}$$

For $\vec{E}_{point\ charge\ at\ (1,2)\ m}$

$$\begin{aligned}
(to) - (from) & \\
(1,2) - (4,3) &\rightarrow (-3,-1) \\
\vec{r} &= [3(-\hat{\imath}) + 1(-\hat{\jmath})]\ m \\
|\vec{r}| &= \sqrt{(3)^2 + (1)^2}\ m = \sqrt{10}\ m \\
\frac{\vec{r}}{|\vec{r}|} &= \frac{[3(-\hat{\imath}) + 1(-\hat{\jmath})]\ m}{\sqrt{10}\ m} \\
&= \frac{3}{\sqrt{10}}(-\hat{\imath}) + \frac{1}{\sqrt{10}}(-\hat{\jmath}) \qquad (627)
\end{aligned}$$

$$\begin{aligned}
\vec{E}_{point\ charge} &= \frac{1}{4\pi\epsilon_o}\left[\frac{q}{|\vec{r}|^2}\right]\frac{\vec{r}}{|\vec{r}|} \\
\vec{E}_{point\ charge\ at\ (1,2)\ m} &= \frac{1}{(4\pi)(8.85\times10^{-12})}\left[\frac{-.8\times10^{-6}}{(\sqrt{10})^2}\right]\frac{\vec{r}}{|\vec{r}|} \\
&\approx -719.34\ \frac{N}{C}\left[\frac{3}{\sqrt{10}}(-\hat{\imath}) + \frac{1}{\sqrt{10}}(-\hat{\jmath})\right] \\
&\approx 719.34\ \frac{N}{C}\left[\frac{3}{\sqrt{10}}(+\hat{\imath}) + \frac{1}{\sqrt{10}}(+\hat{\jmath})\right] \qquad (628)
\end{aligned}$$

Equation (628) is in magnitude unit-vector form. We need to be in component form so we can add the two $\vec{E}$ fields together.

$$\begin{aligned}
\vec{E}_{point\ charge\ at\ (1.2)\ m} &\approx 719.34\ \frac{N}{C}\left[\frac{3}{\sqrt{10}}(+\hat{\imath}) + \frac{1}{\sqrt{10}}(+\hat{\jmath})\right] \\
&\approx [682.43(+\hat{\imath}) + 227.48(+\hat{\jmath})]\ \frac{N}{C}\ , \qquad (629)
\end{aligned}$$

so that

$$\begin{aligned}
\vec{E}_{total\ at\ (1,2)\ m} &= \vec{E}_{line\ charge\ at\ (1,2)\ m} + \vec{E}_{point\ charge\ ar\ (1,2)\ m} \\
&\approx [0(+\hat{\imath}) + 539.5(+\hat{\jmath})]\ \frac{N}{C} + [682.43(+\hat{\imath}) + 227.48(+\hat{\jmath})]\ \frac{N}{C} \\
&\approx [682.43(+\hat{\imath}) + 766.98(+\hat{\jmath})]\ \frac{N}{C}
\end{aligned}$$

$$\begin{aligned}
|\vec{E}|_{total\ at\ (1,2)\ m} &\approx \sqrt{(682.43)^2 + (766.98)^2}\ \frac{N}{C} \approx 1026.63\ \frac{N}{C}
\end{aligned}$$

$$\begin{aligned}
\vec{E}_{total\ at\ (1,2)\ m} &\approx 1026.63\ \frac{N}{C}\left[\frac{682.43}{1026.63}(+\hat{\imath}) + \frac{766.98}{1026.63}(+\hat{\jmath})\right] \\
&\approx 1026.63\ \frac{N}{C}[.66(+\hat{\imath}) + .75(+\hat{\jmath})]\ . \qquad (630)
\end{aligned}$$

Figure 6.9 shows a picture of $\vec{E}_{total}$ as the superposition of $\vec{E}_{lc} + \vec{E}_{pc}$.

Quiz 6.3 The $\vec{E}$ field at $(1, 2)\ m$ due to a $+63\ nC$ charge located at $(-1, 2)\ m$ is $\vec{E} \approx 141.62\ \frac{N}{C}\ (+\hat{\imath})$. Find $\vec{E}_{total}$ at $(1, 2)\ m$ if there is also a $+63\ nC$ charge placed at $(1, 0)\ m$. Leave your answer in component form.

$$\boxed{\vec{F}_{electric} = q\vec{E}}$$

Equation (614) says $\vec{E} = \frac{\vec{F}}{q}$. Multiplying both sides by q we get

$$\vec{F} = q\vec{E} \qquad (631)$$

for the force on an electric charge placed in an electric field. If the electric charge is positive, then

$$\vec{F} = +|q|\vec{E}\ , \qquad (632)$$

and the force goes in the same direction as the $\vec{E}$ field. If the electric charge is negative, then

$$\vec{F} = -|q|\vec{E}\ , \qquad (633)$$

and the force goes in the opposite direction as the $\vec{E}$ field. From equations (632), and (633), we get the idea that *Electric fields push positive charges and pull negative charges.*

Example 6.4

The electric field around a $+4.5\ nC$ charge located at the origin is given by

$$\vec{E} = \left[\frac{40.46\ x}{\left(\sqrt{x^2 + y^2}\right)^3}(+\hat{\imath}) + \frac{40.46\ y}{\left(\sqrt{x^2 + y^2}\right)^3}(+\hat{\jmath})\right]\ \frac{N}{C}\ .$$

Find the force on a $-15\ \mu C$ charge placed at $(.03, .04)\ m$ and express your answer in magnitude unit vector form.

<u>Solution 6.4</u>

First we need to find the electric field at the point $(.03, .04)\ m$. Plugging in .03 for x and .04 for y,

$$\vec{E}_{at\ (.03,.04)\ m} = \left[\frac{40.46(.03)}{\left(\sqrt{(.03)^2+(.04)^2}\right)^3}(+\hat{\imath}) + \frac{40.46(.04)}{\left(\sqrt{(.03)^2+(.04)^2}\right)^3}(+\hat{\jmath})\right]\frac{N}{C}$$

$$= \left[\frac{1.2138}{.000125}(+\hat{\imath}) + \frac{1.6184}{.000125}(+\hat{\jmath})\right]\frac{N}{C}$$

$$\vec{E}_{at\ (.03,.04)\ m} = \left[9710.4(+\hat{\imath}) + 12947.2(+\hat{\jmath})\right]\frac{N}{C}\ . \qquad (634)$$

Notice that we did not carry the m units with the .03 and .04 when we plugged those numbers in. That's because $\vec{E}$ was already expressed in $\frac{N}{C}$. (In other words the m's had already been accounted for.)

At some point we have to convert to magnitude unit vector form. It is easier to do the conversion before we multiply $\vec{E}$ by q.

$$|\vec{E}_{at\ (.03,.04)\ m}| = \sqrt{(9710.4)^2 + (12947.2)^2}\ \frac{N}{C}$$

$$= 16184\ \frac{N}{C}$$

$$\vec{E}_{at\ (.03,.04)\ m} = 16184\ \frac{N}{C}\left[\frac{9710.4}{16184}(+\hat{\imath}) + \frac{12947.2}{16184}(+\hat{\jmath})\right]$$

$$= 16184\ \frac{N}{C}\left[.6(+\hat{\imath}) + .8(+\hat{\jmath})\right] \qquad (635)$$

Finally we are ready for,

$$\vec{F} = q\vec{E}$$

$$= (-15 \times 10^{-6}\ C)\left\{16184\ \frac{N}{C}\ \left[.6(+\hat{\imath}) + .8(+\hat{\jmath})\right]\right\}$$

$$\approx -.243\ N\ \left[.6(+\hat{\imath}) + .8(+\hat{\jmath})\right]$$

$$\vec{F} \approx .243\ N\ \left[.6(-\hat{\imath}) + .8(-\hat{\jmath})\right]\ . \qquad (636)$$

The signs of the $\hat{\imath}$ and $\hat{\jmath}$ components of $\vec{F}$ indicate that $\vec{F}$ is opposite to $\vec{E}$. That's what we are expecting since the electric field should "pull" a negative charge.

Quiz 6.4 A .6 m line of charge is placed along the y axis with its midpoint at $(0, 0)$. Find the force on a $+20\ \mu C$ charge located at $(.4, 0)\ m$ if the $\vec{E}$ field along the x axis is given by

$$\vec{E} = \frac{5000}{x\sqrt{x^2 + .09}}(+\hat{\imath})\ \frac{N}{C}\ .$$

Voltage $\equiv$ Electric Potential Difference

Back in Chapter 4, we had an expression for the work done by a constant force

$$Work_{\,by\ cf} = \vec{F} \bullet \vec{d}\,, \tag{637}$$

where $\vec{F}$ is the constant force that is doing the work. Sometimes it is useful to find the work done *against* a constant force. That expression looks like

$$Work_{\,against\ cf} = -\vec{F} \bullet \vec{d}\,, \tag{638}$$

where $\vec{F}$ is the constant force that is opposing the work. For example, suppose you want to know how much energy (work) is required to lift a 3 kg rock 2 m straight up against the force due to gravity.

$$\begin{aligned} Work_{\,against\ cf} &= -\vec{F} \bullet \vec{d} \\ &= -m\vec{g} \bullet \vec{d} \\ &= -(3\ kg)\left(9.8\ \frac{m}{s^2}\right)(-\hat{\jmath}) \bullet (2\ m)(+\hat{\jmath}) \\ &= \left(29.4\ \frac{kg\ m}{s^2}\right)(+\hat{\jmath}) \bullet (2\ m)(+\hat{\jmath}) \\ &= 58.8\ Nm\ =\ 58.8\ J \end{aligned} \tag{639}$$

This example demonstrates why there is a minus sign on the right hand side of equation (638). Clearly it requires positive work to lift something up against gravity. If there were no minus sign on the right side, then the answer would come out to be negative, which wouldn't make any sense. The minus sign is there to "correct" the sign on the final answer, so that the final answer makes sense.

If we divide both sides of equation (638) by a + electric charge q, then

$$\begin{aligned} \frac{Work_{\,against\ cf}}{q} &= \frac{-\vec{F} \bullet \vec{d}}{q} \\ &= -\left(\frac{\vec{F}}{q}\right) \bullet \vec{d}\,. \end{aligned} \tag{640}$$

From equation (614), the $\frac{\vec{F}}{q}$ on the right side of equation (640) equals $\vec{E}$, the electric field. The left side of equation (640) is called the electric potential difference, or voltage, V, and it represents the work per unit charge necessary to move from the beginning of $\vec{d}$ to the end of $\vec{d}$ through a constant $\vec{E}$ field. So

$$V_{c\vec{E}} = -\vec{E} \bullet \vec{d}\,, \tag{641}$$

where the $_{c\vec{E}}$ subscript is there to remind us that equation (641) applies to a constant electric field.

The units of voltage are named for Alessandro Volta who invented the 1st battery around 1799. From equation (641)

$$V \equiv \frac{N\,m}{C} \equiv \frac{J}{C}\,.$$

The units of voltage are Volts (V).

Example 6.5

The electric field in a certain region of space is given by

$$\vec{E} = 225\,\frac{N}{C}\left[\frac{4}{\sqrt{17}}(+\hat{\imath}) + \frac{1}{\sqrt{17}}(+\hat{\jmath})\right]\,.$$

Find the voltage from $(.03, -.03)$ m to $(.01, -.02)$ m.

Solution 6.5

It is a good idea to draw a picture like the one shown in Figure 6.10. The electric field is constant, and its direction is given by the unit vector

$$\frac{\vec{r}}{|\vec{r}|} = \left[\frac{4}{\sqrt{17}}(+\hat{\imath}) + \frac{1}{\sqrt{17}}(+\hat{\jmath})\right]\,.$$

The denominators of the $\hat{\imath}$ and $\hat{\jmath}$ components are the same, so looking at the numerators, we see that $\vec{E}$ goes 4 to the right, then 1 up. If we put a point at $(0, 0)$ on our picture, and another point at $(.04, .01)$, then $\vec{E}$ is a straight line passing through those two points, with its arrowhead drawn up and to the right. Of course $\vec{E}$ fills all of the space in this problem, so it is a good idea to draw in a couple more $\vec{E}$ field lines parallel to the first one.

The distance vector $\vec{d}$ is given by

$$\begin{array}{rcl} (to) - (from) & & \\ (.01, -.02) - (.03, -.03) & \rightarrow & (-.02, .01) \\ \vec{d} & = & [.02(-\hat{\imath}) + .01(+\hat{\jmath})]\; m\,, \end{array} \qquad (642)$$

and $\vec{d}$ is shown as a dotted line in Figure 6.10.

We wanted to draw a picture for this problem because the picture can show us whether $\vec{d}$ is going with $\vec{E}$ or against $\vec{E}$. In this case, Figure 6.10 reveals that $\vec{d}$ is going against $\vec{E}$. That tells us that our answer for the electric potential difference (voltage) should be positive, since we would have to push a + charge to make it go against $\vec{E}$.

Let's see if it is positive.

$$\begin{aligned}
V_{c\vec{E}} &= -\vec{E} \bullet \vec{d} \\
&= -225\,\frac{N}{C}\left[\frac{4}{\sqrt{17}}(+\hat{\imath}) + \frac{1}{\sqrt{17}}(+\hat{\jmath})\right] \bullet \left[.02(-\hat{\imath}) + .01(+\hat{\jmath})\right]\ m \\
&= -225\left[\left(\frac{4}{\sqrt{17}}\right)(-.02) + \left(\frac{1}{\sqrt{17}}\right)(.01)\right]\ \frac{N\ m}{C} \\
&\approx -225(-.0194 + .0024)\ V \\
V_{c\vec{E}} &\approx 3.83\ V
\end{aligned} \tag{643}$$

As expected, the voltage from $(.03, -.03)\ m$ to $(.01, -.02)\ m$ is positive, because we went against the $\vec{E}$ field.

Quiz 6.5 Find the voltage from $(0, .01)\ m$ to $(.03, .02)\ m$ if $\vec{E} = [600(+\hat{\imath}) + 300(-\hat{\jmath})]\ \frac{N}{C}$ between those two points.

Things to Remember

Notation

$\vec{F}_{12} \rightarrow$ the force on 2 due to 1

Relationships

$$\vec{F}_{12} = \frac{1}{4\pi\epsilon}\left[\frac{q_1 q_2}{|\vec{r}_{12}|^2}\right]\frac{\vec{r}_{12}}{|\vec{r}_{12}|}$$

$$\vec{E}_{point\ charge} = \frac{1}{4\pi\epsilon}\left[\frac{q}{|\vec{r}|^2}\right]\frac{\vec{r}}{|\vec{r}|}$$

$$\vec{E}_{total} = \sum \vec{E}_{individual}$$

$$\vec{F}_{electric} = q\vec{E} \qquad V_{due\ to\ constant\ \vec{E}} = -\vec{E} \bullet \vec{d}$$

Units

$$q \rightarrow C \qquad \epsilon \rightarrow \frac{C^2}{Nm^2}$$

$$\vec{E} \rightarrow \frac{N}{C} \qquad \text{Voltage(V)} \rightarrow \frac{\text{J}}{\text{C}} = \text{V}$$

Constants and Conversions

$$\epsilon_o \approx 8.85 \times 10^{-12}\ \frac{C^2}{Nm^2}$$

$$\mu \rightarrow \text{micro} = \times 10^{-6}$$

$$n \rightarrow \text{nano} = \times 10^{-9}$$

Homework Problems Chapter 6

6.1 Find the force on a $+15\,\mu C$ charge located at $(-1,-2)\,m$ due to a $-34\,\mu C$ charge located at $(3,-1)\,m$.

6.2 Find the force on a $+12\,\mu C$ charge located at $(2,-1)\,m$ due to a $+8\,\mu C$ charge located at $(-2,2)\,m$.

6.3 Find the expression for the $\vec{E}$ field at $(x,y)\,m$ due to a $+q$ point charge located at the origin. Leave your answer all in symbols.

6.4 Find $\vec{E}$ at $(1,2)\,m$ due to a $50\,nC$ charge located at $(1,1)\,m$.

6.5 One $.28\,nC$ charge is located at $(-.03,\,0)\,m$ and another $.28\,nC$ charge is located at $(+.03,\,0)\,m$. Find the $\vec{E}$ field midway between the two charges and $.04\,m$ above the x-axis. (i.e.- Find $\vec{E}$ at $(0,.04)\,m$.)

6.6 The $\vec{E}$ field at $(1,1)\,m$ due to a $+16\,nC$ charge located at $(-1,-1)\,m$ is given by $\vec{E} \approx 18\frac{N}{C}\left[\frac{1}{\sqrt{2}}(+\hat{i})+\frac{1}{\sqrt{2}}(+\hat{j})\right]$. The $\vec{E}$ field at $(1,1)\,m$ due to a $+52\,nC$ charge located at $(3,0)\,m$ is given by $\vec{E} \approx \left[83.642(-\hat{i})+41.821(+\hat{j})\right]\frac{N}{C}$. Find $\vec{E}_{total}$ at $(1,1)\,m$ and express your answer in magnitude unit vector form.

6.7 The $\vec{E}$ field from one particular infinite line of charge placed co-incident with the x axis is given by $\vec{E} = \frac{1079}{y}\frac{N}{C}(+\hat{j})$. Find the force on a $-24\,nC$ charge located at $(.03,-.02)\,m$.

6.8 The $\vec{E}$ field in a certain region of space is given by

$$\vec{E} = \frac{42926}{\left(\sqrt{x^2+y^2}\right)^2}\left[\frac{x}{\sqrt{x^2+y^2}}(-\hat{i})+\frac{y}{\sqrt{x^2+y^2}}(-\hat{j})\right]\frac{N}{C}.$$

Find the force on a $+25\,\mu C$ charge located at $(.5,\,1.2)\,m$.

6.9 In a certain region of space, $\vec{E} = 50\,\frac{N}{C}\left(+\hat{\imath}\right)$. Find the voltage from $(.2, .1)\,m$ to $(0, 0)\,m$ by - a) Going straight there, and

b) Going 1 st from $(.2, .1)\,m$ to $(.5, .3)\,m$ to find V_a;. Then next from $(.5, .3)\,m$ to $(0, 0)\,m$ to find V_b; So that $V_{total} = V_a + V_b$.

6.10 Find the electric potential difference from $(.1,.2)\,m$ to $(-.2,.1)\,m$ through

$$\vec{E} = 120\,\frac{N}{C}\left[\frac{3}{5}\left(+\hat{\imath}\right) + \frac{4}{5}\left(+\hat{\jmath}\right)\right]$$

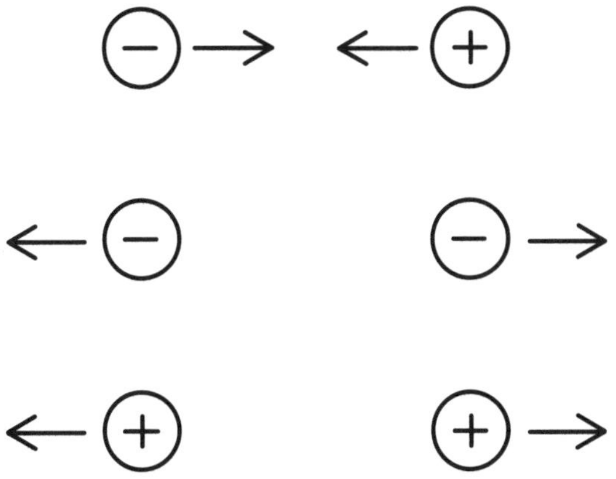

Figure 6.1 Unlike charges attract. Like charges repel.

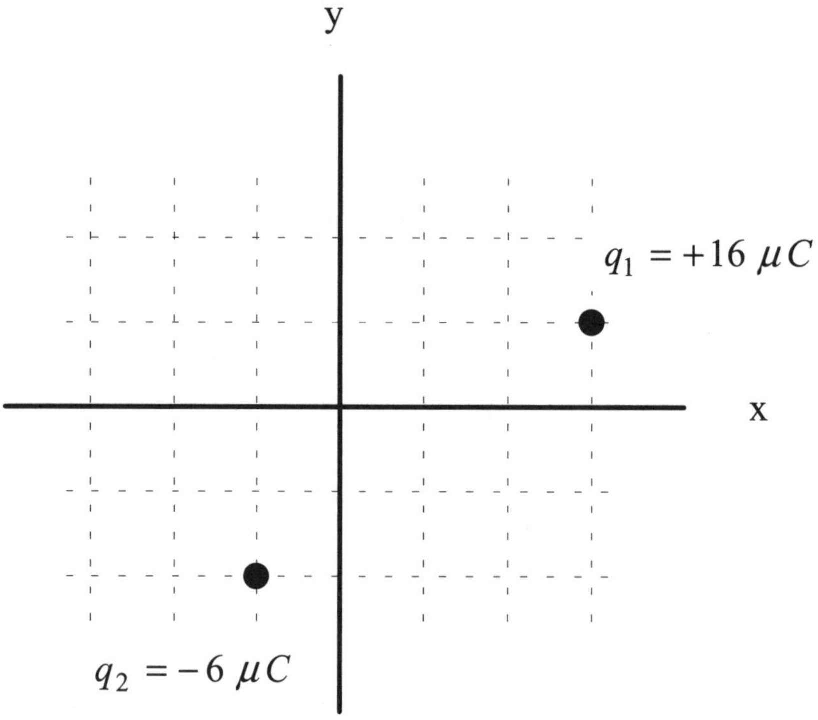

Figure 6.2 The two charges for Example 6.1

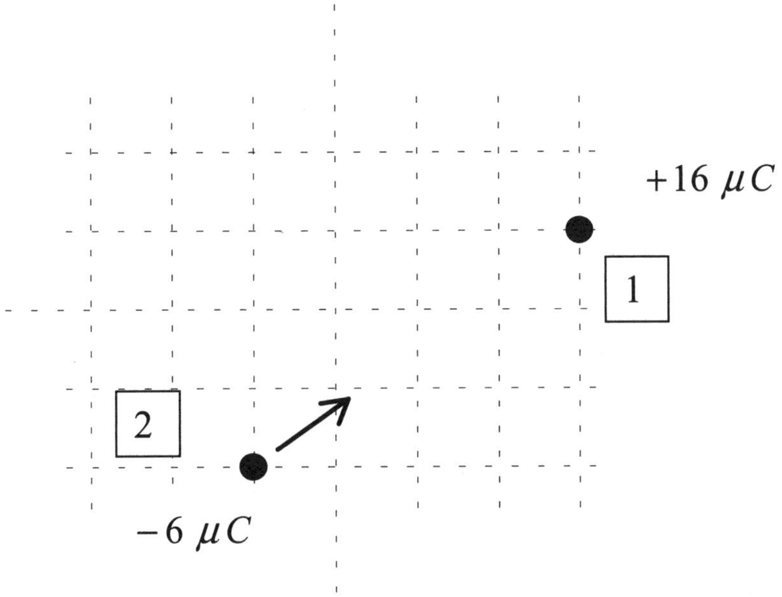

Figure 6.3 The direction of $\vec{F}_{12}$ from Example 6.1

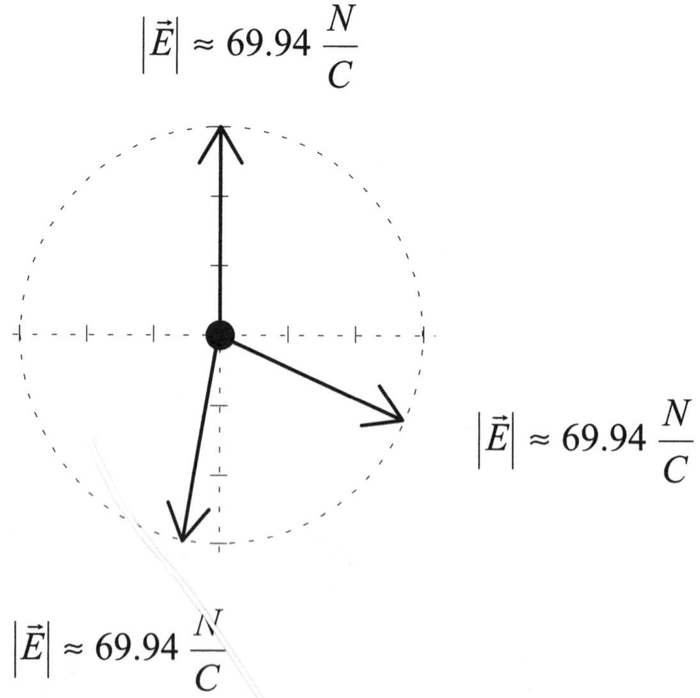

Figure 6.4 Spherical symmetry of $\left|\vec{E}\right|$ around a point charge

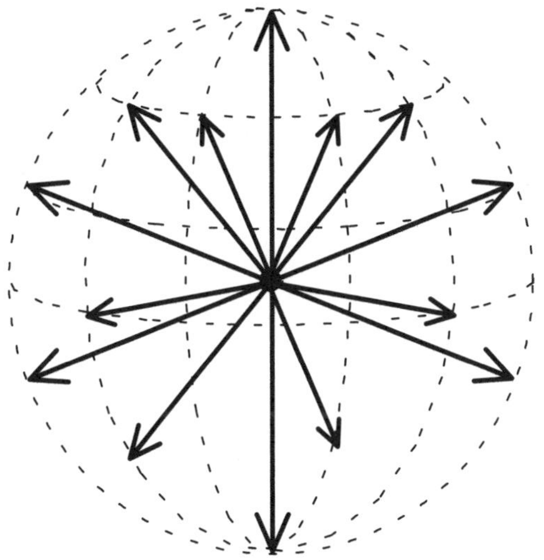

Figure 6.5 3 – dimensional $\vec{E}$ field around a positive point charge

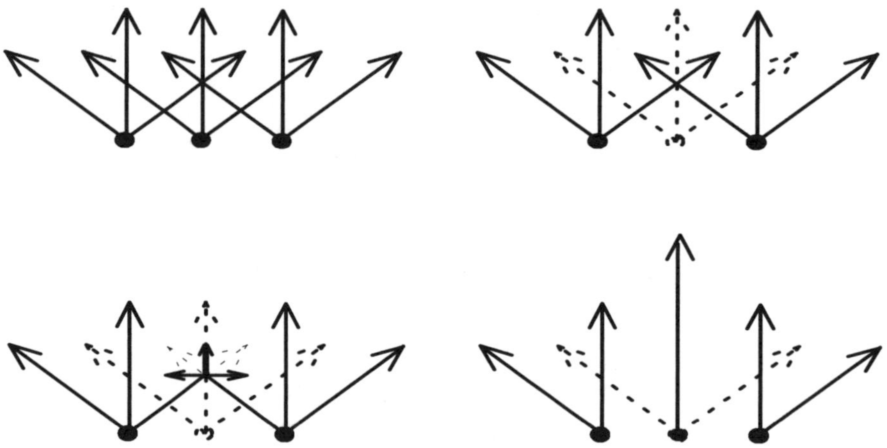

Figure 6.6 Side-to-side components of $\vec{E}$ cancel along the interior of a line of charge

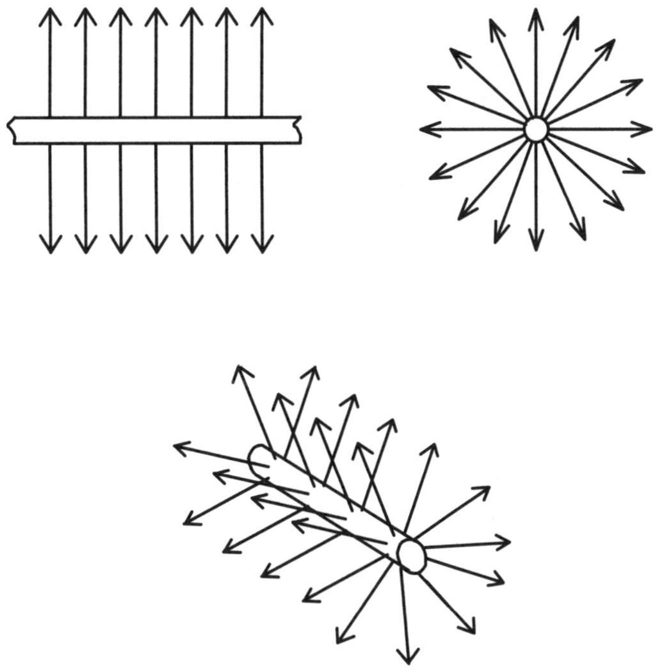

Figure 6.7 $\vec{E}$ field around the middle of a long line of positive Charge

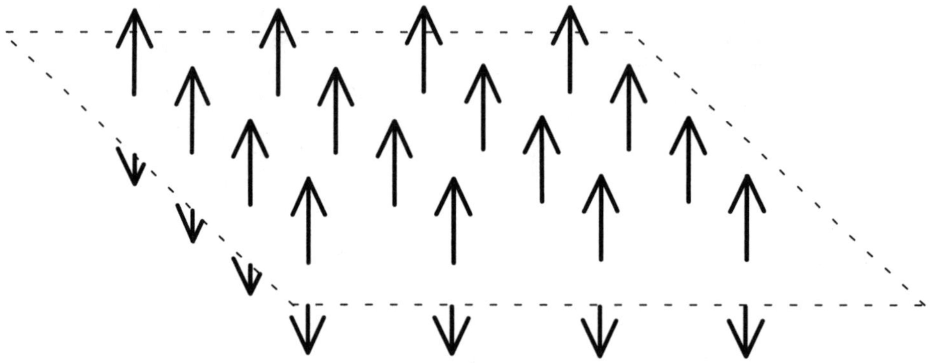

Figure 6.8 $\vec{E}$ field from a plane of positive charge

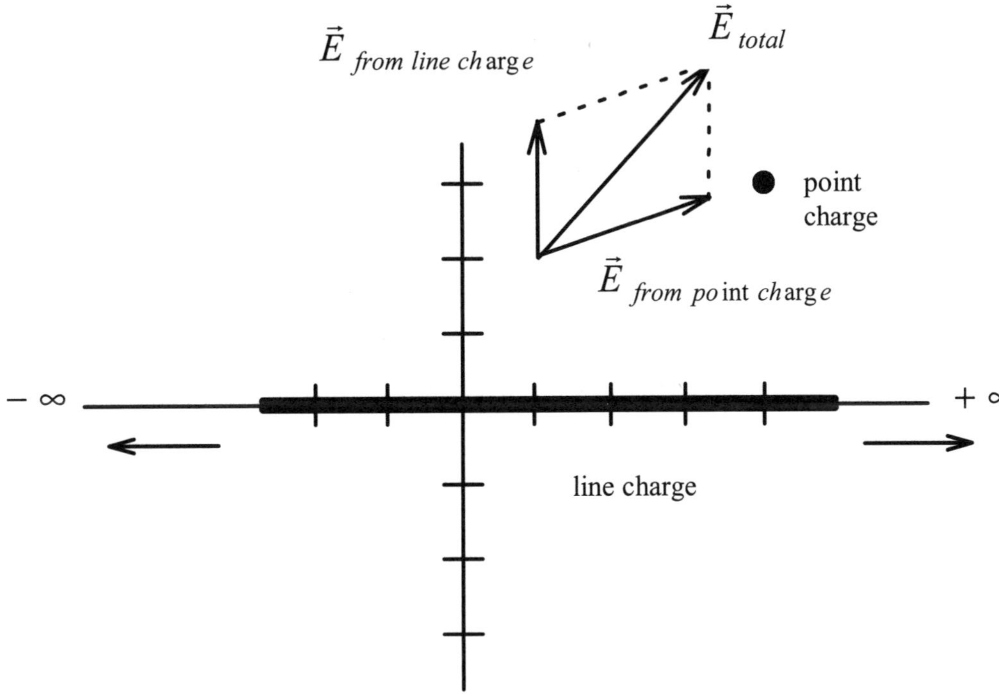

Figure 6.9 Superposition of $\vec{E}$ from Example 6.3

$$\vec{E} = 225\frac{N}{C}\left[\frac{4}{\sqrt{17}}\left(+\hat{\imath}\right) + \frac{1}{\sqrt{17}}\left(+\hat{\jmath}\right)\right]$$

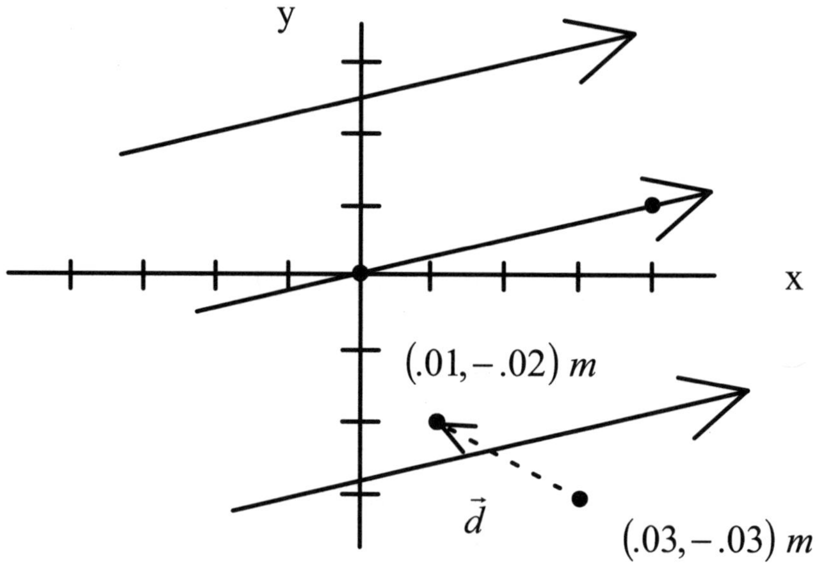

Figure 6.10 Electric potential difference from Example 6.5

Chapter 7 - Special Relativity

Timeline

290 BC The Greek philosopher-scientist Strato is an early proponent of absolute space (and time). His contemporary, Theophrastus, believes instead that space is defined by the position and order of the bodies that it contains.

240 BC Chrysippus, a Stoic philosopher in ancient Greece, suggests that a 'breath-like spirit', *pneuma*, fills space, penetrates solid bodies, and holds the cosmos together by elastic tension.

1584 Italian philosopher Giordano Bruno clearly describes an example of what would later become Einstein's 1st postulate of Special Relativity.

1630's The old style velocity addition law is attributed to Galileo, although it does not appear explicitedly in his writings.

1644 In order to explain 'action at a distance', French mathematician and physicist Rene Descartes proposes that all of space is filled with an *aether* substance capable of transmitting force.

1686 In his famous book the *Principia*, Issac Newton asserts that time and space are absolute and unchanging. His contemporary, Gottfried von Leibniz, adopts a more 'relativistic' view of time and space.

1887 American physicists Albert Michelson and Edward Morley perform an experiment to measure the speed of the Earth relative to the *aether*. The experiment fails, but one of its results suggests that stationary observers and moving observers will both measure the same value for the speed of light. Later on the concept of an *aether* is discarded from physics.

1892 In an attempt to explain the Michelson-Morley result, Irish physics professor George Fitzgerald derives the correct expression for the contraction of space in the direction of a moving object's motion.

1900-04 Two other physics professors, Joseph Larmor in England, and Hendrik A. Lorentz in Holland, independently derive space and time coordinate transformations. Their equations lead to the Fitzgerald contraction, and would later become the cornerstone of Einstein's theory of Special Relativity. Lorentz's work receives more attention, and the transformations are named after Lorentz, even though Larmor had them first. (Interestingly, both men started with theories that were later rejected.)

1905 Albert Einstein publishes his theory of Special Relativity. His paper includes yet another independent derivation of the Lorentz space and time transformations.

1905 In a separate paper Einstein concludes, "The mass of a body is a measure of its energy content." ($E = mc^2$)

1966 Physicists at the CERN high-energy laboratory in Switzerland confirm the time dilation effect for sub-atomic particles traveling at $.997c$, to within 2 % of the theoretical prediction.

TEXT

Albert Einstein created his 1905 theory of Special Relativity in order to explain certain aspects of constant speed motion. The theory is based on two articles of faith called postulates:

1. The laws of physics are the same in all "inertial reference frames".

2. Everyone measures the speed of light to be the same number, even if they are moving at a constant velocity when they take the measurement.

An inertial reference frame is a co-ordinate system that is moving at a constant velocity with respect to another co-ordinate system. Figure 7.1 shows a pool player and a ball bouncer. In Figure 7.1 a, they are doing their stuff on solid ground. In Figure 7.1 b, they are inside a railroad car that is moving at a constant velocity. Einstein's 1st postulate says that everything will work the same way as long as the relative speed between the railroad car and the ground remains constant. This postulate grew out of experiments done a long time ago by Galileo. It seems reasonable, you can try it yourself, and it is not too hard to swallow.

Einstein's second postulate is bizarre. Imagine you are driving down an interstate highway at 60 miles per hour. A car going the other way at 70 miles per hour zips by. The 70 mile per hour car looks to you like it is going much faster, and it seems reasonable to suppose that your relative speed would be $60+70 = 130$ miles per hour. Now imagine that a car going the same way at 75 miles per hour passes you. That car seems to crawl by at a relative speed of $75 - 60 = 15$ miles per hour. (Figure 7.2.) We all see this happen every day, and it seems perfectly natural to us. Einstein however, says that things will not work that way if the second car becomes a beam of light. No matter how fast you are going in your car, you would measure the beam of light coming towards you, and the beam of light passing you, to both be going at the same speed. Incredibly, that speed would be exactly the same speed that you would measure if you were standing still. (The speed of light in a vacuum is symbolized by c, and $c \approx 3 \times 10^8 \ \frac{m}{s}$).

Nothing in our everyday experience prepares us for Einstein's second postulate, and nobody would believe it, except that the famous Michelson-Morley experiment in 1887 demonstrated that it was true. Other experiments, carried out all through the 20th century, found the same thing, and it looks like the 2nd postulate is a fact of Nature, whether we like it or not.

Velocity Addition

One consequence of the second postulate is that the old velocity addition rule.

$$v_1' = v_1 \pm v_2 \ , \tag{701}$$

has to be replaced by a new velocity addition rule,

$$v_1' = \frac{v_1 \pm v_2}{1 \pm \frac{v_1 v_2}{c^2}} \ , \tag{702}$$

Actually equations (701) and (702) are written in terms of speeds, not velocities. Remember speed is the magnitude of velocity, not the velocity itself. Here v_1 and v_2 are ground speeds, c is the speed of light, and v_1' is the relative speed between 1 and 2 as seen by 2. Both 1 and 2 are traveling along the x axis. And you use the $-$ sign when they are both traveling in the same direction, the $+$ sign when they are traveling in different directions.

Example 7.1

A spaceship traveling at $\frac{1}{2}$ c is being overtaken by a beam of light as shown in Figure 7.3. How fast is the light beam going relative to the space ship ?

Solution 7.1

The speed of the spaceship is v_2, and the speed of the light beam is v_1, They are traveling in the same direction so that

$$\begin{aligned} v_1' &= \frac{v_1 - v_2}{1 - \frac{v_1 v_2}{c^2}} \\ &= \frac{c - \frac{1}{2}c}{1 - \frac{(c)\left(\frac{1}{2}c\right)}{c^2}} \\ &= \frac{c\left(1 - \frac{1}{2}\right)}{1 - \frac{1}{2}} \\ v_1' &= c \, . \end{aligned} \tag{703}$$

An observer on the spaceship sees the light beam go by at a speed of c, in accordance with Einstein's second postulate.

Quiz 7.1 One spaceship moves to the right at .9 c. Another moves to the left at .76 c. What is the relative speed between the two ships ?

Special Relativity makes new and dramatic predictions about the nature of space and time. Two of them involve time dilation and length contraction.

Time Dilation

Figure 7.4 shows an astronaut with a clock, and a ground controller with a clock. The spaceship is moving at a constant v with respect to the ground. As shown on page 333, the ground controller will calculate the astronaut's clock to run slow in accordance with

$$\Delta t_s = \Delta t_g \sqrt{1 - \frac{v^2}{c^2}}, \tag{704}$$

where Δt_s is the number of seconds that go by on the ship, and Δt_g is the number of seconds that go by on the ground.

If $v < c$, then $\sqrt{1 - \frac{v^2}{c^2}}$ is always less than 1, which means that $\Delta t_s < \Delta t_g$ in equation (704). In other words, **moving clocks run slow**.

Example 7.2

How fast must an astronaut travel so that 45 seconds go by on the ship for every for every 60 seconds that go by on the ground ?

Solution 7.2

In principle it is possible to plug the numbers of seconds directly into equation (704), then solve for v. But in practice, it is much easier to first solve for v algebraically, then plug in the numbers.

$$\begin{aligned}
\Delta t_s &= \Delta t_g \sqrt{1 - \frac{v^2}{c^2}} \\
\frac{\Delta t_s}{\Delta t_g} &= \sqrt{1 - \frac{v^2}{c^2}} \\
\left(\frac{\Delta t_s}{\Delta t_g}\right)^2 &= 1 - \frac{v^2}{c^2} \\
\frac{v^2}{c^2} &= 1 - \left(\frac{\Delta t_s}{\Delta t_g}\right)^2 \\
v^2 &= c^2 \left[1 - \left(\frac{\Delta t_s}{\Delta t_g}\right)^2\right] \\
v &= c\sqrt{1 - \frac{(\Delta t_s)^2}{(\Delta t_g)^2}} \qquad (705)
\end{aligned}$$

It is now straightforward to plug the numbers into equation (705).

$$\begin{aligned}
v &= c\sqrt{1 - \frac{(\Delta t_s)^2}{(\Delta t_g)^2}} \\
&= c\sqrt{1 - \frac{(45\ s)^2}{(60\ s)^2}}
\end{aligned}$$

$$
\begin{aligned}
&= c\sqrt{1-\frac{2025\ s^2}{3600\ s^2}} \\
&= c\sqrt{1-.5625} \ = \ c\sqrt{.4375} \\
v &\approx .66\ c \\
& \textit{or} \\
v &\approx .66\left(3\times 10^8\ \frac{m}{s}\right) \\
&\approx 1.98\times 10^8\ \frac{m}{s}
\end{aligned}
\tag{706}
$$

If the spaceship travels at about $\frac{2}{3}$ the speed of light, then 45 seconds go by on the ship for every 60 seconds that go by on the ground.

Quiz 7.2 A spaceship is traveling at .4 c. How many seconds go by on the ground for every 100 seconds that go by on the ship ?

Length Contraction

Another radical prediction of Special Relativity is that the space through which an object moves is contracted in the direction of motion, so that the object itself becomes contracted. In symbols,

$$
L = L_o\sqrt{1-\frac{v^2}{c^2}}\ , \tag{707}
$$

where L is the length of the moving object (as measured by the stationary observer), L_o is the length of the same object when it is stationary (again measured by the stationary observer), and v is the object's speed. Actually the Irish physicist G.F. FitzGerald worked out the form of equation (707) several years before Einstein. For that reason this equation is sometimes called the FitzGerald Contraction. **Moving objects are contracted in the direction of motion.**

Example 7.3

The stationary observer in Figure 7.5a measures a stationary square piece of wood to be .75 m by .75 m. What will the stationary observer in Figure 7.5b measure for the dimensions of the same piece of wood as it zooms by at $2.64\times 10^8\ \frac{m}{s}$?

Solution 7.3

The height of the piece of wood, h, is perpendicular to the direction of motion. Length contraction only applies to the dimension that is parallel to the direction of motion. So the height of the moving piece of wood is the same as the height of the stationary piece of wood, $h = .75\ m$.

The length of the piece of wood is in the direction of motion, so the length dimension will be Fitzgerald contracted into

$$\begin{aligned} L &= L_o\sqrt{1-\frac{v^2}{c^2}} \\ &= .75\ m\sqrt{1-\left(\frac{2.64\times 10^8\ \frac{m}{s}}{3\times 10^8\ \frac{m}{s}}\right)^2} \\ &= .75\ m\sqrt{1-.7744} \\ &\approx .75\ m(.4749737) \\ &\approx .356\ m \end{aligned} \tag{708}$$

Example 7.3 emphasizes that only the dimension that lies along the direction of travel gets FitzGerald contracted. The other dimensions are unchanged.

Quiz 7.3 A meter stick is moving with constant speed along the direction of its length. How fast is it going if a stationary observer measures it to be .8 m long ?

Why haven't we seen this before ?

Equations (704) and (707) raise an interesting question, "If moving clocks run slow, and moving objects get contracted, why haven't we seen this happen long before Einstein ?" In 5,000 years of recorded history, why is there no mention of anybody ever seeing this ? The answer involves how fast an object has to go before relativistic effects become noticeable.

Suppose something was moving at one million miles per hour. Let's see how much slower its clock would run, and how much its length would be contracted. First we need to convert miles per hour into meters per second.

$$\left(\frac{1,000,000}{1}\frac{miles}{hr}\right)\left(\frac{1}{60}\frac{hr}{min}\right)\left(\frac{1}{60}\frac{min}{sec}\right)\approx 277.778\frac{miles}{sec}$$

$$\left(\frac{277.778}{1}\frac{miles}{sec}\right)\left(\frac{5280}{1}\frac{ft}{mile}\right)\left(\frac{12}{1}\frac{in}{ft}\right)\left(\frac{2.54}{1}\frac{cm}{in}\right)\left(\frac{1}{100}\frac{m}{cm}\right)\approx 4.47\times 10^5\ \frac{m}{s}\ .$$

So

$$1,000,000\ \frac{mi}{hr}\approx 4.47\times 10^5\ \frac{m}{s}\ .$$

For the number of seconds that would go by on a clock traveling at 1,000,000 $\frac{mi}{hr}$, from equation (704)

$$\Delta t_s = \Delta t_g\sqrt{1-\frac{v^2}{c^2}}$$

$$
\begin{aligned}
&\approx \Delta t_s \sqrt{1 - \frac{\left(4.47 \times 10^5 \ \frac{m}{s}\right)^2}{\left(3 \times 10^8 \ \frac{m}{s}\right)^2}} \\
&\approx \Delta t_g \underbrace{\sqrt{1 - .0000022}}_{\approx 1} \\
\Delta t_s &\approx \Delta t_g \ . \qquad (709)
\end{aligned}
$$

For the contracted length of an object going 1,000,000 $\frac{mi}{hr}$, from equation (707)

$$
\begin{aligned}
L &= L_o \sqrt{1 - \frac{v^2}{c^2}} \\
&\approx L_o \underbrace{\sqrt{1 - \frac{\left(4.47 \times 10^5 \ \frac{m}{s}\right)^2}{\left(3 \times 10^8 \ \frac{m}{s}\right)^2}}}_{\approx 1} \\
L &\approx L_o \ . \qquad (710)
\end{aligned}
$$

Equations (709) and (710) point out that even if something is moving with a speed of 1,000,000 $\frac{mi}{hr}$, the relativistic effects are still way too small to be noticed. An object must be going at an appreciable fraction of the speed of light before relativity will click in. Nothing big enough for us to see goes anywhere near that fast, so length contraction and time dilation were never recognized prior to 1887.

Those effects do occur however. They happen every day in particle accelerators all over the world. Nuclear physicists are now able to accelerate subatomic particles almost to the speed of light, and none of their experiments will work unless they also account for the effects of Special Relativity.

$E = mc^2$

Albert Einstein's $E = mc^2$ is certainly the most famous equation in the world. It is also one of his greatest contributions to science.

Before Einstein, a material object could possess kinetic energy due to its motion, and/or it could possess potential energy due to its location in some kind of field. But that was all. If the object was stationary, way out in empty space, far from any fields, then its total energy would be equal to zero. Einstein said there was more. The total energy would not just add up to zero, because the object would also possess a "rest mass" energy given by

$$E = m_o c^2 \ , \qquad (711)$$

where m_o is the "rest mass" of the object. Einstein's idea is that any material object has a kind of "internal" energy equal to the oject's mass times the speed of light squared. This idea was radical, and totally unexpected at the time.

If the object is moving with constant v in outer space, then it seems reasonable that

$$\begin{aligned} E_{total} &= \textit{rest mass energy} \;+\; \textit{kinetic energy} \\ &= m_o c^2 + \frac{1}{2} m_o v^2 \\ E_{total} &= m_o c^2 \left(1 + \frac{1}{2}\frac{v^2}{c^2}\right) . \end{aligned} \tag{712}$$

There is a kind of mathmatical series, called a binominal expansion, that reduces to

$$(1-x)^{-n} \approx 1 + nx \tag{713}$$

when x is much less than 1. If we let $n = \frac{1}{2}$ and $x = \frac{v^2}{c^2}$, then

$$\left(1 - \frac{v^2}{c^2}\right)^{-\frac{1}{2}} = \frac{1}{\sqrt{1-\frac{v^2}{c^2}}} \approx 1 + \frac{1}{2}\frac{v^2}{c^2} . \tag{714}$$

Substituting equation (714) into equation (712) leads to

$$\begin{aligned} E_{total} &= E = \textit{rest mass energy} \;+\; \textit{kinetic energy} \\ &= m_o c^2 + \frac{1}{2} m_o v^2 \\ &= m_o c^2 \left(1 + \frac{1}{2}\frac{v^2}{c^2}\right) \approx m_o c^2 \left(\frac{1}{\sqrt{1-\frac{v^2}{c^2}}}\right) \\ &= \left(\frac{m_o}{\sqrt{1-\frac{v^2}{c^2}}}\right) c^2 \\ E &= mc^2 . \end{aligned} \tag{715}$$

The quantity

$$m = \frac{m_o}{\sqrt{1-\frac{v^2}{c^2}}} \tag{716}$$

is called the relativistic mass. Notice that the relativistic mass is always greater than the rest mass when $0 < v < c$. That happens because $\frac{1}{\sqrt{1-\frac{v^2}{c^2}}}$ is always greater than 1 when $v > 0$ but less than c. That brings us to another unusual prediction of Special Relativity. **The mass of a moving object increases with respect to a stationary observer**.

Also notice that

$$mc^2 \approx \textit{rest mass energy} \;+\; \textit{kinetic energy}$$

not

$$mc^2 = rest\ mass\ energy\ +\ kinetic\ energy\ .$$

That happens because the binominal approximation says that

$$\frac{1}{\sqrt{1-\frac{v^2}{c^2}}} \approx 1 + \frac{1}{2}\frac{v^2}{c^2} \qquad \text{not} \qquad \frac{1}{\sqrt{1-\frac{v^2}{c^2}}} = 1 + \frac{1}{2}\frac{v^2}{c^2}\ .$$

The approximation is very good for small v, but as v gets closer and closer to c, the approximation gets worse and worse. Einstein's position is that mc^2 is the correct expression for E regardless of the size of v. It was the historical $KE = \frac{1}{2}m_o v^2$ term that had always been slightly inaccurate. Again the error would not become noticeable until the object was moving at a significant fraction of the speed of light.

Let's look at the units.

$$mc^2 \rightarrow kg\left(\frac{m}{s}\right)^2 \rightarrow \left(\frac{kg\ m}{s^2}\right)m \rightarrow N\ m \rightarrow J$$

We would expect energy to have units of Joules (J), and it does.

Example 7.4

How fast does an object have to go so that a stationary observer finds that it has twice as much energy as it would have standing still ?

Solution 7.4

Here we want the total energy, mc^2, to equal twice the rest mass energy, m_oc^2.

$$mc^2 = 2(m_oc^2) \tag{717}$$

We need to divide out the c^2's, substitute for m from equation (716), and solve for v.

$$\begin{aligned}
mc^2 &= 2(m_oc^2)\\
m &= 2m_o\\
\frac{m_o}{\sqrt{1-\frac{v^2}{c^2}}} &= 2m_o\\
m_o &= 2m_o\sqrt{1-\frac{v^2}{c^2}}\\
\frac{1}{2} &= \sqrt{1-\frac{v^2}{c^2}}\\
\frac{1}{4} &= 1-\frac{v^2}{c^2}\\
\frac{v^2}{c^2} &= 1-\frac{1}{4}\\
\frac{v^2}{c^2} &= \frac{3}{4}\\
v^2 &= \frac{3}{4}c^2\\
v &= \frac{\sqrt{3}}{2}c \approx .866\ c
\end{aligned} \tag{718}$$

The object has to go extremely fast in order to double its rest mass energy because the rest mass energy is such a huge number to begin with.

Quiz 7.4 A penny minted in 1995 contains about 2.5 grams of mass. Suppose your 4 person household uses 950 kilowatt-hours = 3.42×10^9 J of electricity each month. For how many years could you provide electricity to the house if all of the penny's rest mass could be converted into energy ? (1 kg = 1000 g.)

The Spacetime Interval

Figure 7.6A shows a classic Pythagorean Theorem right triangle. Figure 7.6B shows the same right triangle, but with co-ordinate system notation (CSN). In Figure 7.7, the CSN triangle is moving in the + x direction with velocity v. According to Special Relativity, the side of the triangle along the direction of motion will be contracted, so that $(\Delta x') = (\Delta x)\sqrt{1 - \frac{v^2}{c^2}}$. Meanwhile the y side is perpendicular to the direction of motion, so it is not contracted and $(\Delta y')$ is still $= (\Delta y)$.

The stationary CSN triangle in Figure 7.6B has a Pythagorean Theorem hypotenuse given by

$$d^2 = (\Delta x)^2 + (\Delta y)^2 \,. \tag{719}$$

The moving CSN triangle in Figure 7.7 has a Pythagorean Theorem hypotenuse given by

$$\begin{aligned} (d')^2 &= (\Delta x')^2 + (\Delta y')^2 \\ (d')^2 &= \left[(\Delta x)\sqrt{1 - \frac{v^2}{c^2}}\right]^2 + (\Delta y)^2 \,. \end{aligned} \tag{720}$$

From equations (719) and (720) it is apparent that $d^2 \neq (d')^2$, because

$$(\Delta x)^2 + (\Delta y)^2 \neq (\Delta x')^2 + (\Delta y')^2 \,. \tag{721}$$

Equation (721) reveals another important aspect of Special Relativity:

A stationary observer measues different Pythagorean distances between the same two points in different inertial reference frames.

Albert Einstein published the theory of Special Relativity a few years after he graduated from the Swiss Federal Institute of Technology. One of his former professors, a man named Hermann Minkowski, was impressed by Einstein's ideas, but bothered by the variability of Pythagorean distance. Minkowski began to search for a "distance-like" quantity that would stay the same from reference frame to reference frame. After awhile he came up with

$$(\Delta S)^2 = (\Delta x)^2 + (\Delta y)^2 - [c(\Delta t)]^2 \,, \tag{722}$$

where ΔS is called the *spacelike* spacetime interval. Let's look at the units.

$$\begin{aligned}
(\Delta S)^2 &\rightarrow (m-m)^2 + (m-m)^2 - \left[\frac{m}{s}(s-s)\right]^2 \\
&\rightarrow m^2 + m^2 - \left[\frac{m}{s}(s)\right]^2 \\
&\rightarrow m^2 + m^2 - m^2 \\
(\Delta S)^2 &\rightarrow m^2 \\
\Delta S &\rightarrow \sqrt{m^2} \rightarrow m
\end{aligned}$$

The spacetime interval has units of meters just like the Pythagorean distance has units of meters. But unlike the Pythagorean distance, the spacetime interval includes a dimension for time together with the dimensions of space.

Here's the idea. With the Pythagorean concept of length, x, y co-ordinates are assigned to each end of a rod. A calculation then gives us the *distance between the two ends.* For the Relativistic concept of interval, x, y and t co-ordinates are assigned to each end of the rod. A calculation then gives us the *interval between two events.* One event is the back of the rod at t_1. The other event is the front of the rod at t_2. Maybe $t_1 = t_2$ and maybe it doesn't. If it does, then $\Delta t = 0$, and the interval reduces to the Pythagorean theorem. If it doesn't, then $\Delta t \neq 0$, and every term in the interval has to come into play.

The big advantage is that the spacetime interval between two events is the same number, even when calculated in different inertial references frames. In other words

$$(\Delta x)^2 + (\Delta y)^2 - c^2(\Delta t)^2 = (\Delta x')^2 + (\Delta y')^2 - c^2(\Delta t')^2 \,. \tag{723}$$

Example 7.5

An electron traveling along the x-axis at $\frac{1}{2}$ the speed of light inside a laboratory passes through a detector placed at $x = 0\ m$, and a detector placed at $x = 3\ m$. Calculate the square of the *spacelike* interval between those two events in a) the laboratory frame, and b) the electron frame.

Solution 7.5

a) Figure 7.8 shows the situation from a laboratory frame observer's point of view. He is stationary with respect to the dectector apparatus. The first event he observes is the electron passing through the $D1$ detector located at $x = 0\ m$ at time t_1. The second event is the electron passing through $D2$ a little while later at time t_2. The spacial separation between the 2 events is just $\Delta x = (3\ m - 0\ m) = 3\ m$. (There is no movement in the y direction, so $\Delta y = 0$) The time separation between the two events can be found from

$$\begin{aligned}
\Delta x &= v(\Delta t) \\
\Delta t &= \frac{\Delta x}{v} = \frac{3\ m}{\frac{1}{2}c} \\
\Delta t &= \frac{6\ m}{c}
\end{aligned} \tag{724}$$

So the laboratory frame observer calculates the square of the *spacelike* interval to be

$$\begin{aligned}
(\Delta S)^2 &= (\Delta x)^2 + (\Delta y)^2 - c^2(\Delta t)^2 \\
&= (3\ m)^2 + (0\ m)^2 - c^2\left(\frac{6\ m}{c}\right)^2 \\
&= 9\ m^2 - c^2\left(\frac{36\ m^2}{c^2}\right) = 9\ m^2 - 36\ m^2 \\
(\Delta S)^2 &= -27\ m^2\ . \qquad (725)
\end{aligned}$$

b) Figure 7.9 shows the same situation from the point of view of an observer riding on the electron. She is stationary with respect to the electron. The first event that she observes is detector $D1$ passing by at time t_1'. Detector $D2$ passes by a little while later at time t_2'. In the electron frame, both events happen at the position of the electron so that $\Delta x' = 0$. Again there is no movement in the y direction so $\Delta y'$ also $= 0$. And again the difference in time can be found from distance divided by speed. This time however, d, the separation distance between the detectors is Fitzgerald contracted because the detector apparatus is moving at a speed of v with respect to the electron riding observer. (She observes the electron to be stationary while the entire laboratory moves by at speed v.) So in the electron frame

$$\begin{aligned}
\Delta t' &= \frac{d}{v} = \frac{\Delta x\sqrt{1-\frac{v^2}{c^2}}}{v} \\
&= \frac{6\ m}{c}\sqrt{1-\frac{\left(\frac{1}{2}c\right)^2}{c^2}} \\
&= \frac{6\ m}{c}\sqrt{1-\frac{\frac{1}{4}c^2}{c^2}} \\
&= \frac{6\ m}{c}\sqrt{1-\frac{1}{4}} = \frac{6\ m}{c}\sqrt{\frac{3}{4}} \\
\Delta t' &= \frac{3\sqrt{3}\ m}{c}\ . \qquad (726)
\end{aligned}$$

The electron frame observer calculates the square of the *spacelike* interval to be

$$\begin{aligned}
(\Delta S')^2 &= (\Delta x')^2 + (\Delta y')^2 - c^2(\Delta t')^2 \\
&= (0\ m)^2 + (0\ m)^2 - c^2\left(\frac{3\sqrt{3}\ m}{c}\right)^2 \\
&= -c^2\left(\frac{(9)(3)\ m^2}{c^2}\right) \\
(\Delta S')^2 &= -27\ m^2\ . \qquad (727)
\end{aligned}$$

As expected, $(\Delta S)^2 = (\Delta S')^2$. The unexpected part is the negative sign. $(\Delta S)^2$ is going to be negative any time that $c\Delta t$ is greater than the spacial separation between the two events. For this particular example $c\Delta t$ in the laboratory frame was $c\Delta t = 6\ m$, and the spacial separation was $\Delta x = 3\ m$. In the electron frame,

$c\Delta t' = 3\sqrt{3}\ m$, and the spacial separation was $\Delta x' = 0\ m$. It turns out that $c\Delta t$ usually is the bigger number, and that fact has led to the use of a *timelike* spacetime interval defined such that $(\Delta S_t)^2 = -(\Delta S)^2$, so that

$$(\Delta S_t)^2 = c^2(\Delta t)^2 - (\Delta x)^2 - (\Delta y)^2 \,, \tag{728}$$

Notice that the *timelike* interval will also stay the same from frame to frame.

Quiz 7.5 A ground observer sees a particle go from $x_1 = -3\ m$ to $x_2 = 9\ m$ in 160 nano seconds. Calculate the square of the *timelike* interval in both the ground frame and the particle frame. (Remember $5\ ns = 5 \times 10^{-9} s$.)

Things to Remember

Relationships

$$v_1' = \frac{v_1 \pm v_2}{1 \pm \frac{v_1 v_2}{c^2}}$$

$$\Delta t_s = \Delta t_g \sqrt{1 - \frac{v^2}{c^2}} \qquad L = L_o \sqrt{1 - \frac{v^2}{c^2}}$$

$$E = mc^2 \qquad m = \frac{m_o}{\sqrt{1 - \frac{v^2}{c^2}}}$$

$$(\Delta S)^2 = (\Delta x)^2 + (\Delta y)^2 - [c(\Delta t)]^2$$

$$(\Delta S_t)^2 = c^2 (\Delta t)^2 - (\Delta x)^2 - (\Delta y)^2$$

Units

$$\Delta S \rightarrow m$$

Constants and Conversions

$$c \approx 3 \times 10^8 \ \frac{m}{s}$$

$$1kg = 1000g$$

Homework Problems Chapter 7

7.1 Two spaceships are moving towards each other, and each one is traveling at $.99c$. What is their relative speed a) according to Galileo, and b) according to Einstein?

7.2 A spaceship moving at $.4c$ is overtaken and passed by a spaceship moving at $.7c$. What is the relative speed between the two ships?

7.3 How many seconds go by on a spaceship traveling at $.8c$ for every 60 seconds that go by on the ground?

7.4 At what speed is the number of seconds that goes by on the ship equal to $\frac{1}{2}$ the number of seconds that goes by on the ground?

7.5 A spaceship traveling at $.5c$ is 72 m long according to an observer on the ground. How long is it according to a passenger on the ship? (Note that the ship is stationary with respect to the passenger.)

7.6 A meter stick is traveling along the direction of its own length at $.25c$. How long is it according to a stationary observer on the ground?

7.7 A chunk of rock with a rest mass equal to 26 kg is moving through outer space at a constant $.7c$. How much energy does the rock possess a) according to a stationary observer, and b) according to an alien riding on the rock?

7.8 How fast is an outer space object going if its energy is 3 times what it would be standing still?

7.9 A ground observer sees a particle go from $x = -4m$ to $x = 14m$ in $100ns$. Calculate the square of the timelike interval in both the ground frame and the particle frame.

7.10 A ground observer sees the front of a light beam travel from $x = 1m$ to $x = 9m$. Calculate the square of the timelike interval in both the ground frame and the light beam frame.

a.

b.

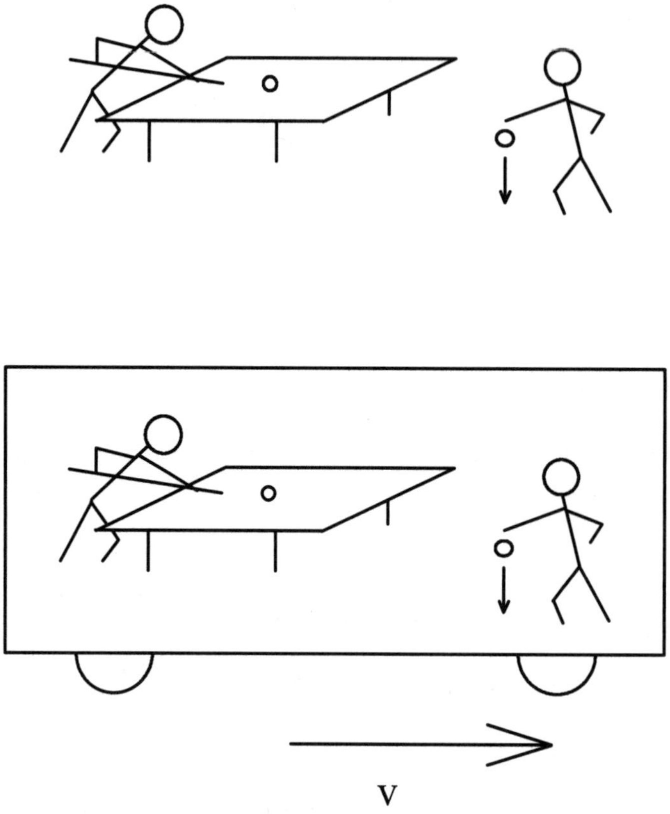

Figure 7.1 Pool player and ball bouncer; a) on solid ground
b) inside a constant velocity railroad car

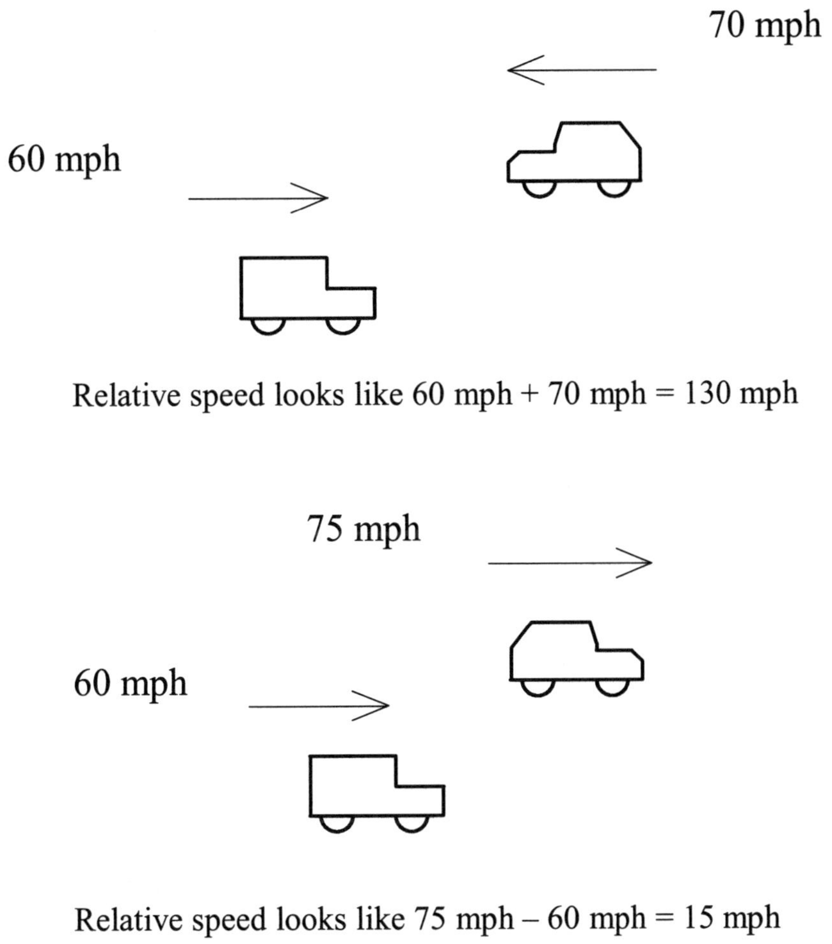
70 mph
60 mph
Relative speed looks like 60 mph + 70 mph = 130 mph
75 mph
60 mph
Relative speed looks like 75 mph – 60 mph = 15 mph

Figure 7.2 Highway Physics

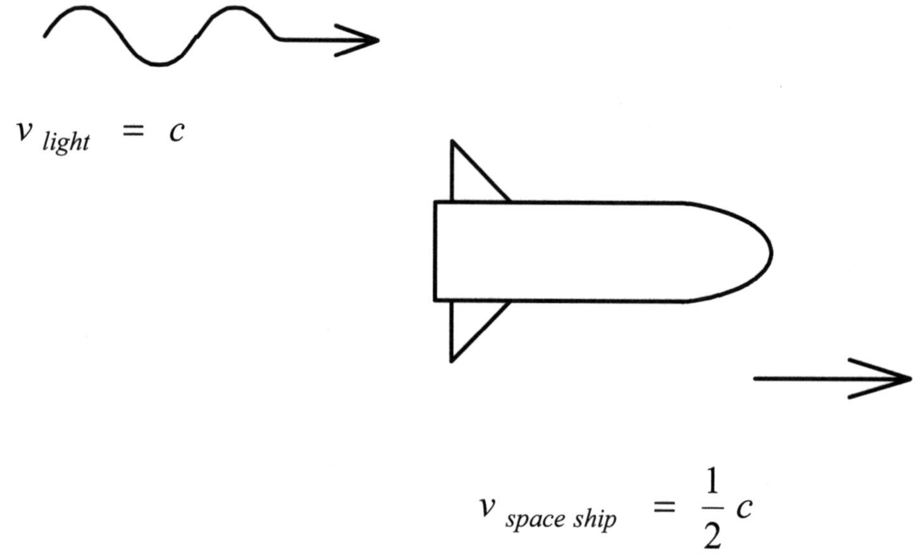

Figure 7.3 Light beam and spaceship from Example 7.1

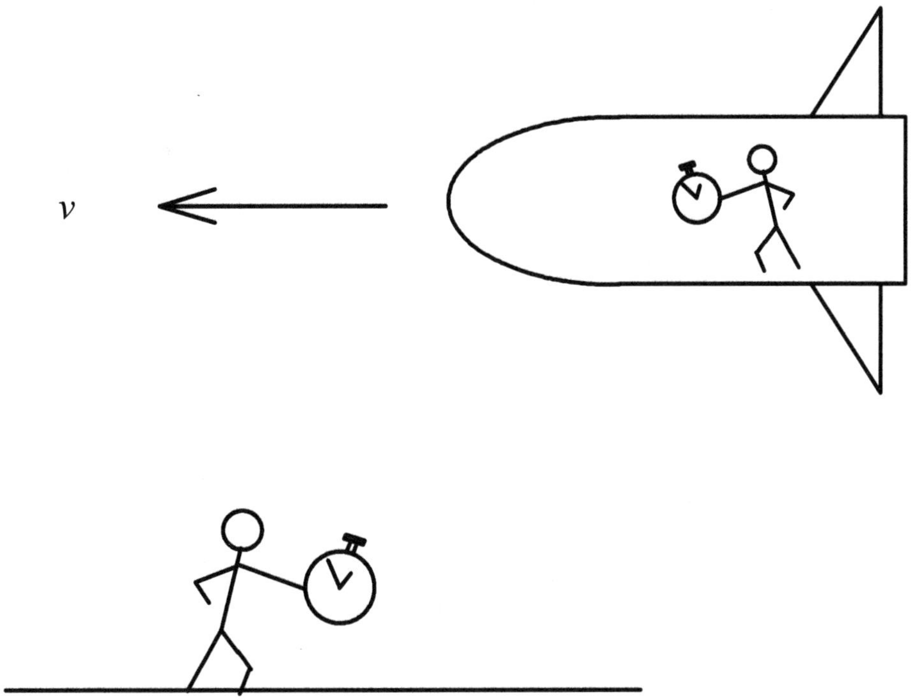

Figure 7.4 Astronaut's clock runs slow compared to ground controller's clock

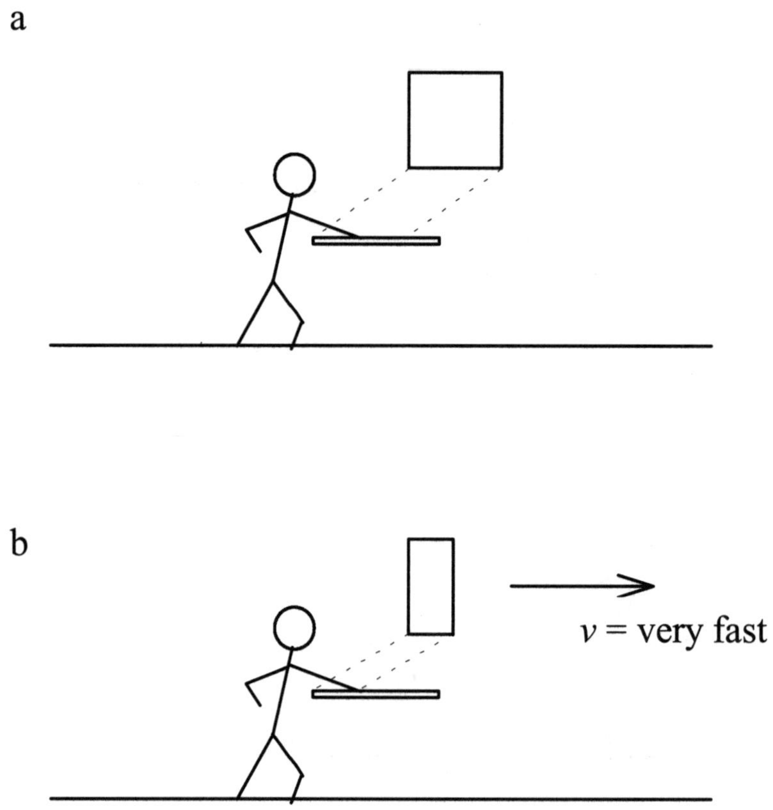

Figure 7.5 Moving square is contracted along the direction of Motion

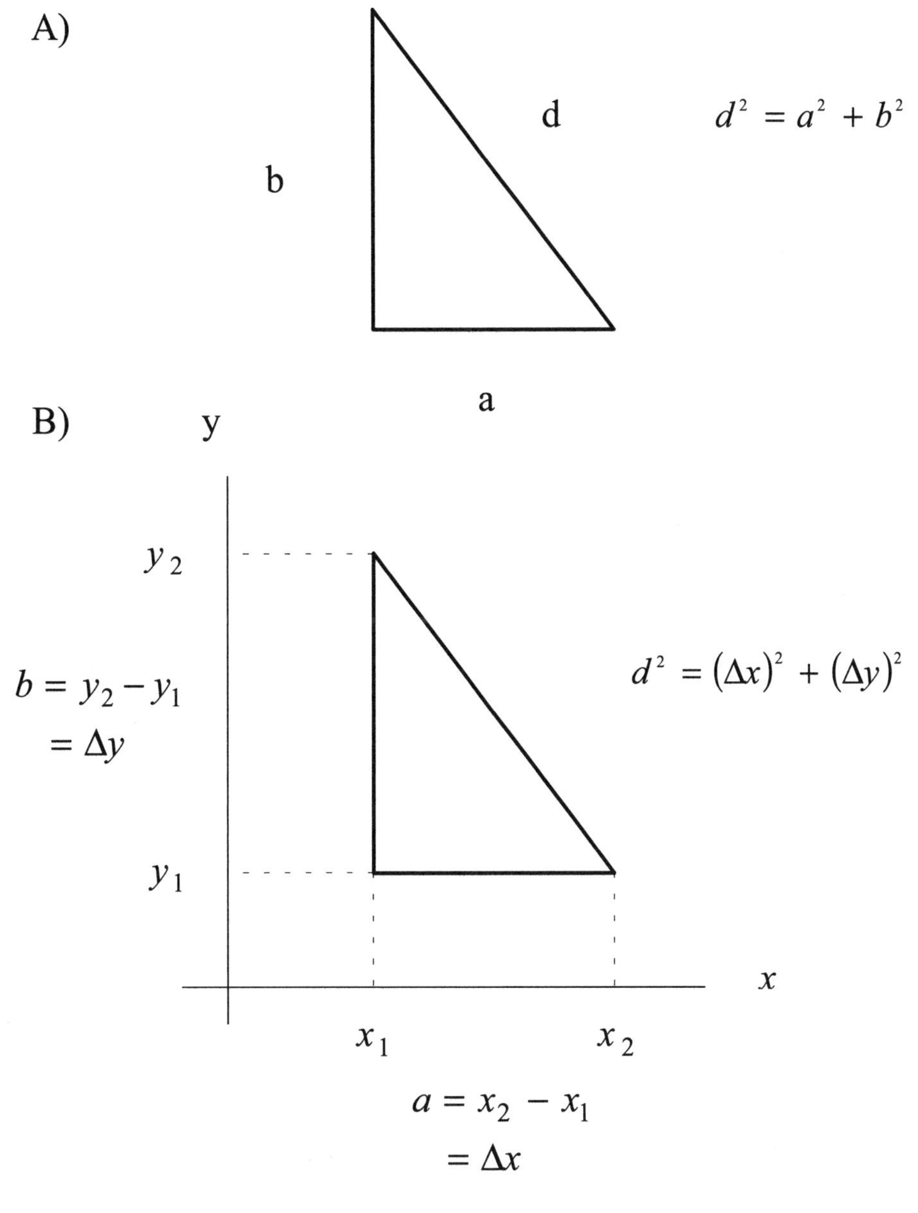

Figure 7.6 A) Classic Pythagorean Theorem right triangle
B) Pythagorean Theorem right triangle with co-ordinate system notation (CSN)

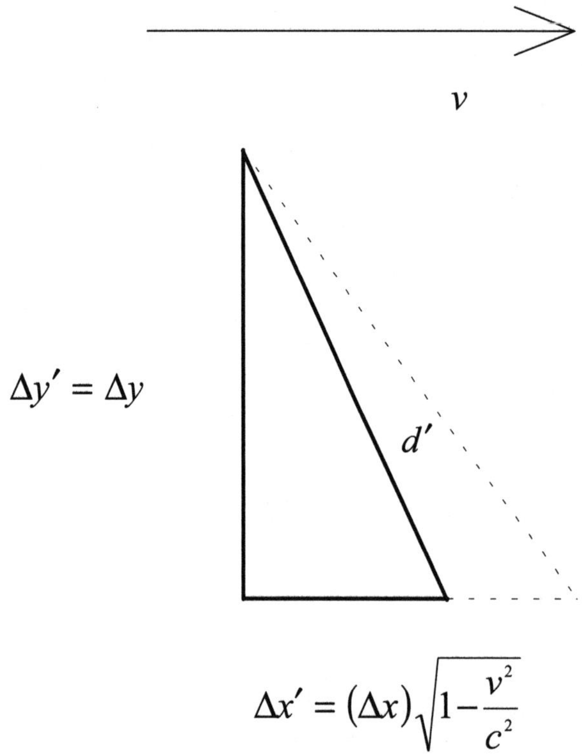

Figure 7.7 CSN triangle moving in the + x direction

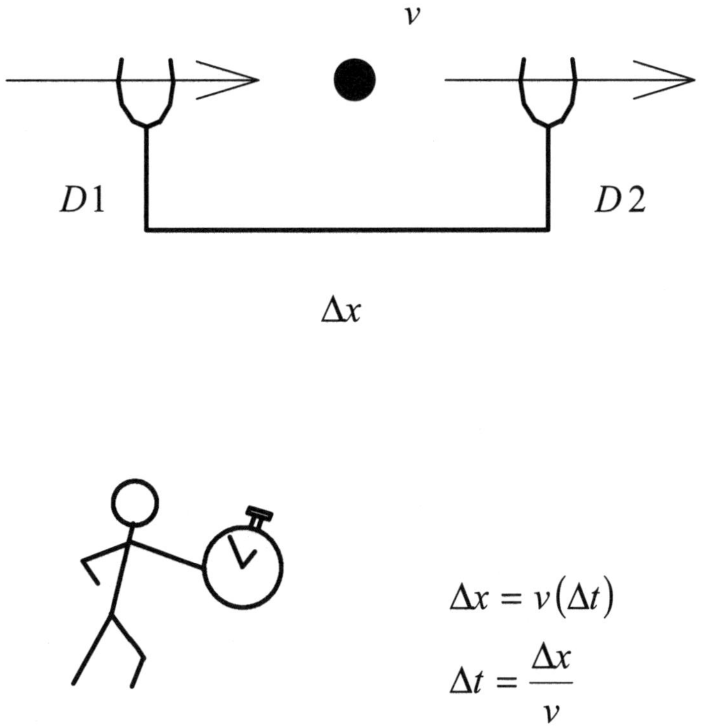

Figure 7.8 Laboratory frame for Example 7.5

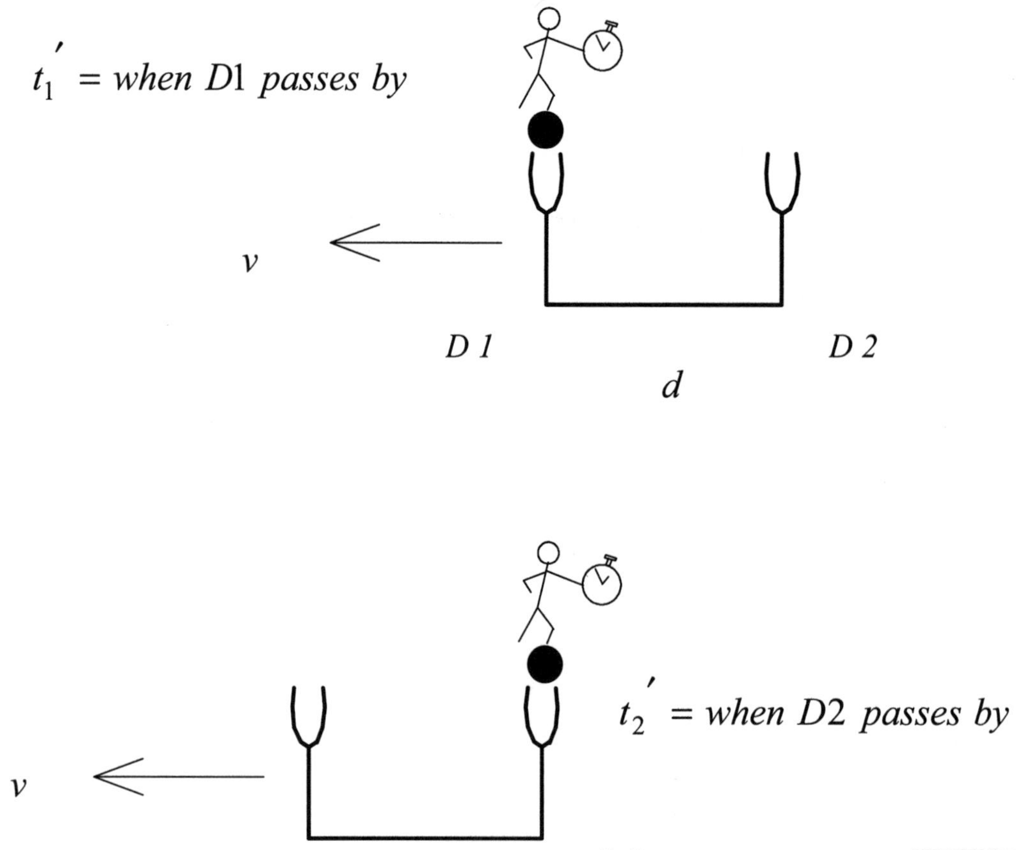

$$d = \Delta x \sqrt{1 - \frac{v^2}{c^2}}$$

$$t_2' - t_1' = \Delta t' = \frac{d}{v} \qquad \Delta t' = \frac{\Delta x \sqrt{1 - \frac{v^2}{c^2}}}{v} = \Delta t \sqrt{1 - \frac{v^2}{c^2}}$$

Figure 7.9 Electron frame for Example 7.5

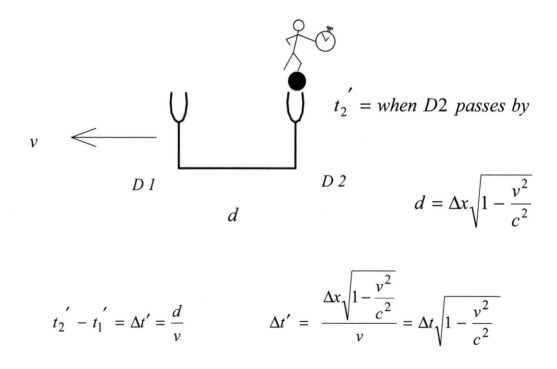

Chapter 8 - Electric Current and the Magnetic Field

Timeline

450 BC A 'scientific' explanation of magnetic attraction is attributed to Empedocles, one of the early Greek scientists.

83 AD A manuscript from the Han dynasty in China seems to reference a south-pointing magnetic "spoon" compass.

1600 In his book *On the Magnet*, William Gilbert, physician to Queen Elizabeth of England, mentions that bits of iron placed near a magnet on a table tend to arrange themselves into a definite pattern.

1729 British scientist Stephen Gray discovers electrical conduction.

1799 Italian physicist Alessandro Volta invents a battery to produce electricity.

1802 Gian Romagnosi, an Italian amateur scientist, notices that a magnetic needle would move when placed close to an electric current. Eighteen years later Danish physicist Hans Christian Oersted rediscovers the same effect.

1820 French scientists Jean-Baptiste Biot and Felix Savart perform experiments to determine the force exerted on a magnet due to a nearby electric current. Their results are eventually incorporated into the Biot-Savart Law for the magnetic field intensity produced by a current carrying wire.

1827 German physics professor Georg Ohm publishes what is now known as Ohm's Law, $V = IR$.

1830's After repeating Gilbert's experiment with bits of iron, British scientist Michael Faraday begins talking about lines of force in the air around a magnet. Later he introduces the term 'magnetic field'.

1845 While still a student, German future physics professor Gustav Kirchhoff extends Ohm's Law into a set of rules for analyzing electric circuits.

1895 Hendrik A. Lorentz, a physics professor at the University of Leiden in Holland, mathematically describes the force experienced by an electric charge moving in a magnetic field.

1924 German physics professor Max Born publishes a popular book called *Einstein's Theory of Relativity.* The text includes the idea that a magnetic field in one reference frame can look like an electric field in another reference frame.

TEXT

Scientists are always delighted when they can uncover a relationship bewteen two phenomena previously thought to be unrelated. Such was the case with electricity and magnetism.

Electricity and magnetism have both been around for a long time. The ancient Chinese were aware that an iron bar stroked with a "lodestone" would acquire a directional North-South property. By the 10th century that idea had spread to Europe, and crude magnetic compasses were used in the Mediterranean before 1200. Static electricity on the other hand, was known to the ancient Greeks. In the late 1700's, Galvani and Volta discovered dynamic electricity in the form of electric current. Electricity and magnetism however, were thought to be two completely different things. That viewpoint began to change in the early 1800's, when first Romagnosi, and then Hans Christian Orestead noticed that an electric current would deflect a magnetic compass needle.

Today we believe that magnetic fields actually originate in moving electric charge. We picture all materials being made up of atoms, and each atom containing a positively charged nucleus surrounded by negatively charged electrons. The atoms of certain materials called conductors, are characterized by the fact that the outer electrons are not very tightly bound to the nucleus. The conductor is typically a metal wire, and a battery can be used to "pump" those loose outer electrons along the wire in a closed loop called an electric circuit. Electric current, I, is defined in terms of the amount of charge on the electrons, passing through a cross-section of the wire every second. So current is measured in Coulombs per second, and

$$1\,\frac{C}{s} = 1\,A\,,$$

where A stands for *Amps*, which is short for Amperes.

The units of current are Amps (A).

Ohm's Law and KVL

If one end of a short wire is connected to the positive terminal of a battery, and the other end is connected to the negative terminal, then the flow of current will be too intense, and too much energy will be released. Sparks will fly, and the wire will quickly melt. Melting circuits are not very useful, so partially conducting materials called resistors, are placed in the circuit in order to limit current flow.

In 1827, a German math teacher named Georg Ohm published a book containing the now famous Ohm's Law,

$$V = IR\,. \tag{801}$$

Ohm's Law relates the voltage *across* the resistor V, to the current *through* the resistor I, times the value of the resistance R. Figure 8.1 shows a picture. Voltage has units of volts V, and current has units of Amps A. Resistance is actually defined as voltage divided by current. It's units are called Ohms, Ω, and

$$1\,\Omega = 1\,\frac{V}{A}\,.$$

The units of Resistance are Ohms (Ω).

Figure 8.2 shows a very simple electric circuit. It consists of a battery and a resistor connected in series by zero-resistance wires. (Real wires have a little bit of resistance, but it is so small that you can usually just ignore it.) Notice that the + sign goes with the wide part of the battery symbol, and the − sign goes with the narrow part of the battery symbol. The + sign represents the positive or "high" side of the battery, and the − sign represents the negative or "low" side of the battery. Early researchers mistakenly pictured electric current as some sort of positively charged fluid that would flow *out of* the + side of the battery. Today we picture electric current as the flow of negatively charged electrons *into* the + side of the battery. Even though we now know better, the earlier convention has survived, and electric current is defined to be the flow of positive charge out of the + side. In other words, when there is just one battery in a circuit, the electric current I *always comes out of the + side of the battery.*

Gustav Kirchhoff (the 2 h's are not a mistake) published his groundbreaking circuit laws in 1854. Kirchhoff's Voltage Law, KVL, says that the sum of the voltage "drops" around a loop equals zero. In symbols,

$$\sum V's_{\,around\ a\ loop} = 0\,. \tag{802}$$

The inspiration for KVL comes from conservation of energy. Look at the circuit of Figure 8.2. Let's start at the bottom of the battery, which we'll take to be the zero point, and walk around the loop clockwise. As we go up through the battery (− to +), we get an increase in energy provided by the chemicals inside the battery. When we go down through the resistor (+ to −), we get a decrease in energy because the electrons, struggling to make it through the resistor, radiate heat. By the time we get back to the bottom of the battery, we have lost as much energy as we gained, and we are back to zero. Energy is proportional to voltage. So if the energy around the loop adds up to zero, the voltage around the loop must also add up to zero.

Notice that KVL, together with the idea that I flows out of the + side of the battery, implies that *current always flows from + to − through a resistor.*

Example 8.1

Use KVL and Ohm's Law to find the current in the Figure 8.3 circuit.

<u>Solution 8.1</u>

Kirchhoff's Voltage Law states that

$$V_{battery} + V_{R\,1} + V_{R\,2} = 0\,. \tag{803}$$

Notice that something has to be negative in equation (803), otherwise the 3 terms could not add to zero. Going clockwise around Figure 8.3, the battery is "polarized" $-$ to $+$, while both resistors are polarized $+$ to $-$. We could make the voltages across both resistors negative, since they are both polarized the same way, or we could make the battery voltage negative, since the battery is polarized opposite to the resistors.

Either scheme would work. There is only one battery however, while there are two resistors. If we make the battery voltage negative, we will have only one $-$ sign instead of two, so let's do it that way.

The voltage across each resistor is given by Ohm's Law, so we have

$$\begin{aligned} V_{battery} + V_{R\,1} + V_{R\,2} &= 0 \\ -\,9\,V + I\,(80\,\Omega) + I\,(100\,\Omega) &= 0 \\ I\,(80\,\Omega + 100\,\Omega) &= 9\,V \\ I\,(180\,\Omega) &= 9\,V \\ I &= \frac{9\,V}{180\,\Omega} \\ I &= .05\,A \end{aligned} \tag{804}$$

The current that flows in the Figure 8.3 circuit is equal to .05 A.

Quiz 8.1 Find the current that flows through the circuit of Figure 8.4.

A New Dimension

So far, we have dealt with 2 dimensions of space, x and y, and in the last chapter, 1 dimension involving time, $c\Delta t$. We won't need the time dimension in this chapter, but we are going to need a third dimension of space, z. In the 3 dimensional co-ordinate system, up is $+z$. Down is $-z$. Left is $-y$. Right is $+y$. Coming straight out of the paper, so that it is perpendicular to both y and z would be $+x$. Going back into the paper is $-x$. The unit vector associated with the z direction is $\pm\hat{k}$, and $+\hat{k}$ points up. Figure 8.5 shows a picture.

Suppose we wanted to sketch the 3 dimensional vector,

$$\vec{A} = 2(+\hat{\imath}) + 3(+\hat{\jmath}) + 2(-\hat{k}) \; , \tag{805}$$

Figure 8.6 shows how to do it. Just like in two dimensions, the component form of the 3 dimensional vector is a road map that tells you how to get from the tail of the vector to the tip of the vector. Equation (805) says to first go 2 in the $+\hat{\imath}$ direction. If we put the tail at the origin, that means we walk out 2, along dotted line path a. Next we are supposed to go 3 in the $+\hat{\jmath}$ direction. That means we walk 3 to the right, along dotted line path b. It is important to realize that when you are walking from the tail to the tip of the vector, you must keep going from where you last stopped. In other words, after you finish moving in the x direction, you are located at $x = +2$.

So you begin your y direction move from $x = +2$. You do not go back to the origin to start the y direction move. Finally, equation (805) says to go 2 in the $-\hat{k}$ direction. So we now go down 2 along dotted line path c. The $\vec{A}$ vector has its tail at the origin, and its tip at the end of the three segment dotted line path.

The Magnetic Field

The magnetic field, $\vec{B}$, around a long, straight, current-carrying wire is given by

$$\vec{B} = \left(\frac{\mu I}{2\pi|\vec{r}|}\right)\hat{a}_{\,r.h.r.} \tag{806}$$

Here I is the current that flows through the wire, and $|\vec{r}|$ is the perpendicular distance from the wire to the point of interest. The symbol μ represents the "permeability" of the medium that $\vec{B}$ is going through. Permeability for the magnetic field is a lot like permittivity for the electric field. They both reflect how much the medium affects the strength of the field. All of our magnetic fields will be going through air. So μ becomes μ_o, the permeability of free space, and

$$\mu_o = 4\pi \times 10^{-7}\,\frac{N}{A^2}\;. \tag{807}$$

There are no units on the 2π in the denominator of equation (806). The current in the numerator has units of Amps, A, and the $|\vec{r}|$ in the denominator has units of meters, m. So the units of $\vec{B}$ become

$$\frac{\left(\frac{N}{A^2}\right)A}{m} \longrightarrow \frac{N}{A\,m}\;.$$

A Newton divided by an Amp times a meter is called a Tesla, after Nikola Tesla who did brilliant work with magnetic fields in the early 1900's.

$$1\,\frac{N}{A\,m} = 1\,T$$

The units of magnetic field are called Teslas (T).

The magnetic field is a vector, and $\hat{a}_{\,r.h.r.}$ is the unit vector that indicates the direction of $\vec{B}$. The subscript $_{r.h.r.}$ stands for "right hand rule". Here's the way it works. A straight wire is basically a very long, small diameter cylinder. When you look at the end of the wire, you just see a small circle. The end view of a current-carrying wire is just a circle. The current in the wire is either flowing in the direction of your eye, which, seen from the end, would be "out of the paper", or it is flowing away from your eye, which, seen from the end, would be "into the paper". If the current comes out of the paper, a dot is placed in the middle of the end view circle like this, $\odot$. If the current goes into the paper, an x is placed in the middle of the end view circle like this, $\otimes$. Figure 8.7 shows a picture.

The magnetic field goes around a current-carrying wire in circles. Once you have an end view of the wire drawn, all you need to know about the direction is whether the $\vec{B}$ field circle is pointing clockwise, or counterclockwise. That's where $\hat{a}_{r.h.r.}$ comes into play. The right hand rule says to point the thumb of your right hand in the direction of current flow. Curl the fingers of your right hand a little bit, and they will curl around in the direction of $\vec{B}$. Figure 8.8a shows an example for current flowing out of the paper. Figure 8.8b shows an example for current flowing into the paper.

Example 8.2

The long wire shown in Figure 8.9 carries a current of .04 A. Find $\vec{B}$ at $(0, .2, 0)$ m.

Solution 8.2

This problem has 2 parts. The direction of $\vec{B}$ is found by drawing a series of little pictures. The magnitude of $\vec{B}$ is found by doing a calculation.

1.) This particular wire is parallel to the z axis, so we look down from the top in order to sketch our end view. All end views have this much in common. They all consist of a small circle situated at the center of two co-ordinate axes. The small circle represents the end of the wire, and it is surrounded by a larger circle representing $\vec{B}$. Every end view picture starts this same way, and the second step of Figure 8.10 shows the general setup.

The trick is to make the general setup fit the particular problem. First the co-ordinate axes have to be labeled. This is done by comparing the end view with the original 3 dimensional picture. In the original picture, the $+y$ axis sticks out to the right. Hopefully you can see that the $+y$ axis will also be to the right in the end view. That means that the $-y$ axis is on the left. In the original picture, the $+x$ axis comes out of the paper. When you look down from the top, the $+x$ axis will be pointing down in your end view. That means the $-x$ axis will be pointing up. (Labeling the co-ordinate axes requires a certain amount of spacial visualization, and sometimes that doesn't come easy. In the beginning it may help to actually make a 3 dimensional co-ordinate system using toothpicks stuck into a small ball of clay. That way you can rotate the toothpick co-ordinate system and keep track of the axes as they change position in space.)

Once the axes have been labeled, you must decide whether a dot or an x goes in the small circle. In this problem the current is coming towards your eye, so a dot goes in the small circle.

Next, apply the right hand rule. Since you have a dot in the little circle, current comes out of the paper. You point the thumb of your right hand up, out of the paper, and the fingers of your right hand curl around in a counterclockwise direction. Somewhere on the big circle, (anywhere will work) you draw an arrowhead indicating that $\vec{B}$ points counterclockwise.

For the direction of $\vec{B}$, you slide the arrowhead around to the axis of interest. Here we are looking for $\vec{B}$ at $(0, .2, 0)\ m$. Since the co-ordinate specification goes (x, y, z), the point $(0, .2, 0)$ is located on the $+y$ axis. From the last part of Figure 8.10, $\vec{B}$ will point in the $-x$ direction when it crosses the $+y$ axis.

The direction of $\vec{B}$ at the point $(0, .2, 0)\ m$ is $(-\hat{\imath})$.

2.) For the magnitude of $\vec{B}$, from equation (806),

$$|\vec{B}| = \frac{\mu_o I}{2\pi|\vec{r}|} . \tag{808}$$

We are looking for $\vec{B}$ at $(0, .2, 0)\ m$, so the perpendicular distance from the point of interest to the wire is $|\vec{r}| = .2\ m$. The current in the wire is $I = .04\ A$, and $\mu_o = 4\pi \times 10^{-7}\ \frac{N}{A^2}$. Plugging those numbers into equation (808),

$$\begin{aligned} |\vec{B}| &= \left[\frac{(4\pi \times 10^{-7})(.04)}{(2\pi)(.2)}\right] T \\ |\vec{B}| &= 4 \times 10^{-8}\ T . \end{aligned} \tag{809}$$

Here we can just carry the the Tesla unit as we go along. It is not necessary to redo the unit analysis since we've already done it once and it will be the same each time.

Combining the magnitude of the magnetic field with its direction, we finally get

$$\begin{aligned} \vec{B} &= |\vec{B}|\ \hat{a}_{\,r.h.r.} \\ \vec{B} &= 4 \times 10^{-8}\ T\ (-\hat{\imath}) \end{aligned} \tag{810}$$

for $\vec{B}$ at the point $(0, .2, 0)\ m$.

Quiz 8.2 The wire shown in Figure 8.11 carries a current of $.01\ A$. Find $\vec{B}$ at $(.05, 0, 0)\ m$.

Cross Product

There are two different kinds of vector "multiplication". The dot product we have already seen. It is symbolized by $\vec{A} \bullet \vec{B}$, and the result is always a scalar. The cross product is symbolized by $\vec{A} \times \vec{B}$, and the result is always a vector.

Suppose

$$\vec{A} = 2(-\hat{\imath}) + 1(+\hat{\jmath}) + 3(-\hat{k})$$

and

$$\vec{B} = 1(\hat{\imath}) + 4(+\hat{\jmath}) + 2(-\hat{k}) .$$

To find $\vec{A} \times \vec{B}$, you make a table,

$$\vec{A} \times \vec{B} \qquad \begin{array}{ccc} \hat{\imath} & \hat{\jmath} & \hat{k} \\ -2 & 1 & -3 \\ 1 & 4 & -2 \end{array} \tag{811}$$

The 1st line in the table contains the unit vectors. The 2nd line represents the vector that is to the <u>left</u> of the $\times$ symbol, and it contains the "coefficients" of the unit vectors, with the signs included. The 3rd line comes from the vector that is to the right of the $\times$ symbol. The order is important! $\vec{A} \times \vec{B} \neq \vec{B} \times \vec{A}$, and if you get the order of the lines backwards, your answer will be wrong. *The 1st vector in the cross product always comes 1st in the table.*

But the table in equation (811) is not yet complete. In order to finish it we have to recopy the 1st two columns, and place them on the right side.

$$\vec{A} \times \vec{B} \rightarrow \quad \begin{array}{ccccc} \hat{\imath} & \hat{\jmath} & \hat{k} & \hat{\imath} & \hat{\jmath} \\ -2 & 1 & -3 & -2 & 1 \\ 1 & 4 & -2 & 1 & 4 \end{array} \tag{812}$$

The cross product is constructed from the completed table, and it is always going to be of the form

$$\begin{aligned} \vec{A} \times \vec{B} &= [(\textit{something}) - (\textit{something})]\, \hat{\imath} \\ &\quad + [(\textit{something}) - (\textit{something})]\, \hat{\jmath} \\ &\quad + [(\textit{something}) - (\textit{something})]\, \hat{k}\,. \end{aligned} \tag{813}$$

In order to find out what the *somethings* are in the big square brackets, you have to go back to the table and draw diagonals,

$$\begin{array}{ccccccccc} \hat{\imath} & & \hat{\jmath} & & \hat{k} & & \hat{\imath} & & \hat{\jmath} \\ & \searrow & & \searrow & & \searrow & & & \\ \boxed{-2} & & 1 & & -3 & & -2 & & \boxed{1} \\ & & & \searrow & & \searrow & & \searrow & \\ 1 & & 4 & & -2 & & 1 & & 4 \end{array} \tag{814}$$

The multiplications that go to the left of the minus signs in the big square brackets of equation (813) are indicated by the left-to-right diagonals of table (814). Putting those in, we have so far

$$\begin{aligned} \vec{A} \times \vec{B} &= \left[(1) \overset{\searrow}{(} -2) - \qquad \right] \hat{\imath} \\ &\quad + \left[(-3) \overset{\searrow}{(}\, 1) - \qquad \right] \hat{\jmath} \\ &\quad + \left[(-2) \overset{\searrow}{(}\, 4) - \qquad \right] \hat{k} \end{aligned} \tag{815}$$

(The arrows over the products in equation (815) are just there to remind us which way we multiplied to get those products. You won't need them when you do a cross product.)

The multiplications that go to the right of the minus signs are indicated by the right-to-left diagonals of table (816).

$$\begin{array}{ccccccccc} \hat{\imath} & & \hat{\jmath} & & \hat{k} & & \hat{\imath} & & \hat{\jmath} \\ & & & \swarrow & & \swarrow & & \swarrow & \\ \boxed{-2} & & 1 & & -3 & & -2 & & \boxed{1} \\ & \swarrow & & \swarrow & & \swarrow & & & \\ 1 & & 4 & & -2 & & 1 & & 4 \end{array} \tag{816}$$

Just looking at the multiplications on the right of the minus signs,

$$\begin{aligned} \vec{A}\times\vec{B} &= \Big[\qquad - (-3)\overset{\swarrow}{(\ 4)}\Big]\,\hat{\imath} \\ &\quad + \Big[\qquad - (-2)\overset{\swarrow}{(\ -2)}\Big]\,\hat{\jmath} \\ &\quad + \Big[\qquad - (1)\overset{\swarrow}{(\ 1)}\Big]\,\hat{k} \end{aligned} \tag{817}$$

Notice that the coefficients on the ends, in the middle, never get used. In this particular example the $\boxed{-2}$ and the $\boxed{1}$ do not get used.

The diagonals tell you how to multiply. The diagonals that go down from left to right give you the products on the left sides of the minus signs. The diagonals that come back the other way, from right to left, give you the products on the right sides of the minus signs. Putting everything together,

$$\begin{aligned} \vec{A}\times\vec{B} &= [(1)\overset{\searrow}{(\ -2)} - (-3)\overset{\swarrow}{(\ 4)}]\,\hat{\imath} \\ &\quad + [(-3)\overset{\searrow}{(\ 1)} - (-2)\overset{\swarrow}{(\ -2)}]\,\hat{\jmath} \\ &\quad + [(-2)\overset{\searrow}{(\ 4)} - (1)\overset{\swarrow}{(\ 1)}]\,\hat{k}\,. \end{aligned} \tag{818}$$

It is wise to proceed in baby steps to the final answer.

$$\begin{aligned} \vec{A}\times\vec{B} &= [-2-(-12)]\,\hat{\imath} + [-3-(4)]\,\hat{\jmath} + [-8-(1)]\,\hat{k} \\ &= [+10]\,\hat{\imath} + [-7]\,\hat{\jmath} + [-9]\,\hat{k} \\ \vec{A}\times\vec{B} &= 10(\hat{\imath}) + 7(-\hat{\jmath}) + 9(-\hat{k})\,. \end{aligned} \tag{819}$$

Vector (819) is the answer, but in order to get there, we had to do a lot of arithmetic with a lot of minus signs. There were certainly plenty of opportunities to make a mistake, and it would be nice to have some way to know whether or not the answer is correct. Two facts can help us with that.

1. The cross product of two vectors is always perpendicular ($\perp$) to each of the original vectors , and
2. The dot product of two perpendicular vectors equals zero.

In symbols 1 says , $(\vec{A} \times \vec{B}) \perp (\vec{A})$ and $(\vec{A} \times \vec{B}) \perp (\vec{B})$, so that from 2

$$(\vec{A} \times \vec{B}) \bullet (\vec{A}) = 0 \quad \text{and} \quad (\vec{A} \times \vec{B}) \bullet (\vec{B}) = 0\,.$$

You can use the dot product to check your cross product ! Let's try it.

For the 1st one

$$\begin{aligned} (\vec{A} \times \vec{B}) \bullet (\vec{A}) &= [10(\hat{\imath}) + 7(-\hat{\jmath}) + 9(-\hat{k})] \bullet [2(-\hat{\imath}) + 1(\hat{\jmath}) + 3(-\hat{k})] \\ &= (10)(-2) + (-7)(1) + (-9)(-3) \\ &= -20 - 7 + 27 \\ (\vec{A} \times \vec{B}) \bullet (\vec{A}) &= 0\,. \end{aligned} \tag{820}$$

For the 2nd one

$$\begin{aligned} (\vec{A} \times \vec{B}) \bullet (\vec{B}) &= [10(\hat{\imath}) + 7(-\hat{\jmath}) + 9(-\hat{k})] \bullet [1(\hat{\imath}) + 4(\hat{\jmath}) + 2(-\hat{k})] \\ &= (10)(1) + (-7)(4) + (-9)(-2) \\ &= 10 - 28 + 18 \\ (\vec{A} \times \vec{B}) \bullet (\vec{B}) &= 0\,. \end{aligned} \tag{821}$$

Both dot products check, and we are confident that equation (819) is the right answer. (It is important to resist the temptation to stop checking after the 1st dot product equals zero. One of the two will almost always equal zero, even when the answer is wrong. You have to check both dot products to be confident that the cross product is right.)

Example 8.3

$$\vec{L} = 3(\hat{\imath}) + 1(-\hat{\jmath}) + 5(-\hat{k})$$

$$\vec{K} = 2(-\hat{\imath}) + 1(\hat{k})$$

Find $\vec{K} \times \vec{L}$ and check your answer by verifying that
$(\vec{K} \times \vec{L}) \bullet (\vec{K}) = 0 \quad \text{and} \quad (\vec{K} \times \vec{L}) \bullet (\vec{L}) = 0.$

Solution 8.3

Here $\vec{K}$ is going to come first in the table, and the coefficient of the $\hat{\jmath}$ component of $\vec{K}$ is equal to zero.

$$\vec{K} \times \vec{L} \rightarrow \begin{array}{ccccc} \hat{\imath} & \hat{\jmath} & \hat{k} & \hat{\imath} & \hat{\jmath} \\ -2 & 0 & 1 & -2 & 0 \\ 3 & -1 & -5 & 3 & -1 \end{array} \tag{822}$$

$$\begin{aligned} \vec{K} \times \vec{L} &= [(0)(-5) - (1)(-1)]\,\hat{\imath} + [(1)(3) - (-2)(-5)]\,\hat{\jmath} \\ &\quad + [(-2)(-1) - (0)(3)]\,\hat{k} \\ &= [0 - (-1)]\,\hat{\imath} + [3 - (10)]\,\hat{\jmath} + [2 - (0)]\,\hat{k} \end{aligned}$$

$$\vec{K} \times \vec{L} = 1(\hat{\imath}) + 7(-\hat{\jmath}) + 2(\hat{k}) \tag{823}$$

Let's check. For the 1st one

$$\begin{aligned} (\vec{K} \times \vec{L}) \bullet (\vec{K}) &= [1(\hat{\imath}) + 7(-\hat{\jmath}) + 2(\hat{k})] \bullet [2(-\hat{\imath}) + 0(\hat{\jmath}) + 1(\hat{k})] \\ &= (1)(-2) + (-7)(0) + (2)(1) \\ &= -2 + 2 \\ (\vec{K} \times \vec{L}) \bullet (\vec{K}) &= 0\,. \end{aligned} \tag{824}$$

For the 2nd one

$$\begin{aligned} (\vec{K} \times \vec{L}) \bullet (\vec{L}) &= [1(\hat{\imath}) + 7(-\hat{\jmath}) + 2(\hat{k})] \bullet [3(\hat{\imath}) + 1(-\hat{\jmath}) + 5(-\hat{k})] \\ &= (1)(3) + (-7)(-1) + (2)(-5) \\ &= 3 + 7 - 10 \\ (\vec{K} \times \vec{L}) \bullet (\vec{L}) &= 0\,. \end{aligned} \tag{825}$$

Both dot products check, so the answer looks good.

Quiz 8.3 $\vec{A} = 3(\hat{\imath}) + 4(-\hat{\jmath}) + 2(-\hat{k})$ and $\vec{B} = 1(\hat{\imath}) + 1(\hat{\jmath}) + 2(\hat{k})$
Find $\vec{B} \times \vec{A}$ and check the answer.

The Lorentz Force Law

In 1895, the Dutch physicist H. A. Lorentz introduced his expression for the force on a charged particle moving in a magnetic field. The Lorentz force law says that

$$\vec{F}_{mag} = q(\vec{v} \times \vec{B}) \ , \tag{826}$$

where q is the amount of charge on the particle, $\vec{v}$ is the velocity of the particle, and $\vec{B}$ is the magnetic field through which the particle is moving.

Let's look at the units. The cross product is a type of multiplication, so the units on the right hand side need to be multiplied together.

$$\begin{aligned} q(\vec{v} \times \vec{B}) \ &\Rightarrow \ C\left(\frac{m}{s}\right)T \rightarrow \left(\frac{C\,m}{s}\right)\left(\frac{N}{A\,m}\right) \\ &\rightarrow \ \left(\frac{C}{s}\right)\left(\frac{N}{\frac{C}{s}}\right) \\ &\rightarrow \ N \end{aligned}$$

$\vec{F}_{mag}$ is a force. So the units on the right hand side must reduce to N, and they do.

Example 8.4

A $-6\mu C$ charge moving with $\vec{v} = 1200 \ \frac{m}{s} \ (+\hat{k})$ enters a region of space where $\vec{B} = .35 \ T \ (-\hat{\imath})$. Find the force on the charge and express the answer in magnitude unit vector form.

Solution 8.4

This is basically a straight plug in. The 1st thing to do is find $\vec{v} \times \vec{B}$ and expess it in magnitude unit vector form.

$$\vec{v} \times \vec{B} \rightarrow \begin{array}{ccccc} \hat{\imath} & \hat{\jmath} & \hat{k} & \hat{\imath} & \hat{\jmath} \\ 0 & 0 & 1200 & 0 & 0 \\ -.35 & 0 & 0 & -.35 & 0 \end{array} \tag{827}$$

$$\begin{aligned} \vec{v} \times \vec{B} \ &= \ [(0)(0) - (1200)(0)]\,\hat{\imath} \ + \ [(1200)(-.35) - (0)(0)]\,\hat{\jmath} \\ &\quad + [(0)(0) - (0)(-.35)]\,\hat{k} \\ &= \ [0 - (0)]\,\hat{\imath} \ + \ [-420 - (0)]\,\hat{\jmath} \ + \ [0 - (0)]\hat{k} \end{aligned}$$

$$\vec{v} \times \vec{B} \ = \ 420(-\hat{\jmath}) \tag{828}$$

Usually $\vec{v} \times \vec{B}$ does not come out in magnitude unit vector form. But this one did. So it is not necessary to go through all that square root business.

We just need to multiply by q,

$$\begin{aligned}\vec{F}_{mag} &= q(\vec{v} \times \vec{B}) \\ &= (-6 \times 10^{-6})(420)(-\hat{j})\ N \\ &\approx .0025\ N\ (+\hat{j}) \qquad (829)\end{aligned}$$

We have already demonstrated that the units on $\vec{F}_{mag}$ are N. So, just like with $\vec{B}$ from a wire, it is not necessary to show the unit analysis over and over. We can just carry the N as we go.

The appearance of a cross product in the Lorentz force law leads to a very interesting result. The cross product vector is always perpendicular to each of the original vectors. Since $(\vec{v} \times \vec{B}) \perp (\vec{v})$ and $(\vec{v} \times \vec{B}) \perp (\vec{B})$, the force on the charge is also perpendicular to both $\vec{v}$ and $\vec{B}$. When q enters the magnetic field $\vec{B}$, it is pushed off at a right angle to both $\vec{B}$ and to its original velocity $\vec{v}$. Figure 8.12 shows a picture for this particular example. The "right angle" behavior of the magnetic force seems like a completely different thing compared to the straight line behavior of the electric force. Special Relativity provides a way to tie the two together.

Quiz 8.4 A $+4\ \mu C$ charge moving at $\vec{v} = [1800(-\hat{j}) + 2400(+\hat{k})]\ \frac{m}{s}$ enters $\vec{B} = .2\ T\ (+\hat{i})$. Find the force on the charge and express the answer in magnitude unit vector form.

The Magnetic Force as a Relativistic Electric Force

Imagine a $+q$ particle located close to a current-carrying wire. Now let the particle suddenly be moving parallel to the wire. Conventional wisdom says that the current-carrying wire has to be surrounded by a magnetic field. Because the charged particle would then be moving through a magnetic field, the Lorentz Force Law predicts that the magnetic field will exert a force on the particle. Figure 8.13 shows a picture. Einstein's Theory of Special Relativity however, makes it possible to explain the force shown in Figure 8.13 without ever mentioning the concept of a magnetic field. Here's how it works.

In the relativistic picture, the current in a current-carrying wire is modeled as two oppositely moving lines of charge. In Figure 8.14, a stationary, or "laboratory frame" observer sees plus charge moving to the right with velocity $\vec{v}_+ = |\vec{v}|(+\hat{j})$, and an equal amount of minus charge moving to the left with velocity $\vec{v}_- = |\vec{v}|(-\hat{j})$. Both lines of charge will be Fitzgerald contracted in accordance with $L = L_o\sqrt{1 - \frac{v^2}{c^2}}$, but they will be equally contracted since $v = |\vec{v}|$ is the same for both lines. Relativity does not affect the amount of charge, so the laboratory frame observer sees an equal amount of + and − charge, and the line looks electrically neutral to him.

Each line of charge contains a linear charge density, λ, of so many Coulombs per meter. For example, if the total amount of uniformly distributed charge on a 2.5 m

line was $+15 \times 10^{-6}\ C$, then the charge density would be

$$\lambda = \frac{q}{L} = \frac{+15 \times 10^{-6}}{2.5}\ \frac{C}{m} = +6 \times 10^{-6}\ \frac{C}{m}\ . \tag{830}$$

Current is defined to be in the direction of positive charge flow. Here there are two contributions to the total current. One is from the + charged line,

$$\vec{I}_{from\ +\ line} = +\lambda\vec{v}_+ = \lambda|\vec{v}|(+\hat{\jmath})\ , \tag{831}$$

and one is from the − charged line,

$$\vec{I}_{from\ -\ line} = -\lambda\vec{v}_- = -\lambda|\vec{v}|(-\hat{\jmath}) = \lambda|\vec{v}|(+\hat{\jmath})\ . \tag{832}$$

The total current then is given by

$$\vec{I} = \vec{I}_{from\ +} + \vec{I}_{from\ -} = 2\lambda v(+\hat{\jmath})\ . \tag{833}$$

Notice that in terms of current, a negatively charged line moving to the left, is the same thing as a positively charged line moving to the right. So the two currents add instead of canceling. Let's look at the units.

$$\lambda|\vec{v}| \Rightarrow \left(\frac{C}{m}\right)\left(\frac{m}{s}\right) \rightarrow \frac{C}{s} \rightarrow A$$

The units turn out to be *Amps*, which is what we expect for a current.

So from a laboratory frame observer's point of view, a current-carrying wire can be modeled as a line of equally spaced plus charges, and a line of identically spaced minus charges. Each line carries the same magnitude of charge, but they each move in opposite directions at the same speed. Figure 8.14 shows a picture.

Notice that equations (831) through (833) describe current as a vector. Technically, current should be a vector since it has a direction. In practice however, current is almost always found inside a wire, so it can only be going one of two different ways. That fact leads most people to keep track of the direction by means of a + or − sign. In other words, instead of writing $\vec{I} = 5\ A\ (-\hat{\jmath})$ for example, you would usually just write $I = -5\ A$.

Back to our example. From the laboratory frame observer's point of view, the current-carrying wire is electrically neutral since, according to him, the wire contains equal amounts of + and − charge. He sees an $\vec{F}_{mag}$ force on the moving charged particle, which he attributes to the motion of the particle through the magnetic field of the wire. Figure 8.15 is the same as Figure 8.13.

Things looks quite different however, to an observer riding on the charged particle. Figure 8.15 indicates that the charged particle moves in the same direction as the wire's + charge, but in the opposite direction as the wire's − charge. Because the charge riding observer moves against the − charges, they look to her like they are moving faster. At the same time, she is moving with the + charges, so they look to be moving slower. The two lines of charge are not equally Fitzgerald contracted from the viewpoint of a charge riding observer. According to her, the − line goes faster than the + line, so the − charges look to be closer together. She does not percieve the charged particle to have any velocity. (Since she is standing on it, the charged particle is stationary with respect to her.) So she cannot attribute the force on the particle to come from a magnetic field. From her viewpoint,

$$\vec{F}_{mag} = q(\vec{v} \times \vec{B}) = q(\vec{0} \times \vec{B}) = 0 \,. \tag{834}$$

She is still going to see a force, but it is not going to be magnetic, because, according to her, the charged particle is not moving. But also according to her, the "current-carrying wire" is not electrically neutral. Instead, it looks to her like there are more − charges per meter than there are + charges. So she sees a negatively charged wire. Figure 8.16 shows a picture. She does concludes that there is a force on her + charged particle, but as she sees it, the force is purely electric, caused by

$$\vec{F}\,' = q\vec{E}\,' \,. \tag{835}$$

The $'$'s mean that we are talking about the force in the charge rider's reference frame.

The bottom line is this: Special Relativity provides the mechanism by which a magnetic force in one reference frame can be understood as an electric force in another reference frame. In this example, the laboratory frame observer sees a neutrally charged wire because from his point of view, the two lines of charge are equally Fitzgerald contracted. The charge riding observer sees a negatively charged wire because from her point of view, the two lines of charge are unequally Fitzgerald contracted. They both see a force. But he believes the force comes from a magnetic field, while she believes the force comes from an electric field.

Example 8.5

Figure 8.17 shows a negatively charged particle moving parallel to a current-carrying wire. Show that the direction of the force on the charged particle will be the same from both a laboratory frame observer, and a charge riding observer's point of view.

Solution 8.5

Let's first find the direction of the magnetic force seen by the laboratory frame observer. From Figure 8.17, the charge is moving in the positive y direction, so that $\vec{v} = |\vec{v}|(+\hat{\jmath})$. Figure 8.18 shows the steps necessary to determine that $\vec{B}$ points in the negative x direction when it crosses the $+z$ axis where $-q$ is located. So $\vec{B} = |\vec{B}|(-\hat{\imath})$ right at $-q$, and we need to find $\vec{F}_{mag} = q(\vec{v} \times \vec{B})$.

$$\vec{v} \times \vec{B} \rightarrow \begin{matrix} \hat{\imath} & \hat{\jmath} & \hat{k} & \hat{\imath} & \hat{\jmath} \\ 0 & |\vec{v}| & 0 & 0 & |\vec{v}| \\ -|\vec{B}| & 0 & 0 & -|\vec{B}| & 0 \end{matrix} \tag{836}$$

$$\vec{v} \times \vec{B} = [0-0]\hat{\imath} + [0-0]\hat{\jmath} + [0-(|\vec{v}|)(-|\vec{B}|)]\hat{k}$$

$$\vec{v} \times \vec{B} = vB(+\hat{k}) \tag{837}$$

Finally,

$$\begin{aligned} \vec{F}_{mag} &= q(\vec{v} \times \vec{B}) \\ &= -qvB(+\hat{k}) \\ \vec{F}_{mag} &= qvB(-\hat{k}) \end{aligned} \tag{838}$$

According to the laboratory frame observer, the $-q$ charge experiences a magnetic force pointing down towards the wire. That force comes about because $-q$ moves with velocity $\vec{v}$ through a magnetic field $\vec{B}$. Figure 8.19 shows a picture.

Figure 8.17 indicates that the $-q$ charge is moving against I. Inside the wire, the + charges move in the direction of I. (Remember I is defined as the flow of positive charge.) So $-q$ moves against the wire's + charges, and with the wire's − charges. From the charge rider's point of view, the + charges are closer together, the − charges are farther apart, and the wire appears positively charged. Electric fields point away from positive charges, so the charge rider sees an electric field along the $+z$ axis pointing up. From the charge rider's point of view,

$$\begin{aligned} \vec{F}'_{elect} &= q\vec{E}' \\ &= -q|\vec{E}'|(+\hat{k}) \\ \vec{F}'_{elect} &= qE'(-\hat{k}) \, . \end{aligned} \tag{839}$$

Figure 8.20 shows a picture.

Both the laboratory frame observer and the charge riding observer see a force pointing down. The laboratory frame observer thinks that it is an $\vec{F}_{magnetic}$. The charge riding observer thinks that it is an $\vec{F}_{electric}$.

Quiz 8.5 Figure 8.21 shows a positively charged particle moving parallel to a current carrying wire. Show that the direction of the force on the charged particle will be the same from both a laboratory frame observer, and a charge riding observer's point of view.

Things to Remember

Relationships

$$V = IR \qquad \sum V's_{\,around\ a\ loop} = 0$$

$$\vec{B} = \left(\frac{\mu_o I}{2\pi|\vec{r}|}\right) \hat{a}_{\,r.\,h.\,r.}$$

$$\vec{F}_{mag} = q\left(\vec{v} \times \vec{B}\right)$$

Units

$$I \rightarrow \frac{C}{s} = A \qquad R \rightarrow \frac{V}{A} = \Omega$$

$$\vec{B} \rightarrow \frac{N}{A\,m} = T$$

Constants and Conversions

$$\mu_o = 4\pi \times 10^{-7}\,\frac{N}{A^2}$$

Homework Problems Chapter 8

8.1

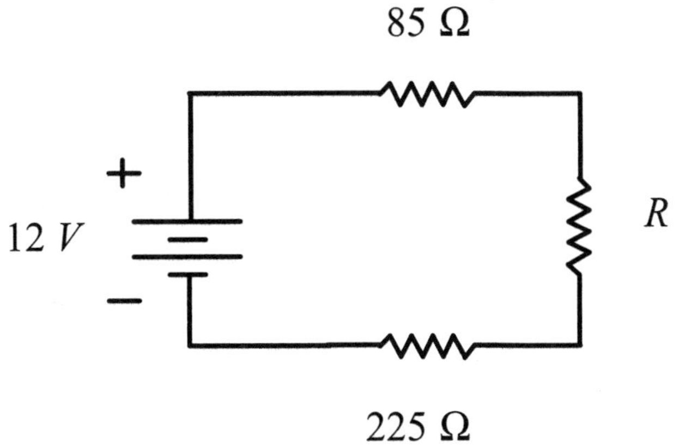

Find R so that the current in the circuit will be .03 A.

8.2

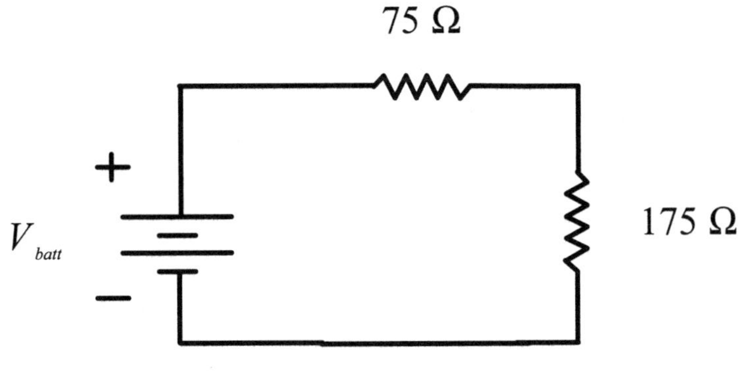

Find V_{batt} so that the current in the circuit will be .036 A.

8.3

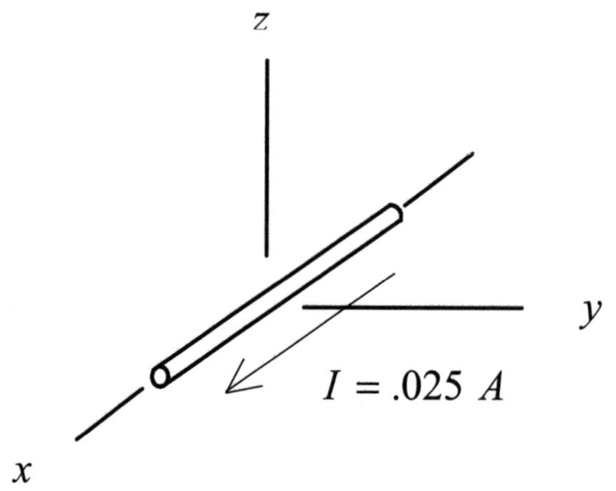

Find $\vec{B}$ at $(0,-.005,0)\,m$.

8.4

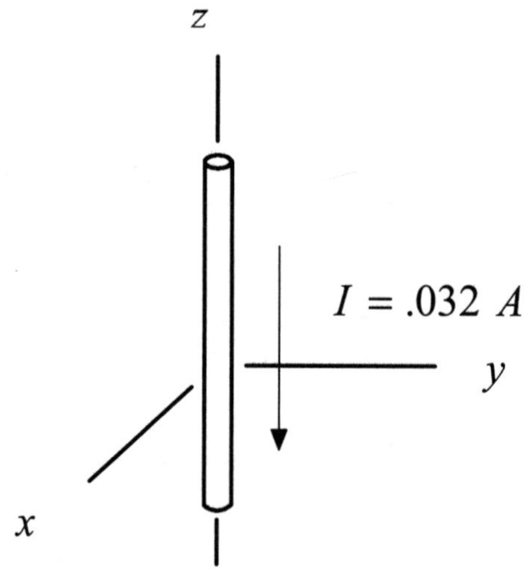

Find $\vec{B}$ at $(-.08,0,0)\,m$.

8.5 $\vec{H} = 2(+\hat{i}) + 3(-\hat{j}) + 1(-\hat{k})$ $\quad\quad$ $\vec{K} = 5(-\hat{i}) + 2(+\hat{k})$

Find $\vec{H}\times\vec{K}$ and check your answer.

8.6 Rework 8.5, but this time find $\vec{K}\times\vec{H}$ instead of $\vec{H}\times\vec{K}$.

8.7 A $-120\ nC$ charge traveling with $\vec{v} = 1.6\times10^5 \frac{m}{s}(-\hat{j})$ enters a region of space where $\vec{B} = [.15(+\hat{i}) + .34(+\hat{j})]\ T$. Find the force on the charge.

8.8 A $1\times10^{-4}\ C$ charge traveling with $\vec{v} = 13000 \frac{m}{s}(+\hat{k})$ enters a region of outer space where $\vec{B} = \left[\frac{5}{130}(-\hat{i}) + \frac{12}{130}(+\hat{j})\right]\ T$. Find $\vec{F}$.

8.9

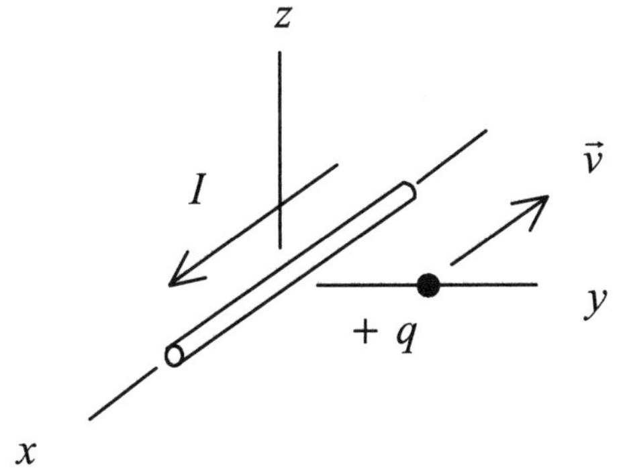

Show that the direction of the force on $+q$ will be the same from both a laboratory frame observer, and a charge riding observer's point of view.

8.10

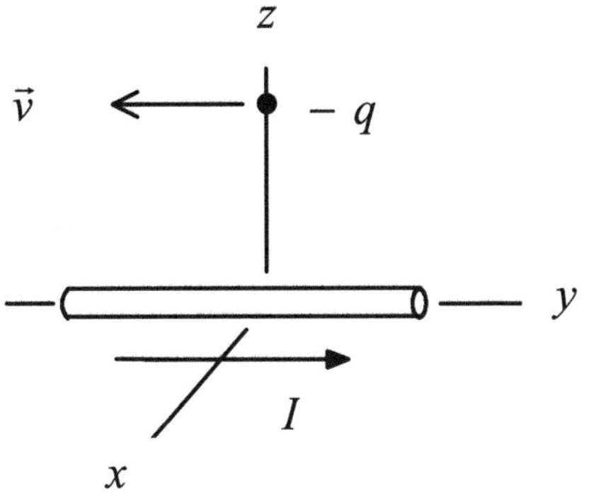

Show that the direction of the force on $-q$ will be the same from both a laboratory frame observer, and a charge riding observer's point of view.

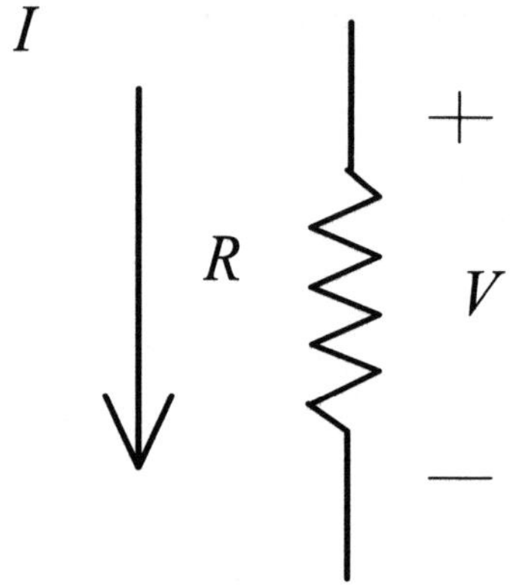

Figure 8.1 Voltage across a resistor, and current through a resistor are related by $V = IR$.

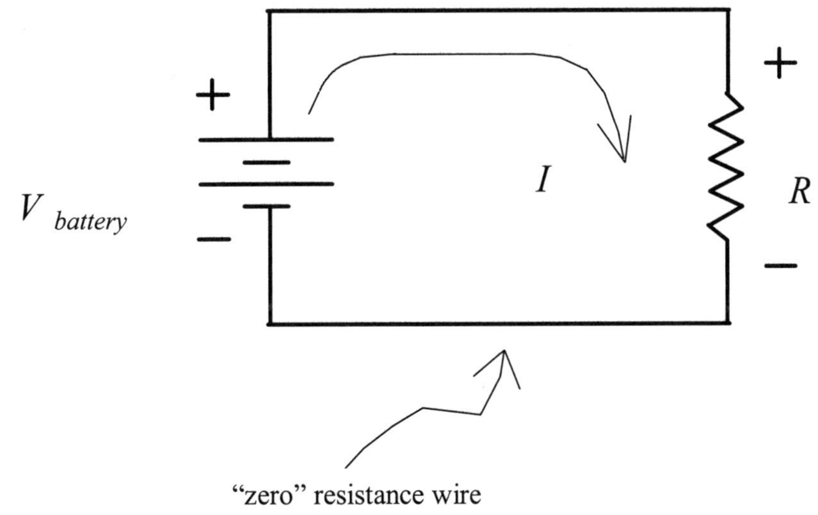

Figure 8.2 Simple electric circuit

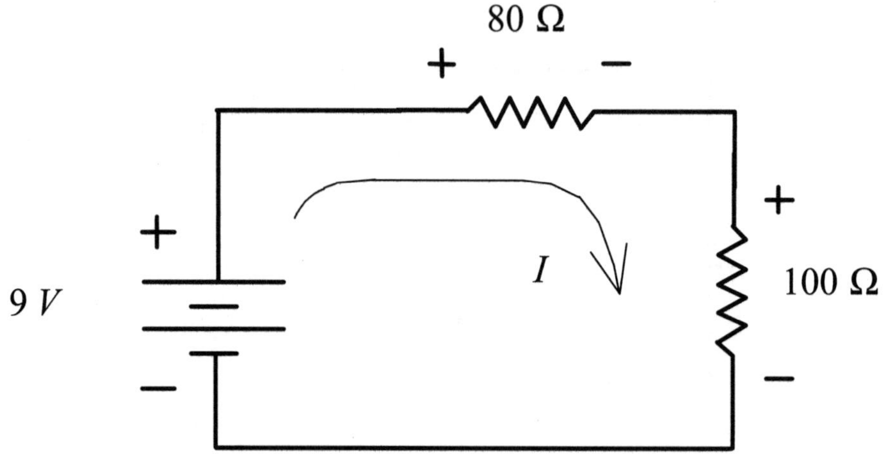

Figure 8.3 Electric circuit for Example 8.1

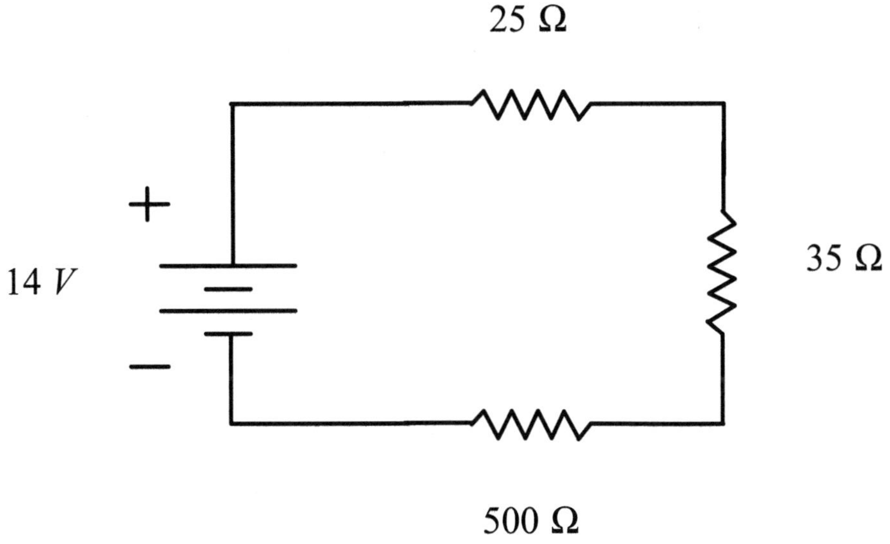

Figure 8.4 Electric circuit for Quiz 8.1

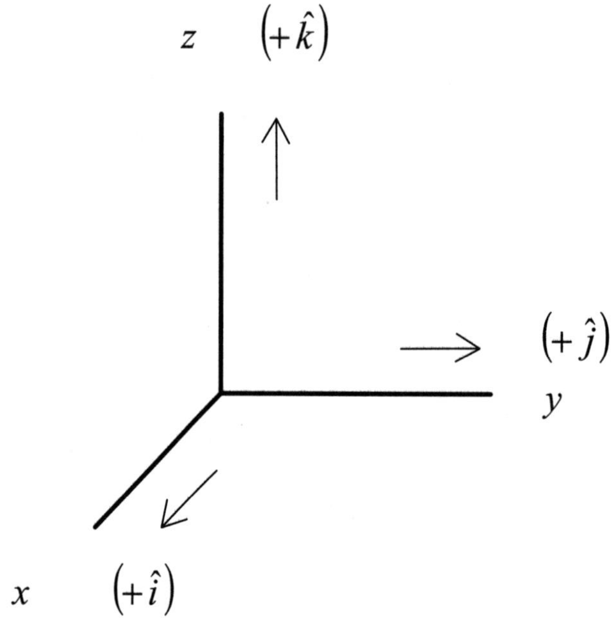

Figure 8.5 3 dimensions

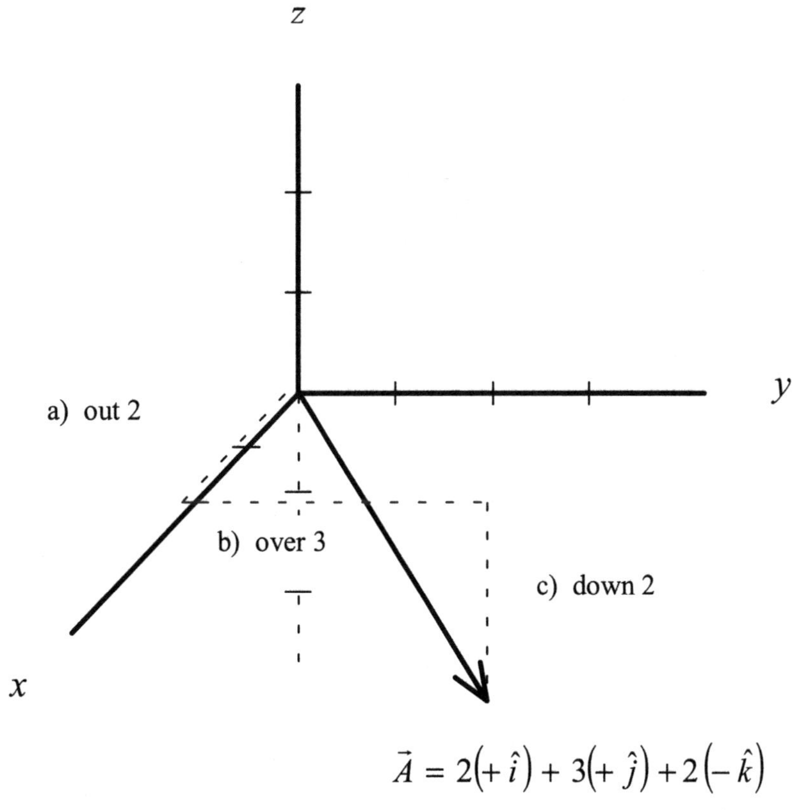

Figure 8.6 Vector $\vec{A}$ in 3 dimensions

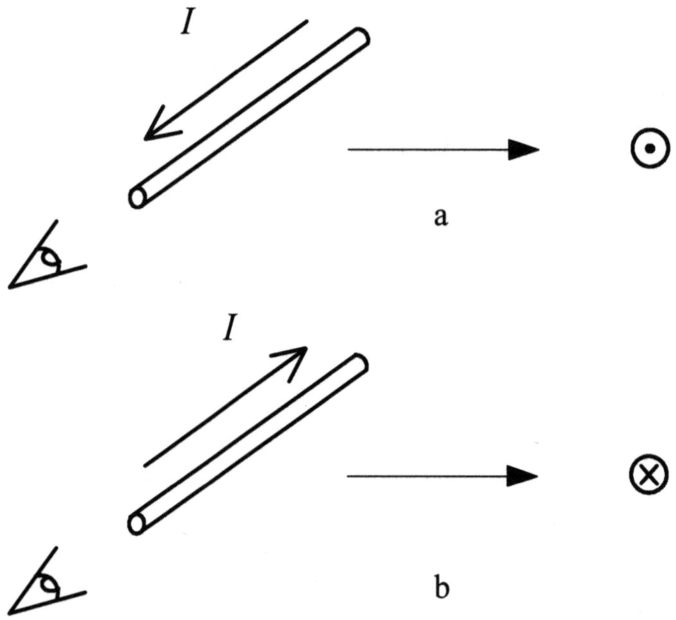

Figure 8.7 a) Current comes out of the paper towards your eye.
b) Current goes into the paper away from your eye.

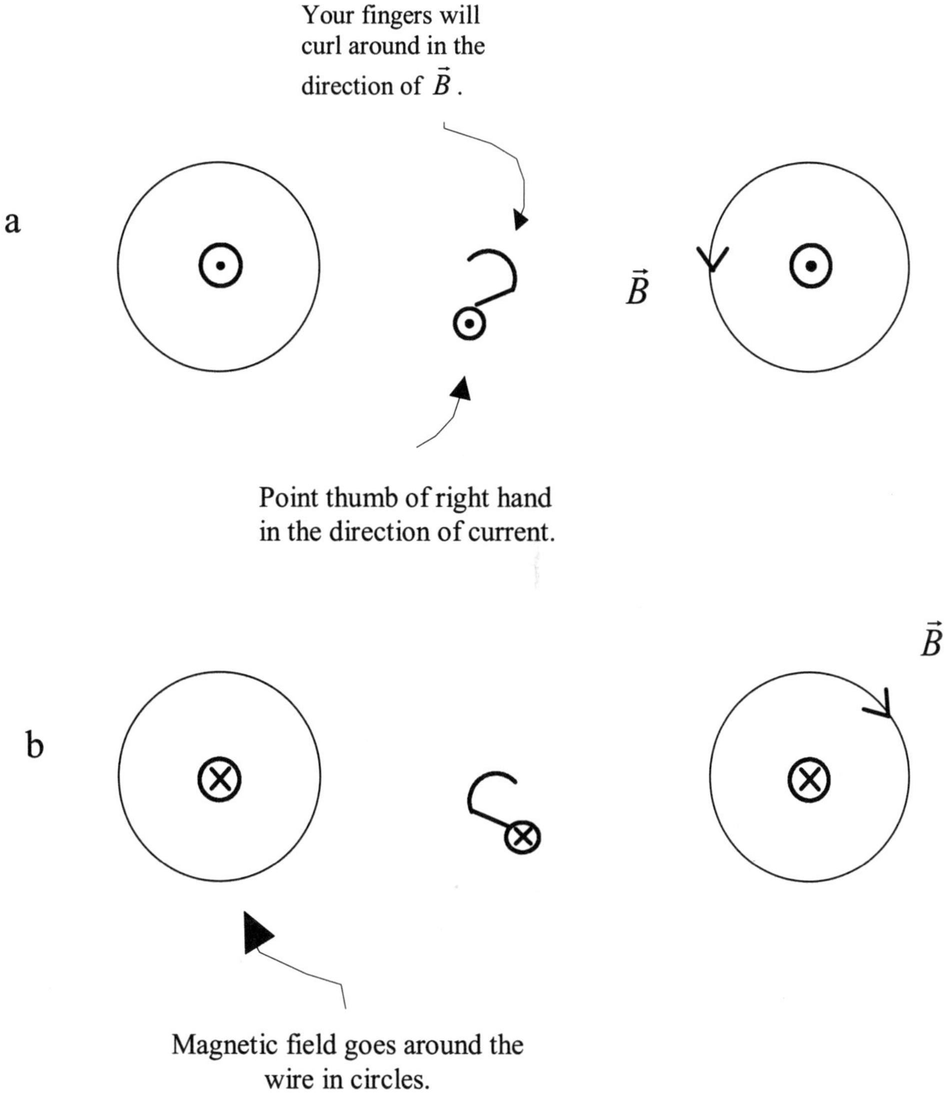
Your fingers will curl around in the direction of $\vec{B}$.
a
$\vec{B}$
Point thumb of right hand in the direction of current.
$\vec{B}$
b
Magnetic field goes around the wire in circles.

Figure 8.8 Right hand rule gives the direction of $\vec{B}$ for
a) current coming out of the paper, and
b) current going into the paper.

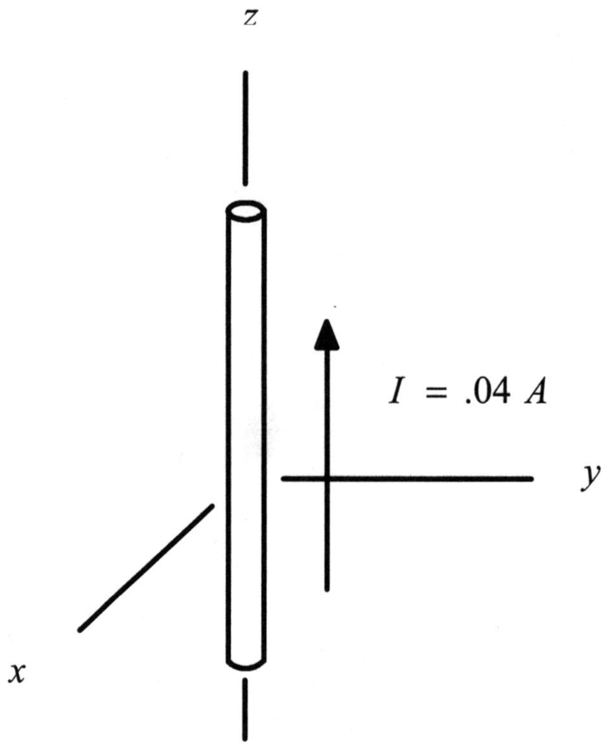

Figure 8.9 Long straight wire for Example 8.2

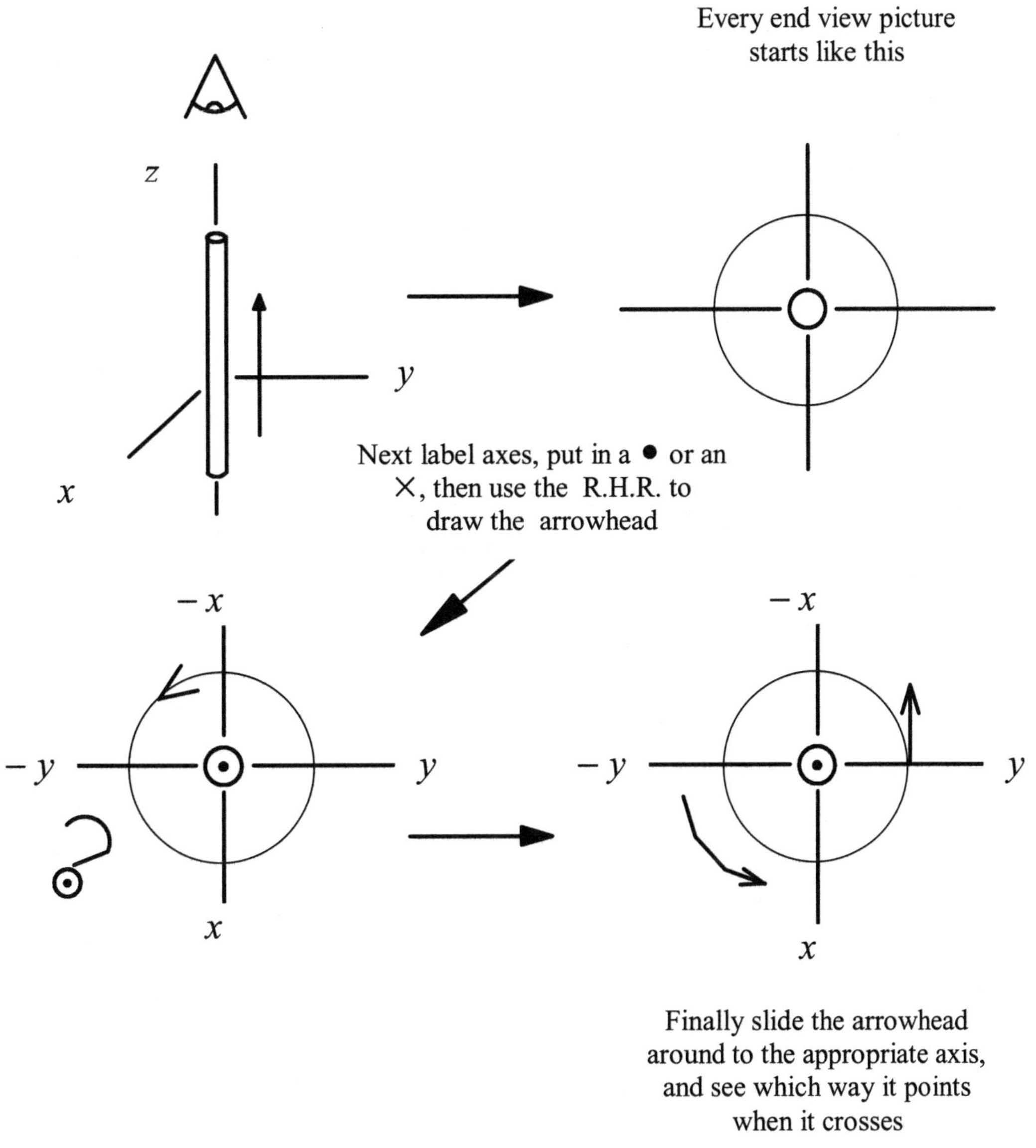
Every end view picture starts like this
z
y
x
Next label axes, put in a • or an ×, then use the R.H.R. to draw the arrowhead
− x
− y
y
x
− x
− y
y
x
Finally slide the arrowhead around to the appropriate axis, and see which way it points when it crosses

Figure 8.10 Steps in finding the direction of $\vec{B}$

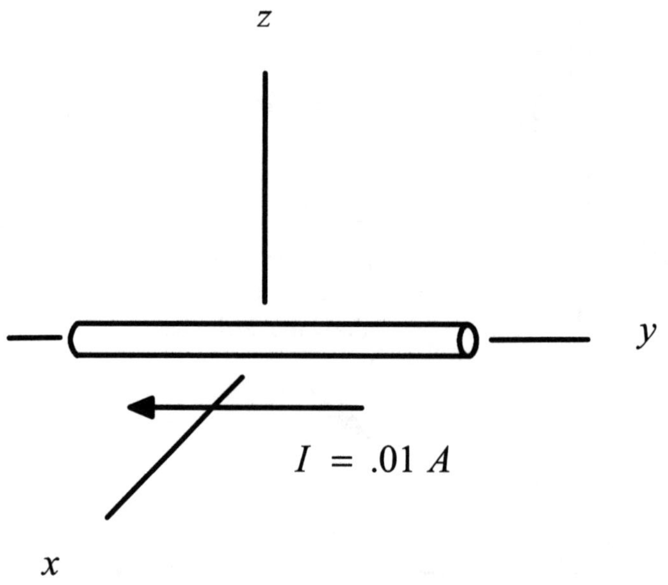

Figure 8.11 Long wire for Quiz 8.2

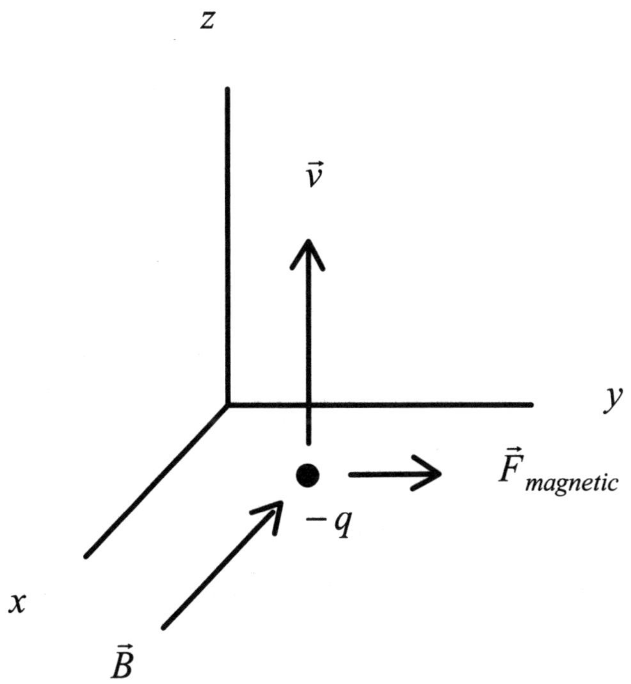

Figure 8.12 "Right Angle" characteristic of $\vec{F}_{magnetic}$

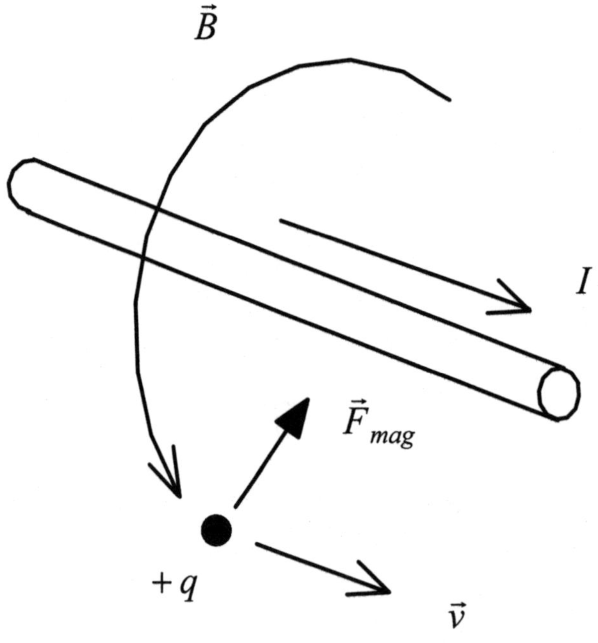

Figure 8.13 Electric charge moving parallel to a current carrying wire

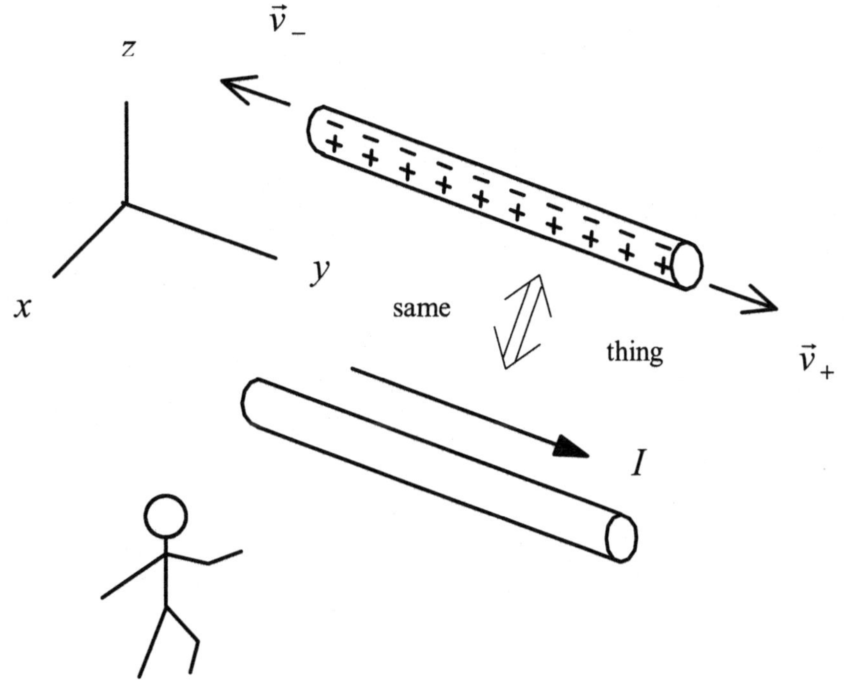

Figure 8.14 A laboratory frame observer can model I as two lines of equally spaced, oppositely moving charge.

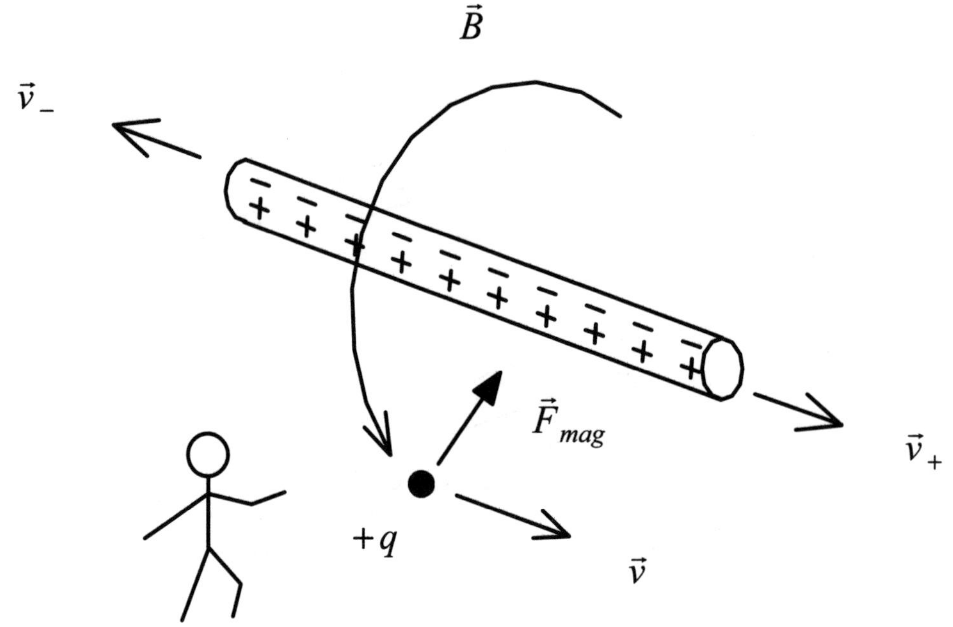

Figure 8.15 Laboratory frame observer sees a magnetic force caused by a $+q$ charge moving through the $\vec{B}$ field of an electrically neutral current carrying wire

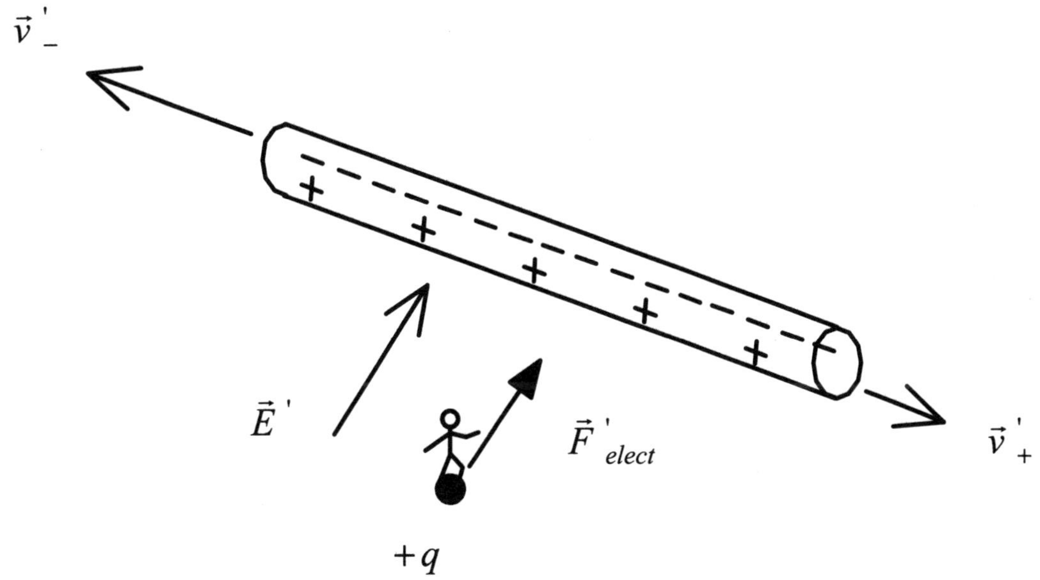

Figure 8.16 Charge riding observer sees an electric force caused by a stationary $+q$ charge placed in the $\vec{E}$ field of a negatively charged wire

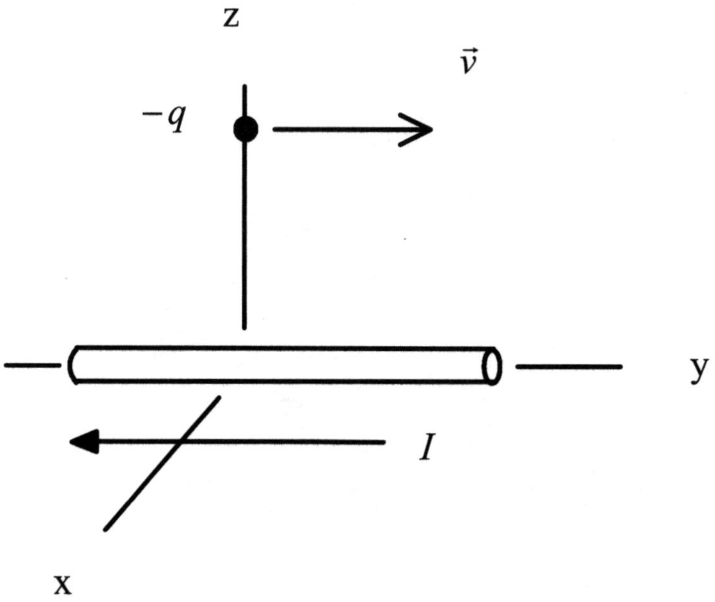

Figure 8.17 Setup for Example 8.5

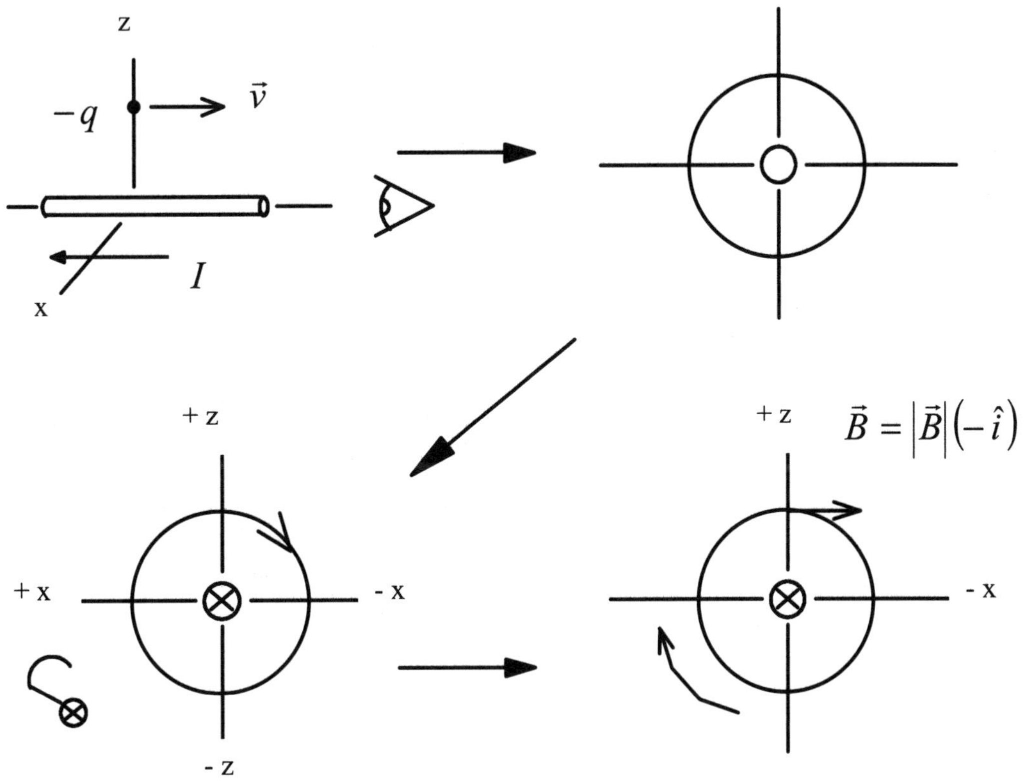

Figure 8.18 Steps in finding the direction of $\vec{B}$ where it crosses the $+z$ axis

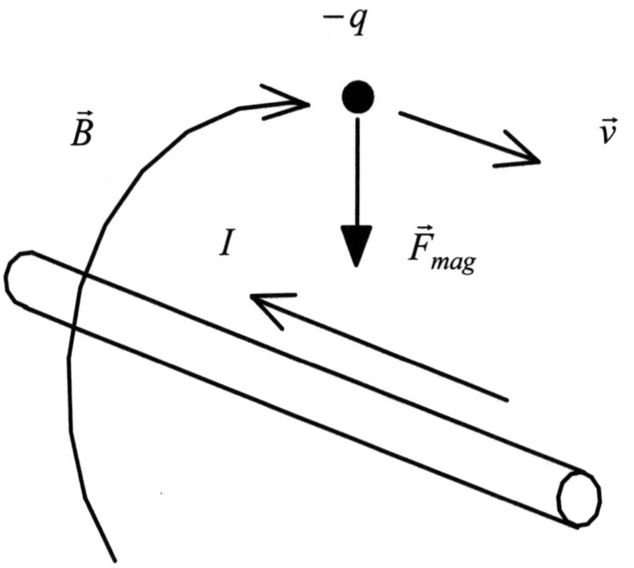

Figure 8.19 $\vec{F}_{magnetic}$ for Example 8.5

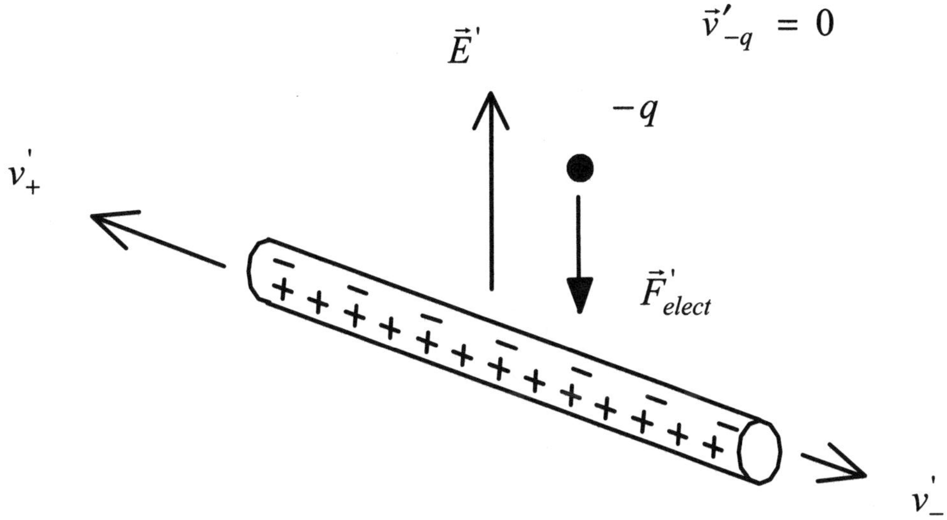

Figure 8.20 $\vec{F}'_{electric}$ for Example 8.5

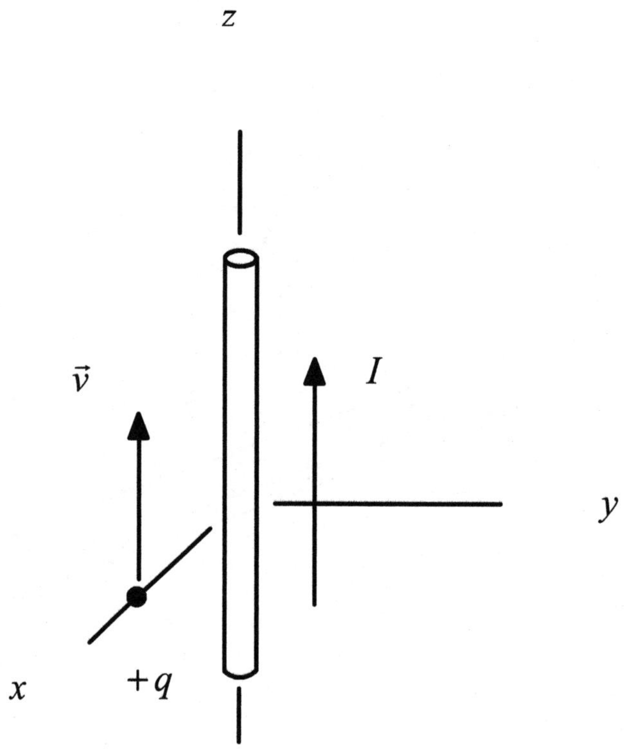

Figure 8.21 Setup for Quiz 8.5

Chapter 9 - Gravity

Timeline

590 BC Thales of Miletus, one of the 1st natural philosophers (scientists) recorded in history, is believed to have taught that the Earth is spherical.

440 BC Another Greek philosopher, Empedocles, wrote that a 'force' called *love* attracts all things together.

350 BC Aristotle, ancient Greek scientist and founder of the Lyceum school in Athens, incorrectly concludes that a heavy rock will fall faster than a lighter rock.

280 BC Strato, new headmaster of the Lyceum school in Athens, uses observation and experiment to determine that falling bodies speed up as they fall.

60 BC Contradicting Aristotle, the Roman poet Lucretius suggests that all objects will fall with the same (increasing) speeds through a vacuum, even though they might have different weights.

1604 Galileo Galilei performs experiments in Italy to demonstrate that objects of different weights all experience the same constant acceleration due to gravity. Which means that Lucretius was right. All objects would fall with the same speeds in a vacuum.

1609 The German astronomer Johannes Kepler suggests that the force due to gravity between two stones is mutually attractive, and that each stone would approach the other.

1645 The French librarian Ismael Boulliau claims that if a planetary moving force exits, it should vary as $1/r^2$, instead of the $1/r$ suggested by Kepler.

1651 Italian astronomer and Jesuit priest, Giambattista Riccioli publishes a reasonably accurate value for the acceleration of a falling body.

1659 The Dutch scientist Christiaan Huygens improves Riccioli's measurement, finding the acceleration of a falling body to be close to 9.8 $\frac{m}{s^2}$. Huygens also points out the similarity between gravity and centripetal force.

1687 Issac Newton publishes his universal law of gravitation, $|\vec{F}| = G\left(\frac{m_1 m_2}{r^2}\right)$, in order to explain gravity.

1845 Two different astronomers, John Couch Adams in England and Jean Joseph Leverrier in France, use Newton's theory of gravity to predict the existence of a planet beyond Uranus. Ten months later Neptune is discovered right where they predicted it would be.

1854 The German mathematician Bernhard Riemann develops the mathematics of curvature necessary for Einstein's theory of gravity.

1915 Albert Einstein publishes his General Theory of Relativity in order to explain gravity.

1971 Apollo 15 astronaut David Scott confirms Galileo (and Lucretius) by watching a feather and a hammer fall with the same speeds on the airless surface of the moon.

1971 American physicists J.C. Hafele and Richard Keating use clocks on board commercial airliners to verify Einstein's General Relativity prediction that gravity slows down time.

TEXT

The 20th century gave birth to two great revolutions in physical science. One of them involves an idea that was completely new, called quantum mechanics. The other involves an idea that is as old as time, called gravity.

Around 350 BC, the ancient Greek philosopher Aristotle wrote that a spherical, stationary Earth was located at the center of the universe. Heavier elements, such as earth and water, just "naturally" moved down (towards the Earth), while lighter elements, like air and fire, naturally moved up (towards the sky). Aristotle believed that a greater quanity of a heavy element would move down (fall) more swiftly than a lesser quanity of the same element.

Today we no longer believe that the Earth is the center of the universe. And in 1607 AD, Aristotle's "more swiftly" idea was also proven wrong. After a series of ingenious experiments using pendulums and inclined planes, Galileo Galilei concluded that all bodies will fall at the same rate if there is no air resistance to slow them down. That observation set the stage for Issac Newton's Universal Law of Gravitation.

Newton's Gravity

Issac Newton's *Principia* is dated 1686, although Newton supposedly developed much of the theory 20 years earlier. The *Principia* is perhaps the most influential scientific book of all time. In it Newton proposes his famous 3 laws, and also describes the form of what is now called the Universal Law of Gravitation. In modern notation,

$$|\vec{F}| = G\left(\frac{m_1 m_2}{r^2}\right) , \tag{901}$$

where $|\vec{F}|$ represents the magnitude of the force on either one of the two objects, due to the other object, m_1 is the mass of the 1st object, m_2 is the mass of the 2nd object, $r^2 = |\vec{r}|^2$ is the square of the distance between the centers of mass, and G is the Universal Gravitation Constant, now believed to be about $6.673 \times 10^{-11}\ (Nm^2)/kg^2$. Figure 9.1 shows a picture.

Let's look at the units.

$$G\left(\frac{m_1 m_2}{r^2}\right) \longrightarrow \left(\frac{Nm^2}{kg^2}\right)\frac{(kg)(kg)}{m^2} \rightarrow N$$

Notice that the units on the right hand side turn out to be Newtons (N) because big G carries "designer units" that have intentionally been rigged to make the right side come out right. Units on constants are almost always determined exactly that way. Scientists know in advance what the final units have to be, so they give their constants whatever units are necessary to make the unit analysis work.

Example 9.1

A 3 kg crystal ball and a 2 kg metal sphere are placed far out in deep space with .25 m between their centers of mass. How much force does the sphere exert on the ball ?

Solution 9.1

"How much force" means $|\vec{F}|$, so this is a straight plug in into equation (901).

$$\begin{aligned} |\vec{F}| &= \frac{Gm_1 m_2}{r^2} \\ &= \left[\frac{(6.673 \times 10^{-11})(3)(2)}{(.25)^2}\right] N \\ |\vec{F}| &\approx 6.4 \times 10^{-9}\ N \end{aligned} \tag{902}$$

We have already done the unit analysis, and there has been no algebraic manipulation of the equation, so it's probably OK to just carry the N unit as we go along.

Example 9.1 could just as well have asked, "How much force does the ball exert on the sphere?" The solution would look exactly the same. Newton's gravity is always attractive, and each object exerts the same amount of force on the other object. The forces are in opposite directions, but the magnitudes are always the same.

Quiz 9.1 Electrons carry a charge of about $q_e = -1.6 \times 10^{-19}\ C$ and have a mass of about $m_e = 9.11 \times 10^{-31}\ kg$. Use equation (901) to calculate the strength of the gravitational attraction between two electrons that are placed 1×10^{-9} m apart. Then use the magnitude of equation (603) on page 125 to calculate the strength of the electric repulsion between the two electrons. How much stronger is the electric force?

Equation (901) is frequently used to determine the gravitational force that a planet exerts on objects close to its surface. Planets are nearly spherical, and it is customary to locate the center of the planet at the center of a spherical co-ordinate system. That way the $+r$ direction will always point up, and the $-r$ direction will always point down, no matter where you are located on the surface. Figure 9.2 shows a picture.

In terms of spherical co-ordinates, a customized version of equation (901) would look like

$$\vec{F}_{grav\ (close\ to\ surface)} = m\left(\frac{G\,M_p}{r_p^2}\right)(-\hat{r})\ , \tag{903}$$

where $\vec{F}_{grav}$ is the gravitational force pulling down on an object of mass m, M_p is the mass of the planet that is doing the pulling, r_p is the radius of the planet, and $(-\hat{r})$ is a unit vector pointing down towards the center of the planet. (Here we are using r_p because we are talking about the force due to gravity on an object located close to the surface. If the object had been very high above the surface, we would have used r, the distance from the center of the planet out to the center of the object.)

Newton's second law says that all forces have to equal $m\vec{a}$, which means

$$\vec{F}_{grav} = m\vec{a}_{grav}\ . \tag{904}$$

Setting equation (904) equal to equation (903) leads to

$$\begin{aligned} \vec{F}_{grav} &= \vec{F}_{grav} \\ m\vec{a}_{grav} &= m\left(\frac{G\,M_p}{r^2}\right)(-\hat{r}) \\ \vec{a}_{grav} &= \frac{G\,M_p}{r^2}(-\hat{r})\ . \end{aligned} \tag{905}$$

Notice that the m's on both sides of equation (905) cancel out. This is an important and necessary feature of Newton's theory. Galileo had already demonstrated that all objects fall with the same acceleration, even if their masses are different. Newton's gravity accounts for that fact by making the acceleration depend only on the mass of the planet, not on the mass of the object.

The acceleration due to gravity occurs frequently enough to be given its own name. It is called $\vec{g}$, and

$$\vec{F} = m\vec{g} \tag{906}$$

is always taken to mean the force on m due to gravity. *Weight* is the name given to the magnitude of the force due to gravity, so

$$Weight = m|\vec{g}| = mg \tag{907}$$

Example 9.2

Earth's moon has a mass of about $7.35 \times 10^{22}\ kg$, and a radius close to $1.74 \times 10^{6}\ m$. Find the acceleration due to gravity near the surface of the moon.

Solution 9.2

From equation (905),

$$\vec{g}_{\,moon} = G\left(\frac{M_p}{r^2}\right)(-\hat{r})\,. \tag{908}$$

Let's look at the units first.

$$\begin{aligned} G\left(\frac{M_p}{r^2}\right) &\longrightarrow \left(\frac{N\,m^2}{kg^2}\right)\frac{kg}{m^2} \rightarrow \frac{N}{kg} \\ &\longrightarrow \frac{kg\;m}{s^2}\left(\frac{1}{kg}\right) \rightarrow \frac{m}{s^2} \end{aligned}$$

Any acceletation should have units of m/s^2, and this one does, so the units look OK.

Plugging in the numbers,

$$\begin{aligned} \vec{g}_{\,moon} &= \frac{G\,M_p}{r^2}(-\hat{r}) \\ &= \frac{(6.673 \times 10^{-11})(7.35 \times 10^{22})}{(1.74 \times 10^{6})^2}(-\hat{r})\,\frac{m}{s^2} \\ \vec{g}_{\,moon} &\approx 1.62\,\frac{m}{s^2}\,(-\hat{r}) \end{aligned} \tag{909}$$

Quiz 9.2 The Earth has a mean radius close to $6.37 \times 10^{6}\ m$, and a mass of about $5.974 \times 10^{24}\ kg$. Find the acceleration due to gravity near the surface of the Earth.

Einstein's Gravity

Issac Newton's Universal Law of Gravitation works very well inside our solar system, where the forces due to gravity are comparatively weak. (Well enough in fact, that we used it to go to the moon in Apollo 11.) There are however, some minor differences between what we actually observe, and what Newton's gravity predicts that we should observe. Albert Einstein was bothered by those differences, and in 1915 he proposed a completely fresh approach.

Einstein's Theory of General Relavity is based on geometry instead of the concept of attractive force. Here's how it works. Figure 9.3a shows an observer standing in a "normal" xy co-ordinate system. The observer is looking at a triangle with a hypotenuse whose length is given by the Pythagorean theorem. He sees,

$$\begin{aligned} (\Delta L)^2 &= (\Delta x)^2 + (\Delta y)^2 \\ \Delta L &= \sqrt{(\Delta x)^2 + (\Delta y)^2} \\ &= \sqrt{(4)^2 + (3)^2} = \sqrt{25} \\ \Delta L &= 5 \end{aligned} \tag{910}$$

Figure 9.3b shows a different observer standing in a "squeeze world" co-ordinate system. That observer is also looking at a triangle with a hypotenuse whose length is given by the Pythagorean theorem. He sees,

$$\begin{aligned} (\Delta L_{sq})^2 &= (\Delta x_{sq})^2 + (\Delta y_{sq})^2 \\ \Delta L_{sq} &= \sqrt{(\Delta x_{sq})^2 + (\Delta y_{sq})^2} \\ &= \sqrt{(4)^2 + (3)^2} = \sqrt{25} \\ \Delta L_{sq} &= 5 \end{aligned} \tag{911}$$

Both observers see a 3, 4, 5 right triangle as long as they are looking inside their own co-ordinate system. But when the normal world observer looks at the squeeze world triangle, he sees something different. That happens because the squeeze world co-ordinates are not the same size as the normal world co-ordinates.

For this particular example the co-ordinates are related by

$$\begin{aligned} x_{sq} &= \frac{4}{5}\,x \\ y_{sq} &= \frac{3}{2}\,y \end{aligned} \tag{912}$$

So the Pythagorean theorem for the squeeze world triangle, in terms of the normal world co-ordinates, becomes

$$\begin{aligned} (\Delta L_{sq})^2 &= (\Delta x_{sq})^2 + (\Delta y_{sq})^2 \\ &= \left(\frac{4}{5}\Delta x\right)^2 + \left(\frac{3}{2}\Delta y\right)^2 \\ (\Delta L_{sq})^2 &= \frac{16}{25}(\Delta x)^2 + \frac{9}{4}(\Delta y)^2 \end{aligned} \tag{913}$$

In this case, the normal world observer sees the squeeze world triangle to have a length of

$$\begin{aligned} (\Delta L_{sq})^2 &= \frac{16}{25}(\Delta x)^2 + \frac{9}{4}(\Delta y)^2 \\ &= \frac{16}{25}(4)^2 + \frac{9}{4}(3)^2 \;=\; \frac{256}{25} + \frac{81}{4} \\ &= 30.49 \\ \Delta L_{sq} &= \sqrt{30.49} \approx 5.52 \end{aligned} \tag{914}$$

Equation (913) is a sort of "cross-over" Pythagorean theorem. It gives the squeeze world length in terms of the normal world co-ordinates.

Example 9.3

Construct the cross-over Pythagorean theorem for a "stretch world" in which $x_{st} = 1.3\,x$ and $y_{st} = .7\,y$.

Solution 9.3

Inside stretch world

$$\begin{aligned}\Delta x_{st} &= (x_{st})_2 - (x_{st})_1\\ &= 1.3x_2 - 1.3x_1 = 1.3(x_2 - x_1)\\ \Delta x_{st} &= 1.3\Delta x \end{aligned} \tag{915}$$

Similarlly, $\Delta y_{st} = .7\Delta y$. So the cross-over Pythagorean theorem becomes,

$$\begin{aligned}(\Delta L_{st})^2 &= (\Delta x_{st})^2 + (\Delta y_{st})^2\\ &= (1.3\Delta x)^2 + (.7\Delta y)^2\\ (\Delta L_{st})^2 &= 1.69(\Delta x)^2 + .49(\Delta y)^2 \end{aligned} \tag{916}$$

Quiz 9.3 Construct the cross-over Pythagorean theorem for a "big world" where $x_{\,big} = 4\,x$ and $y_{\,big} = 3\,y$.

In General Relativity, you have to talk about the spacetime interval instead of the Pythagorean theorem, and Albert Einstein's concept of gravity is based on a "cross-over" spacetime interval. From Chapter 7 equation (728), the timelike spacetime interval was

$$(\Delta S_t)^2 = c^2(\Delta t)^2 - (\Delta x)^2 - (\Delta y)^2\,, \tag{917}$$

where $c \approx 3 \times 10^8\ \frac{m}{s}$ is the speed of light. Expanding that interval to include all 3 space dimensions results in

$$(\Delta S_t)^2 = c^2(\Delta t)^2 - (\Delta x)^2 - (\Delta y)^2 - (\Delta z)^2\,. \tag{918}$$

Equation (918) represents the spacetime interval for *flatspace*. In other words, it describes the interval far away from a planet or any other kind of body that has mass. Einstein's theory of gravity is based on the idea that the presence of mass will somehow "squeeze" the spacetime interval away from its flatspace value. Einstein visualized the new interval as looking like

$$(\Delta S_t)^2 = g_{11}c^2(\Delta t)^2 - g_{22}(\Delta x)^2 - g_{33}(\Delta y)^2 - g_{44}(\Delta z)^2\,, \tag{919}$$

where the g_{aa}'s are "crossover" factors similar to the $\frac{16}{25}$ and $\frac{9}{4}$ in equation (913).

Equation (918) represents the flatspace interval, and it is expressed in terms of the familiar (x, y, z) rectangular co-ordinate system. That would be fine if we were going to stay out in flatspace, far away from anything with mass. But the whole point is to see what the interval will look like up close to a body that does have mass. Many of those bodies, planets and stars for example, are roughly spherical in shape. When you are going to be close to a spherical gravity source, it is more efficient to express the interval in the (r, θ, ϕ) spherical co-ordinate system. In those co-ordinates, r is radial, θ is the angle that comes down from the North Pole, and ϕ is an angle measured around the equator.

In spherical co-ordinates the flatspace equation (918) looks like

$$(\Delta S_t)^2 = c^2(\Delta t)^2 - (\Delta r)^2 - r^2(\Delta\theta)^2 - r^2 sin^2\theta(\Delta\phi)^2 . \qquad (920)$$

Here (Δr) represents a straight up-and-down distance, measured along a line that goes from the center of the planet out. The $(\Delta\theta)$ and $(\Delta\phi)$ terms are side-to-side terms that are parallel to the surface of the planet (Figure 9.4), and $\sin^2\theta = (\sin\theta)^2$.

We should make one last change. When r_2 and r_1 are very close together, so close that you need a microscope to tell them apart, then (Δr) is usually written as dr. In other words,

$$(\Delta r)^2 \longrightarrow dr^2 \ when \ (\Delta r) \rightarrow \ very \ very \ small . \qquad (921)$$

So we finally get

$$dS_t^2 = c^2dt^2 - dr^2 - r^2d\theta^2 - r^2\sin^2\theta d\phi , \qquad (922)$$

for the *flatspace* timelike interval in spherical co-ordinates.

Equation (922) is in spherical co-ordinates because we are about to go up close to the surface of a spherical planet. But right now we are still far out in deep space, way away from any kind of mass or field. So equation (922) represents the flat spacetime interval, which people usually call the "flatspace" interval.

Einstein's idea is that the presence of mass will warp the spacetime interval away from its flatspace value. Up close to the surface of a planet for example, Einstein thought that the cross-over interval might look like

$$dS_t^2 = g_{11}c^2dt^2 - g_{22}dr^2 - g_{33}r^2d\theta^2 - g_{44}r^2\sin^2\theta d\phi^2 . \qquad (923)$$

With that idea in mind he began to search for the g_{aa}'s.

Albert Einstein himself never did find an exact expression for the g's. But a contemporary of Einstein's did. A German astronomer named Karl Schwarzschild, used Einstein's theory to find the g's for the interval up close to the surface of a stationary, uniformly dense, spherical mass. Schwarzschild's interval looks like

$$dS_t^2 = \left(1 - \frac{2GM}{rc^2}\right)c^2dt^2 - \left(\frac{1}{1 - \frac{2GM}{rc^2}}\right)dr^2 - r^2d\theta^2 - r^2sin^2\theta d\phi^2 , \qquad (924)$$

where G is the Universal Gravitation Constant, and M is the mass of the sphere.

Comparing the cross-over interval in equation (924) to the flatspace interval in equation (922) reveals that the last two terms are the same. That means that $g_{33} = 1$ and $g_{44} = 1$. The side-to-side terms do not change when you go up close to a planet like Earth. That's because our gravity doesn't work side-to-side. Gravity just works straight up and down. (Otherwise we would all be walking around slanted!)

Of course the Earth is not stationary. It rotates on its axis, and it revolves around the sun. It is neither uniformly dense, nor perfectly spherical. So real planets do not exactly fit the assumptions that Schwarzchild made when he worked out his interval. Today more accurate intervals do exist. They are complicated however, and as a matter of practice the Schwarzchild interval is often used as an approximation to the actual interval around real planets and stars.

If we just look at intervals that go straight up and down, which means intervals with two events that both fall on a line going from the center of the planet straight out, then θ and ϕ will not change, so $d\theta = 0$, $d\phi = 0$, and

$$\begin{aligned} dS^2_{t\ \textit{up \& down}} &= c^2dt^2\left(1-\frac{2GM}{rc^2}\right)-\left(\frac{1}{1-\frac{2GM}{rc^2}}\right)dr^2 - r^2(0)^2 - r^2\sin^2\theta(0)^2 \\ dS^2_{t\ u\,\&\,d} &= c^2dt^2\left(1-\frac{2GM}{rc^2}\right)-\frac{dr^2}{1-\frac{2GM}{rc^2}} \end{aligned} \qquad (925)$$

Equation (925) is the cross-over up & down interval. It expresses $dS^2_{t\ u\,\&\,d}$ in terms of the flatspace co-ordinates dt and dr. The close-to-the-surface interval,

$$dS^2_{t\ u\,\&\,d} = c^2dt^2_{\ planet} - dr^2_{\ planet}, \qquad (926)$$

expresses that same $dS^2_{t\ u\,\&\,d}$ in terms of the close-to-surface co-ordinates, $dt_{\ planet}$ and $dr_{\ planet}$.

Comparing equation (926) to equation (925) reveals that

$$\begin{aligned} dt^2_{\ planet} &= dt^2\left(1-\frac{2GM}{rc^2}\right) \\ dt_{\ planet} &= dt\sqrt{1-\frac{2GM}{rc^2}} \end{aligned} \qquad (927)$$

and,

$$\begin{aligned} dr^2_{\ planet} &= \frac{dr^2}{1-\frac{2GM}{rc^2}} \\ dr_{\ planet} &= \frac{dr}{\sqrt{1-\frac{2GM}{rc^2}}}\ . \end{aligned} \qquad (928)$$

The crossover factor, $\sqrt{1-\frac{2GM}{rc^2}}$, is always a number less than 1.0. That means equations (927) and (928) actually predict that *time slows down*, and *space is stretched out* up close to the surface of a spherical mass. Both of those predictions are brand new with Einstein. Newton doesn't have anything like that, because in Newton's theory there is no such thing as a cross-over. Newton thought that $dt_{\ planet}$ would equal dt

and dr_{planet} would equal dr everywhere in space and time.

Imagine that the entire universe is empty. Now visualize a 3 dimensional Cartesian co-ordinate system that extends throughout the whole thing. Every side on every co-ordinate system cube would have a length of one. Both Newton and Einstein would agree on that. Now put in a bunch of stars, planets, and other masses. According to Newton, those masses would have no effect on the co-ordinates. Every cube would still have dimensions of $1 \times 1 \times 1$. But according to Einstein, the cubes that are up close to the masses will be stretched or squeezed so that they are no longer $1 \times 1 \times 1$. In Einstein's theory, the difference in the size of the far away co-ordinates, and the size of the up close co-ordinates would be expressed as a difference in Pythagorean theorem length, if you could ignore time. But you cannot ignore time, so the difference winds up being expessed as a difference in the spacetime interval. The presence of mass warps the spacetime interval away from its flatspace value.

Example 9.4

The Earth has a mass of about $5.974 \times 10^{24}\ kg$, and a radius close to $6.37 \times 10^{6}\ m$. One day = 24 hours = 86,400 seconds. How many seconds go by on Earth for every 86,400 seconds that go by deep in outer space?

<u>Solution 9.4</u>

First we need to write equation (927) in terms of the elapsed time at the surface of the Earth,

$$dt_{\,Earth} = dt\sqrt{1 - \frac{2G(M_{\,Earth})}{(r_{\,Earth})c^2}}\ . \tag{929}$$

Now let's calculate the 2nd term under the square root sign.

$$\frac{2G(M_{\,Earth})}{(r_{\,Earth})c^2} = \frac{2(6.673 \times 10^{-11})(5.974 \times 10^{24})}{(6.37 \times 10^{6})(3 \times 10^{8})^2} \approx 1.39 \times 10^{-9} \tag{930}$$

The units on that term wind up to be

$$\begin{aligned}\frac{2G(M_{\,Earth})}{(r_{\,Earth})c^2} &\longrightarrow \frac{\left(\frac{N\,m^2}{kg^2}\right)kg}{m\left(\frac{m}{s}\right)^2} \rightarrow \left(\frac{N\,m^2}{kg}\right)\left(\frac{s^2}{m^3}\right) \\ &\longrightarrow \left(\frac{N}{kg}\right)\left(\frac{s^2}{m}\right) \rightarrow \left(\frac{kg\,m}{s^2}\right)\left(\frac{s^2}{kg\,m}\right) \\ &\longrightarrow \textit{no units}\ .\end{aligned}$$

We were expecting *no units* because the 2nd term under the radical has to be subtracted from 1, and 1 doesn't have any units. So the unit analysis looks OK.

So far we have

$$dt_{\,Earth} = dt\sqrt{1 - 1.39 \times 10^{-9}}\ . \tag{931}$$

The next step is to get a number for the right hand side. But if we try that on our calculator, it probably won't work. When you enter $(1 - 1.39 \times 10^{-9})$, your calculator probably just says 1. The number is too small to find that way. Fortunately there is another way.

Chapter 7, equation (713) states that

$$(1-x)^{-n} \approx 1 + nx \; . \tag{932}$$

For this example we have a $+n$ exponent instead of a $-n$ exponent. The binominal expansion for the $+n$ case looks like

$$(1-x)^{n} \approx 1 - nx \; . \tag{933}$$

Applying equation (933) to equation (931) leads to

$$\begin{aligned} dt_{\ Earth} &= dt(1 - 1.39 \times 10^{-9})^{\frac{1}{2}} \approx dt\left[1 - \frac{1}{2}(1.39 \times 10^{-9})\right] \\ dt_{\ Earth} &\approx dt(1 - .695 \times 10^{-9}) \; . \end{aligned} \tag{934}$$

Plugging in 86,400 seconds for dt,

$$\begin{aligned} dt_{\ Earth} &\approx (86,400\ sec)(1 - .695 \times 10^{-9}) \\ dt_{\ Earth} &\approx 86,400\ sec \ - \ 60 \times 10^{-6}\ sec \; . \end{aligned} \tag{935}$$

The time dilation term predicts that clocks on the surface of the Earth will run about 60 μs a day slower than clocks out in deep space. Even though 60 μs a day sounds insignificant, it turns out to be a very big deal for the designers of Global Positioning Systems. GPS requires almost perfect synchronization between the clocks in the satellites and the clocks on the ground. General Relavity has to be taken into account, otherwise GPS will not work the right way.

Quiz 9.4 Jupiter has a mass of about $1.9 \times 10^{27}\ kg$, and an average radius close to $7.1 \times 10^{7}\ m$. How many seconds go by on the surface of Jupiter for every 86,400 s that go by deep in outer space?

Black Holes

Almost as soon as the Schwarzschild interval appeared, people noticed that a far away flatspace observer would see $c^2 dt^2 \left(1 - \frac{2GM}{rc^2}\right)$ become zero, and $\frac{dr^2}{1-\frac{2GM}{rc^2}}$ become infinite if $\frac{2GM}{rc^2}$ became equal to 1. The specific r value that could make that happen is called the Schwarzschild radius, and it is calculated from

$$\begin{aligned} \frac{2GM}{r_{sch}\ c^2} &= 1 \\ 2GM &= r_{sch}\ c^2 \\ r_{sch} &= \frac{2GM}{c^2} \; . \end{aligned} \tag{936}$$

Example 9.5

Calculate the Schwarzchild radius for the Earth.

Solution 9.5

Starting with equation (938)

$$r_{sch} = \frac{2GM}{c^2} , \tag{937}$$

Let's look first at the units on the right hand side.

$$\begin{aligned}
\frac{2GM}{c^2} &\longrightarrow \frac{\left(\frac{N\,m^2}{kg^2}\right) kg}{\left(\frac{m}{s}\right)^2} \rightarrow \left(\frac{N\,m^2}{kg}\right)\left(\frac{s^2}{m^2}\right) \\
&\longrightarrow N\left(\frac{s^2}{kg}\right) \rightarrow \left(\frac{kg\,m}{s^2}\right)\left(\frac{s^2}{kg}\right) \\
&\longrightarrow m\,.
\end{aligned}$$

We would expect a radius to have units of m, and this one does so the units look OK. Plugging in the numbers for Earth,

$$\begin{aligned}
r_{sch} &= \frac{2GM}{c^2} = \frac{2(6.673 \times 10^{-11})(5.974 \times 10^{24})}{(3 \times 10^8)^2}\, m \\
r_{sch} &\approx .0089\, m\,.
\end{aligned} \tag{938}$$

The Schwarzchild interval describes spacetime around the *outside* of a spherical mass. So in order to make $c^2dt^2\left(1 - \frac{2GM}{r_{sch}c^2}\right) = 0$, all of the mass has to be in a ball that would fit *inside* a circle whose circumference is given by $C = 2\pi r_{sch}$. Equation (938) indicates that the circle for Earth is about the size of a wedding ring !

At first no one could concieve of any process that could compact the entire mass of the Earth into a ball that would fit through a wedding ring. So the Schwarzchild radius was originally thought to be a curiousity, without any physical significance. Then in 1939, Robert Oppenheimer and Hartland Snyder described a process by which the enormous gravity of certain types of dying stars could cause those stars to actually shrink down through the Schwarzchild radius. Gravity around one of those tiny shrunken stars would be so strong that nothing physical, not even light, could ever escape from inside the Schwarzchild radius. That's why they are called "black holes". They are black because light cannot get out. And if light can not get out, then the outside universe can never learn about events that take place inside. For that reason, the name "event horizon" is sometimes given to the boundary formed by a circle with $C = 2\pi r_{sch}$.

Quiz 9.5 In order for a black hole to form, physicists believe that the mass of the dying star needs to be at least 3 times the mass of our sun (i.e.- $m_{star} \approx 6 \times 10^{30}\ kg$). What would be the circumference of the event horizon around one of these "minimal" black holes?

Black holes are so bizzare that it has been difficult for the scientific community to believe that they could really exist. Starting in the 1960's however, astronomers began seeing things far out in space to suggest that black holes do exist. The evidence is not yet 100 % conclusive, but it is already strong enough that most of today's physicists are convinced.

Comparing Einstein and Newton

Black holes are not the only thing new with Einstein. General Relativity also makes several other predictions that are unheard of in Newton's gravity. It seems natural to compare the two theories to find out why. But any attempt to do that quickly reveals that they contrast rather than compare.

Newton and Einstein describe the same phenomena in completely different terms. Newton's gravity is very much like Newton's 2nd Law. $\vec{F} = m\vec{a}$, with $\vec{a}$ being the acceleration due to gravity. The magnitude of that acceleration depends on the mass of the planet and one over the square of the distance out to the object being attracted. In Newton's worldview, space and time are absolute and separate. Neither one is affected by the presence of mass. Straight lines in space remain straight even when they are up close to a planet, and the rate at which time flows always stays everywhere the same.

In Einstein's worldview, space and time are both part of spacetime, and spacetime definitely is affected by the presence of mass. Einstein's gravity does not mention a force, so it is not at all like Newton's 2nd Law. Instead it is more like Newton's 1st Law, which says that objects moving in a straight line want to keep moving in a straight line. Einstein's straight lines are straight lines in spacetime called *geodesics.*

Far away from a planet, r is very big, and the Schwarzchild interval becomes the flatspace interval. In symbols,

$$\begin{aligned} dS_t^2|_{r\to\infty} &= \left(1 - \frac{2GM}{(\infty)c^2}\right) c^2dt^2 - \left(\frac{1}{1 - \frac{2GM}{(\infty)c^2}}\right) dr^2 - r^2d\theta^2 - r^2\sin^2\theta d\phi^2 \\ &= (1-0)\, c^2dt^2 - \left(\frac{1}{1-0}\right) dr^2 - r^2d\theta^2 - r^2\sin^2\theta d\phi^2 \\ &= c^2dt^2 - dr^2 - r^2d\theta^2 - r^2\sin^2\theta d\phi^2 \\ dS_t^2|_{r\to\infty} &= dS_t^2{}_{\ flatspace} \end{aligned} \tag{939}$$

Way out there, Einstein's geodesics match up with Newton's idea of straight lines in absolute space.

Einstein's gravity however, warps spacetime. So up close to a planet, the geodesics curve in towards the surface of the planet. When a stone falls to the ground it is really just traveling straight, on the straightest possible geodesic path through spacetime. (In the study of geometry, a geodesic is defined as the shortest possible distance between two points. On a flat table top that distance would be a straight line. On the surface of a sphere it would be a great circle. So if the co-ordinate systen is curved, the geodesic might not look "straight" even though it is still the shortest distance between the two points.)

Figure 9.5 tries to show the way that Newton would view a falling rock together with Einstein's view of the same rock.

Things to Remember

Relationships

$$|\vec{F}| = G\left(\frac{m_1 m_2}{r^2}\right) \qquad \vec{g} = G\left(\frac{M_p}{r^2}\right)(-\hat{r})$$

$$Weight = m|\vec{g}|$$

$$dS^2_{t\ flatspace} = c^2dt^2 - dr^2 - r^2d\theta^2 - r^2\sin^2\theta d\phi^2$$

$$dS^2_{t\ Schwarzschild} = \left(1 - \frac{2GM}{rc^2}\right)c^2dt^2 - \left(\frac{1}{1-\frac{2GM}{rc^2}}\right)dr^2 - r^2d\theta^2 - r^2\sin^2\theta d\phi^2$$

$$dt_{\ planet} = dt\sqrt{1 - \frac{2GM}{rc^2}}$$

$$dr_{\ planet} = \frac{dr}{\sqrt{1-\frac{2GM}{rc^2}}}$$

$$(1-x)^{\frac{1}{2}} \approx 1 - \frac{1}{2}x \qquad r_{\ sch} = \frac{2GM}{c^2}$$

Constants and Conversions

$$G \approx 6.673 \times 10^{-11}\ \frac{Nm^2}{kg^2}$$

$$2.2\ lbs = 9.8\ N$$

Homework Problems Chapter 9

9.1 The sun's mass is about $2 \times 10^{30}\ kg$ and the earth's mass is close to $6 \times 10^{24}\ kg$. Find the strength of the gravitational force that the sun exerts on the earth when they are $1.5 \times 10^{11}\ m$ apart.

9.2 Algebraically solve equation (901) for r, and do a unit analysis to make sure that the units turn out to be meters.

9.3 The mass of planet Mars is about $6.42 \times 10^{23}\ kg$ and its radius is $3.43 \times 10^{6}\ m$. Find the acceleration due to gravity on Mars.

9.4 How many pounds does a 14 kg rock weigh on a.) the earth ?
b.) Mars ?
c.) the moon ?

9.5 The sides of a normal world right triangle are $\Delta x = 12,\ \Delta y = 5,\ \Delta L = 13$. The sides of a "squish" world right triangle are also $\Delta x_{sq} = 12,\ \Delta y_{sq} = 5,\ \Delta L_{sq} = 13$. Find the length of the squish world hypotenuse in terms of the normal world co-ordinates if $\Delta x_{sq} = \frac{4}{3}\Delta x$, and $\Delta y_{sq} = \frac{3}{4}\Delta y$.

9.6 World B co-ordinates are related to the normal world co-ordinates by $x_B = \frac{2}{3}x$, and $y_B = \frac{3}{2}y$. Construct the crossover Pythagorean theorem for World B.

9.7 Neutron stars are believed to be ultra compact spheres that can pack the mass of 1.4 to 3 suns in a ball the size of a city (diameter $\approx 2.7 \times 10^{4}\ m$). Although they are supposed to rotate very quickly (which means the Schwarzschild interval doesn't really apply), we can imagine one that is somehow stationary. How many earth days would go by on the surface of a stationary neutron star for every 10 earth days that go by in outer space, if the neutron star has 1.8 times as much mass as our sun ?

9.8 What does the mass to radius ratio, $\frac{M}{r}$, need to be so that $\frac{9}{10}$ as much time goes by on the surface of a stationary star? (Hint: Let $dt_{star} = \frac{9}{10}dt$, and solve for $\frac{M}{r}$.)

9.9 British physicist Stephen Hawking has proposed a process by which a black hole can slowly evaporate. How much mass would be left in a "Hawking black hole" that is down to an event horizon with a circumference the size of a basketball (C = .78 *m*) ?

9.10 Along the way in H.W. 9.9 you should have come up with $M = \frac{c^2 r_{sch}}{2G}$. Redo the unit analysis for this equation and show that the units really do come out to be *kg*.

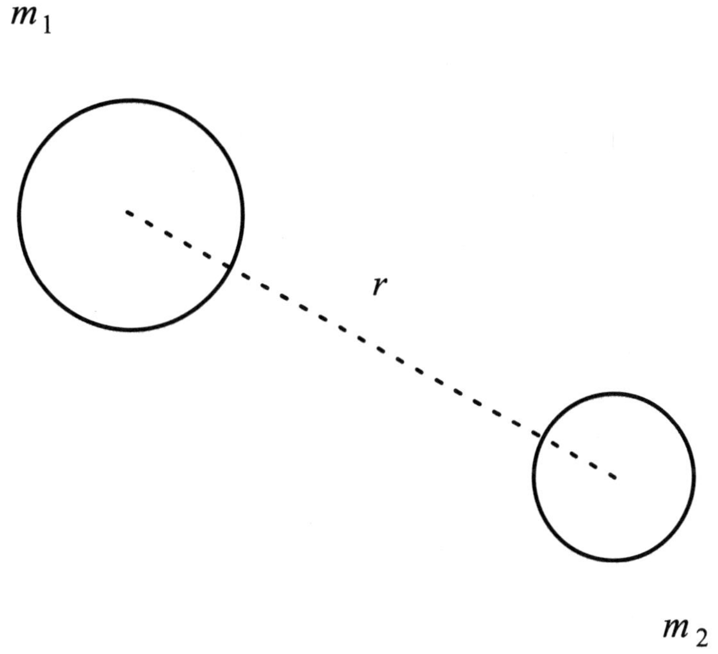

Figure 9.1 Two masses in space

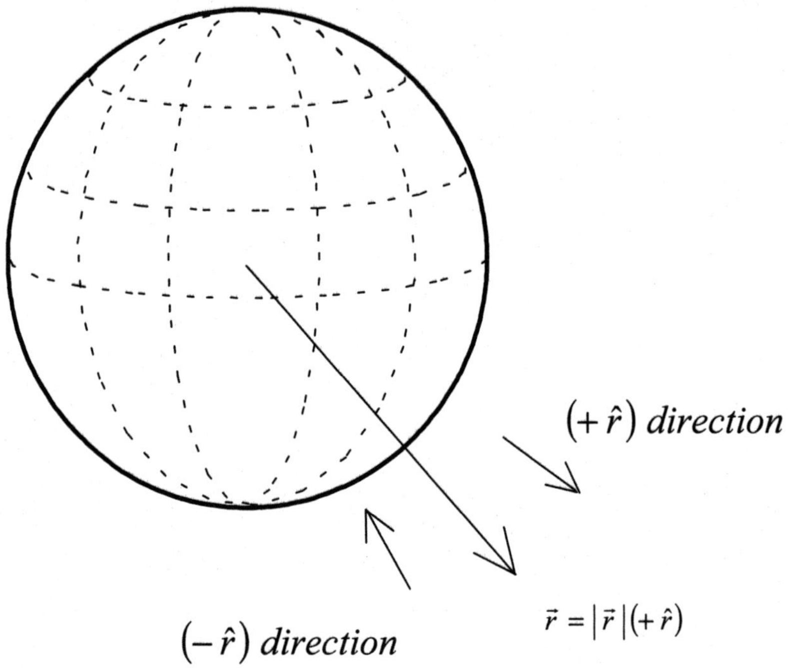

Figure 9.2 Anywhere on the planet the $(+\hat{r})$ unit vector points "out" (or up), and the $(-\hat{r})$ unit vector points "in" (or down).

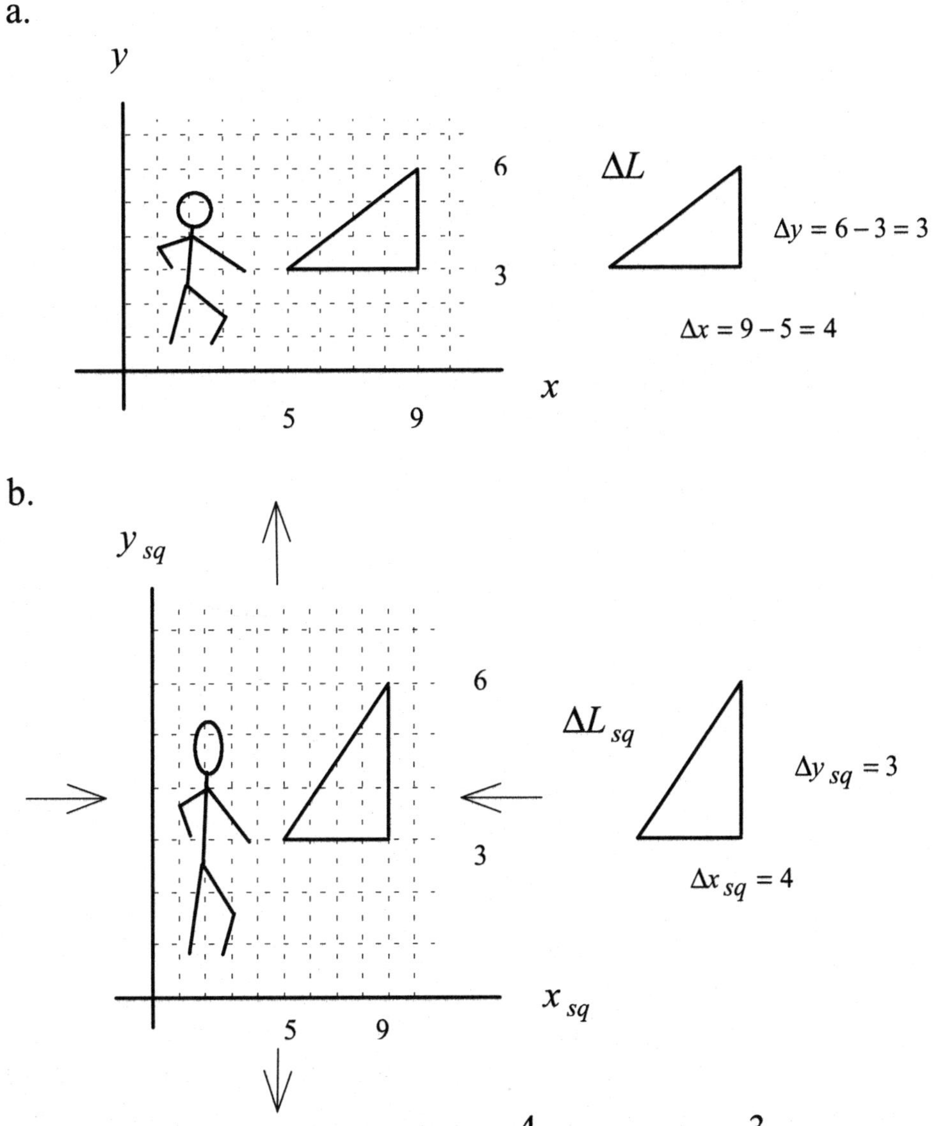

$$x_{sq} = \frac{4}{5}x \qquad y_{sq} = \frac{3}{2}y$$

Figure 9.3 a.) Normal World
b.) Squeeze World

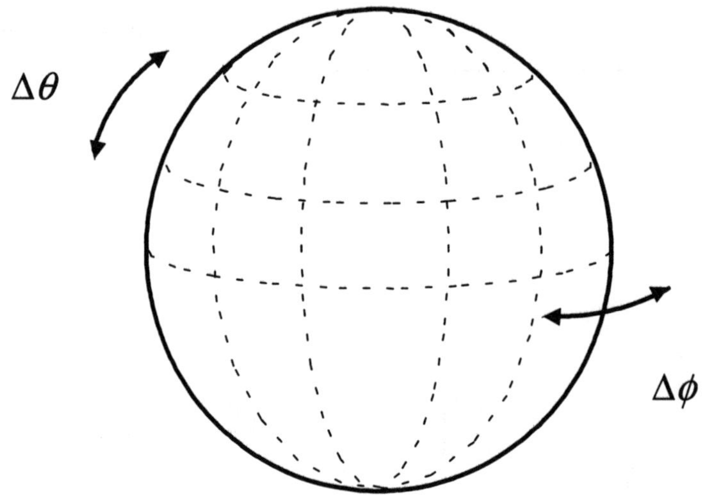

Figure 9.4 Changes in the angular spherical co-ordinates θ and ϕ lead to paths that are parallel to the surface of the planet.

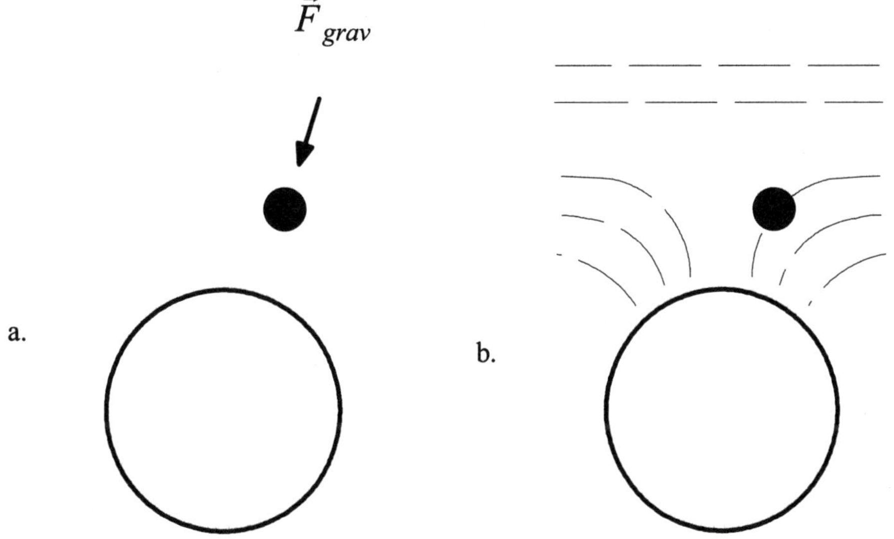

Figure 9.5 a.) Newton's rock falls because it is pulled through space by a force due to gravity.

b.) Einstein's rock falls because it is moving along a "straight line" geodesic in spacetime.

Chapter 10 - Quantum Mechanics

Timeline

1900 British scientist Lord Rayleigh uses classical physics to derive the incorrect Rayleigh-Jeans radiation law.

1900 Max Planck in Germany introduces 'energy elements' (energy quanta) in order to accomplish his derivation of a much more correct radiation law.

1926 Austrian physicist Erwin Schrödinger publishes his equation for the quantum mechanical wave function Ψ.

1926 German physicists and mathematicians Werner Heisenberg, Max Born, and Pascual Jordan formulate a matrix approach to Quantum Mechanics.

1926 Max Born realizes that the Ψ function can be expanded as a series of orthonormal eigen vectors, and suggests a probabilistic interpretation for the eigen vector coefficients.

1935 Erwin Schrödinger introduces his famous cat example in order to point out the problems associated with applying the rules of Quantum Mechanics to objects that are big enough to see.

1953 A similar objection, brought up by applying Quantum Mechanics to a visible 'Particle in a Box', causes Albert Einstein to conclude that Ψ really represents a statistical ensemble of partices, and cannot be said to describe an individual system.

TEXT

Right around the time that Albert Einstein was putting the finishing touches on his Special Theory of Relativity, another great revolution in scientific thought was about to take place.

Early in 1900, a noted British scientist called Lord Rayleigh derived a formula to predict the color that an object would glow as it was heated to a very high temperature. His result is known as the Rayleigh-Jeans law. It was based on existing physics, and it predicted that heated objects would glow blue. That was bad news for existing physics because everybody knows real heated objects glow red. Clearly something was wrong somewhere. This problem was so serious that it was called the *Ultraviolet Catastrophe*, and for a while, nobody knew how to fix it.

Quantum drops

A German professor named Max Planck came to the rescue with a radical idea. Think about water. Water comes in drops. For all practical purposes, when you are working with water, the smallest amount that you can get is a drop. Late in 1900, Max Planck was able to fix the Ultraviolet Catastrophe by suggesting that energy comes in drops too.

Planck proposed that the vibrating molecules in a heated object could only receive or emit light energy in discrete bundles. Soon after, Albert Einstein suggested that light itself consited of discrete bundles that were eventually called photons. Each photon would contain a "drop" of energy given by

$$E_{photon} = hf \ , \tag{1001}$$

where f is the frequency of the light in H_z (= 1/s), and h is Planck's constant, approximately $6.626 \times 10^{-34}\ J\,s$.

Example 10.1

Max Planck called his drop of energy a "quantum" after the Greek word for quota. Yellow light has a wavelength of about 590 nm. How much energy makes up one quantum of yellow light?

Solution 10.1

We are given the wavelength of yellow light. But we need the frequency in order to use equation (1001). Fortunately the two are related in Chapter 5, by equation (523). We are talking about light, so $v = c$ and,

$$\begin{aligned} v &= \lambda f \\ c &= \lambda f \\ f &= \frac{c}{\lambda} = \frac{3 \times 10^{8}\ \frac{m}{s}}{590 \times 10^{-9}\ m} \\ &\approx 5.08 \times 10^{14} \left(\frac{m}{s}\right)\left(\frac{1}{m}\right) \\ f &\approx 5.08 \times 10^{14}\ \frac{1}{s} \ . \end{aligned} \tag{1002}$$

From here it's a straight plug in to equation (1001).

$$\begin{aligned} E_{photon} &= hf \\ &\approx (6.626 \times 10^{-34}\ Js)\left(5.08 \times 10^{14}\ \frac{1}{s}\right) \\ E_{photon} &\approx 3.37 \times 10^{-19}\ J. \end{aligned} \tag{1003}$$

Quiz 10.1 The energy in one photon of blue light is $4.32 \times 10^{-19}\ J$. What is the wavelength of that particular shade of blue?

The second part of Planck's hypothesis calls for the vibrating molecules that emit radiation to have energies restricted to an integer number of quantum drops.

$$E_n = n(hf)\ , \tag{1004}$$

where n is a positive integer. This means that the energy of vibration could be for example, 23 times hf, or 24 times hf, but it could never be 23.5 times hf. There are no fractional in-between values. That was Max Planck's radical idea. In classical physics, the energy could take on any value. Here it was "quantized" into discrete units.

Planck's result does not just apply to hot vibrating molecules. Subsequent calculations revealed that any harmonically oscillating system contains $E_n = n(hf) + \frac{1}{2}hf$, where $\frac{1}{2}hf$ is called the 'zero point' energy (because it is still there even if $n = 0$). All of the examples that we will consider are low frequency spring oscillators, so that we can effectively ignore the $\frac{1}{2}hf$ term and always use $E_n \approx n(hf)$.

Example 10.2

Suppose a small mass hangs at the end of a light spring. The mass is then pulled down and released so that it oscillates up and down with what is called "simple harmonic motion". (One oscillation is all the way up, then all the way back down again.) Calculate the number of energy drops in the oscillating spring-mass system if the frequency of oscillation is 3 H_z and the total energy is .08 J.

Solution 10.2

We are given the total energy, so we just need to solve $E_n = n(hf)$ for n.

$$\begin{aligned} E_n &= n(hf) \\ n &= \frac{E_n}{hf} \end{aligned} \tag{1005}$$

Let's look at the units.

$$\begin{aligned} \frac{E_n}{hf} &\longrightarrow \frac{J}{(Js)(H_z)} \\ &\longrightarrow \frac{J}{(Js)\left(\frac{1}{s}\right)} \rightarrow \frac{J}{J} \\ &\longrightarrow \textit{no units} \end{aligned} \tag{1006}$$

We were expecting no units since n represents a pure number. Continuing on,

$$\begin{aligned} n &= \frac{E_n}{hf} \\ &\approx \frac{.08}{(6.626 \times 10^{-34})(3)} \\ n &\approx 4 \times 10^{31}\ . \end{aligned} \tag{1007}$$

In this example the total amount of energy, .08 J, is pretty small. The number of quanta however, is huge beyond imagination, 4×10^{31}. That means each drop is incredibly tiny ($\approx 2 \times 10^{-33}$ J in this case). Before Planck, no one ever noticed that energy comes in drops because the drops are just way too small to detect. The effect is sort of like looking down on a white beach from a 4th story balcony. The beach is made up of grains of sand. But you certainly can't see any individual grains from the 4th floor.

Quiz 10.2 A spring-mass oscillator contains 2×10^{32} drops of energy, and bobs up and down 20 times a second. How much energy of vibration does the system possess?

Quantum Operators

Planck's "quantized energy" allowed him to derive a realistic expression for the colors of a heated object. Rayleigh-Jeans was out, and the Ultraviolet Catastrophe was over. Before long, other researchers were also able to achieve spectacularly successful results by applying the concept of quantum to a wide variety of situations. Gradually the physics of "Quantum Mechanics" began to emerge. Many scientists contributed, and it came out looking very, very weird.

For one thing, theory and experiment both revealed that sub-atomic entities like electrons and photons do not follow the same Newtonian guidelines that govern big things like baseballs and water waves.

In some types of experiments the sub-atomic guys behaved like they were particles. In other types of experiments they behaved like they were waves. What they really are, is still not at all clear.

In addition to energy, other observables were also quantized. (An observable is a measurable physical quantity.) A particle's momentum, or an electron's spin for example, could only have certain discrete values.

The concept of particle trajectory was replaced by the idea of "probable position". In classic Newtonian physics, when you throw a baseball into the air, it is possible to calculate exactly where the baseball will be, together with its exact momentum, at any time during its flight. The path that the baseball will take is called a trajectory, and it is 100 % deterministic. But in 1927, Werner Heisenberg published a paper questioning the wisdom of assigning a definite trajectory to a sub-atomic particle. One problem arises from the fact that a sub-atomic particle is so small. If you shine a light on it to see where it is going, the light will knock it off course and change it's momentum. The very act of observing the particle introduces uncertainty into the trajectory. Physics is supposed to talk about things that can be observed. Heisenberg argued that if the trajectory can't be observed (without messing it up), then (from the physics point of view) it just doesn't exist. After a while his "uncertainty principle" argument caused the concept of trajectory to disappear entirely from Quantum

Mechanics.

Instead of an equation for trajectory, there is an equation for the "wave function", Ψ (Greek letter *psi*). By itself, Ψ does not have a physical interpretation, but $|\Psi|^2$ is related to the *probability* that a particle can be found in a certain location.

So Quantum Mechanics winds up dealing with probabilities. A quantum calculation does not give you the actual value that an observable will take on. Instead you get the possible values that the observable could take on, together with the odds on that particular value coming up. Here's how it works.

Each observable has its own "operator". So there would be an energy operator for example, or a momentum operator, etc. The wavefunction, Ψ, that governs the "system", can be expressed as a series of orthonormal "eigen vectors" that are generated by the operator.

$$\Psi = C_1\hat{\Phi}_1 + C_2\hat{\Phi}_2 + \cdots + C_n\hat{\Phi}_n \ . \tag{1008}$$

Here the $\hat{\Phi}_n$'s are the eigen vectors, and the C_n's are probability coefficients. (Eigen is a German word pronounced eye-gun.) Orthonormal means two things. The "ortho" part means that the eigen vectors are perpendicular to each other. The "normal" part means that the length of the eigen vector equals one (i.e. - $|\hat{\Phi}_n|^2 = 1$). The word "system" refers to the particle together with certain aspects of its environment. The system could be a completely free particle. It could be a particle trapped in an energy well. It could be the electron in a hydrogen atom. Many different systems are possible, and each different system would have a different Ψ.

The operator, which we'll call $\overline{\Lambda}$, operates in turn on each one of the $\hat{\Phi}_n$'s. After the operation is over, what's left is a constant (called an eigen value) multiplied by that same $\hat{\Phi}_n$. In other words,

$$\overline{\Lambda}\hat{\Phi}_n = \lambda_n\hat{\Phi}_n \ , \tag{1009}$$

where λ_n is the specific eigen value that goes with the specific eigen vector $\hat{\Phi}_n$.

The λ_n from equation (1009) represents a possible value of the observable. The $|C_n|^2$ from equation (1008) is the probability that a measurement will find the observable equal to that particular λ_n.

Let's look at an example. We will start with a "practice operator" that has been stripped down for ease of calculation. Practice operators work mathematically, but they do not necessarily apply to anything physical. They have been made up to demonstrate the ideas behind Quantum in a simple fashion.

Example 10.3

Find the eigen values associated with the practice operator $\overline{\Lambda}_{practice} = \begin{bmatrix} 2 & 3 \\ 3 & -6 \end{bmatrix}$.

Solution 10.3

We start by subtracting λ from each main diagonal element of $\overline{\Lambda}_{practice}$ so that we get

$$\begin{bmatrix} (2-\lambda) & 3 \\ 3 & (-6-\lambda) \end{bmatrix} . \tag{1010}$$

Next the so-called "secular equation" is formed by setting the determinant of matrix (1010) equal to zero.

$$\begin{aligned} (2-\lambda)(-6-\lambda)-(3)(3) &= 0 \\ -12+4\lambda+\lambda^2-9 &= 0 \\ \lambda^2+4\lambda-21 &= 0\,. \end{aligned} \tag{1011}$$

The quadratic formula states that the solutions of $ax^2+bx+c=0$ can be found from

$$x=\frac{-b\pm\sqrt{b^2-4ac}}{2a}\,. \tag{1012}$$

Comparing equation (1011) to the quadratic formula gives us

$$\begin{aligned} \lambda &= \frac{-4\pm\sqrt{(4)^2-(4)(1)(-21)}}{(2)(1)} \\ &= \frac{-4\pm\sqrt{16-(-84)}}{2} \\ &= \frac{-4\pm\sqrt{100}}{2}=\frac{-4\pm 10}{2} \\ \lambda_1 &= \frac{6}{2}=3 \\ \lambda_2 &= \frac{-14}{2}=-7 \end{aligned} \tag{1013}$$

The eigen values for this particular practice matrix are $\lambda_1=3$, and $\lambda_2=-7$.

Quiz 10.3 One famous problem from Quantum Mechanics involves a particle that can only move back and forth along the x axis between $x=0$ and $x=L$ (Figure 10.1). The problem is called "Particle in a Box", and the momentum operator is given by $\overline{\Lambda}_{mom}=\begin{bmatrix} \frac{nh}{2L} & 0 \\ 0 & -\frac{nh}{2L} \end{bmatrix}$, where h is Planck's constant, L is the length of the box, and n is a positive quantum number (Either 1 or 2 or 3 or 56; n could be any non-zero positive integer.) Find the possible values of the particle's momentum. (i.e. - Find the eigenvalues, $\lambda_1=p_1$ and $\lambda_2=p_2$.)

Example 10.4

The eigen values from Example 10.3 were $\lambda_1 = 3$ and $\lambda_2 = -7$. Find the eigen vectors associated with each eigen value. Normalize each vector, then check to make sure that the answer satisfies equation (1009). Also check to make sure that the two vectors are orthogonal (perpendicular).

Solution 10.4

Equation (1009) states that $\overline{\Lambda}\hat{\Phi}_n = \lambda\hat{\Phi}_n$, so that for $\lambda_1 = 3$,

$$\begin{bmatrix} 2 & 3 \\ 3 & -6 \end{bmatrix}\begin{bmatrix} A \\ B \end{bmatrix} = 3\begin{bmatrix} A \\ B \end{bmatrix}. \tag{1014}$$

We need to find $\begin{bmatrix} A \\ B \end{bmatrix}$.

Multiplying out both sides of equation (1014),

$$\begin{bmatrix} 2A + 3B \\ 3A - 6B \end{bmatrix} = \begin{bmatrix} 3A \\ 3B \end{bmatrix}, \tag{1015}$$

which reduces to

$$\begin{aligned} -A + 3B &= 0 \\ 3A - 9B &= 0\,. \end{aligned} \tag{1016}$$

The 2nd equation in (1016) is equal to the 1st equation multiplied by -3. So the two equation cannot be solved simultaneously. Instead we will let $A = 1$, and solve the 1st equation for B. (We could let A equal any number, but the answer will come out in its most reduced form if $A = 1$.) So

$$\begin{aligned} -A + 3B &= 0 \\ -(1) + 3B &= 0 \\ 3B &= 1 \\ \\ B &= \frac{1}{3}\,. \end{aligned} \tag{1017}$$

Let's check A and B by plugging them into the 2nd equation.

$$\begin{aligned} 3A - 9B &= 0 \\ 3(1) - 9\left(\frac{1}{3}\right) &= 0 \\ 3 - 3 &= 0 \\ 0 &= 0\,. \end{aligned} \tag{1018}$$

It looks like the eigen vector that goes with $\lambda_1 = 3$ is $\Phi_1 = \begin{bmatrix} 1 \\ \frac{1}{3} \end{bmatrix}$. Now we need to "normalize" by finding $\hat{\Phi}_1 = \frac{\Phi_1}{|\Phi_1|}$. In this case, all of the elements of Φ_1 are real numbers so that,

$$\begin{aligned} |\Phi_1| &= \left| \left[\begin{array}{c} 1 \\ \frac{1}{3} \end{array} \right] \right| = \sqrt{(1)^2 + \left(\frac{1}{3}\right)^2} \\ &= \sqrt{\frac{9}{9} + \frac{1}{9}} = \sqrt{\frac{10}{9}} \\ |\Phi_1| &= \frac{\sqrt{10}}{3} \, . \end{aligned} \tag{1019}$$

Each element of Φ_1 has to be divided by $|\Phi_1|$.

$$\begin{aligned} \hat{\Phi}_1 &= \frac{\Phi_1}{|\Phi_1|} = \frac{1}{|\Phi_1|} \begin{bmatrix} 1 \\ \frac{1}{3} \end{bmatrix} = \frac{1}{\frac{\sqrt{10}}{3}} \begin{bmatrix} 1 \\ \frac{1}{3} \end{bmatrix} \\ &= \frac{3}{\sqrt{10}} \begin{bmatrix} 1 \\ \frac{1}{3} \end{bmatrix} = \begin{bmatrix} \left(\frac{3}{\sqrt{10}}\right)(1) \\ \left(\frac{3}{\sqrt{10}}\right)\left(\frac{1}{3}\right) \end{bmatrix} \\ \hat{\Phi}_1 &= \begin{bmatrix} \frac{3}{\sqrt{10}} \\ \frac{1}{\sqrt{10}} \end{bmatrix} \end{aligned} \tag{1020}$$

It is not a bad idea to make sure that $|\hat{\Phi}_1| = 1$.

$$|\hat{\Phi}_1| = \left| \left[\begin{array}{c} \frac{3}{\sqrt{10}} \\ \frac{1}{\sqrt{10}} \end{array} \right] \right| = \sqrt{\left(\frac{3}{\sqrt{10}}\right)^2 + \left(\frac{1}{\sqrt{10}}\right)^2} = \sqrt{\frac{9}{10} + \frac{1}{10}} = \sqrt{\frac{10}{10}} = 1 \, . \tag{1021}$$

The normalization looks OK, so we can go on to the equation check for $\hat{\Phi}_1$.

That check consists of verifying $\overline{\Lambda}\hat{\Phi}_1 = \lambda_1 \hat{\Phi}_1$ from equation (1009).

$$\begin{aligned} \begin{bmatrix} 2 & 3 \\ 3 & -6 \end{bmatrix} \begin{bmatrix} \frac{3}{\sqrt{10}} \\ \frac{1}{\sqrt{10}} \end{bmatrix} &= 3 \begin{bmatrix} \frac{3}{\sqrt{10}} \\ \frac{1}{\sqrt{10}} \end{bmatrix} \\ \begin{bmatrix} 2\left(\frac{3}{\sqrt{10}}\right) + 3\left(\frac{1}{\sqrt{10}}\right) \\ 3\left(\frac{3}{\sqrt{10}}\right) - 6\left(\frac{1}{\sqrt{10}}\right) \end{bmatrix} &= \begin{bmatrix} 3\left(\frac{3}{\sqrt{10}}\right) \\ 3\left(\frac{1}{\sqrt{10}}\right) \end{bmatrix} \\ \begin{bmatrix} \frac{6}{\sqrt{10}} + \frac{3}{\sqrt{10}} \\ \frac{9}{\sqrt{10}} - \frac{6}{\sqrt{10}} \end{bmatrix} &= \begin{bmatrix} \frac{9}{\sqrt{10}} \\ \frac{3}{\sqrt{10}} \end{bmatrix} \\ \begin{bmatrix} \frac{9}{\sqrt{10}} \\ \frac{3}{\sqrt{10}} \end{bmatrix} &= \begin{bmatrix} \frac{9}{\sqrt{10}} \\ \frac{3}{\sqrt{10}} \end{bmatrix} . \end{aligned} \tag{1022}$$

Again everything looks OK, and we can move to the next eigen vector.

For Φ_2,

$$
\begin{aligned}
\begin{bmatrix} 2 & 3 \\ 3 & -6 \end{bmatrix} \begin{bmatrix} A \\ B \end{bmatrix} &= -7 \begin{bmatrix} A \\ B \end{bmatrix} \\
\begin{bmatrix} 2A + 3B \\ 3A - 6B \end{bmatrix} &= \begin{bmatrix} -7A \\ -7B \end{bmatrix} \\
9A + 3B &= 0 \\
3A + B &= 0\,.
\end{aligned} \tag{1023}
$$

This time the 1st equation is 3 times the 2nd equation. Again they won't solve simultaneously, so again we let $A = 1$. (If we let A equal a different number, Φ will be different, but $\hat{\Phi}$ will still be the same.) Solving the 1st equation for B,

$$
\begin{aligned}
9A + 3B &= 0 \\
9(1) + 3B &= 0 \\
3B &= -9 \\
B &= -3\,,
\end{aligned} \tag{1024}
$$

then using the 2nd equation to check,

$$
\begin{aligned}
3A + B &= 0 \\
3(1) + (-3) &= 0 \\
0 &= 0\,.
\end{aligned} \tag{1025}
$$

It looks like the eigen vector that goes with $\lambda_2 = -7$ is $\Phi_2 = \begin{bmatrix} 1 \\ -3 \end{bmatrix}$.

We need to normalize.

$$
\begin{aligned}
|\Phi_2| &= \left\| \begin{bmatrix} 1 \\ -3 \end{bmatrix} \right\| = \sqrt{(1)^2 + (-3)^2} = \sqrt{1+9} = \sqrt{10} \\
\frac{1}{|\Phi_2|} &= \frac{1}{\sqrt{10}}
\end{aligned} \tag{1026}
$$

$$
\begin{aligned}
\hat{\Phi}_2 &= \left(\frac{1}{|\Phi_2|} \right) (\Phi_2) = \frac{1}{\sqrt{10}} \begin{bmatrix} 1 \\ -3 \end{bmatrix} \\
\hat{\Phi}_2 &= \begin{bmatrix} \frac{1}{\sqrt{10}} \\ -\frac{3}{\sqrt{10}} \end{bmatrix}.
\end{aligned} \tag{1027}
$$

Now check to make sure that $\hat{\Phi}_2$ satisfies $\overline{\Lambda}\hat{\Phi}_2 = \lambda_2 \hat{\Phi}_2$.

$$
\begin{bmatrix} 2 & 3 \\ 3 & -6 \end{bmatrix} \begin{bmatrix} \frac{1}{\sqrt{10}} \\ -\frac{3}{\sqrt{10}} \end{bmatrix} = -7 \begin{bmatrix} \frac{1}{\sqrt{10}} \\ -\frac{3}{\sqrt{10}} \end{bmatrix}
$$

$$\begin{bmatrix} \frac{2}{\sqrt{10}} - \frac{9}{\sqrt{10}} \\ \frac{3}{\sqrt{10}} + \frac{18}{\sqrt{10}} \end{bmatrix} = \begin{bmatrix} -\frac{7}{\sqrt{10}} \\ \frac{21}{\sqrt{10}} \end{bmatrix}$$

$$\begin{bmatrix} -\frac{7}{\sqrt{10}} \\ \frac{21}{\sqrt{10}} \end{bmatrix} = \begin{bmatrix} -\frac{7}{\sqrt{10}} \\ \frac{21}{\sqrt{10}} \end{bmatrix} \tag{1028}$$

The equation check looks OK. The last thing to do is a test to make sure that $\hat{\Phi}_1$ is orthogonal to $\hat{\Phi}_2$.

$$\begin{aligned} \begin{bmatrix} \frac{3}{\sqrt{10}} & \frac{1}{\sqrt{10}} \end{bmatrix} \begin{bmatrix} \frac{1}{\sqrt{10}} \\ -\frac{3}{\sqrt{10}} \end{bmatrix} &= \left(\frac{3}{\sqrt{10}}\right)\left(\frac{1}{\sqrt{10}}\right) + \left(\frac{1}{\sqrt{10}}\right)\left(-\frac{3}{\sqrt{10}}\right) \\ &= \frac{3}{10} - \frac{3}{10} \\ &= 0 \,. \end{aligned} \tag{1029}$$

The two eigen vectors are orthogonal, and our final result is

$$\text{for} \quad \lambda_1 = 3 \quad \hat{\Phi}_1 = \begin{bmatrix} \frac{3}{\sqrt{10}} \\ \frac{1}{\sqrt{10}} \end{bmatrix}$$

and

$$\text{for} \quad \lambda_2 = -7 \quad \hat{\Phi}_2 = \begin{bmatrix} \frac{1}{\sqrt{10}} \\ -\frac{3}{\sqrt{10}} \end{bmatrix}$$

Quiz 10.4 Find the momentum eigen vectors for the Particle in a Box of **Quiz 10.3**. Normalize and check to make sure that the $\hat{\Phi}$'s are orthogonal.

Example 10.5

Continuing with the practice operator from Example 10.3 and given that $\Psi = \begin{bmatrix} 1 \\ 0 \end{bmatrix}$, find the C_n's, assemble the series for Ψ, check to make sure that all of the probabilities add up to 1.0, then interpret the results.

Solution 10.5

For this particular example, equation (1008) reduces to

$$\begin{aligned} \Psi &= C_1\hat{\Phi}_1 + C_2\hat{\Phi}_2 \\ \Psi &= C_1 \begin{bmatrix} \frac{3}{\sqrt{10}} \\ \frac{1}{\sqrt{10}} \end{bmatrix} + C_2 \begin{bmatrix} \frac{1}{\sqrt{10}} \\ -\frac{3}{\sqrt{10}} \end{bmatrix} . \end{aligned} \tag{1030}$$

We still need to find C_1 and C_2. They can be found from the fact that

$$C_n = \hat{\Phi}_n \bullet \Psi \ , \tag{1031}$$

so that

$$\begin{aligned} C_1 &= \hat{\Phi}_1 \bullet \Psi = \begin{bmatrix} \frac{3}{\sqrt{10}} & \frac{1}{\sqrt{10}} \end{bmatrix} \begin{bmatrix} 1 \\ 0 \end{bmatrix} \\ &= \frac{3}{\sqrt{10}}(1) + \frac{1}{\sqrt{10}}(0) \\ C_1 &= \frac{3}{\sqrt{10}} \ , \end{aligned} \tag{1032}$$

and

$$\begin{aligned} C_2 &= \hat{\Phi}_2 \bullet \Psi = \begin{bmatrix} \frac{1}{\sqrt{10}} & -\frac{3}{\sqrt{10}} \end{bmatrix} \begin{bmatrix} 1 \\ 0 \end{bmatrix} \\ &= \frac{1}{\sqrt{10}}(1) + \left(-\frac{3}{\sqrt{10}}\right)(0) \\ C_2 &= \frac{1}{\sqrt{10}} \ . \end{aligned} \tag{1033}$$

Plugging in the appropriate values from equations (1032) and (1033), this particular wavefunction becomes

$$\Psi = \frac{3}{\sqrt{10}} \begin{bmatrix} \frac{3}{\sqrt{10}} \\ \frac{1}{\sqrt{10}} \end{bmatrix} + \frac{1}{\sqrt{10}} \begin{bmatrix} \frac{1}{\sqrt{10}} \\ -\frac{3}{\sqrt{10}} \end{bmatrix} \ . \tag{1034}$$

The probabilities are calculated from $|C_n|^2$, and all of them have to add up to 1.0. So the probability check looks like

$$\begin{aligned} |C_1|^2 + |C_2|^2 &= 1 \\ \left(\frac{3}{\sqrt{10}}\right)^2 + \left(\frac{1}{\sqrt{10}}\right)^2 &= 1 \\ \frac{9}{10} + \frac{1}{10} &= 1 \\ 1 &= 1 \end{aligned} \tag{1035}$$

The probabilities add up the way that they should, and it's time to interpret the results.

Quantum mechanics has told us there are only 2 possible values that our make believe observable could take on, $\lambda_1 = +3$ and $\lambda_2 = -7$. If the observable was some kind of acceleration for example, $+3$ could mean $3 \frac{m}{s^2}$ to the right, -7 could mean $7 \frac{m}{s^2}$ to the left.

Quantum does not tell us however, which of the two values will actually come up. Instead it gives us the "Vegas betting odds". For this example, when we actually make the observation (i.e. - when we measure), the odds say there ia a 90 % chance we will see a 3, and a 10 % chance we will see a -7.

In probability notation,

$$\begin{aligned} P(observable &= +3) &= |C_1|^2 &= \frac{9}{10} \\ P(observable &= -7) &= |C_2|^2 &= \frac{1}{10}, \end{aligned} \tag{1036}$$

where $P(observable = 4)$ reads "the probability that $observable = 4$".

We have to get one value or the other. But we can never know for certain which value we will get, until we actually do the measurement.

Quiz 10.5 The wave function for the particle-in-a-box of Quiz 10.3 is given by $\Psi = \begin{bmatrix} -\frac{i}{\sqrt{2}} \\ \frac{i}{\sqrt{2}} \end{bmatrix}$. Find the C_n's, assemble Ψ, then find $P(p = +\frac{nh}{2L})$ and $P(p = -\frac{nh}{2L})$. Don't forget that little p stands for momentum. Also remember that $|C_n|^2 = C_n^{\star} C_n$ if C_n is an imaginary number.

There is a striking similarity between the quantum wave vector Ψ of equation (1034) and the ordinary unit vector $\frac{\vec{r}}{|\vec{r}|}$ that we used back in Chapters 1, 2, and 6. Figure 10.2 shows a picture of the two together.

Interpretation of the Operator

Let's forget for a moment that we actually used the $\overline{\Lambda}$ operator to obtain the eigen values and eigen vectors of Ψ, and ask ourselves what is the stated role of $\overline{\Lambda}$. Our Example 10.5 practice wavefunction turned out to be

$$\Psi = \frac{3}{\sqrt{10}} \begin{bmatrix} \frac{3}{\sqrt{10}} \\ \frac{1}{\sqrt{10}} \end{bmatrix} + \frac{1}{\sqrt{10}} \begin{bmatrix} \frac{1}{\sqrt{10}} \\ -\frac{3}{\sqrt{10}} \end{bmatrix} . \tag{1037}$$

The question that we want to answer is, "Once you have the eigen vector expansion for Ψ, what can you get from $\overline{\Lambda}$?" The answer goes like this: Equation (1009) stated that

$$\overline{\Lambda} \hat{\phi}_n = \lambda_n \hat{\phi}_n , \tag{1038}$$

where λ_n was a possible value of the observable being studied, and ϕ_n was one of the eigen vectors. So let's actually "operate" on one of the eigen vectors and see what happens. Since $\overline{\Lambda} = \begin{bmatrix} 2 & 3 \\ 3 & -6 \end{bmatrix}$, for $\overline{\Lambda}\hat{\phi}_1$ we will get

$$\overline{\Lambda}\hat{\phi}_1 = \begin{bmatrix} 2 & 3 \\ 3 & -6 \end{bmatrix} \begin{bmatrix} \frac{3}{\sqrt{10}} \\ \frac{1}{\sqrt{10}} \end{bmatrix}$$

$$
\begin{aligned}
&= \begin{bmatrix} 2\left(\frac{3}{\sqrt{10}}\right) + 3\left(\frac{1}{\sqrt{10}}\right) \\ 3\left(\frac{3}{\sqrt{10}}\right) + (-6)\left(\frac{1}{\sqrt{10}}\right) \end{bmatrix} \\
&= \begin{bmatrix} \frac{9}{\sqrt{10}} \\ \frac{3}{\sqrt{10}} \end{bmatrix}
\end{aligned}
$$

$$
\overline{\Lambda}\hat{\phi}_1 = (3)\begin{bmatrix} \frac{3}{\sqrt{10}} \\ \frac{1}{\sqrt{10}} \end{bmatrix} = \lambda_1\hat{\phi}_1 \,. \tag{1039}
$$

Equation (1039) reveals that λ_1, the possible value of the observable, equals 3. We already knew this from equation (1013), but here we are getting it from a direct operation on the eigen vector. And that's exactly what the operator is supposed to do. It "uncovers" the possible value of the observable that was "hidden" inside $\hat{\phi}$. (Figure 10.3)

Schrödinger's Cat

The quantum wave function Ψ consists of a summation, or "superposition", of probability coefficients times eigen vectors. Associated with each eigen vector is a definite possible value of the observable under consideration. So the eigen vectors are in some sense real *states* of the system. In other words, each eigen vector associates with a value that actually might come up when the measurement is taken. The Ψ vector however, blends together all of the different possible eigen states into a sort of ghostly hodge-podge, where the observable seems to take on all values, or parts of all values, at once. Only when the measurement is actually taken, is the Ψ function thought to "collapse" to one of its component eigen states.

Consider the Ψ vector from Example 10.3,

$$
\begin{aligned}
\Psi &= C_1\hat{\Phi}_1 + C_2\hat{\Phi}_2 \\
\Psi &= \frac{3}{\sqrt{10}}\begin{bmatrix} \frac{3}{\sqrt{10}} \\ \frac{1}{\sqrt{10}} \end{bmatrix} + \frac{1}{\sqrt{10}}\begin{bmatrix} \frac{1}{\sqrt{10}} \\ -\frac{3}{\sqrt{10}} \end{bmatrix} \,.
\end{aligned} \tag{1040}
$$

This Ψ, the Ψ that we calculated, really refers to the system before anybody looks at it (i.e.- before the measurement takes place). When somebody does look (when the measurement does take place), they will find that the observable takes on just a single value. Let's say they see -7 in this case. The eigen vector associated with -7 is Φ_2, so just as soon as we know that the observable $= -7$, the Ψ function has to collapse onto Φ_2.

$$
\begin{aligned}
\Psi_{before} &= \left(\frac{3}{\sqrt{10}}\right)\hat{\Phi}_1 + \left(\frac{1}{\sqrt{10}}\right)\hat{\Phi}_2 \\
&\xrightarrow{look} \text{find out } \lambda = -7 \\
\Psi_{after} &= (0)\hat{\Phi}_1 + (1)\hat{\Phi}_2 = (1)\begin{bmatrix} \frac{1}{\sqrt{10}} \\ -\frac{3}{\sqrt{10}} \end{bmatrix} \,.
\end{aligned} \tag{1041}
$$

Here the probability coefficient that used to be $\frac{1}{\sqrt{10}}$ has become 1. That happens because we are now 100 % certain that the observable is in the state described by $\hat{\Phi}_2$. So $|C_1|^2 + |C_2|^2 = 1$ becomes $(0)^2 + |C_2|^2 = 1$, which means $C_2 = 1$. (Figure 10.4)

None of this seems to make sense. How can an object be in a superposition of all possible states at once, then suddenly collapse into a single state just because it is measured? It sounds too weird to be true. Nevertheless, we human beings do not have any direct perception of the sub-atomic world where Quantum Mechanics is supposed to apply. For all we know, maybe it **is** appropriate to describe sub-atomic particles with a Ψ vector that is a superposition of all possible states. Serious misgivings occur however, if we try to apply Ψ to objects that we can see.

In a 1935 paper, Erwin Schrödinger, one of the founding fathers of Quantum Mechanics, had this to say. " One can even set up quite ridiculous cases. A cat is penned up in a steel chamber, along with the following diabolical device (which must be secured against direct interference by the cat.): in a Geiger counter there is a tiny bit of radioactive substance, *so* small, that *perhaps* in the course of one hour one of the atoms decays, but also, with equal probability, perhaps none; if it happens, the counter tube discharges and through a relay releases a hammer which shatters a small flask of hydrocyanic acid. If one has left this entire system to itself for an hour, one would say the cat still lives *if* meanwhile no atom has decayed. The first atomic decay would have poisoned it. The Ψ-function of the entire system would express this by having in it the living and the dead cat (pardon the expression) mixed or smeared out in equal parts."

Tongue in cheek, let's set up an operator to describe the condition of Schrödinger's cat. We'll call it the "Life & Death" operator,

$$L \,\&\, D = \begin{bmatrix} 0 & life \\ life & 0 \end{bmatrix} . \tag{1042}$$

The eigen values for this operator are found from,

$$\begin{aligned} (0-\lambda)(0-\lambda) - (life)(life) &= 0 \\ \lambda^2 - (life)^2 &= 0 \\ \lambda^2 &= (life)^2 \\ \lambda &= \pm\, life\,. \end{aligned} \tag{1043}$$

So that

$$\begin{aligned} \lambda_1 &= life \\ \lambda_2 &= -life \;=\; death\,. \end{aligned} \tag{1044}$$

For the eigen vector that goes with life,

$$\begin{bmatrix} 0 & life \\ life & 0 \end{bmatrix} \begin{bmatrix} A \\ B \end{bmatrix} = life \begin{bmatrix} A \\ B \end{bmatrix}$$

$$\begin{array}{rcl} life(B) & = & life(A) \\ life(A) & = & life(B) \end{array} \Rightarrow \begin{array}{rcl} A & = & 1 \\ B & = & 1 \end{array},$$

$$|\Phi_1| = \left\| \begin{bmatrix} 1 \\ 1 \end{bmatrix} \right\| = \sqrt{(1)^2 + (1)^2} = \sqrt{2}\,,$$

$$\lambda_1 = life \iff \hat{\Phi}_1 = \begin{bmatrix} \frac{1}{\sqrt{2}} \\ \frac{1}{\sqrt{2}} \end{bmatrix} . \tag{1045}$$

For the eigen vector that goes with death (= −life),

$$\begin{bmatrix} 0 & life \\ life & 0 \end{bmatrix} \begin{bmatrix} A \\ B \end{bmatrix} = -life \begin{bmatrix} A \\ B \end{bmatrix}$$

$$\begin{array}{rcl} life(B) & = & -life(A) \\ life(A) & = & -life(B) \end{array} \Rightarrow \begin{array}{rcl} A & = & 1 \\ B & = & -1 \end{array},$$

$$|\Phi_2| = \left\| \begin{bmatrix} 1 \\ -1 \end{bmatrix} \right\| = \sqrt{(1)^2 (-1)^2} = \sqrt{2}\,,$$

$$\lambda_2 = death \iff \hat{\Phi}_2 = \begin{bmatrix} \frac{1}{\sqrt{2}} \\ -\frac{1}{\sqrt{2}} \end{bmatrix} . \tag{1046}$$

Schrödinger tells us that there is an equal probability of decay, or no decay. So

$$|C_1|^2 = |C_2|^2\,. \tag{1047}$$

We also know that

$$|C_1|^2 + |C_2|^2 = 1\,. \tag{1048}$$

Solving equations (1044) and (1045) simultaneously, leads to

$$|C_1|^2 = |C_2|^2 = \frac{1}{2}\,. \tag{1049}$$

If we let

$$C_1 = C_2 = \frac{1}{\sqrt{2}}\,, \tag{1050}$$

then the assembled Ψ function would look like,

$$\Psi_{cat} = C_1 \hat{\Phi}_{life} + C_2 \hat{\Phi}_{death}$$

$$\Psi_{cat} = \frac{1}{\sqrt{2}} \begin{bmatrix} \frac{1}{\sqrt{2}} \\ \frac{1}{\sqrt{2}} \end{bmatrix} + \frac{1}{\sqrt{2}} \begin{bmatrix} \frac{1}{\sqrt{2}} \\ -\frac{1}{\sqrt{2}} \end{bmatrix} . \tag{1051}$$

Figure 10.5 shows a picture.

We would interpret Ψ_{cat} to mean that before we open the box,

$$P(cat\ is\ alive) = |C_1|^2 = \frac{1}{2}$$

$$P(cat\ is\ dead) = |C_2|^2 = \frac{1}{2}, \quad (1052)$$

which were the original conditions that Schrödinger set up.

Of course when we actually do open the box, we either find the cat alive, in which case Ψ_{cat} has collapsed to $\Psi_{cat} = (1)\hat{\Phi}_{life}$, or we find it dead, in which case Ψ_{cat} has collapsed to $\Psi_{cat} = (1)\hat{\Phi}_{death}$ (Figure 10.6). Those Ψ's make sense. What Schrödinger was talking about when he called this a "ridiculous case", was Ψ_{cat} before anybody looks in the box. Quamtum Mechanics seems to suggest that before anybody looks, the cat is somehow in a superposition of life and death - i.e. part alive and part dead (Figure 10.7).

That aspect of Quantum Mechanics - the idea that an observable can somehow be in a superposition of all possible values, then suddenly collapse onto just one value when it is measured - has been a persistent thorn in the side of the theorists almost from the beginning. The Copenhagen Interpretation and the Many Worlds Interpretation both attempt to explain how a single outcome can emerge from a multitude of potentialities. Neither one is very appealing. A more recent theory called Decoherence states that the object must always interact with it's environment (especially if the object is big). That way, it is the environment that sort of "measures" the observable into a collapsed state.

Whether or not Decoherence will finally explain Schrödinger's "measurement problem" remains to be seen. The problem itself is only troubling from a philosophical point of view however. From a practical point of view, it has never seemed to matter. Quantum Mechanics has been a very successful theory. The behaviors of solids, transistors, and lasers, the structure of DNA, and the colors of the stars are just a few of the phenomena that lend themselves to a Quantum Mechanical description.

Things to Remember

Relationships

$$E_{photon} = hf \qquad E_n \approx n(hf)$$

$$\Psi = C_1\hat{\Phi}_1 + C_2\hat{\Phi}_2 + ... + C_n\hat{\Phi}_n$$

$$\overline{\Lambda}\hat{\phi}_n = \lambda_n\hat{\phi}_n \qquad |C_n|^2 = C_n^{\star}C_n$$

$$C_n = \Psi \bullet \hat{\Phi}_n \qquad |C_1|^2 + |C_2|^2 + ... + |C_n|^2 = 1$$

$$P(observable = \lambda_n) = |C_n|^2$$

Constants and Conversions

$$h \approx 6.626 \times 10^{-34}\ Js$$

Homework Problems Chapter 10

10.1 How much energy is contained in one photon of 520 nm green light?

10.2 One photon of $5\times10^{14}\ H_z$ light contains $3.313\times10^{-19}\ J$ of energy. Use that information to calculate Planck's constant.

10.3 A spring-mass system oscillates at $1.13\ H_z$ with a total energy of $.16\ J$. How many quanta of energy does the system contain?

10.4 One particular spring-mass system contains 3×10^{32} energy quanta when it oscillates. What is the frequency of oscillation if the total energy is $.3\ J$?

10.5 Find the eigen values for $\overline{\Lambda}_{practice} = \begin{bmatrix} 2 & 6 \\ 6 & -3 \end{bmatrix}$.

10.6 Find the eigen values for the Pauli matrix, $\sigma_y = \begin{pmatrix} 0 & -i \\ i & 0 \end{pmatrix}$.

10.7 Find the eigen vectors for $\overline{\Lambda}_{practice} = \begin{bmatrix} 2 & 6 \\ 6 & -3 \end{bmatrix}$. Normalize and check to make sure that the normalized vectors are orthogonal.

10.8 Your answer to HW 10.6 should have been $\lambda_1 = 1,\ \lambda_2 = -1$. Use those values to find the eigen vectors for $\sigma_y = \begin{pmatrix} 0 & -i \\ i & 0 \end{pmatrix}$. Normalize and check for orthogonality. Remember $|\Phi| = \sqrt{\Phi^* \bullet \Phi}$. Also, when the $\hat{\Phi}$'s have imaginary components, the test for orthogonality is $\hat{\Phi}_1^* \bullet \hat{\Phi}_2 = 0$.

10.9 If the wave function for $\overline{\Lambda}_{practice} = \begin{bmatrix} 2 & 6 \\ 6 & -3 \end{bmatrix}$ is $\Psi = \begin{bmatrix} 12/13 \\ -5/13 \end{bmatrix}$, find $P(\lambda{=}6)$ and $P(\lambda{=}-7)$.

10.10 Assemble the eigen vector expansion for Ψ from 10.9. Look at the right hand side of the equation. Multiply in the C's. Then add the two vectors together using the fact that

$$\begin{bmatrix} A \\ B \end{bmatrix} + \begin{bmatrix} C \\ D \end{bmatrix} = \begin{bmatrix} A+C \\ B+D \end{bmatrix}.$$

The idea is to make sure that the right side really does $= \begin{bmatrix} 12/13 \\ -5/13 \end{bmatrix}$.

Recommended:

Given $\overline{\Lambda}_{practice} = \begin{bmatrix} 2 & 2 \\ 2 & -1 \end{bmatrix}$, and $\Psi = \begin{bmatrix} 3/5 \\ 4/5 \end{bmatrix}$, verify the following expansion:

$$\begin{bmatrix} 3/5 \\ 4/5 \end{bmatrix} = 2/\sqrt{5} \begin{bmatrix} 2/\sqrt{5} \\ 1/\sqrt{5} \end{bmatrix} - 1/\sqrt{5} \begin{bmatrix} 1/\sqrt{5} \\ -2/\sqrt{5} \end{bmatrix} \qquad \begin{matrix} P(\lambda = 3) = .8 \\ P(\lambda = -2) = .2 \end{matrix}$$

(i.e. – Find the eigen values. Find & check the normalized eigen vectors, Find & check the probability coefficients, etc.)

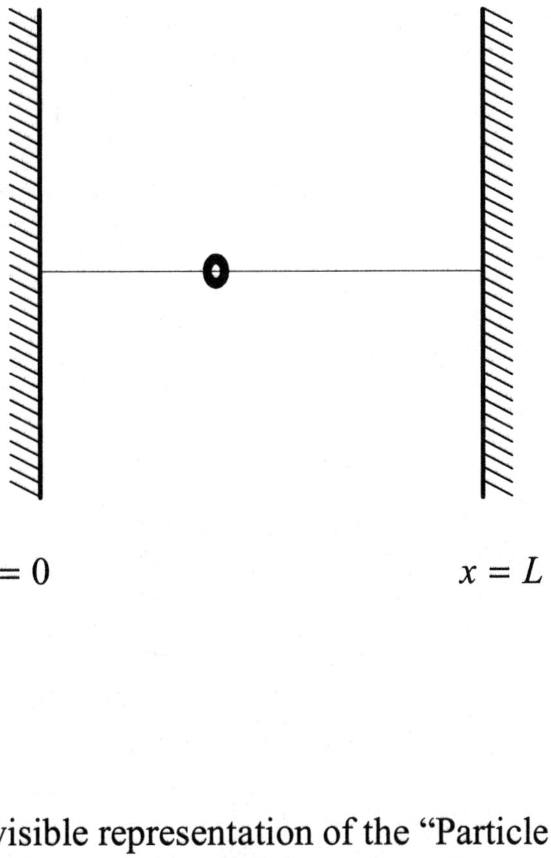

Figure 10.1 A visible representation of the "Particle in a Box" could be a very small bead, traveling back and forth along the x axis between $x = 0$ and $x = L$.

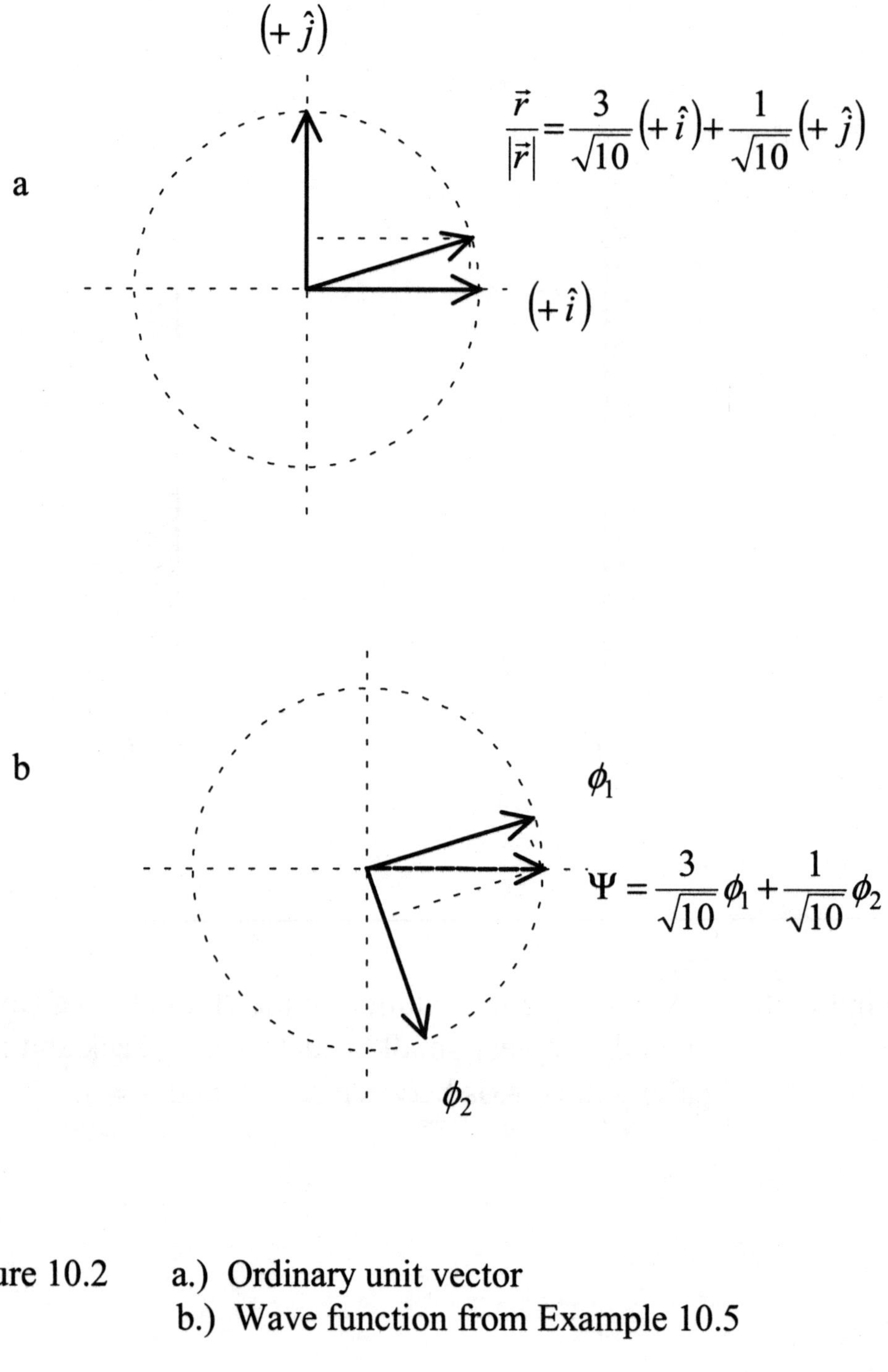

Figure 10.2 a.) Ordinary unit vector
b.) Wave function from Example 10.5

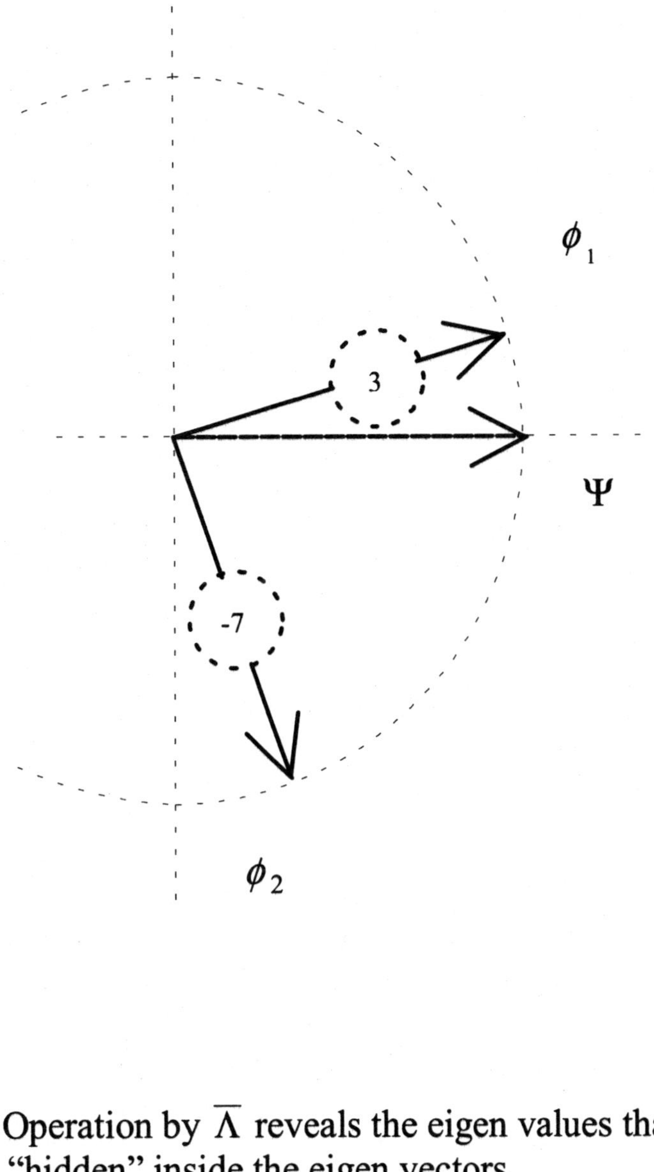

Figure 10.3 Operation by $\overline{\Lambda}$ reveals the eigen values that were "hidden" inside the eigen vectors.

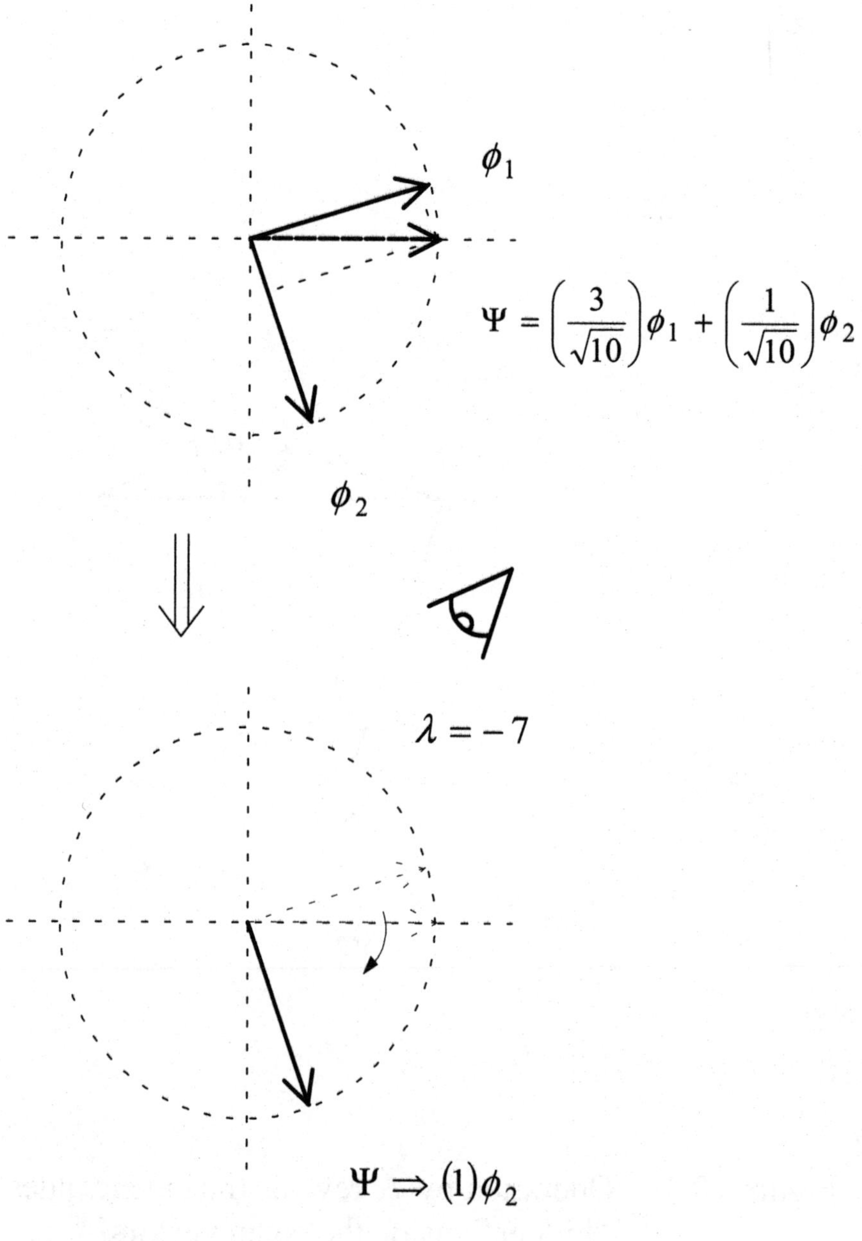

Figure 10.4 The wavefunction Ψ is thought to collapse onto one of its eigen vectors just as soon as the measurement is taken.

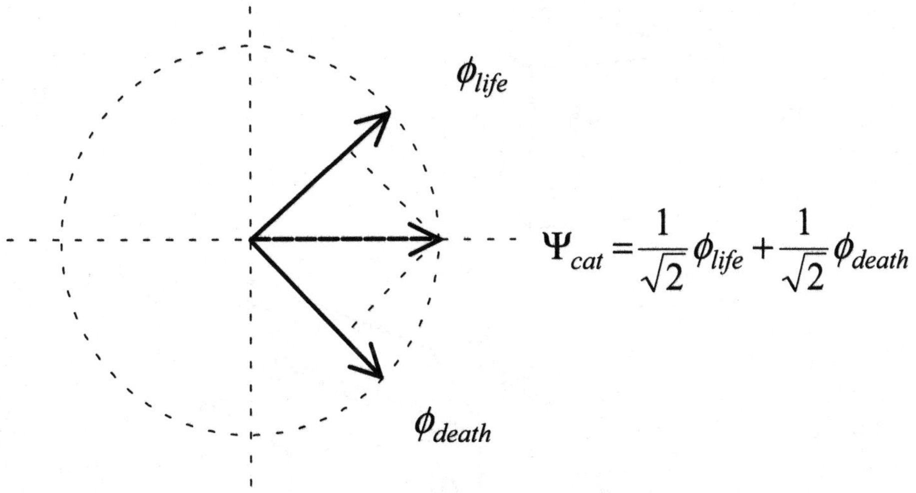

Figure 10.5 Wave function for Schrödinger's cat

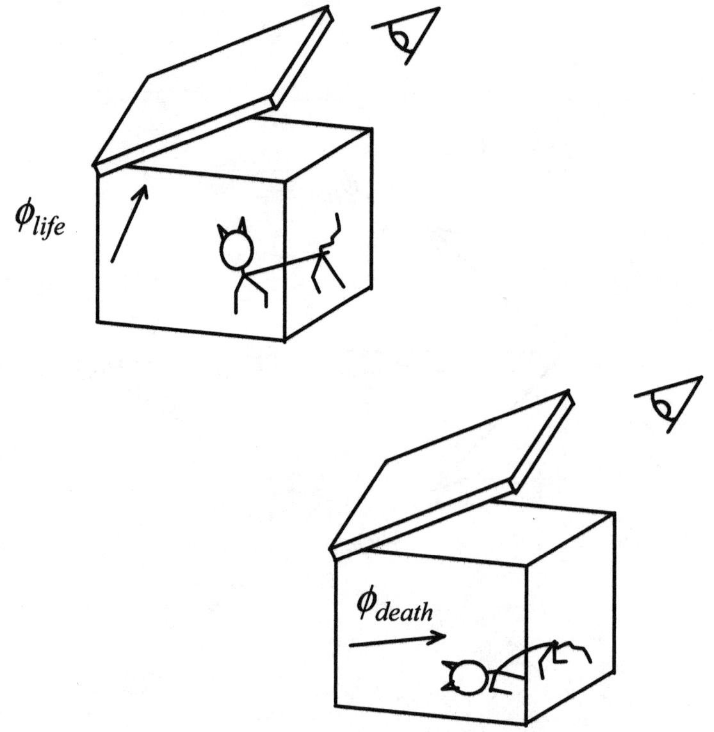

Figure 10.6 When the box is opened, Ψ_{cat} must collapse into either ϕ_{life} or ϕ_{death}.

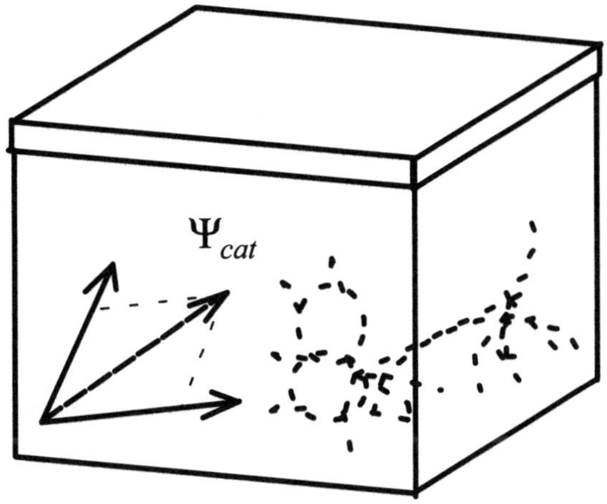

Figure 10.7 Before the box is opened, Schrödinger implies that Quantum Mechanics calls for the cat to be part alive, and part dead.

Chapter 11 - Light

Timeline

450 BC The Greek philosopher Empedocles talks about a fire iside the eye, shinning out like a lantern and giving rise to sight.

300 BC Euclid of Alexandria writes that seeing takes place because of straight line rays that emanate from the eyes and enclose the object in a cone. He also uses the Law of Reflection in his *Optics* textbook.

55 BC The Roman poet Lucretius writes about light from the sun being composed of particles.

1020 Contrary to Euclid, the Arab mathematician Alhazen suggests that seeing takes place because straight line rays of light are reflected from an object into the eye.

1621 Willebrord Snell, a Dutch lawyer and mathematician, discovers the Law of Refraction (Snell's Law).

1637 French philosopher and scientist Rene Descartes proposes that light is like a pulse traveling through an elastic medium. (Descartes' pulse is not periodic, so his idea is almost, but not quite, a wave theory of light.)

1663 After a series of experiments, Italian physics professor Francesco Grimaldi concludes that light is actually a wave.

1676 The Danish astronomer Ole Romer demonstrates that the speed of light is not infinite.

1678 Dutch scientist Christiaan Huygens publishes a wave theory of light.

1704 English scientist Issac Newton publishes a particle theory of light.

1802 Thomas Young, an English physicist, obtains strong experimental evidence that light behaves like a wave.

1850 The French scientists A.H.L. Fizeau and J.B.L. Focault measure the speed of light in water to be less than the speed of light in air.

1864 Scottish mathematician James Clerk Maxwell predicts the existence of electromagnetic waves, and proposes that light itself is an electromagnetic wave.

1888 Heinrich Hertz. a German physics professor, actually produces electromagnetic waves in the laboratory. (The age old wave-particle controversy of light seemed to be settled in favor of waves.)

1905 Albert Einstein's explanation of the photoelectric effect reopens the wave-particle issue by introducing a quantized, "particle-like" aspect of light.

1926 American chemist Gilbert Lewis coins the name 'photon', which is eventually applied to Einstein's light quanta.

1970's The results of several experiments suggest the existence of photons, but there is disagreement about whether or not the evidence is conclusive.

1986 French physicists P. Grangier, G. Roger, and A. Aspect unambiguously demonstrate that individual photons do exist.

TEXT

Human beings cannot see light. We see objects that are illuminated by light, but light itself is invisible to us. Interplanetary space for example, is full of light from the sun. But when it is empty, that space appears to be jet black. The sun's light does not reveal itself until it strikes a physical object. Because we cannot see light, it is hard to tell just what light really is.

We do know some things, and one of them is that light travels fast through outer space. Its speed through a vacuum is close to $3 \times 10^8 \ \frac{m}{s}$. The Earth's atmosphere doesn't slow it down very much. You can use that same vacuum speed for air. Light does however, slow down when it travels through substances that are more dense. The index of refraction, n, is defined as the speed of light in air, divided by the speed of light in the medium.

$$n = \frac{c}{v} \, , \tag{1101}$$

where c is the speed of light in air, and v is its speed in the medium. (Notice that the $\frac{m}{s}$ in the numerator and the $\frac{m}{s}$ in the denominator cancel so that n does not have units.)

The speed of light through a certain type of glass for example might be $v = 1.875 \times 10^8 \ \frac{m}{s}$. In that case,

$$n = \frac{c}{v} = \frac{3 \times 10^8 \frac{m}{s}}{1.875 \times 10^8 \frac{m}{s}} = 1.60 \, . \tag{1102}$$

So the index of refraction for that type of glass would be $n = 1.60$.

Usually the index of refraction for the medium is the quanity that's given, and the speed of light in the medium is the quanity that is calculated. Equation (1101) would then rearrange into

$$v = \frac{c}{n} \, . \tag{1103}$$

Light as a Ray

Right now, look at the period at the end of this sentence. Imagine a straight line through space connecting your eye to that period. It's almost as though a single ray of light traveled straight from that point into your eye so that you could see the point. The Law of Reflection, and the Law of Refraction are both conveniently described in terms of straight line light rays.

Figure 11.1 shows an interface between air on the top, and water on the bottom. An incoming ray of light is "incident" on the air-water interface from the air side. A dotted line is drawn normal (perpendicular) to the interface, and the incoming ray makes an angle θ_1 with the normal. Experience tells us that part of the incoming ray will be reflected, and part will go on through, which is called being refracted. (After it rains for example, you can easily see through to the bottoms of the puddles that form in the street, but you can also see the houses and trees reflected from the tops of those puddles.)

The Law of Reflection tells us that the reflected ray and the incident ray make equal angles with the normal. If θ_1' is the angle of the reflected ray then:

$$\text{Law of Reflection} \qquad \theta_1 = \theta_1' \,.$$

The Law of Refraction, which most people call Snell's Law, is also written in terms of angles that are measured to the normal. It is however a little more complicated. If θ_2 is the angle that the refracted ray makes with the normal then:

$$\text{Law of Refraction (Snell's Law)} \qquad n_1 \sin(\theta_1) = n_2 \sin(\theta_2) \,,$$

where the two n's are the two indices of refraction.

Example 11.1

A light ray traveling through a medium whose index of refraction is 1.26 enters another medium whose index of refraction is 1.49. If the ray makes an angle to the normal of 37° in the 1.49 medium, what is its angle to the normal in the 1.26 medium?

Solution 11.1

Mostly this is a straight plug-in to Snell's Law. The only trick is to keep the n's and θ's straight, and for that you need to draw a picture. Figure 11.2 shows the interface between the 2 media. (This time the interface is vertical.)

The light ray comes in from the $n = 1.26$ side, and the 37° angle is on the $n = 1.49$ side. That means,

$$n_1 \sin(\theta_1) = n_2 \sin(\theta_2)$$

$$\begin{aligned}
(1.26)\sin(\theta_1) &= (1.49)\sin(37^o) \\
\sin(\theta_1) &\approx \frac{(1.49)(.601815)}{(1.26)} \\
\sin(\theta_1) &\approx .7116701 \\
\theta_1 &\approx \sin^{-1}(.7116701) \\
\theta_1 &\approx 45.37^o\ .
\end{aligned} \tag{1104}$$

Note: $\sin^{-1}(.7116701)$ stands for the *inverse sine* of (.7116701), and it means, "the angle whose sine is .7116701". On most calculators, you find it by entering .7116701, then hitting 2nd function, then sin. (Make sure that you are in degree mode.)

It is easy to check the calculation part of equation (1104). We just need to ask,

$$\begin{aligned}
\text{Is}\quad n_1\sin(\theta_1) &= n_2\sin(\theta_2)\ ? \\
(1.26)\sin(45.37^o) &= (1.49)\sin(37^o) \\
(1.26)(.7116583) &= (1.49)(.601815) \\
.89669 &\approx .8967
\end{aligned} \tag{1105}$$

Of course equation (1105) just gives us a check on the numbers. It does not tell us whether or not the problem was set up right to begin with.

Quiz 11.1 A light ray travels through the wall of a plastic aquarium into the $n = 1.33$ water inside. In the plastic it makes an angle of 23° with the normal. In the water it makes an angle of 26.9^o with the normal. What is the speed of the light in the plastic?

The straight-line ray picture of light is also useful for determining characteristics of the image formed by a lens or by a curved mirror. For example, consider the converging lens shown in Figure 11.3. Mirrors and lenses use reflection and refraction to direct incoming light rays to a single point. That point is called the focal point, and a symmetric converging lens like the one in Figure 11.3, would have two equidistant focal points, one on either side of the lens.

Light entering the Figure 11.3 lens would actually be refracted twice, once when it goes into the lens, and once again when it comes out. It can be hard to draw that double refraction, so ray tracing typically makes use of a "thin lens approximation." In the thin lens approximation, you draw the lens fat (so everyone can tell that it's a lens), but you do the ray tracing as if the entire lens was contained in the center-line. That way there is only one refraction for each incoming ray.

Ray tracing involves following 3 rules. We will illustrate them by way of example.

Example 11.2

Determine the 2 characteristics, orientation and relative size, of the image formed by the lens shown in Figure 11.4. (In other words, is the image erect or inverted? And is the image same size, larger, or smaller?)

Solution 11.2

For a converging lens: Ray one is drawn from the top of the object to the center-line, parallel to the optic axis. From the center-line, it is drawn straight through the far focal point. (Figure 11.5.)

Ray two is drawn from the top of the object straight through the center of the lens, and it keeps right on going. (Figure 11.6.)

Ray three is drawn from the top of the object through the focal point on the same side of the lens, to the center-line. It is then refracted so that it emerges from the lens parallel to the optic axis. (Figure 11.7.)

If the drawing was done carefully and the picture is accurate, the 3 rays should all intersect at the same point. The image is now drawn with its top (the arrowhead) at the point where the rays intersect, and its bottom perpendicular to and touching the optic axis. (Figure 11.8.) Inspection reveals that the image is smaller than the object, and that it is inverted with respect to the object. The image is not inverted because it is pointing down. It is inverted because its arrowhead (top) points in the opposite direction as the arrowhead on the object.

Actually the image could have been drawn back in Figure 11.6 after the first 2 rays were in place. But there is a reason that we need the rules for all 3 rays, instead of just rules for 2 rays. Depending on where the object is located along the optic axis, it might not be possible to draw all 3 rays. Usually however you can draw at least 2 of the rays if you know the rules for all 3. So you try to draw all 3, but if one of them doesn't work, you use the other 2.

Quiz 11.2 Use ray tracing to determine the 2 characteristics of the image formed by the lens shown in Figure 11.9. (Trace 11.9 onto your paper, so that you maintain the correct proportions. Then use the edge of a different sheet of paper to measure the height of the image and to draw lines.)

Light as a Wave

Early scientists imagined light to be a stream of particles. That idea fit very well into the straight-line ray representation (Figure 11.10). In 1637 however, Rene Descartes pointed out that a blind man senses objects by tapping with his cane. The vibration from the tap travels down the cane to the blind man's hand, and that is how he knows the object is there. Descartes hypothesized that light might somehow be like the vibration in the cane. Objects are seen because some kind of a pulse travels from the object to the eye.

Descartes idea eventually developed into a wave theory of light. Figure 11.11 shows a top view of water waves moving away from a stone that has been dropped into a pond. Figure 11.12 shows a side view of the same thing. In this case it is the water that is doing the "waving". As time went on, many experiments seemed to support the wave theory of light, but the question always remained, "What was doing the waving?" If light is a wave, what is it a wave of?

That question was answered by James Clerk Maxwell, a brilliant Scottish scientist working in the mid 1800's. Maxwell had collected all of the then-known facts about electricity and magnetism. He assembled them into a consistent set of 4 equations. By substituting one equation into another, Maxwell predicted that electric and magnetic fields, coupled together, could travel through space as "electromagnetic" waves. The speed of those waves turned out to be c, the speed of light. Because an electromagnetic wave travels at the speed of light, and a light wave travels at the speed of light, Maxwell concluded that light actually is an electromagnetic wave. (In today's terms, Maxwell would say that a light wave is the same thing as a radio wave, except that it has a much higher frequency.)

Electromagnetic waves can take on many forms, but a sinusoidal representation for a wave far from it's source, and traveling through free space in the $+x$ direction, might look like,

$$\vec{E} = |\vec{E}_{max}| \sin(kx - \omega t)(+\hat{j}) \; , \tag{1106}$$

and

$$\vec{B} = |\vec{B}_{max}| \sin(kx - \omega t)(+\hat{k}) \; . \tag{1107}$$

Here $\vec{E}$ represents the electric field, and $|\vec{E}_{max}|$ is its maximum strength, while $\vec{B}$ is the accompanying magnetic field, with its maximum strength of $|\vec{B}_{max}|$. Figure 11.13 attempts a picture.

Maxwell's equations also predict that

$$|\vec{E}_{max}| = c|\vec{B}_{max}| \tag{1108}$$

where c is the speed of light. Let's look at the units of equation 1108 to see if they work out right.

$$\begin{aligned} |\vec{E}_{max}| &\rightarrow \left(\frac{m}{s}\right)\left(\frac{N}{A\,m}\right) \rightarrow \left(\frac{1}{s}\right)\left(\frac{N}{\frac{C}{s}}\right) \\ &\rightarrow \left(\frac{1}{s}\right)\left(\frac{N\,s}{C}\right) \rightarrow \frac{N}{C} \end{aligned}$$

An electric field should have units of Newtons per Coulomb, and $|\vec{E}_{max}|$ does, so the units look OK.

When the wave is far from its source, the electric and magnetic fields are usually perpendicular to each other. Figure 11.13 shows a Maxwell-style light wave (i.e.- an electromagnetic wave) traveling through space.

The intensity, or power per unit area, of an electromagnetic wave is defined to be,

$$I = \frac{1}{2}\epsilon_o c|\vec{E}_{max}|^2 \ , \tag{1109}$$

where $\epsilon_o \approx 8.85 \times 10^{-12} \frac{C^2}{N\,m^2}$ is the permittivity of free space, and c is the speed of light.

Let's look at the units.

$$\begin{aligned} I &\rightarrow \left(\frac{C^2}{N\,m^2}\right)\left(\frac{m}{s}\right)\left(\frac{N^2}{C^2}\right) \\ &\rightarrow \left(\frac{N\,m}{s}\right)\left(\frac{1}{m^2}\right) \rightarrow \left(\frac{J}{s}\right)\left(\frac{1}{m^2}\right) \end{aligned}$$

One Joule (J) is a unit of energy equivalent to 1 Newton-meter ($N\ m$). One Joule per second $\left(\frac{J}{s}\right)$ is a unit of power called a Watt (W). You might see for example, the electric energy that you use every month expressed as 24 kilowatt hours on your electric bill. Power multiplied by time equals energy. In this case

$$\begin{aligned} 24\ kW\ hr &= 24\left(\frac{kW}{1}\right)\left(\frac{1000\ W}{kW}\right) hr = 24000\ W\ hr \\ 24000\ W\ hr &= 24000\left(\frac{J}{s}\right)\left(\frac{hr}{1}\right)\left(\frac{60\ min}{hr}\right)\left(\frac{60\ s}{min}\right) \\ &= 86.4 \times 10^6\left(\frac{J}{s}\right)\left(\frac{s}{1}\right) = 86.4 \times 10^6\ J\ . \end{aligned}$$

So 24 kilowatt hours equals 86.4 million Joules, a lot of energy.

Back to the units on intensity.

$$I \rightarrow \left(\frac{J}{s}\right)\left(\frac{1}{m^2}\right) \rightarrow \frac{W}{m^2} \tag{1110}$$

Intensity is measured in Watts per meter squared, power divided by area. The intensity of the incoming light is a good thing to know if you are trying to convert light into electricity using a panel of solar cells. You need to know how much power per square meter is available from the light, and that is just what intensity gives you.

Example 11.3

Solve equation (1109) for $|\vec{E}_{max}|$, and carry out a unit analysis to verify that the units are correct.

Solution 11.3

Solving for $|\vec{E}_{max}|$ is easy enough.

$$\begin{aligned} I &= \frac{1}{2}\epsilon_o c|\vec{E}_{max}|^2 \\ |\vec{E}_{max}|^2 &= \frac{2I}{\epsilon_o c} \\ |\vec{E}_{max}| &= \sqrt{\frac{2I}{\epsilon_o c}} \end{aligned} \tag{1111}$$

The unit analysis is a little more complicated.

$$\begin{aligned} |\vec{E}_{max}| &\rightarrow \sqrt{\frac{\frac{W}{m^2}}{\left(\frac{C^2}{N\,m^2}\right)\left(\frac{m}{s}\right)}} \rightarrow \sqrt{\left(\frac{W}{m^2}\right)\left(\frac{N\,m^2}{C^2}\right)\left(\frac{s}{m}\right)} \\ &\rightarrow \sqrt{W\left(\frac{N}{C^2}\right)\left(\frac{s}{m}\right)} \rightarrow \sqrt{\left(\frac{J}{s}\right)\left(\frac{N}{C^2}\right)\left(\frac{s}{m}\right)} \\ &\rightarrow \sqrt{\left(\frac{N\,m}{1}\right)\left(\frac{N}{C^2}\right)\left(\frac{1}{m}\right)} \rightarrow \sqrt{\frac{N^2}{C^2}} \\ |\vec{E}_{max}| &\rightarrow \frac{N}{C} \end{aligned}$$

But eventually it turns out OK.

Quiz 11.3 Intensity can also be expressed in terms of the maximum magnetic field, $I = \frac{c}{2\mu_o}|\vec{B}_{max}|^2$. Solve for $|\vec{B}_{max}|$ and include a unit analysis. (Remember that the magnetic field has units of Teslas $\rightarrow \frac{N}{A\,m}$.)

One very satisfying aspect of the "light is an electromagnetic wave" hypothesis is the way in which it explains color. Different colors are associated with different frequencies. And since $v = \lambda f = c$, different frequencies mean different wavelengths. Individual colors exist in a narrow range of wavelengths centered roughly around

$420\ nm$ for violet,
$460\ nm$ for blue,
$520\ nm$ for green,
$575\ nm$ for yellow,
$610\ nm$ for orange,
and
$665\ nm$ for red.

(One nano meter is $1 \times 10^{-9}m$, so that $420\ nm = 420 \times 10^{-9}m$.)

The entire range of visible light only goes from about $400\ nm$ to about $700\ nm$. Visible light is just a small part of the much larger electromagnetic spectrum, which includes wavelengths of more than $10{,}000{,}000{,}000\ nm$ to wavelengths of less than $.0001\ nm$. Figure 11.14 shows a picture.

Example 11.4

A beam of blue light has an intensity of 4 $\frac{kW}{m^2}$. Write down an expression for the magnitude of the magnetic field.

Solution 11.4

Equation (1107) states that

$$\vec{B} = |\vec{B}_{max}| \sin(kx - \omega t)(+\hat{k}) ,$$

so that

$$|\vec{B}| = ||\vec{B}_{max}| \sin(kx - \omega t)| . \tag{1112}$$

In order to specify $|\vec{B}|$ for example 11.4, we will need to find $|\vec{B}_{max}|$, k, and ω. From quiz 11.3

$$\begin{aligned} I &= \frac{c}{2\mu_o}|\vec{B}_{max}|^2 \\ |\vec{B}_{max}| &= \sqrt{\frac{2\mu_o I}{c}} \end{aligned} \tag{1113}$$

Let's look at the units. We are expectiing Teslas $\left(T = \frac{N}{A\,m}\right)$.

$$\begin{aligned} |\vec{B}_{max}| &\rightarrow \sqrt{\frac{\left(\frac{N}{A^2}\right)\left(\frac{W}{m^2}\right)}{\left(\frac{m}{s}\right)}} \rightarrow \sqrt{\left(\frac{N}{A^2}\right)\left(\frac{W}{m^2}\right)\left(\frac{s}{m}\right)} \\ &\rightarrow \sqrt{\left(\frac{N}{A^2}\right)\left(\frac{\frac{J}{s}}{m^2}\right)\left(\frac{s}{m}\right)} \rightarrow \sqrt{\left(\frac{N}{A^2}\right)\left(\frac{J}{s\,m^2}\right)\left(\frac{s}{m}\right)} \\ &\rightarrow \sqrt{\left(\frac{N}{A^2}\right)\left(\frac{N\,m}{m^2}\right)\left(\frac{1}{m}\right)} \rightarrow \sqrt{\frac{N^2}{A^2\,m^2}} \\ |\vec{B}_{max}| &\rightarrow \frac{N}{A\,m} \rightarrow T \end{aligned}$$

So the units look OK. (Providing that we 1st convert our intensity into $\frac{W}{m^2}$ from $\frac{kW}{m^2}$; $I = 4\,\frac{kW}{m^2} = 4000\,\frac{W}{m^2}$.) And

$$\begin{aligned} |\vec{B}_{max}| &= \sqrt{\frac{2\mu_o I}{c}} = \left[\sqrt{\frac{2(4\pi \times 10^{-7})(4000)}{3 \times 10^8}}\right] T \\ |\vec{B}_{max}| &\approx 5.79 \times 10^{-6}\,T . \end{aligned} \tag{1114}$$

The wave number k was defined in Chapter 5 as

$$k = \frac{2\pi}{\lambda} , \tag{1115}$$

where λ is the wavelength in meters. For blue light

$$\lambda \approx 460\ nm = 460 \times 10^{-9}\ m\ ,$$

so that

$$k = \frac{2\pi\ radians}{460 \times 10^{-9}\ m} \approx 1.366 \times 10^{7}\ \frac{rad}{m} \tag{1116}$$

The radian frequency, ω can be found from $c = \lambda f$ and $\omega = 2\pi f$.

$$\begin{aligned}
c &= \lambda f \\
f &= \frac{c}{\lambda} \\
\omega &= 2\pi f = 2\pi\left(\frac{c}{\lambda}\right) \\
&= 2\pi\ radians\left(\frac{3 \times 10^{8}\frac{m}{s}}{460 \times 10^{-9} m}\right) \\
&= 2\pi\left(\frac{3 \times 10^{8}}{460 \times 10^{-9}}\right)\left(\frac{rad}{m}\right)\left(\frac{m}{s}\right) \\
\omega &\approx 4.098 \times 10^{15}\ \frac{rad}{s}
\end{aligned} \tag{1117}$$

Substituting the results of equations (1114), (1116), and (1117) into the expression for the magnitude of $\vec{B}$ we obtain

$$\begin{aligned}
|\vec{B}| &= ||\vec{B}_{max}|\sin(kx - \omega t)| \\
|\vec{B}| &\approx |(5.79 \times 10^{-6}\ T)\sin[(1.366 \times 10^{7})x - (4.098 \times 10^{15})t]|
\end{aligned} \tag{1118}$$

Note that there are no units associated with the sine function, so the units of $|\vec{B}|$ are the same as the units of $|\vec{B}_{max}|$. You should also notice that a Maxwell-style electromagnetic light wave has an extremely small $|\vec{B}|$, a very very short wavelength (λ), and both ω and f are very very high frequencies.

Quiz 11.4 The intensity of yellow sunlight before it passes through the earth's atmosphere is about 1.4 $\frac{kW}{m^2}$. Write down an expression for the strength of the electric field.

Photons

James Maxwell's conception of light as an electromagnetic wave dominated physics in the last half of the 19th century, and even today we still talk about light propagating as an electromagnetic wave. But the 'purely a wave' concept of light received a serious challenge with Albert Einstein's 1905 explanation of the photoelectric effect.

The photoelectric effect was discovered accidentally by Heinrich Hertz in 1887. It works this way: If you shine low frequency light on a metallic surface, nothing happens. If you increase the intensity of the light, still nothing happens. But if you increase the frequency of the light, instead of the intensity, electrons will be "knocked out" of the metal. Figure 11.15 shows a picture.

In order to explain the photoelectric effect, Einstein proposed that light consists of mutually independent energy quanta of magnitude hf, where f is the frequency of the light, and h is Planck's constant (Figure 11.16). One of the incoming light-quanta gives all of its energy to a single electron inside the metal. The electron is being held in the metal by an amount of energy, Φ. If the energy that the electron receives from the photon is is less than Φ, then nothing happens. But if the energy received by the electron is more than Φ, then the electron can come out of the metal with a maximum kinetic energy equal to

$$(KE)_{max} = hf - \Phi \; . \tag{1119}$$

Because the electron might lose some energy on the way out, $(KE)_{max}$ represents the maximum kinetic energy with which the electron could emerge. The energy of the incoming light quanta is given by hf. And Φ is the "work function" of the particular metal, where work function is a term that describes the amount of energy necessary for an electron to escape. (If $hf < \Phi$, the electron does not come out.)

The kinetic energy of subatomic particles is generally very small, and for that reason it is usually expressed in electron-volts (eV) instead of Joules (J). One electron-volt is the amount of kinetic energy acquired by an electron that has been accelerated by 1 volt of electric potential difference. The conversion factor is

$$1 \; eV = 1.60 \times 10^{-19} \; J \; . \tag{1120}$$

Example 11.5

Ultraviolet light with a wavelength of 150 nm falls on a chromium surface (work function = 4.37 eV). If electrons can emerge, what is their maxium possible speed?

Solution 11.5

First let's determine whether or not electrons will come out. We need to answer the question. "Is $hf > \Phi$? From $v = \lambda f = c$,

$$\begin{aligned} c &= \lambda f \\ f &= \frac{c}{\lambda} = \frac{3 \times 10^8 \frac{m}{s}}{150 \times 10^{-9} m} \\ &= 2 \times 10^{15} \left(\frac{m}{s}\right)\left(\frac{1}{m}\right) \\ f &= 2 \times 10^{15} \; \frac{1}{s} \end{aligned} \tag{1121}$$

The energy of the incoming photon is given by

$$\begin{aligned} hf &= (6.626 \times 10^{-34} \; J \; s)\left(2 \times 10^{15} \; \frac{1}{s}\right) \\ &= 1.3252 \times 10^{-18} \; J \; . \end{aligned} \tag{1122}$$

The work function converts to Joules as

$$\Phi = 4.37\ eV \left(\frac{1.6 \times 10^{-19}\ J}{1\ eV}\right) = 6.992 \times 10^{-19}\ J\ . \tag{1123}$$

It looks like hf is $> \Phi$, so electrons will emerge.

In order to find the maximum velocity we can use

$$(KE)_{max} = \frac{1}{2} m_e v_{max}^2\ , \tag{1124}$$

where m_e is the mass of an electron ($m_e \approx 9.11 \times 10^{-31}\ kg$). Solving for v_{max},

$$\begin{aligned} (KE)_{max} &= \frac{1}{2} m_e v_{max}^2 \\ m_e v_{max}^2 &= 2(KE)_{max} \\ v_{max} &= \sqrt{\frac{2(KE)_{max}}{m_e}}\ . \end{aligned} \tag{1125}$$

Let's look at the units.

$$\begin{aligned} v_{max} &\rightarrow \sqrt{\frac{J}{kg}} \rightarrow \sqrt{\frac{N\,m}{kg}} \\ &\rightarrow \sqrt{\left(\frac{kg\ m}{s^2}\right)\left(\frac{m}{kg}\right)} \rightarrow \sqrt{\frac{m^2}{s^2}} \\ &\rightarrow \frac{m}{s} \end{aligned}$$

The units look OK, so the next step is to find $(KE)_{max} = hf - \Phi$. Using the results of equations (1122) and (1123),

$$\begin{aligned} (KE)_{max} &= hf - \Phi \\ &= (1.3252 \times 10^{-18}\ J) - (6.992 \times 10^{-19}\ J) \\ (KE)_{max} &= 6.26 \times 10^{-19}\ J\ . \end{aligned} \tag{1126}$$

Substituting $(KE)_{max}$ into equation (1125), and remembering that we have already done the units,

$$\begin{aligned} v_{max} &= \sqrt{\frac{2(KE)_{max}}{m_e}} \\ &= \left[\sqrt{\frac{2(6.26 \times 10^{-19})}{9.11 \times 10^{-31}}}\right] \frac{m}{s} \\ v_{max} &\approx 1.17 \times 10^6\ \frac{m}{s} \end{aligned} \tag{1127}$$

Quiz 11.5 If $hf > \Phi$, electrons will come out of the metal. If $hf < \Phi$, electrons will not come out of the metal. The dividing point is called the cut off frequency, and it is found by letting $(KE)_{max} = 0$ in equation (1119). Find the cut off frequency for cesium ($\Phi = 1.91\ eV$).

Right now, the propagation of light, how it travels long distances, is best described in terms of Maxwell's electromagnetic wave theory. But the emission and absorption of light, how it comes into being and how it goes away, are best described in terms of Einstein's photons. We do not yet have a clear understanding of the exact nature of light and the way in which our two existing pictures are supposed to fit together.

Things to Remember

Relationships

$$n = \frac{c}{v}$$

$$\theta_1' = \theta_1 \qquad n_1 \sin(\theta_1) = n_2 \sin(\theta_2)$$

$$|\vec{E}| = ||\vec{E}_{max}| \sin(kx - \omega t)|$$
$$|\vec{B}| = ||\vec{B}_{max}| \sin(kx - \omega t)|$$
$$|\vec{E}_{max}| = c|\vec{B}_{max}|$$

$$k = \frac{2\pi}{\lambda} \qquad c = \lambda f \qquad \omega = 2\pi f$$

$$I = \frac{1}{2}\epsilon_o c|\vec{E}_{max}|^2 \qquad I = \frac{c}{2\mu_o}|\vec{B}_{max}|^2$$

$$(KE)_{max} = hf - \Phi$$

Units

$$n \rightarrow no \;\; units$$

$$\vec{E} \rightarrow \frac{N}{C} \qquad \vec{B} \rightarrow T = \frac{N}{A\,m}$$

$$\text{Power} \rightarrow W = \frac{J}{s} \qquad I \rightarrow \frac{W}{m^2} \qquad J = N\,m$$

Constants and Conversions

$$1\ eV = 1.60 \times 10^{-19}\ J \qquad c = 3 \times 10^8\ \frac{m}{s}$$

$$\epsilon_o \approx 8.85 \times 10^{-12}\ \frac{C^2}{Nm^2} \qquad \mu_o = 4\pi \times 10^{-7}\ \frac{N}{A^2}$$

$$h \approx 6.626 \times 10^{-34}\ J\ s$$

$$m_e \approx 9.11 \times 10^{-31}\ kg$$

Homework Problems Chapter 11

1. Light goes from a medium whose index of refraction is 1.62 into a medium whose index of refraction is 1.87. If it makes an angle of 43° with the normal in the 1.62 medium, what angle does it make with the normal in the 1.87 medium?

2. An underwater diver shines a laser beam up towards the surface so that it makes an angle of 45° with the normal in the water. How fast does the light travel through the water if it makes an angle of 70° with the normal when it emerges into the air? ($n_{\text{air}} = 1.0$)

3.

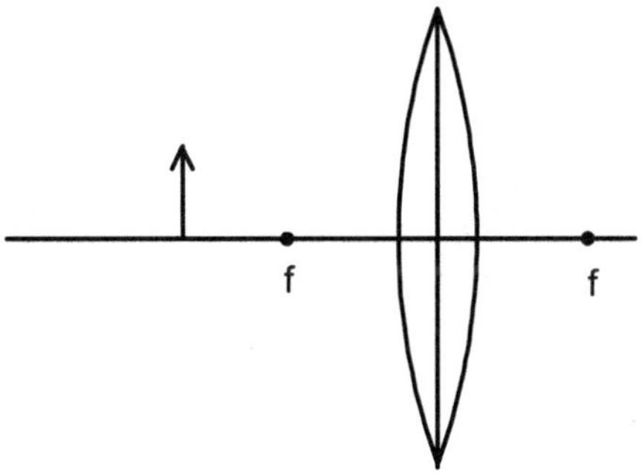

Use ray tracing to determine the 2 characteristics of the image. (Trace the picture.)

4.

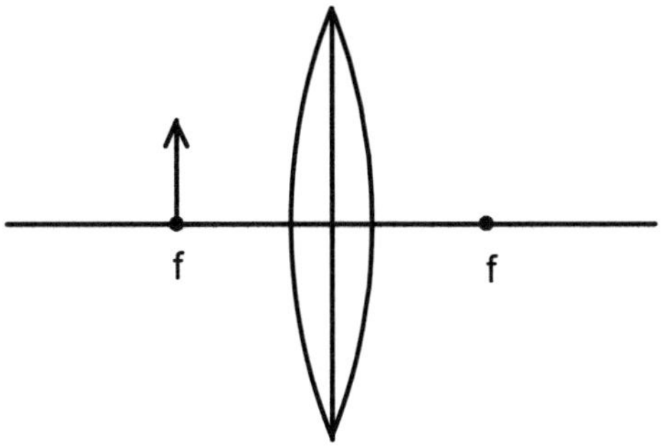

Use ray tracing to determine whether or not an image will form. Be accurate and don't forget to answer Yes or No.

5. Set I from Quiz 11.3 equal to I from equation 1109. Then sub in equation 1108, and algebraically show that $c = \sqrt{\dfrac{1}{\varepsilon_o \mu_o}}$.

6. Do a unit analysis. Then plug in the numbers for ε_o and μ_o, calculate the numerical value for c, and decide whether or not $c = \dfrac{1}{\sqrt{\varepsilon_o \mu_o}}$ is actually true.

7. A beam of green light has an intensity of $450 \dfrac{W}{m^2}$. Write down an expression for the strength of its magnetic field.

8. A beam of light has $\vec{E} = 372 \dfrac{N}{C} \sin\left[\left(9.45\times10^{6}\right)x - \left(2.83\times10^{15}\right)t\right]\left(+\hat{j}\right)$.

   Find a) its intensity
   b) its color
   c) its frequency. (f not ω)

9. Violet light will cause electrons to be ejected from lithium $(\phi \approx 2.9\ eV)$. What is the ejected electron's maximum possible speed? (Keep many decimal places in your intermediate calculations.)

10. Sodium has a work function of about 2.3 eV . Determine what color of visible light (if any) will cause electrons to be ejected from sodium.

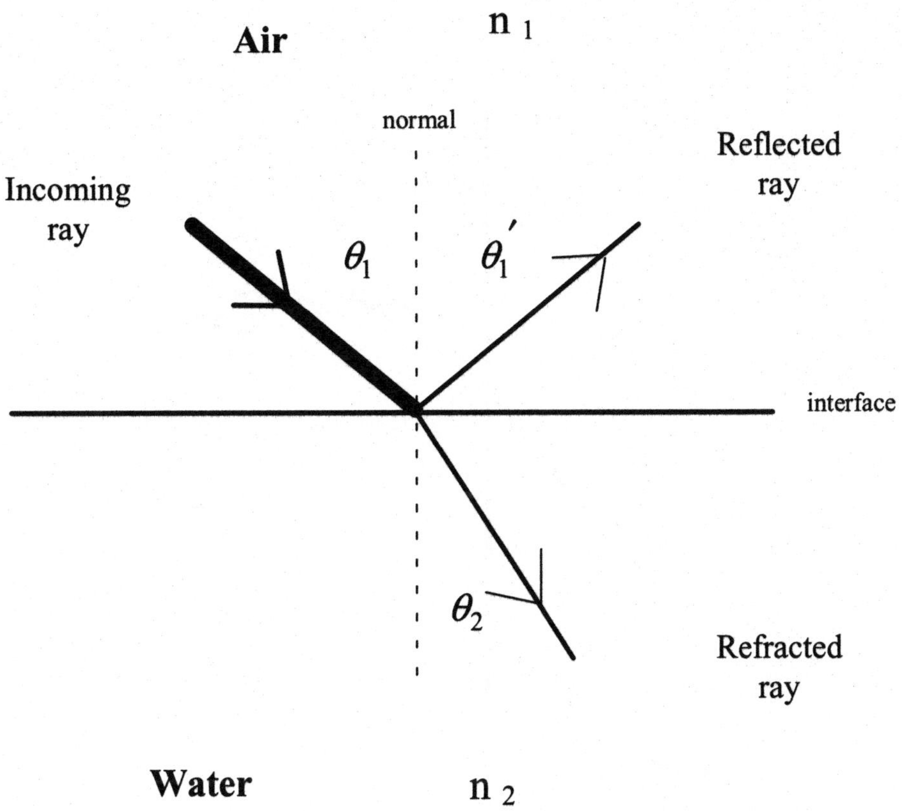

Figure 11.1 An incoming light ray is split into two parts at an air-water interface.

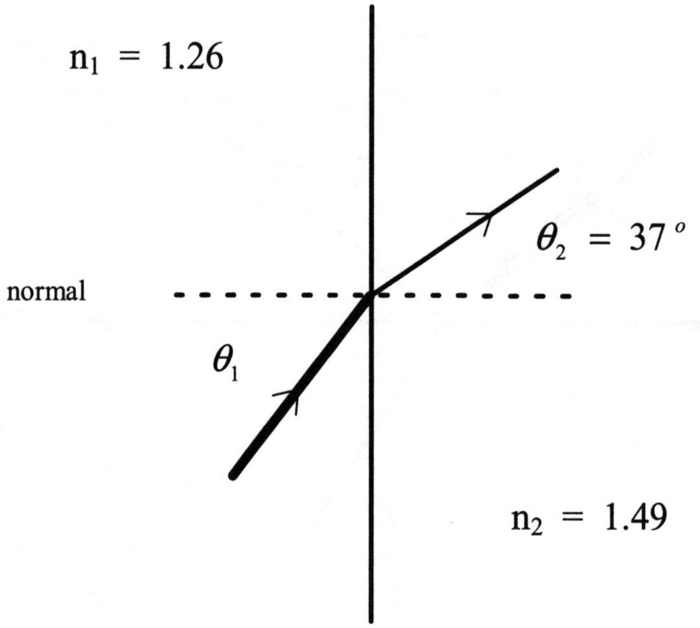

Figure 11.2 Picture for Example 11.1

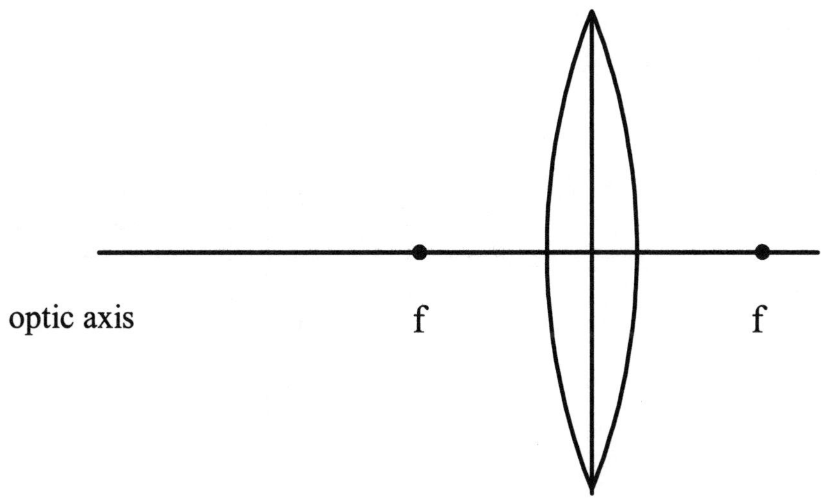

Figure 11.3 “Thin” converging lens

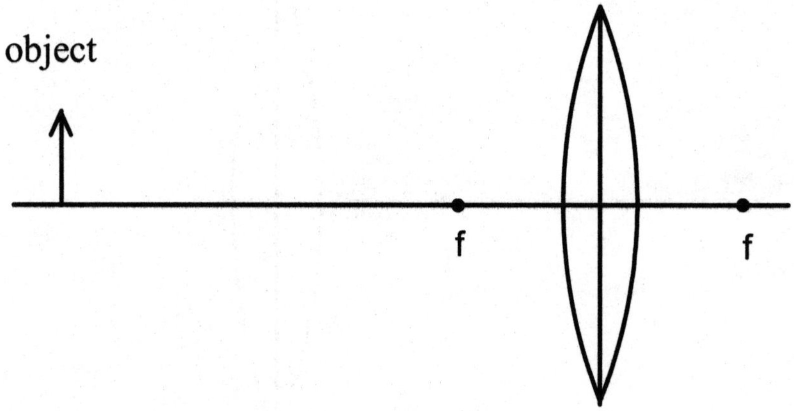

Figure 11.4 Converging lens for Example 11.2

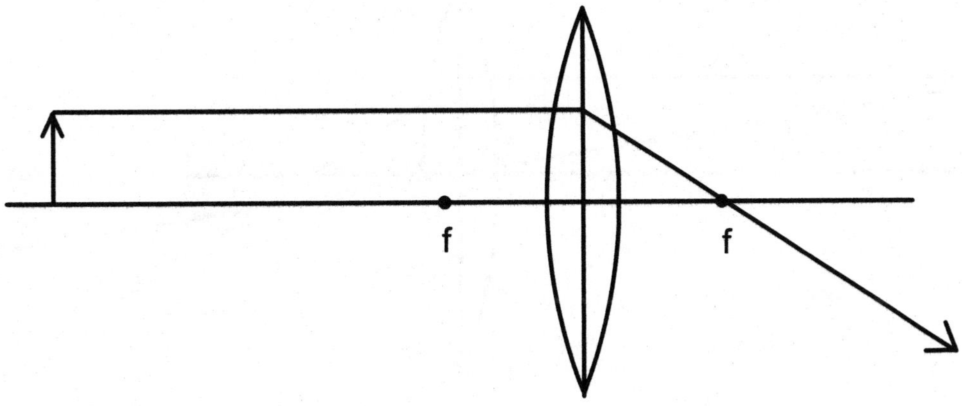

Figure 11.5 Ray 1

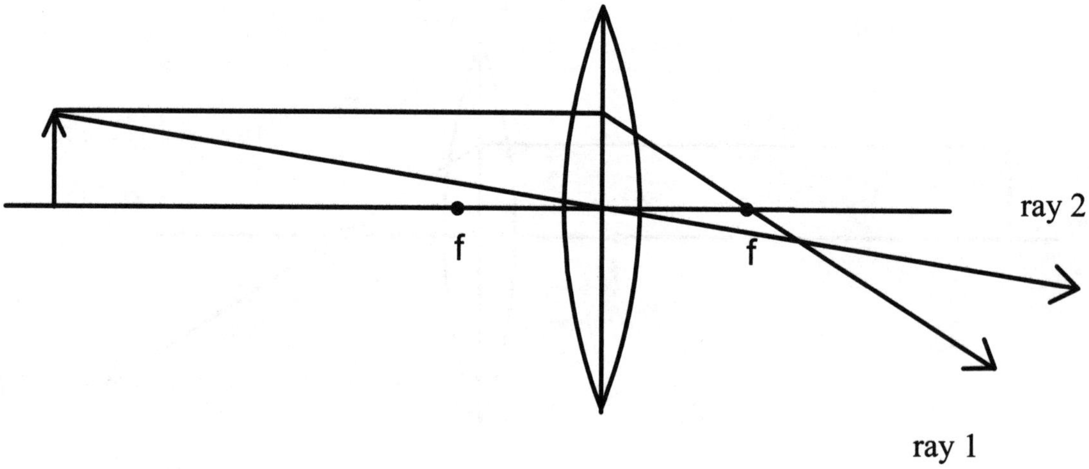

Figure 11.6 Rays 1 and 2

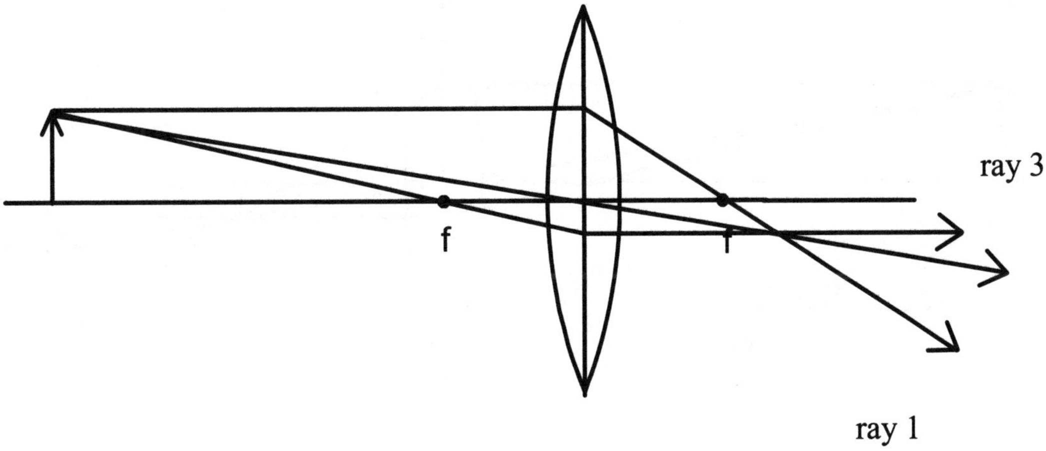

Figure 11.7 Rays 1, 2, and 3

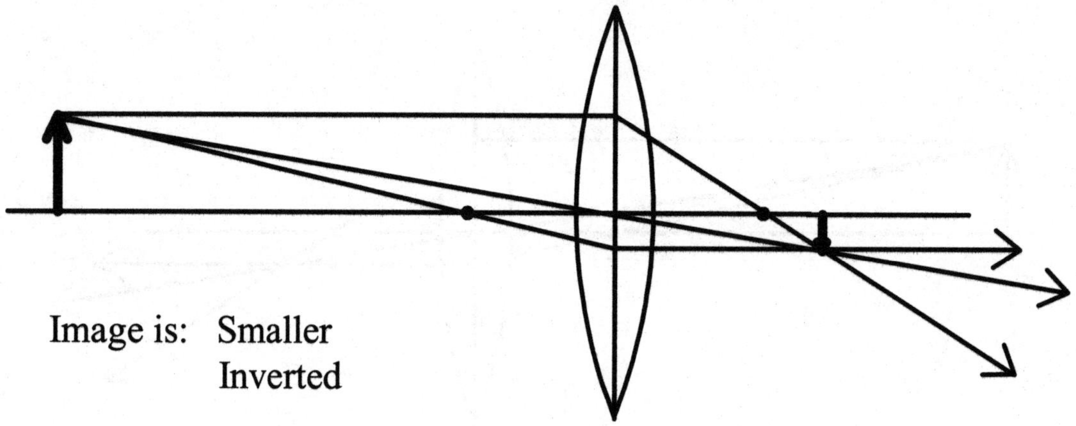

Figure 11.8 Image formation for Example 11.2

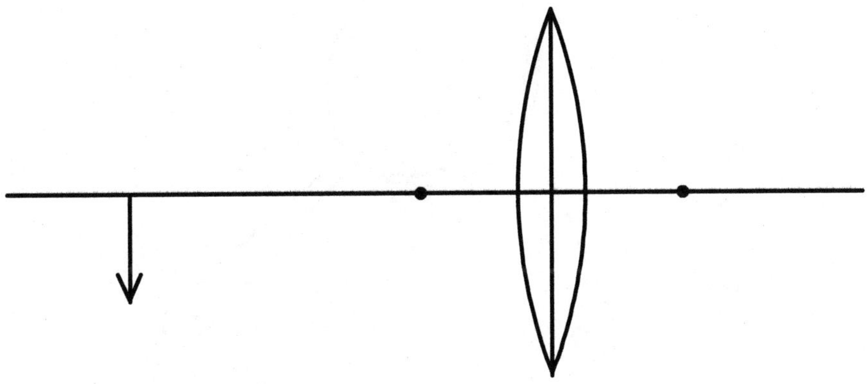

Figure 11.9 Object and lens for Quiz 11.2

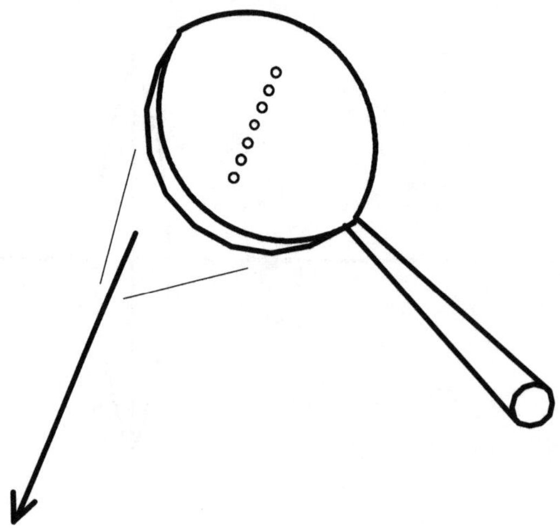

Figure 11.10 Light ray as a stream of particles

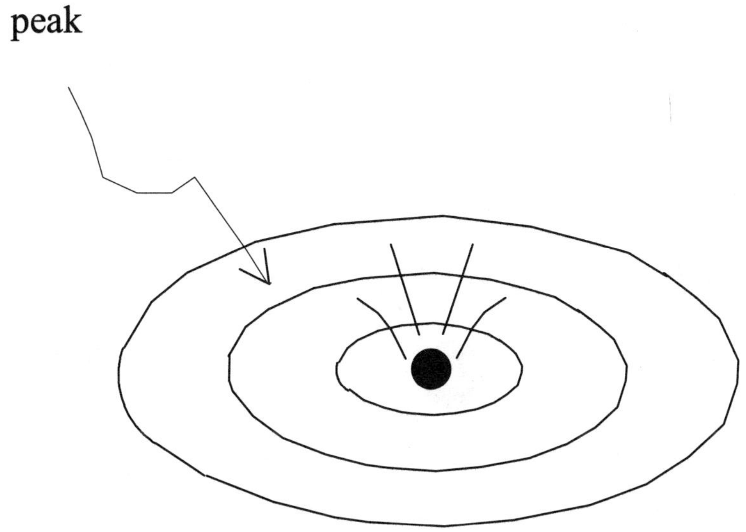

Figure 11.11 Ripples spread out from a stone dropped into a pond (top view)

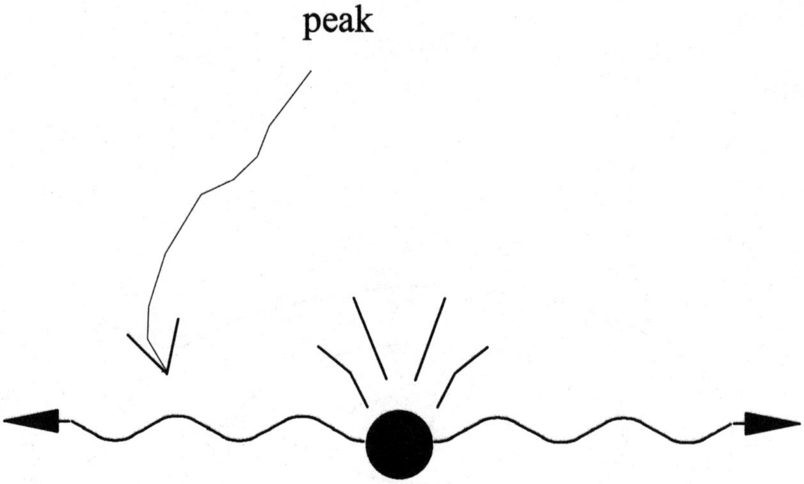

Figure 11.12 Ripples spread out from a stone dropped into a pond (side view}

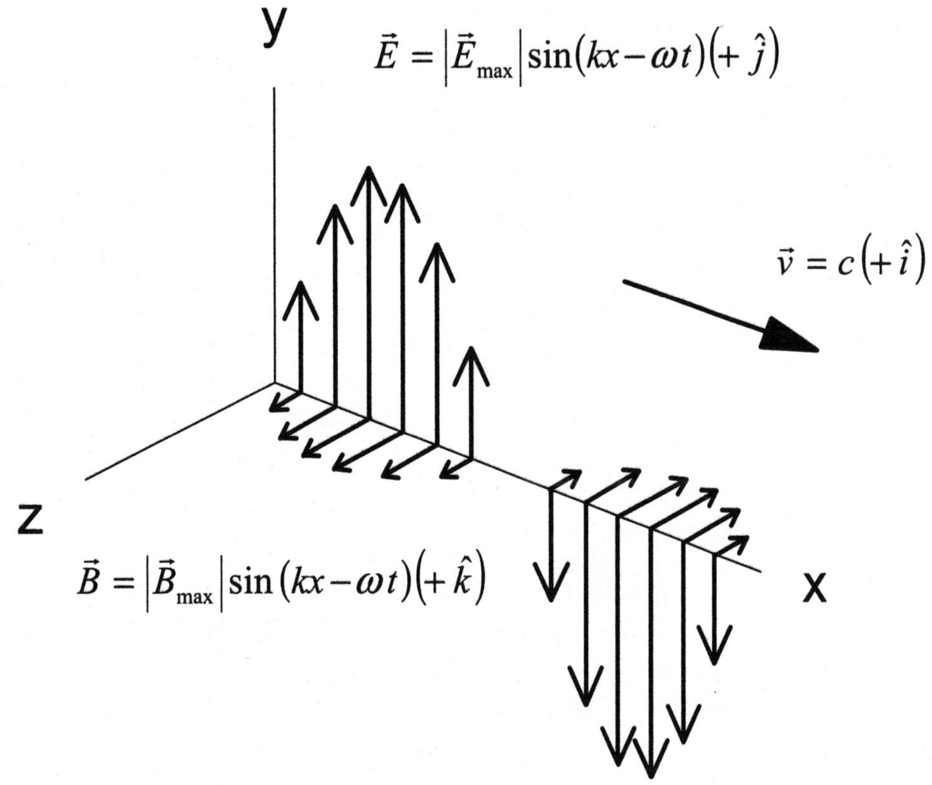

Figure 11.13 One cycle of an electromagnetic wave (Maxwell - style light wave) moving in the positive x direction

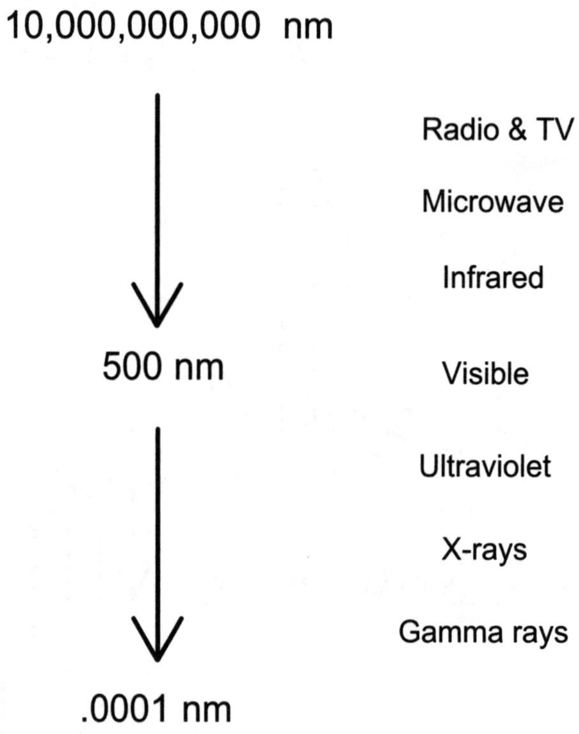

Figure 11.14 Spectrum of electromagnetic wavelengths

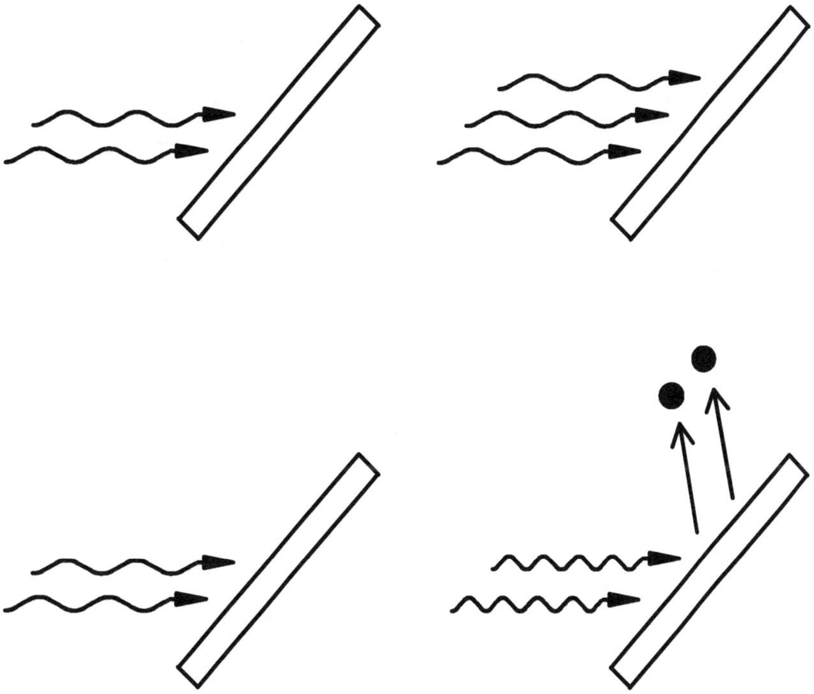

Figure 11.15 Photoelectric effect:

Increasing the amount of light shining on a metallic surface does not cause electrons to be ejected. Increasing the frequency of the light does.

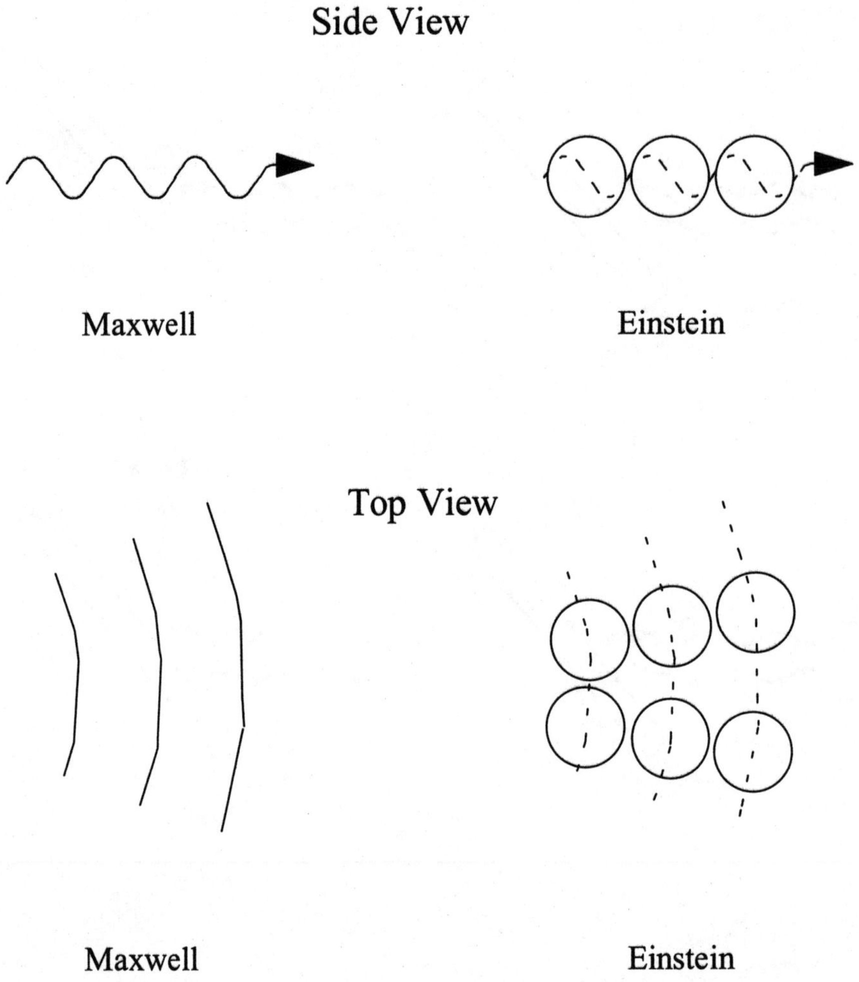

Figure 11.16 Oversimplified "artist's conception" of Einstein light quanta (photons)

Chapter 12 - Torque, Angular Momentum, and the Atom of Bohr

Timeline

420 BC Two Greek philosophers, Leucippus and his student Democritus, reason that a substance cannot be cut in half forever. Eventually you would get to an indivisible particle, or an *atom* of the substance.

240 BC Archimedes of Syracuse discusses the principle of the lever in his treatise *On the Equilibrium of Planes.*

1492 Leonardo da Vinci recognizes that the force ($\vec{F}$), lever arm ($\vec{r}$) product will change when the force is not perpendicular to the lever arm. That principle is incorporated into the modern day vector cross-product definition of torque, $\vec{\tau} = \vec{r} \times \vec{F}$.

1609 Johannes Kepler's 2nd law states that a line from the planet to the Sun sweeps over equal areas in equal intervals of time. Eventually that law would be attributed to Conservation of Angular Momentum.

1686 Issac Newton in England and James Bernoulli in Switzerland independently arrive at the concept of angular momentum.

1703 Writing about pendulum motion, James Bernoulli touches on Conservation of Angular Momentum.

1744 Swiss mathematician and physicist Leonhard Euler reasons that the general law of Conservation of Angular Momentum is in fact independent of Newton's Laws.

1897 J.J. Thompson in England discovers the negatively charged electron and suggests a "plum pudding" model of the atom.

1910 New Zealand physicist Ernest Rutherford discovers the positively charged nucleus and proposes a solar-system (or planetary) model of the atom.

1913 Danish physicist Niels Bohr proposes that the angular momentum of the electron orbiting a hydrogen nucleus should be quantized. The Bohr Atom is extremely successful at predicting the atomic spectrum of hydrogen.

1918 German mathematician Emmy Noether demonstrates that Conservation of Angular Momentum is linked to the isotropic property of space.

1926 Erwin Schrödinger uses his new equation to analyze the hydrogen atom and arrives at the Atomic Orbitals Model.

Baby Torque

Consider the balance shown in Figure 12.1. Both masses experience $|\vec{F}| = mg$ due to gravity. The mass on the left is a distance $d_1 = 3L$ from the fulcrum. The mass on the right is a distance $d_2 = L$ from the fulcrum. If the mass on the left is equal to m, what does the mass on the right have to be in order for the balance beam to stay perfectly flat? Archimedes was fascinated by this problem, and he concluded that the $|\vec{F}|$ lever-arm product on the left, had to equal the $|\vec{F}|$ lever-arm product on the right, in order for the system to stay in balance. For Figure 12.1,

$$\begin{aligned} |\vec{F_{left}}|(3L) &= |\vec{F_{right}}|(L) \\ mg(3L) &= |\vec{F_{right}}|(L) \\ |\vec{F_{right}}| &= 3mg \end{aligned} \tag{1201}$$

Equation 1201 indicates that the mass on the right needs to be 3 times the mass on the left in order for the system to stay balanced. (We are neglecting the mass of the balance beam because it is usually small enough that it does not have an appreciable effect.)

If we call Archimedes' magnitude of $\vec{F}$ lever-arm product "baby torque", then

$$\tau = Fd\,, \tag{1202}$$

where τ is the baby torque, F represents the magnitude of the force that is applied perpendicular to the end of the lever-arm, and d is the length of the lever-arm, or the distance from the fulcrum out to the force.

The units of torque are meters times Newtons ($m\ N$).

In terms of baby torque, the condition for balance beam equlibrium would be,

$$\Sigma\tau_{ccw} = \Sigma\tau_{cw}\,, \tag{1203}$$

where $\Sigma\tau_{ccw}$ represents the sum of the counterclockwise baby torques, and $\Sigma\tau_{cw}$ represents the sum of the clockwise baby torques. In order to tell which is which, you grab the force vector with your hand, and pull it in the direction of it's arrowhead. The lever-arm will swing around the fulcrum in either a clockwise or a counterclockwise direction. Figure 12.2 shows a picture.

Example 12.1

Find m so that the balance beam in Figure 12.3 will stay perfectly flat.

Solution 12.1

A tug on the Figure 12.3 gravity force vectors indicates that the 2 vectors to the left of the fulcrum produce counterclockwise torques, and the vector on the right produces a clockwise torque. Starting with equation (1203), and substituting the right side of equation (1202) for τ,

$$\begin{aligned}
\Sigma\tau_{ccw} &= \Sigma\tau_{cw} \\
F_1d_1 + F_2d_2 &= F_3d_3 \\
m_1gd_1 + m_2gd_2 &= m_3gd_3 \\
m_1d_1 + m_2d_2 &= m_3d_3 \\
(.2\ kg)(.6\ m) + m_2(.4\ m) &= (.8\ kg)(.3\ m) \\
.12\ kg + .4m_2 &= .24\ kg \\
m_2 = m &= .3\ kg \qquad (1204)
\end{aligned}$$

Notice that the g's in equation (1204) all divided out. That does not always happen, and it will not happen in Quiz 12.1.

Quiz 12.1 Find F so that the balance beam in Figure 12.4 will stay flat.

Real Torque

Baby torque provides a useful way to analyze situations where all the forces act in one plane, and the force vectors are always perpendicular to the lever arms. Many times those conditions are not met, and the concept of torque has to be generalized into

$$\vec{\tau} = \vec{r} \times \vec{F}\ , \qquad (1205)$$

where $\vec{r}$ is the distance vector out to the end of the lever arm, $\vec{F}$ is the force applied to the end of the lever arm, and $\times$ represents the vector cross product.

Note that the units of torque are still meters times Newtons ($m\ N$).

Example 12.2

Find the torque acting on the wrench shown in Figure 12.5, and express your answer in magnitude unit-vector form.

Solution 12.2

This is a straight plug-in using equation (1205). From page 184,

$$\vec{r} \times \vec{F} \longrightarrow \qquad \begin{array}{ccccc} \hat{\imath} & \hat{\jmath} & \hat{k} & \hat{\imath} & \hat{\jmath} \\ .2 & .2 & .35 & .2 & .2 \\ 0 & 27 & -39 & 0 & 27 \end{array}$$

$$\vec{r} \times \vec{F} = [(.2)(-39) - (.35)(27)]\,\hat{\imath} + [0 - (.2)(-39)]\,\hat{\jmath} + [(.2)(27) - 0]\,\hat{k}$$

$$\vec{\tau} = \left[17.25(-\hat{\imath}) + 7.8(+\hat{\jmath}) + 5.4(+\hat{k})\right] \;\; m\;N \tag{1206}$$

Equation (1206) is the expression for $\vec{\tau}$, but it is in component form. The problem asks for magnitude unit-vector form, so

$$|\vec{\tau}| = \sqrt{(17.25)^2 + (7.8)^2 + (5.4)^2}\; m\;N = \sqrt{387.5625}\; m\;N,$$

and

$$\vec{\tau} = \sqrt{387.5625}\; m\;N \left[\frac{17.25}{\sqrt{387.5625}}(-\hat{\imath}) + \frac{7.8}{\sqrt{387.5625}}(+\hat{\jmath}) + \frac{5.4}{\sqrt{387.5625}}(+\hat{k})\right]$$

$$\vec{\tau} \approx 19.69\; m\;N \left[.876(-\hat{\imath}) + .396(+\hat{\jmath}) + .274(+\hat{k})\right]. \tag{1207}$$

Magnitude unit-vector form has the advantage of showing you how much torque is there, 19.69 $m\;N$, and which way it is directed, $\left[.876(-\hat{\imath}) + .396(+\hat{\jmath}) + .274(+\hat{k})\right]$. (A quick check reveals that $\sqrt{(.876)^2 + (.396)^2 + (.274)^2} \approx .9996 \approx 1.0$, which means that the unit-vector in equation (1207) is in fact a unit-vector.)

Quiz 12.2 A wrench handle is situated along $\vec{r} = \left[.3(+\hat{\jmath}) + .4(+\hat{k})\right]\; m$. Find the magnitude unit-vector form of $\vec{\tau}$, if a force of $\left[35(-\hat{\jmath}) + 7(+\hat{k})\right]\; N$ is suddenly applied to the end of the handle.

Angular Momentum

Objects that rotate, or revolve around an axis, posses an angular momentum with respect to that axis. For a small individual "point mass" revolving around an external axis, the angular momentum can be expressed as

$$\vec{L} = \vec{r} \times \vec{p}\,, \tag{1208}$$

where $\vec{L}$ represents the angular momentum, $\vec{r}$ is the position vector perpendicular to the axis and stretching from the axis to the center of mass, and $\vec{p} = m\vec{v}$ is the "ordinary" or linear momentum of the mass when it is located at the end of $\vec{r}$.

Let's look at the units. The position vector $\vec{r}$ has units of meters. The momentum $\vec{p} = m\vec{v}$ has units of $(kg)\left(\frac{m}{s}\right)$. So the units on angular momentum are $\frac{kg\;m^2}{s}$. (Most other compound units are named after a pioneering scientist; Newtons or Joules for example. Interestingly, the units of angular momentum have not been named after anybody, so far. They remain just $\frac{kg\;m^2}{s}$.)

Example 12.3

Figure 12.6 shows a .38 kg outer space rock at the end of a string being whirled around at a constant speed. Find $\vec{L}$ if $\vec{v} = \left[4(+\hat{\imath}) + 3(-\hat{\jmath})\right] \frac{m}{s}$ when $\vec{r} = \left[.3(-\hat{\imath}) + .4(-\hat{\jmath})\right]\ m$.

Solution 12.3

The linear momentum is given by

$$\begin{aligned} \vec{p} &= m\vec{v} \\ &= .38\ kg\ \left[4(+\hat{\imath}) + 3(-\hat{\jmath})\right]\ \frac{m}{s} \\ \vec{p} &= \left[1.52(+\hat{\imath}) + 1.14(-\hat{\jmath})\right]\ \frac{kg\ m}{s}\ . \end{aligned} \qquad (1209)$$

From equation (1208), for the angular momentum,

$$\vec{r} \times \vec{p} \longrightarrow \quad \begin{array}{ccccc} \hat{\imath} & \hat{\jmath} & \hat{k} & \hat{\imath} & \hat{\jmath} \\ -.3 & -.4 & 0 & -.3 & -.4 \\ 1.52 & -1.14 & 0 & 1.52 & -1.14 \end{array}$$

$$\begin{aligned} \vec{r} \times \vec{p} &= [0-0]\,\hat{\imath} + [0-0]\,\hat{\jmath} + [(-.3)\,(-1.14) - (-.4)\,(1.52)]\,\hat{k} \\ &= [.342 - (-.608)]\,\hat{k} \\ \vec{L} &= .95\ \left(+\hat{k}\right)\ \frac{kg\ m^2}{s} \end{aligned} \qquad (1210)$$

The direction of $\vec{L}$ can be checked by applying a mayonnaise jar rule to the velocity vector $\vec{v}$. If you twisted the mayonnaise jar top around the way that $\vec{v}$ is going, you would be unscrewing it, which means the top would go up, in the $+\hat{k}$ direction. Figure 12.7 shows a picture. Notice that $\vec{L}$ is located on the axis of revolution.

Quiz 12.3 Figure 12.8 shows the Example 12.3 outer space rock after it has moved a little bit around the circle. Find the angular momentum based on the new position. (Notice that $|\vec{v}| = \sqrt{(4)^2 + (3)^2}\ \frac{m}{s}$, and that you should get the same value for $\vec{L}$ no matter where you do the calculation.)

Conservation of Angular Momentum

Figure 12.9 shows an outer space rock being whirled around with constant speed at the end of a long string. The other end of the string is threaded through a frictionless tube so that the length of $\vec{r}$ can be varied by pulling the string down through the tube. When the r part of the string is long, the angular momentum of the rock is $\vec{L_1} = r_1 m v_1(-\hat{k})$. When the r part of the string is short the angular momentum is

$\vec{L_2} = r_2 m v_2(-\hat{k})$. There is no external torque applied by shortening the string (see page 334), so that

$$\vec{L_1} = \vec{L_2} \tag{1211}$$

due to Conservation of Angular Momentum.

Starting with equation (1211), and plugging in for $\vec{L}$,

$$\begin{aligned} \vec{L_1} &= \vec{L_2} \\ r_1 m v_1(-\hat{k}) &= r_2 m v_2(-\hat{k}) \\ r_1 v_1 &= r_2 v_2 \,. \end{aligned} \tag{1212}$$

Notice that neither the direction of $\vec{L}$, nor the mass of the rock has been changed by shortening r. That's why both of those quantities divide out in equation (1212).

Example 12.4

Just before the string is shortened, the Figure 12.9 rock has $\vec{r} = \left[\frac{\sqrt{2}}{4}\left(+\hat{\imath}\right) + \frac{\sqrt{2}}{4}\left(+\hat{\jmath}\right)\right] m$, and $\vec{v} = \left[3\sqrt{2}\left(+\hat{\imath}\right) + 3\sqrt{2}\left(-\hat{\jmath}\right)\right] \frac{m}{s}$. Just after the string is shortened, the new r is $.15\ m$. Find the new v.

Solution 12.4

Equation (1212) is written in terms of scalars. So the first step is to find $|\vec{r_1}| = r_1$ and $|\vec{v_1}| = v_1$.

$$r_1 = \left[\sqrt{\left(\frac{\sqrt{2}}{4}\right)^2 + \left(\frac{\sqrt{2}}{4}\right)^2}\,\right] m = \frac{1}{2}\, m \tag{1213}$$

and

$$v_1 = \left[\sqrt{\left(3\sqrt{2}\right)^2 + \left(3\sqrt{2}\right)^2}\,\right] \frac{m}{s} = 6\, \frac{m}{s}\,. \tag{1214}$$

The rest of the problem is a straight plug-in into equation (1212).

$$\begin{aligned} r_1 v_1 &= r_2 v_2 \\ \left(\frac{1}{2}\, m\right)\left(6\, \frac{m}{s}\right) &= (.15\ m)\, v_2 \\ .15 v_2 &= 3\, \frac{m}{s} \\ v_2 &= 20\, \frac{m}{s}\,. \end{aligned} \tag{1215}$$

Notice that v_2 is significantly increased by shortening r. A dramatic but familiar example of this same phenomenon occurs when a slowly spinning ice skater pulls in her arms. Conservation of Angular Momentum causes her rate of spin to increase significantly.

Quiz 12.4 A .2 kg outerspace rock is being whirled around at the end of a .18 m string with a speed of 21 $\frac{m}{s}$. The string is then let out so that the rock slows down. How long is the string when the rock is going 14 $\frac{m}{s}$?

The Bohr Atom

The early part of the 1900's was an exciting time for atomic physics. Electrons and protons had just been discovered. Ernest Rutherford had suggested that an atom might be like a tiny solar system, with the negatively charged electrons orbiting around a positively charged nucleus. Then in 1913, Neils Bohr applied Quantum Mechanics to a Rutherford-like model of the hydrogen atom. The Bohr atom has a single proton in its nucleus, and that proton is being orbited by just one electron. Figure 12.10 shows a picture.

Bohr's Quantum Mechanical interpretation starts out by proposing that the magnitude of the angular momentum for the orbiting electron is quantized, so that

$$|\vec{L}| = m_e v r = n\hbar \; , \tag{1216}$$

where m_e is the mass of the electron, v is the electron's speed as it goes around, r is the radius of the electron's circular orbit (the radius ot the atom), n is a non-zero positive integer ($n = 1, 2, 3.....$), and $\hbar$ is Planck's constant divided by 2π ($\hbar = \frac{h}{2\pi}$).

That's why the Figure 12.10 picture has more than one possible orbit for the electron. If $n = 1$, then the electron is in its lowest possible orbit (the one closest to the nucleus). If $n = 2$, then the electron has "jumped" out to the next lowest orbit. If $n = 3$, it would jump out even further, and it would keep on jumping out each time that n increased. Equation (1216) guarantees that no in-between orbits are possible.

Without Bohr's restriction on the electron's angular momentum, it is only possible to get so far by a non-quantum analysis of the atom. For the positions shown in Figure 12.10, the electric force that is exerted by the proton on the electron would be

$$\vec{F}_{elect} = \frac{1}{4\pi\epsilon_o}\left[\frac{q_{proton} q_{electron}}{r^2}\right]\left(+\hat{\imath}\right) \; . \tag{1217}$$

The charges on the proton and electron are thought to be equal in magnitude, but opposite in sign, with the electron charge being negative. In symbols,

$$q_{proton} = +e$$

$$q_{electron} = -e \; ,$$

where e represents the magnitude of the charge ($e \approx 1.6 \times 10^{-19}\ C$). Making those substitutions,

$$\vec{F}_{elect} = \frac{1}{4\pi\epsilon_o}\left[\frac{(+e)\,(-e)}{r^2}\right]\left(+\hat{\imath}\right)$$

$$
\begin{aligned}
&= \frac{1}{4\pi\epsilon_o}\left[\frac{-e^2}{r^2}\right]\left(+\hat{i}\right) \\
\vec{F}_{elect} &= \frac{1}{4\pi\epsilon}\left[\frac{e^2}{r^2}\right]\left(-\hat{i}\right) . \qquad (1218)
\end{aligned}
$$

Equation (1218) shows the force on the electron being directed back towards the proton. Opposite charges attract, so that part looks right.

The electron's speed is assumed constant as it orbits the proton. That means that the centripetal force on the electron, $\vec{F}_c = m\vec{a}_c$, would be

$$
\begin{aligned}
\vec{F}_c &= m_e|\vec{a}_c|\left(-\hat{i}\right) \\
\vec{F}_c &= \frac{m_e v^2}{r}\left(-\hat{i}\right) \qquad (1219)
\end{aligned}
$$

when the electron crosses the x-axis. (Here m_e again means mass of electron.)

Equations (1218) and (1219) are two different expressions of the same force. Setting them equal,

$$
\begin{aligned}
\vec{F}_{elect} &= \vec{F}_c \\
\frac{1}{4\pi\epsilon_o}\left[\frac{e^2}{r^2}\right]\left(-\hat{i}\right) &= \frac{m_e v^2}{r}\left(-\hat{i}\right) ,
\end{aligned}
$$

and solving for v, leads to

$$
v = \sqrt{\frac{e^2}{m_e\left(4\pi\epsilon_o\right) r}} . \qquad (1220)
$$

Equation (1220) is the correct expression for the speed of the electron as it goes around, but it is not very useful because r, the radius of the atom, is still unknown. That's where Bohr's quantum hypothesis comes into play. Equation (1216) can also be soved for v.

$$
\begin{aligned}
m_e v r &= n\hbar \\
v &= \frac{n\hbar}{m_e r} . \qquad (1221)
\end{aligned}
$$

The next step is to set the right side of equation (1220) equal to the right side of equation (1221), and solve for r. We'll do that right now.

Quiz 12.5 Use the two v equations to find an expression for the radius of the Bohr atom.

After a little bit of Algebra,

$$
r = n^2\left[\frac{\hbar^2\left(4\pi\epsilon_o\right)}{m_e e^2}\right] , \qquad (1222)
$$

where

$$n = 1, 2, 3, ...$$

$$\hbar \approx \frac{6.626 \times 10^{-34}}{2\pi} \; J \cdot s$$

$$\epsilon_o \approx 8.85 \times 10^{-12} \frac{C^2}{Nm^2}$$

$$m_e \approx 9.11 \times 10^{-31} \; kg$$

$$e \approx 1.6 \times 10^{-19} \; C \; .$$

Equation (1222) is one of the great triumphs of 20th century physics. All of the quantities on the right hand side are known to a high degree of accuracy. That means r can also be calculated to a high degree of accuracy. For the first time in history, mankind had a believable estimate for the size of an atom.

Bohr's model goes on to make other dramatic predictions. The electron is supposed to jump up to a higher orbit by absorbing a single photon of light, and then to drop down to a lower orbit by emitting a photon of light. Those transitions account for the atomic spectrum of hydrogen. A drop from $n = 4$ to $n = 2$ for example, results in the emission of a 486.1 nm blue-green photon.

The agreement between Bohr's predictions and the observed spectrum was remarkable, and the Bohr atom remains a milestone of scientific thought.

It was however, soon supplanted by a more comprehensive model. In 1926, Erwin Schrödinger at the University of Zurich applied his brand new Schrödinger equation to an analysis of the hydrogen atom. The "Atomic Orbitals" model that emerged from Schrödinger's analysis provides more detail about the structure of an atom, includes the Bohr Atom as a "first approximation", and goes on to make some additional predictions about hydrogen that the Bohr Atom does not make. Schrödinger's approach is also thought to apply to more complicated atoms. (Any kind of atom actually, although the math can get extremely difficult.) Bohr tried, but he was never able to extend his model beyond hydrogen.

Things to Remember

Relationships

$$\Sigma\tau_{cw} = \Sigma\tau_{ccw} \quad \text{where } \tau_1 = F_1 d_1, \;\; \tau_2 = F_2 d_2, \;\; \text{etc.}$$

$$\vec{\tau} = \vec{r} \times \vec{F} \qquad \vec{L} = \vec{r} \times \vec{p} = \vec{r} \times m\vec{v} \qquad \vec{L_1} = \vec{L_2} \;\; \text{if } \vec{\tau}_{ext} = 0$$

$$r = n^2 \left[\frac{\hbar^2 \left(4\pi\epsilon_o\right)}{m_e c^2} \right]$$

Units

$$\vec{\tau} \rightarrow m\ N \qquad \vec{L} \rightarrow \frac{kg\ m^2}{s}$$

Constants and Conversions

n = 1,2,3 ....

$$\hbar \approx \frac{6.626 \times 10^{-34}}{2\pi}\ J\ s \qquad \epsilon_o \approx 8.85 \times 10^{-12} \frac{C^2}{N\ m^2}$$

$$m_e \approx 9.11 \times 10^{-31} kg \qquad e \approx 1.6 \times 10^{-19} C$$

Homework Problems Chapter 12

1.

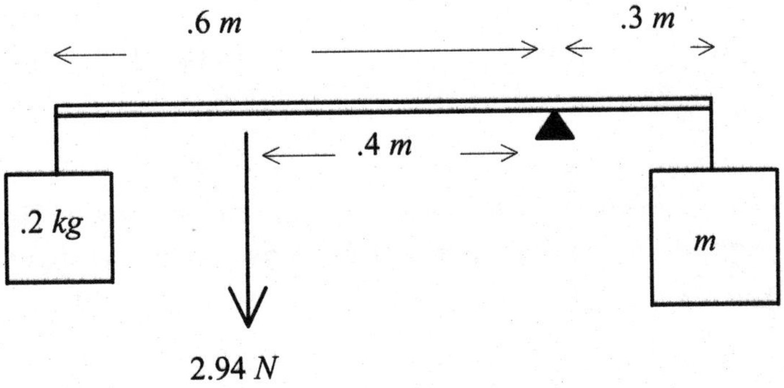

Find m so that the balance beam shown above will stay perfectly flat.

2.

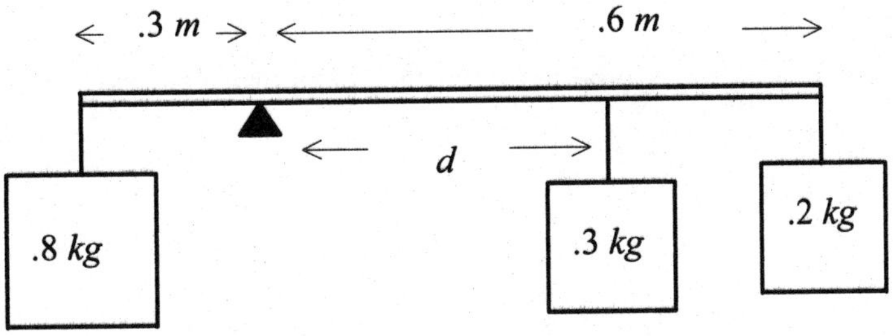

Find d so that the system shown above will stay in balance.

3. The end of a wrench handle located at $\vec{r} = .4\left(+\hat{k}\right)m$ suddenly experiences a force $\vec{F} = \left[20\left(+\hat{i}\right) + 20\left(+\hat{j}\right) + 16\left(-\hat{k}\right)\right]N$. Find the magnitude unit vector form of $\vec{\tau}$.

4. Expressed in terms of "real" torque, equation (1203) becomes $\sum \vec{\tau} = 0$. Applying that equation to the balance shown in Figure 12.4 results in $\vec{\tau}_1 + \vec{\tau}_2 = 0$. Use 3 dimensions so that $\vec{r}_1 = .4\left(+\hat{j}\right)m$, $\vec{r}_2 = .7\left(+\hat{j}\right)m$, $\vec{F}_1 = 13.72\left(+\hat{k}\right)N$, and $\vec{F}_2 = mg\left(-\hat{k}\right)$. Find $\vec{\tau}_1 = \vec{r}_1 \times \vec{F}_1$, $\vec{\tau}_2 = \vec{r}_2 \times \vec{F}_2$, and verify that $\sum \vec{\tau} = 0$.

5. At one point the $.38\ kg$ rock from Example 12.3 has $\vec{v} = \left[\frac{5\sqrt{2}}{2}\left(-\hat{i}\right) + \frac{5\sqrt{2}}{2}\left(+\hat{j}\right)\right]\frac{m}{s}$ and $\vec{r} = \left[\frac{.5}{\sqrt{2}}\left(+\hat{i}\right) + \frac{.5}{\sqrt{2}}\left(+\hat{j}\right)\right]m$. Find $\vec{L}$.

6. The velocity of an object moving with "uniform circular motion" (page 100) is always perpendicular to the radius so that $\vec{v} \bullet \vec{r} = 0$ anywhere on the circle. Verify that $\vec{v} \bullet \vec{r} = 0$ in Example 12.3, Quiz 12.3, and H.W. problem # 5.

7. Suppose the radius of the string in H.W. # 5 is shortened on the next revolution so that $\vec{r} = \left[\frac{.5\sqrt{2}}{4}\left(+\hat{i}\right) + \frac{.5\sqrt{2}}{4}\left(+\hat{j}\right)\right]m$. How would that affect the speed of the rock? (In other words – Find $|\vec{v}_2|$.)

8. How long does $\vec{r}$ have to be in Example 12.4 in order to slow the rock down to $4\frac{m}{s}$?

9. Carry out a unit analysis and verify that the right side of equation (1222) actually does reduce to meters.

10. Calculate the radius of the smallest possible Bohr Atom. Express your answer in nanometers.

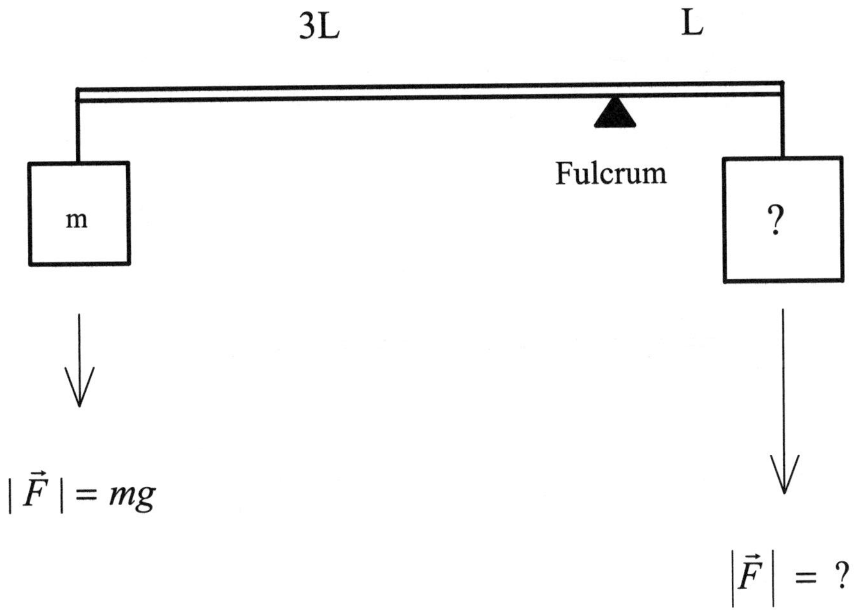

Figure 12.1 Two weights balancing each other

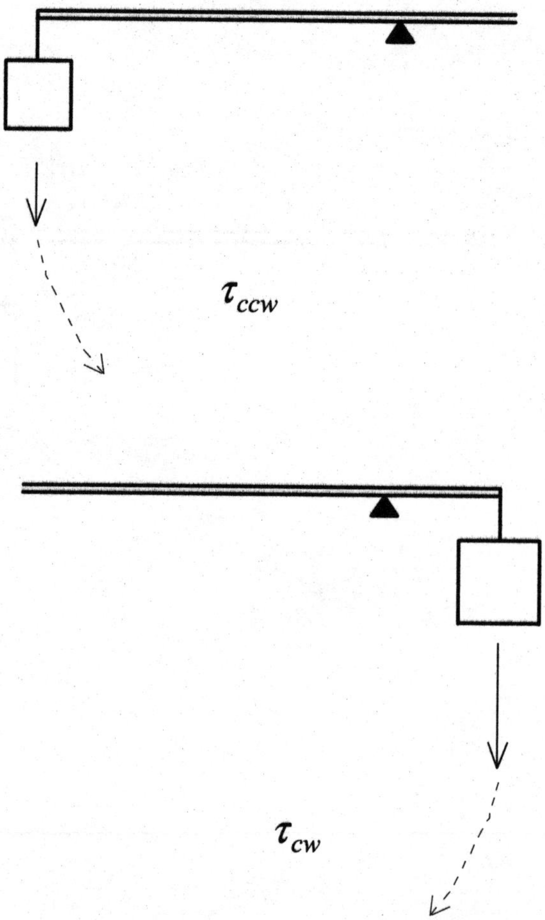

Figure 12.2 Counterclockwise and Clockwise Baby Torque

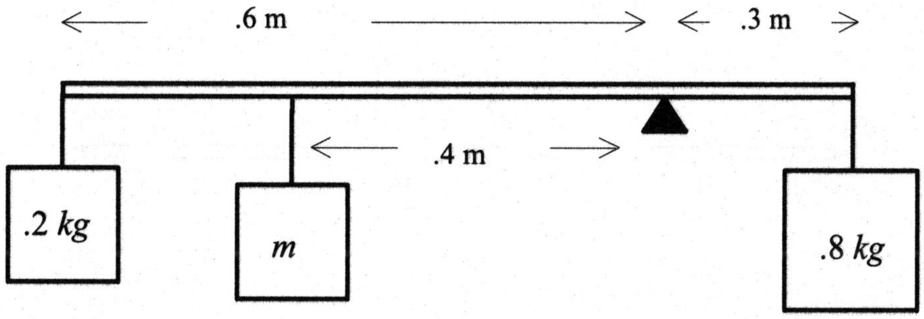

Figure 12.3 Balance for Example 12.1

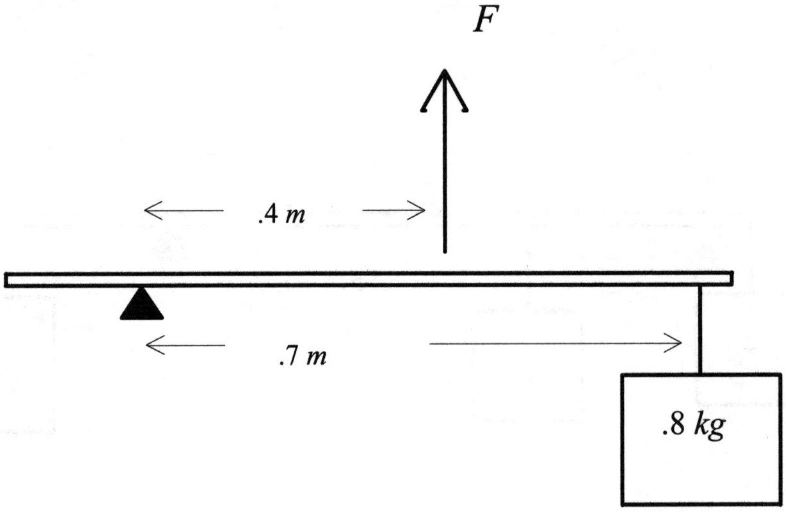

Figure 12.4 Balance for Quiz 12.1

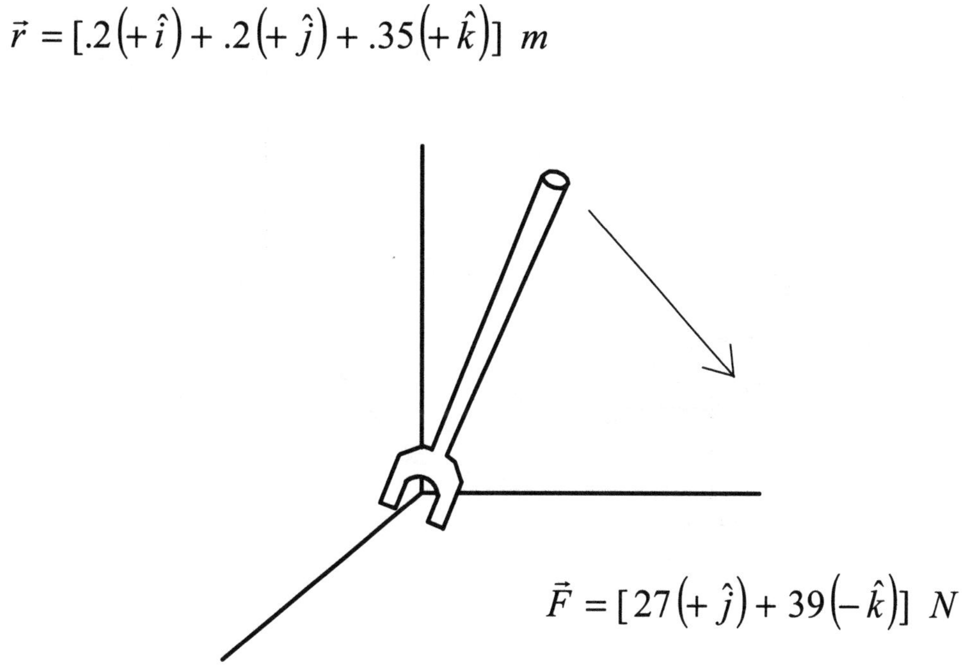

$\vec{r} = [.2(+\hat{i}) + .2(+\hat{j}) + .35(+\hat{k})]\ m$
$\vec{F} = [27(+\hat{j}) + 39(-\hat{k})]\ N$

Figure 12.5 Wrench for Example 12.2

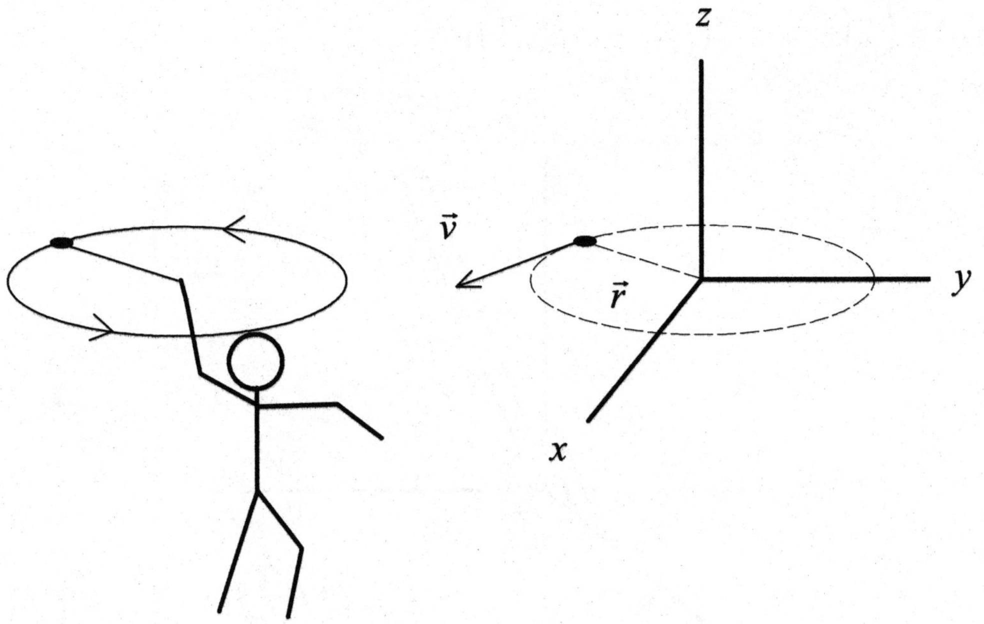

Figure 12.6 Outer space rock for Example 12.3

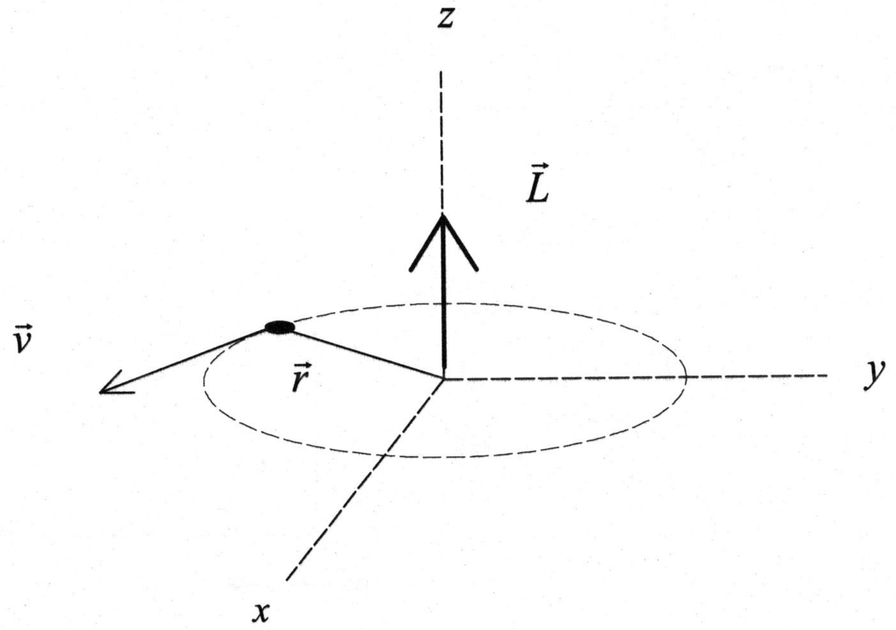

Figure 12.7 Direction of $\vec{L}$ for Example 12.3

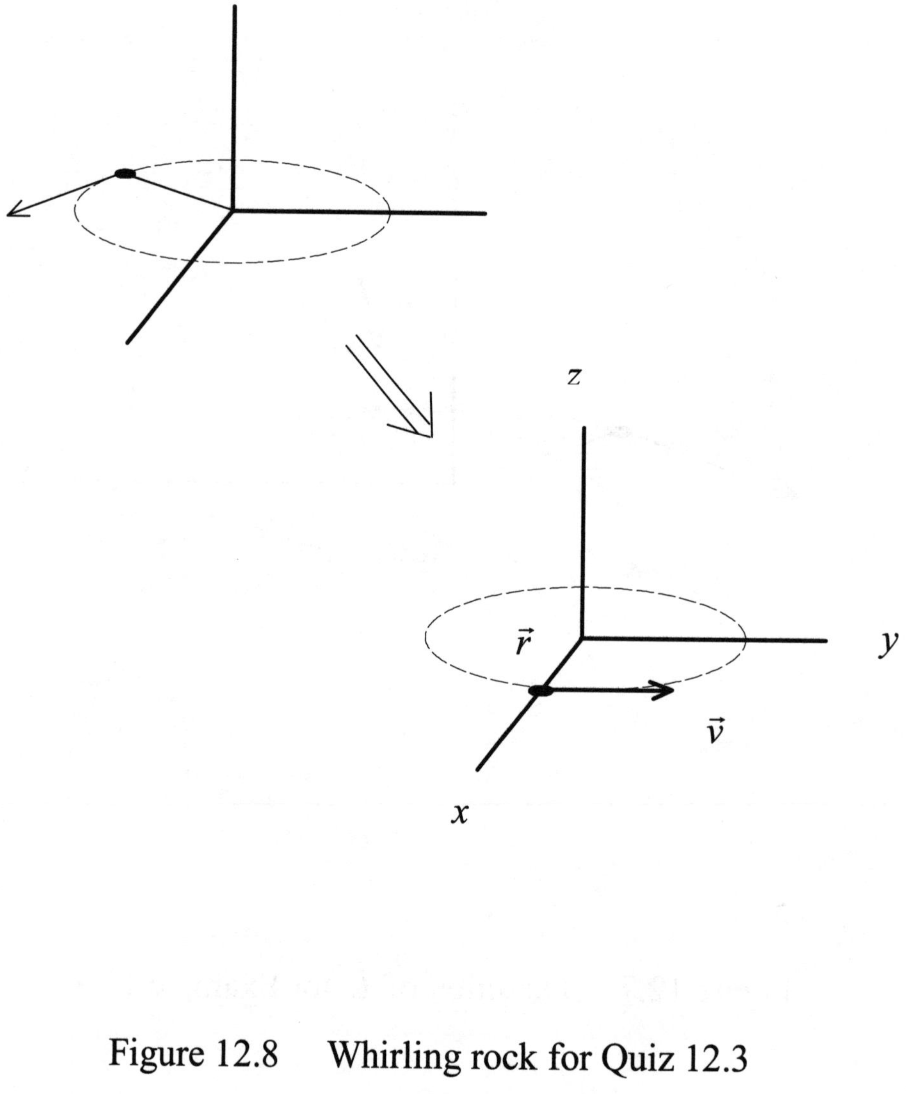

Figure 12.8 Whirling rock for Quiz 12.3

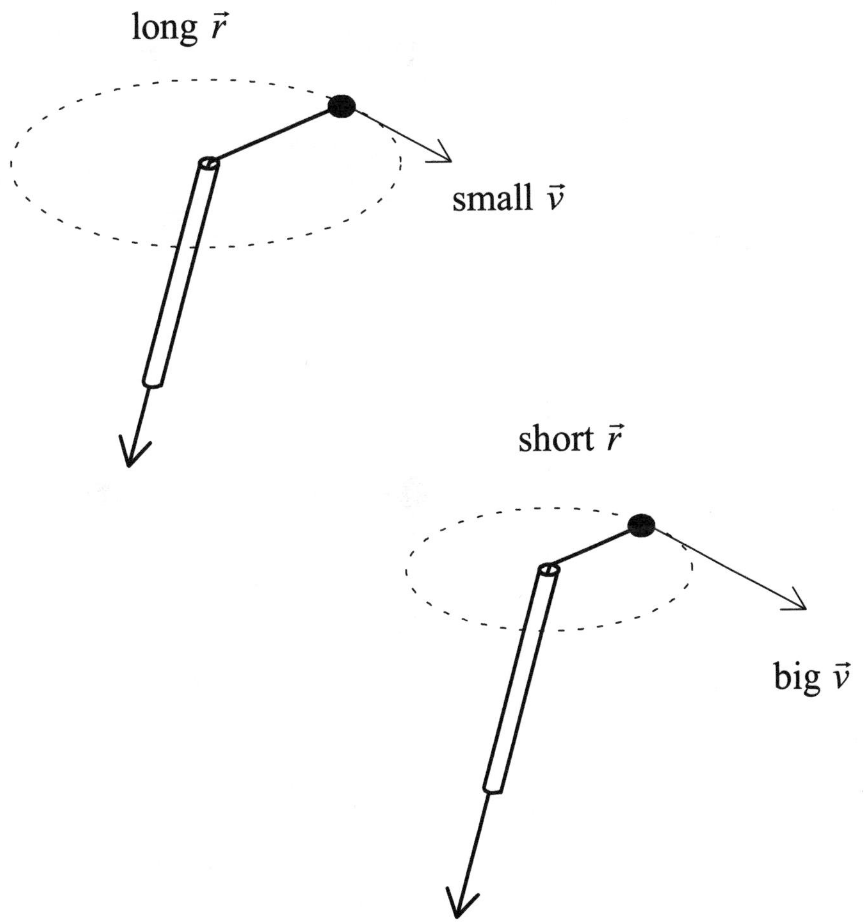

Figure 12.9 Conservation of Angular Momentum; decreasing the radius increases the speed

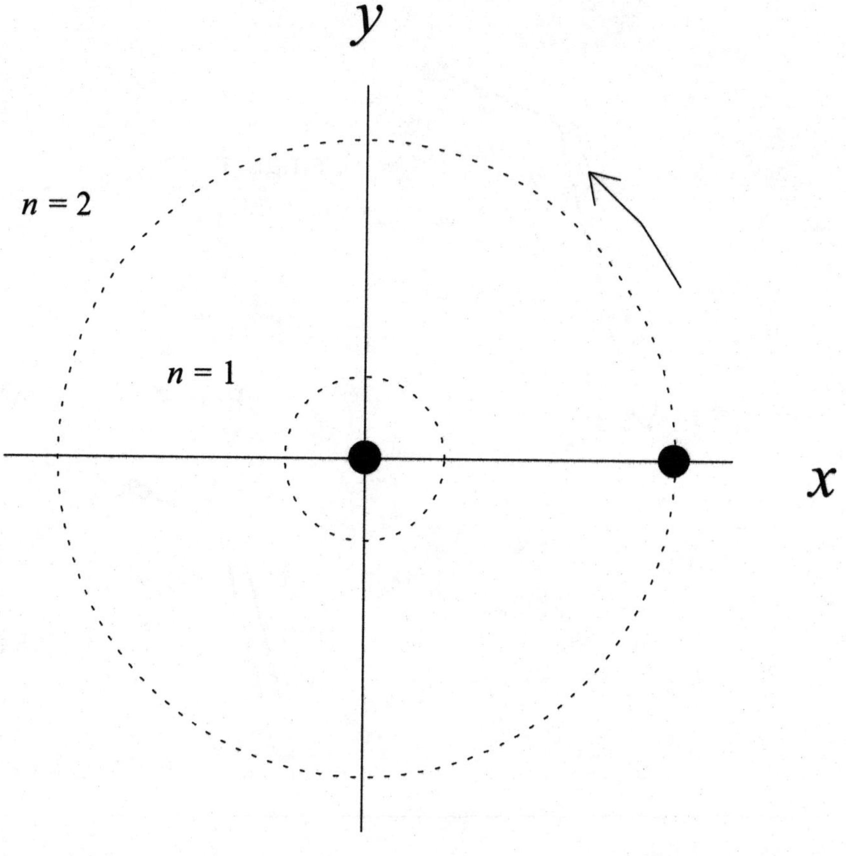

Figure 12.10 First 2 possible radii of the Bohr Atom

Appendix

(A few explanations and derivations)

Galileo's Ball and Ramp Experiment

The ancient Greeks believed that moving objects wanted to stop. But that idea was challenged by John Buridan at the University of Paris around 1325. Three centuries later, Galileo Galilei conducted a brilliant set of experiments using balls and ramps. Figure App.1a shows his original setup. The ramp on the left and the ramp on the right both make the same angle with the ground. When a ball is released from the top of the left ramp, it rolls down the left ramp and then back up the right ramp, until it reaches the same height from which it was released. Then it stops. Next the angle of the right ramp is decreased as in Figure App.1b. This time, when the ball is released from the left it still comes back to its original height on the right, *even though it has farther to go.* Galileo tried this many times with many different angles, and the result was always the same. The ball kept coming back to the height from which it started. With that principle in mind, Galileo extended the idea to the setup in Figure App.1c. Here the right ramp is completely flat. The ball rolling down from the left ramp wants to roll back up to the height from which it was released, but it can't, so Galileo reasoned that it would try to keep on rolling forever. His conclusion: Moving objects want to keep moving.

Conservation of Momentum

Look at the two inelastic (unsqueezeable) balls shown in Figure App.2. They start by moving towards each other, then they collide and move away from each other. Each ball has a incoming velocity before the collision, and each ball has a outgoing velocity after the collision. Note that velocity is a vector quantity. The speed part of velocity is its magnitude. It tells you how many meters the object will travel in one second. The direction part of velocity is its unit vector. It tells you which way the object is going.

During the collision, Newton's 3rd law states that the force exerted on ball 2 by ball 1 has to be equal and opposite to the force exerted on ball 1 by ball 2.

$$\vec{F}_{12} = -\vec{F}_{21} \ . \tag{1}$$

Substituting Newton's 2nd law for $\vec{F}$,

$$m_2\vec{a}_2 = -m_1\vec{a}_1 \ , \tag{2}$$

and then the definition of acceleration for $\vec{a}$, leads to

$$m_2\left(\frac{\vec{v}_{2\,after} - \vec{v}_{2\,before}}{t_{after} - t_{before}}\right) = -m_1\left(\frac{\vec{v}_{1\,after} - \vec{v}_{1\,before}}{t_{after} - t_{before}}\right) \ . \tag{3}$$

Note that the $_{before}$ and $_{after}$ subscripts refer to before and after the collision. The denominators on both sides of equation (3) are the same. So they multiply out leaving

$$\begin{aligned} m_2(\vec{v}_{2\,a} - \vec{v}_{2\,b}) &= -m_1(\vec{v}_{1\,a} - \vec{v}_{1\,b}) \\ m_2\vec{v}_{2\,a} - m_2\vec{v}_{2\,b} &= -m_1\vec{v}_{1\,a} + m_1\vec{v}_{1\,b} \,. \end{aligned} \tag{4}$$

Putting all of the "befores" on the left side of the equation,

$$-m_1\vec{v}_{1\,b} - m_2\vec{v}_{2\,b} = -m_1\vec{v}_{1\,a} - m_2\vec{v}_{2\,a} \,, \tag{5}$$

and multiplying both sides by -1, results in

$$m_1\vec{v}_{1\,b} + m_2\vec{v}_{2\,b} = m_1\vec{v}_{1\,a} + m_2\vec{v}_{2\,a} \,. \tag{6}$$

Equation (6) is a statement of Conservation of linear Momentum. The quantity $m\vec{v}$ is called linear momentum, and its units are $\frac{kg\,m}{s}$. Conservation of Momentum says that the total linear momentum of the balls before the collision has to equal the total linear momentum of the balls after the collision.

Conservation of Energy

The number of meters a straight moving object will travel in some period of time $\Delta t = t_2 - t_1$, can be found by multiplying the average speed of the object by the interval of time: $\left(\frac{m}{s}\right)(s) \rightarrow m$. If you wanted to include direction, and find the vector distance traveled, you would need to substitute average velocity for average speed,

$$\vec{d} = \vec{v}_{avg}\Delta t = \vec{v}_{avg}(t_2 - t_1) \,. \tag{7}$$

Suppose the moving object is being accelerated by a constant force, and we dot that force into both sides of the equation,

$$\vec{F} \bullet \vec{d} = \vec{F} \bullet \vec{v}_{avg}(t_2 - t_1) \,. \tag{8}$$

Now substitute $m\vec{a}$ into the right side

$$\vec{F} \bullet \vec{d} = m\vec{a} \bullet \vec{v}_{avg}(t_2 - t_1) \,. \tag{9}$$

If the force is constant, then from $\vec{F} = m\vec{a}$, the acceleration must be constant too. After all, the mass is not going to change, so if $\vec{F}$ doesn't change and m doesn't change, then $\vec{a}$ can't change either. For constant acceleration, to find $\vec{v}_{avg}$ over some time interval, you just add $\vec{v}_1$ at the beginning of the interval to $\vec{v}_2$ at the end of the interval and divide by 2. It's like finding the average of 4 and 8, $\frac{4+8}{2} = 6$.

The definition of constant acceleration is $\vec{a} = \frac{\vec{v}_2 - \vec{v}_1}{t_2 - t_1}$. And when $\vec{a}$ is constant, $\vec{v}_{avg} = \frac{\vec{v}_1 + \vec{v}_2}{2}$. Making those substitutions into equation (9),

$$\vec{F} \bullet \vec{d} = m\left(\frac{\vec{v}_2 - \vec{v}_1}{t_2 - t_1}\right) \bullet \left(\frac{\vec{v}_1 + \vec{v}_2}{2}\right)(t_2 - t_1) \,. \tag{10}$$

The time intervals will cancel, and $\vec{v}_1 + \vec{v}_2 = \vec{v}_2 + \vec{v}_1$, which leaves

$$\vec{F} \bullet \vec{d} = \frac{1}{2}m(\vec{v}_2 - \vec{v}_1) \bullet (\vec{v}_2 + \vec{v}_1) \,. \tag{11}$$

Distributing the dot product on the right hand side,

$$\vec{F} \bullet \vec{d} = \frac{1}{2}m(\vec{v}_2 \bullet \vec{v}_2 + \overbrace{\vec{v}_2 \bullet \vec{v}_1 - \vec{v}_1 \bullet \vec{v}_2}^{=0} - \vec{v}_1 \bullet \vec{v}_1) \,. \tag{12}$$

The two dot products in the middle add to zero because $\vec{v}_2 \bullet \vec{v}_1 = \vec{v}_1 \bullet \vec{v}_2$. Also, since $\vec{v} \bullet \vec{v} = |\vec{v}|^2$, equation (12) reduces to

$$\begin{aligned} \vec{F} \bullet \vec{d} &= \frac{1}{2}m(|\vec{v}_2|^2 - |\vec{v}_1|^2) \\ &= \frac{1}{2}m|\vec{v}_2|^2 - \frac{1}{2}m|\vec{v}_1|^2 \end{aligned} \tag{13}$$

The magnitude of velocity can be written without the vector and absolute value signs, $|\vec{v}| = v$, so that the final result looks like

$$\vec{F} \bullet \vec{d} = \frac{1}{2}mv_2^2 - \frac{1}{2}mv_1^2 \,. \tag{14}$$

Equation (14) applies to any object being accelerated by a constant force. Let's suppose that object is a ball thrown straight up into the air as shown in Figure App.3. If we neglect air resistance, then gravity is the only force acting on the ball once it leaves the thrower's hand. Gravity is pretty constant close to the surface of the earth where $\vec{a}_{grav} = \vec{g}$. So Newton's 2nd law, $\Sigma\vec{F} = m\vec{a}$, reduces to

$$\vec{F} = m\vec{g} \tag{15}$$

for this case. The ball travels up some distance $\vec{d}$. If we dot the distance vector into both sides of the equation, then

$$\vec{F} \bullet \vec{d} = m\vec{g} \bullet \vec{d} \,. \tag{16}$$

From Figure App.3, $\vec{d} = \vec{h}_2 - \vec{h}_1$, where the heights are referenced to the ground so that $\vec{h}_2 = |\vec{h}_2|(+\hat{\jmath})$ and $\vec{h}_1 = |\vec{h}_1|(+\hat{\jmath})$. The acceleration of the ball is due to gravity, which is constant and always points down, $\vec{g} = |\vec{g}|(-\hat{\jmath})$. Those substitutions lead to

$$\begin{aligned} \vec{F} \bullet \vec{d} &= m\vec{g} \bullet (\vec{h}_2 - \vec{h}_1) \\ &= m\vec{g} \bullet \vec{h}_2 - m\vec{g} \bullet \vec{h}_1 \\ &= m[|\vec{g}|(-\hat{\jmath}) \bullet |\vec{h}_2|(+\hat{\jmath})] + m[|\vec{g}|(+\hat{\jmath}) \bullet |\vec{h}_1|(+\hat{\jmath})] \\ \vec{F} \bullet \vec{d} &= -m|\vec{g}||\vec{h}_2| + m|\vec{g}||\vec{h}_1| \,, \end{aligned} \tag{17}$$

or just

$$\vec{F} \bullet \vec{d} = -mgh_2 + mgh_1 \,, \tag{18}$$

since $|\vec{g}| = g$ and $|\vec{h}| = h$.

Equations (14) and (18) are both expressions for $\vec{F} \bullet \vec{d}$ given a constant acceleration. If we set the two equal, we wind up with one of the most famous relationships in physics,

$$\begin{aligned} \vec{F} \bullet \vec{d} &= \vec{F} \bullet \vec{d} \\ -mgh_2 + mgh_1 &= \frac{1}{2}mv_2^2 - \frac{1}{2}mv_1^2 \\ \frac{1}{2}mv_1^2 + mgh_1 &= \frac{1}{2}mv_2^2 + mgh_2 \; . \end{aligned} \tag{19}$$

Equation (19) is a statement of Conservation of Energy. The $\frac{1}{2}mv^2$ terms are called kinetic energy,

$$Kinetic\ Energy \rightarrow KE = \frac{1}{2}mv^2 \; . \tag{20}$$

The mgh terms are called Gravitational Potential Energy, or just Potential Energy,

$$Potential\ Energy \rightarrow PE = mgh \; . \tag{21}$$

Kinetic energy depends on motion. If the object is not moving, then $\frac{1}{2}mv^2 = \frac{1}{2}m(0)^2 = 0$. The units of KE are

$$\frac{1}{2}mv^2 \rightarrow kg\left(\frac{m}{s}\right)^2 \rightarrow \left(\frac{kg\ m}{s^2}\right) m \rightarrow N\ m \; .$$

Potential energy depends on height. If the object is down on the ground, then $mgh = mg(0) = 0$. The units of PE are

$$mgh \rightarrow kg\left(\frac{m}{s^2}\right) m \rightarrow \left(\frac{kg\ m}{s^2}\right) m \rightarrow N\ m \; .$$

The unit $N\ m$ occurs often enough to have its own name. It is called a Joule, after James Joule, who was the 1st person to demonstrate the equivalence of mechanical energy and heat energy. So

$$1\ N\ m \equiv 1\ J \; .$$

Energy has units of Joules (J).

If air resistance is included, then there would have to be a loss term in equation (19),

$$KE_1 + PE_1 = KE_2 + PE_2 + loss \; . \tag{22}$$

Neglecting air resistance, $loss = 0$ and,

$$KE_1 + PE_1 = KE_2 + PE_2 \; . \tag{23}$$

Conservation of Energy has been interpreted to mean, "Energy can neither be created nor destroyed, but only changed into other forms." We can see that change take place in the fall of a dropped ball. The ball starts out stationary at some height above the ground, h. It has a lot of potential energy, $PE = mgh$, but no kinetic energy, $KE = \frac{1}{2}m(0)^2 = 0$. As the ball falls, it gets closer and closer to the ground so that h is always decreasing. It is losing potential energy. At the same time the ball is going faster and faster so that v is always increasing. It is gaining kinetic energy. By the time it reaches the ground, $PE = mg(0) = 0$, and $KE = \frac{1}{2}mv^2_{max}$. All of its original potential energy has been transformed into kinetic energy. According to equation (23), that transformation takes place in such a way that the total $KE+PE$ at any point during the fall equals the total $KE + PE$ at any other point during the fall.

Centripetal Acceleration

Look at the outer space ball being whirled around with constant speed at the end of the string in Figure App.4. We know from observation that the rock will fly off in a straight line if the string is suddenly cut. That means the velocity vectors are all tangent to the circle. And, if the ball moves with constant speed, they are also all the same length.

The force that is being exerted on the rock comes through the string, and it is pulling the rock in towards the center of the circle. (Strings can't push.) So the centripetal force $\vec{F}_c$ is directed towards the center of the circle. From $\vec{F}_c = m\vec{a}_c$, the centripetal acceleration has to point the same way, in towards the center of the circle. Figure App.5 shows a picture.

For the magnitude of the centripetal acceleration, we can start with the definition,

$$\vec{a}_c = \frac{\vec{v}_2 - \vec{v}_1}{\Delta t} , \tag{24}$$

Then take the magnitude of both sides,

$$|\vec{a}_c| = \left| \frac{\vec{v}_2 - \vec{v}_1}{\Delta t} \right| = \frac{|\vec{v}_2 - \vec{v}_1|}{\Delta t} . \tag{25}$$

(The Δt in the denominator does not need to be written $|\Delta t|$ because we already know that it will always be positive.)

In order to find $|\vec{a}_c|$ we need to find $|\vec{v}_2 - \vec{v}_1|$ and Δt.

Figure App.6a shows a top view of the rock as it goes around, with velocity vectors drawn in at several locations. In Figure App.6b, the length of the string is decreased so that the tails of the velocity vectors are closer together. Finally in Figure App.6c, the length of the string is almost zero. The tails of the velocity vectors are all very close together forming a "wheel of $\vec{v}$'s". That wheel makes it much easier to see the angles between the $\vec{v}$'s.

Figure App.7 shows a famous theorem from geometry. The theorem states that

$$s = r\theta , \tag{26}$$

where s is the arc length, r is the length of the radius, and θ is the radian angle between the two r's.

Figure App.8 shows the vector difference, $\vec{v}_2 - \vec{v}_1$, between two of the velocity vectors from the wheel of $\vec{v}$'s.

Figure App.9 compares the theorem from geometry with $|\vec{v}_2 - \vec{v}_1|$. In Figure App.9a, $arc\ length = v\theta > |\vec{v}_2 - \vec{v}_1|$ because the angle θ between $\vec{v}_1$ and $\vec{v}_2$ is big. But that problem is easy to fix. The rock actually has an infinite number of $\vec{v}$ vectors as it goes around, not just the 8 that are shown in Figure App.6. We are free to choose any of them to be $\vec{v}_2$ and $\vec{v}_1$, so in Figure App.9b we pick two $\vec{v}$'s that are much closer together. Now $v\theta$ is almost equal to $|\vec{v}_2 - \vec{v}_1|$, and if we got infinitesimally close together they actually would be equal.

$$v\theta = |\vec{v}_2 - \vec{v}_1| \,. \tag{27}$$

The difference in time Δt between $\vec{v}_1$ and $\vec{v}_2$ can also be expressed in terms of v and the radian angle θ between the two vectors.

In Figure App.4, the angle for the rock to go all the way around the circle is $360^o = 2\pi$ radians. Big T is called the period, and it is defined as the amount of time that the rock takes to go all the way around. Distance equals speed $\times$ time, so the distance all the way around equals vT. But the distance all the way around a circle is also equal to the circumference, $C = 2\pi r$. It's the same distance, so

$$\begin{aligned} vT &= 2\pi r \\ T &= \frac{2\pi r}{v} \,. \end{aligned} \tag{28}$$

Big T is also the amount of time that it takes for one of the velocity vectors to move all the way around the Figure App.6 wheel of $\vec{v}$'s, and come back to where it started. So big T corresponds to an angle of 2π radians on the wheel of $\vec{v}$'s. From equation (24), Δt is the amount of time that it takes to get from $\vec{v}_1$ to $\vec{v}_2$. So Δt corresponds to an angle of θ on the wheel. The speed v never changes, which means that Δt is the same fraction of big T as θ is of 2π. In other words,

$$\frac{\Delta t}{T} = \frac{\theta}{2\pi} \,. \tag{29}$$

Solving for Δt, and substituting equation (28) for T,

$$\begin{aligned} \frac{\Delta t}{T} &= \frac{\theta}{2\pi} \\ \Delta t &= T\left(\frac{\theta}{2\pi}\right) \\ &= \left(\frac{2\pi r}{v}\right)\left(\frac{\theta}{2\pi}\right) \\ \Delta t &= \frac{r\theta}{v} \,. \end{aligned} \tag{30}$$

Combining equations (25), (27), and (30), we finally obtain

$$
\begin{aligned}
|\vec{a}_c| &= \frac{|\vec{v}_2 - \vec{v}_1|}{\Delta t} \\
&= \frac{v\theta}{\frac{r\theta}{v}} = \left(\frac{v\theta}{1}\right)\left(\frac{v}{r\theta}\right) \\
|\vec{a}_c| &= \frac{v^2}{r} \, .
\end{aligned} \tag{31}
$$

The magnitude of the centripetal accelration is equal to the speed of the rock squared, divided by the length of the string. The direction of $\vec{a}_c$ is down the string, towards the center of the circle.

Time Dilation

The concept of time dilation is a consequence of the two postulates that led to Einstein's theory of Special Relativity.

Look at Figure App.10. In the top half of the Figure, an observer inside the space ship is timing how long it takes for the front of a laser beam to get from the top of the ship to the bottom of the ship. In his reference frame, $\vec{d} = \vec{v}(\Delta t)$, where (Δt) is the number of seconds that it takes the beam to travel the distance $|\vec{d}|$. In magnitudes, $|\vec{d}| = |\vec{v}|(\Delta t)$. If we call the height of the ship, h, then $|\vec{d}| = h$. The beam travels at the speed of light, so that $|\vec{v}| = c$. Also, let's also make note of the fact that the time is being measured on a ship clock by letting $\Delta t = \Delta t_s$. We finally have then,

$$h = c(\Delta t_s) \tag{32}$$

for the distance traveled by the light beam as measured by the on-board observer.

In Figure App.10b, that same light beam is being measured by an obsever standing on the ground, watching the ship move with constant velocity to the right. Just like the on-board observer, the ground observer sees the light beam leave the laser, then arrive at the bottom of the ship right underneath the laser. But while the light beam was traveling, the ship has moved a little bit to the right. According to the ground observer the light beam has to cover a longer distance to get from the top of the ship to the bottom of the ship. Einstein's 1st postulate states that the laws of physics are the same in both inertial reference frames, so the ground observer also uses $\vec{d} = \vec{v}(\Delta t)$ for his measurement. In magnitudes, he gets

$$d = c(\Delta t_g) \, , \tag{33}$$

where Δt_g is the number of seconds that go by on the ground clock.

The ground observer's d is longer than the ship observer's h, $d > h$. Which means

$$c(\Delta t_g) > c(\Delta t_s) \, . \tag{34}$$

A pre-Einstein physicist would have no trouble explaining equation (34). She would say that the two Δt's are equal but that the two c's are not. According to "Galilean" thinking, the ground observer should see a faster speed of light. But Einstein says no. His 2nd postulate states that everybody measures the speed of light to be the same. If that is true, then the c's cancel so that

$$\Delta t_g > \Delta t_s \,. \tag{35}$$

More seconds go by on the ground than go by on the ship.

The exact relationship between Δt_g and Δt_s can be found using the Pythagorean theorem. Figure App.11 shows the triangle. Notice that the length of the bottom side is $v(\Delta t_g)$ because the ship moves with constant speed v as measured on the ground observers clock, Δt_g. Meanwhile the length of the hypotenuse is $c(\Delta t_g)$, so that

$$\begin{aligned}
[c\,(\Delta t_g)]^2 &= [c\,(\Delta t_s)]^2 + [v\,(\Delta t_g)]^2 \\
c^2\,(\Delta t_g)^2 &= c^2\,(\Delta t_s)^2 + v^2\,(\Delta t_g)^2 \\
c^2\,(\Delta t_s)^2 &= c^2\,(\Delta t_g)^2 - v^2\,(\Delta t_g)^2 \\
(\Delta t_s)^2 &= (\Delta t_g)^2 - \frac{v^2}{c^2}\,(\Delta t_g)^2 \\
(\Delta t_s)^2 &= (\Delta t_g)^2\left[1 - \frac{v^2}{c^2}\right] \,.
\end{aligned} \tag{36}$$

Taking the square root of both sides we finally arrive at

$$\Delta t_s = \Delta t_g\sqrt{1 - \frac{v^2}{c^2}} \,, \tag{37}$$

for the exact relationship between the number of seconds that go by on the ship and the number of seconds that go by on the ground.

Conservation of Angular Momentum

Conservation of Angular Momentum is considered to be a fundamental characteristic of Nature, just like Newton's 2nd Law. As such, it is more subject to experimental verification than it is to rigorous derivation. What follows is mainly a "plausibility argument".

At $t = t_1$, an outer space rock is being whirled around in the xy plane with constant speed, as shown at the top of Figure App.12. The rock possesses an angular momentum, $\vec{L}_1 = \vec{r}_1 \times m\vec{v}_1$.

During the interval $t_2 - t_1$, an external force is applied to the rock, which causes a torque, $\vec{\tau}_{average} \approx \vec{r}_{average} \times \vec{F}_{external}$. (The approximately equal to sign comes about because $\vec{r}_{avg}$ is not exactly equal to $\frac{1}{2}(\vec{r}_1 + \vec{r}_2)$. It is however pretty close if Δt is short.)

At $t = t_2$, $\vec{F}_{ext}$ has been removed and the rock's new angular momentum has become $\vec{L}_2 = \vec{r}_2 \times m\vec{v}_2$.

The relationship that describes this evolution of events would be

$$\vec{L}_2 = \vec{\tau}_{avg}\,(\Delta t) + \vec{L}_1\ . \tag{38}$$

(Notice the similarity to the straight line velocity equation, $\vec{v}_2 = \vec{a}\,(\Delta t) + \vec{v}_1$, or to the Impulse-Momentum Theorem, $m\vec{v}_2 = \vec{F}_{avg}\,(\Delta t) + m\vec{v}_1$.) Let's look at the units.

$$\begin{aligned}
m\ kg\left(\frac{m}{s}\right) &= m \cdot N\,(s) + m\ kg\left(\frac{m}{s}\right)\\
\frac{kg\ m^2}{s} &= m\left(\frac{kg\ m}{s^2}\right)s + \frac{kg\ m^2}{s}\\
\frac{kg\ m^2}{s} &= \frac{kg\ m^2}{s} + \frac{kg\ m^2}{s}\\
\frac{kg\ m^2}{s} &= \frac{kg\ m^2}{s}
\end{aligned}$$

Both sides have the same units, which is the way that things are supposed to be.

If $\vec{\tau}_{avg} = 0$, then equation (38) reduces to $\vec{L}_2 = \vec{L}_1$. That could happen in one of two ways.

First, $\vec{\tau}_{avg}$ could equal zero because $\vec{F}_{ext} = 0$. In that case $\vec{L}_2 = \vec{L}_1$ because there has been no change in the system. That case is trival.

But there is another way in which $\vec{\tau}_{avg}$ could equal zero. The cross product of any 2 vectors that are in the opposite (or the same) direction equals zero. Suppose $\vec{F}_{ext}$ is directed down the string by pulling the end of the string that goes down through the tube. We'll say for example that the rock is crossing the $+x$ axis when $\vec{F}_{ext}$ is applied. That way, $\vec{r} = |\vec{r}|(+\hat{\imath})$ when $\vec{F}_{ext} = |\vec{F}_{ext}|(-\hat{\imath})$. In that case.

$$\vec{r} \times \vec{F}_{ext} \longrightarrow \begin{matrix} \hat{\imath} & \hat{\jmath} & \hat{k} & \hat{\imath} & \hat{\jmath} \\ |\vec{r}| & 0 & 0 & |\vec{r}| & 0 \\ -|\vec{F}_{ext}| & 0 & 0 & -|\vec{F}_{ext}| & 0 \end{matrix}$$

$$\begin{aligned}
\vec{\tau}_{avg} = \vec{r} \times \vec{F}_{ext} &= [0-0]\hat{\imath} + [0-0]\hat{\jmath} + [0-0]\hat{k}\\
\vec{\tau}_{avg} &= 0
\end{aligned} \tag{39}$$

Equation (38) again reduces to $\vec{L}_2 = \vec{L}_1$, but this time the system <u>has</u> been changed. The effect of pulling the string down by $\vec{F}_{ext}$ is to shorten $\vec{r}$. Now $\vec{L}_2 = \vec{L}_1$ because

$$\vec{r}_2 \times m\vec{v}_2 = \vec{r}_1 \times m\vec{v}_1\ . \tag{40}$$

Pulling the end of the string to shorten $\vec{r}$ does not affect m, nor does it affect the direction of revolution. That means $\vec{L}$ will still be in the same direction, which would either be $\pm\hat{k}$ depending on which way the rock is going around. Equation (40) then reduces to

$$\begin{aligned} \vec{r}_1 \times m\vec{v}_1 &= \vec{r}_2 \times m\vec{v}_2 \\ r_1 m v_1(\pm\hat{k}) &= r_2 m v_2(\pm\hat{k}) \\ r_1 v_1 &= r_2 v_2 \,. \end{aligned} \tag{41}$$

If the applied torque equals zero, Conservation of Angular Momentum demands that $\vec{L}_1 = \vec{L}_2 \longrightarrow |\vec{L}_1| = |\vec{L}_2|$. For the system shown in Figure App.12, the only way that can happen is if a change in the radius brings about a change in the speed.

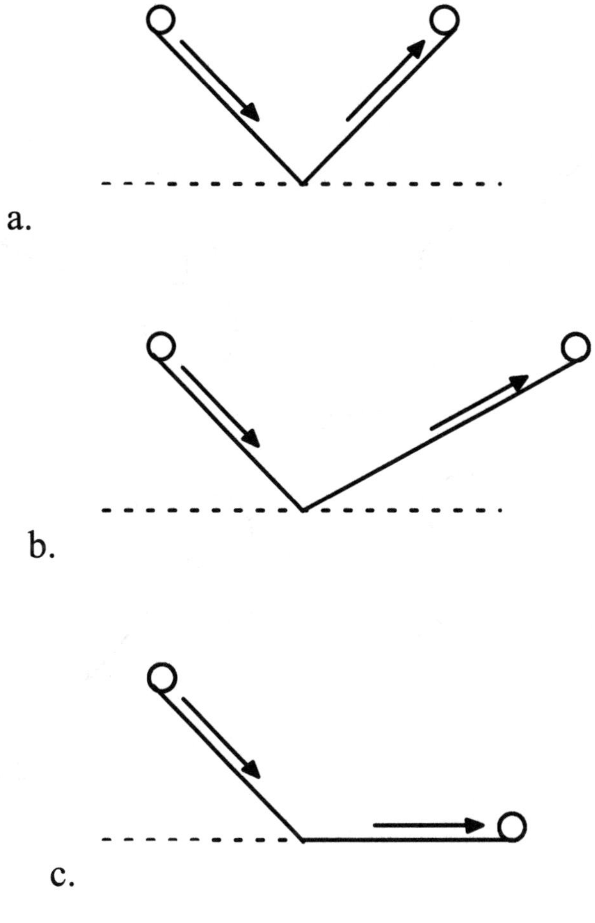

Figure App.1 Galileo's ball and ramp experiment

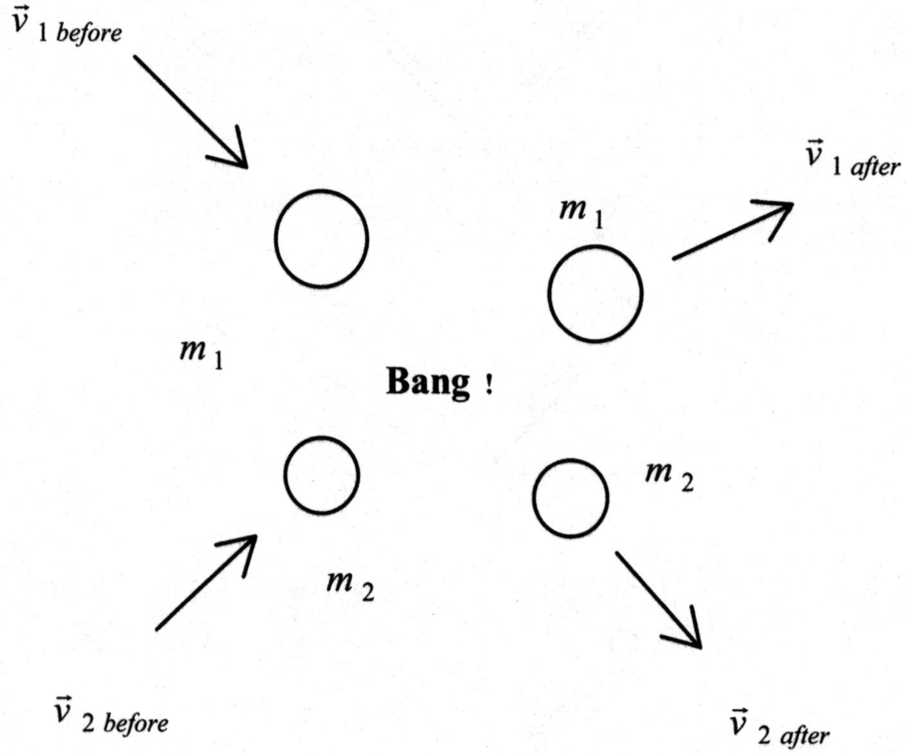

Figure App.2 Colliding Masses

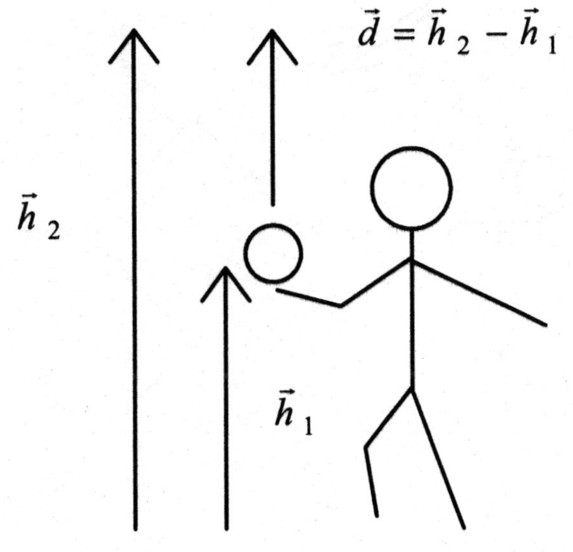

Figure App.3 Ball being thrown straight up

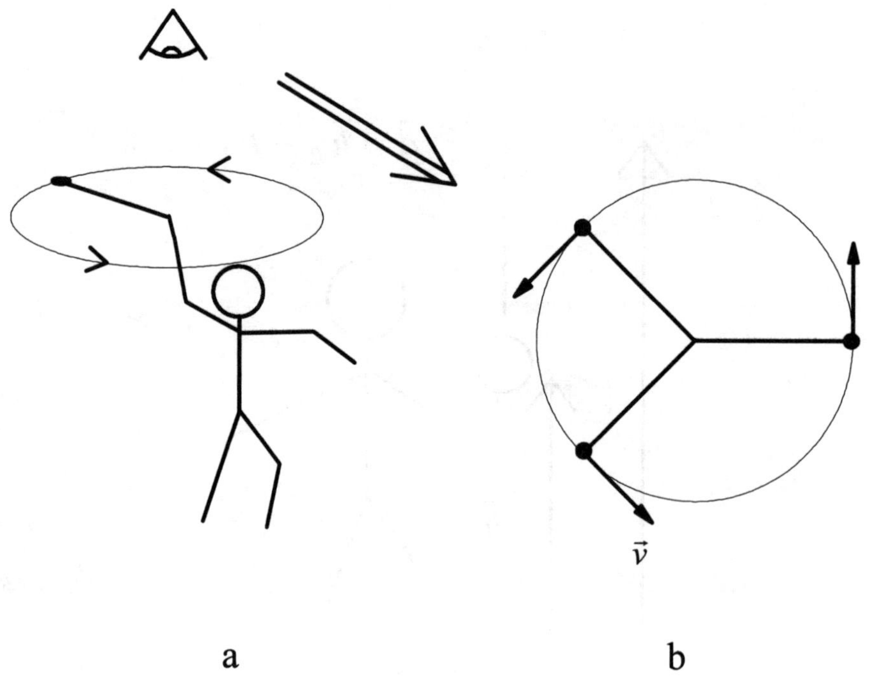

Figure App.4 a.) Rock being whirled around at the end of a string
b.) Velocity vector is always tangent to the circle

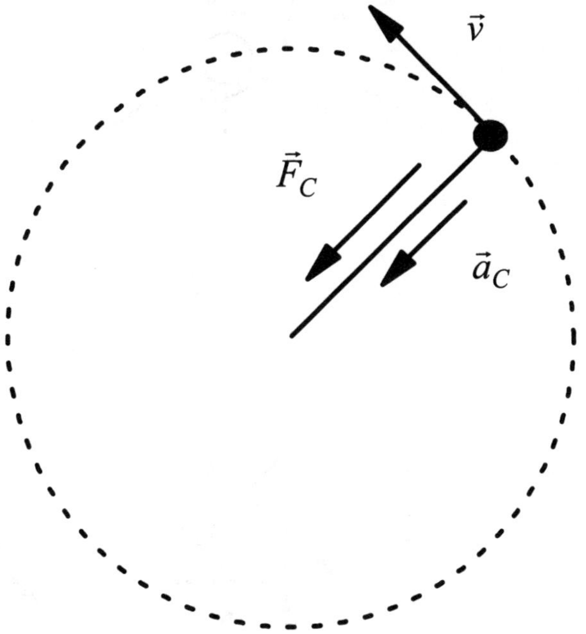

Figure App.5   Centripetal Force and Centripetal Acceleration

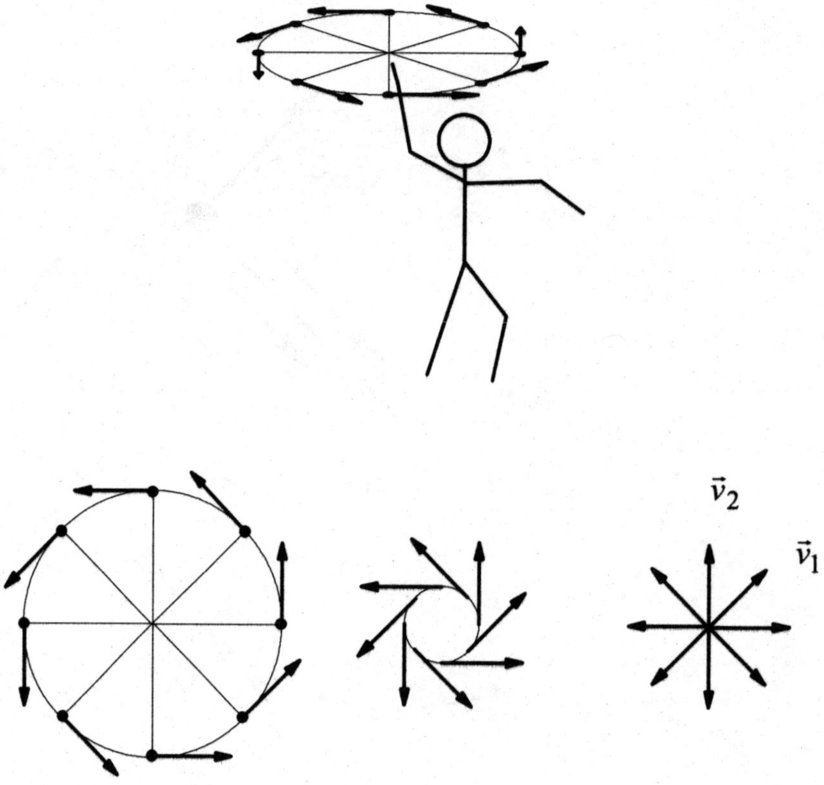

a b c

Figure App.6 String is shortened to form a ``wheel of $\vec{v}$'s''

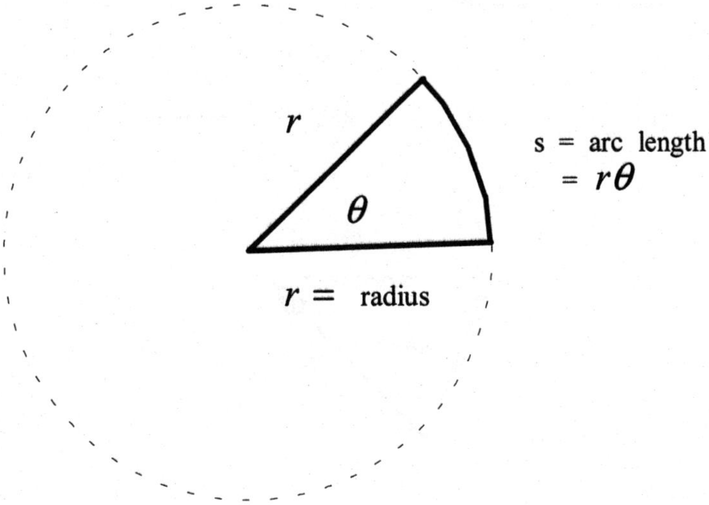

Figure App.7 $s = r\theta$

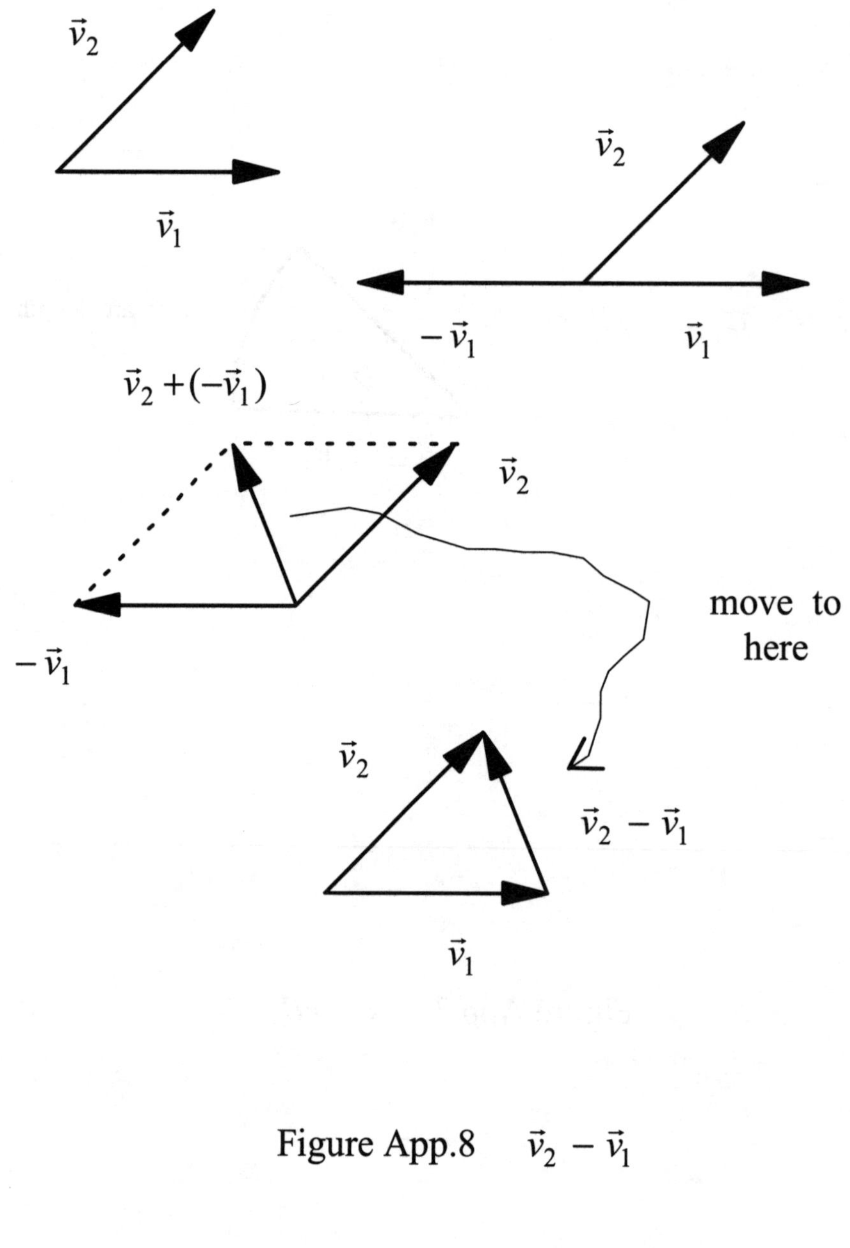

Figure App.8 $\vec{v}_2 - \vec{v}_1$

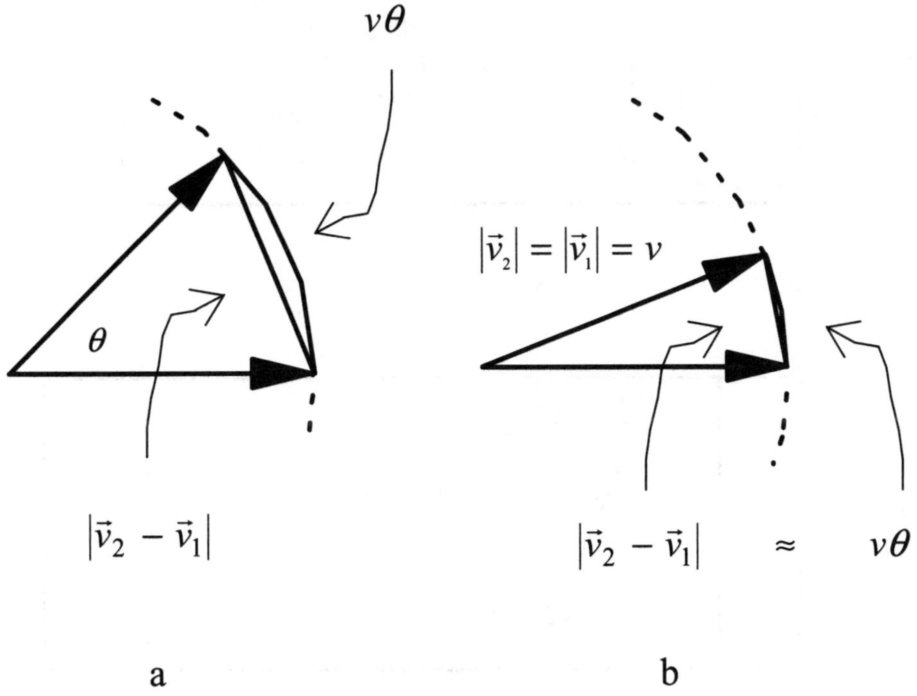

Figure App.9 $|\vec{v}_2 - \vec{v}_1|$ gets close to $v\theta$ as θ gets small

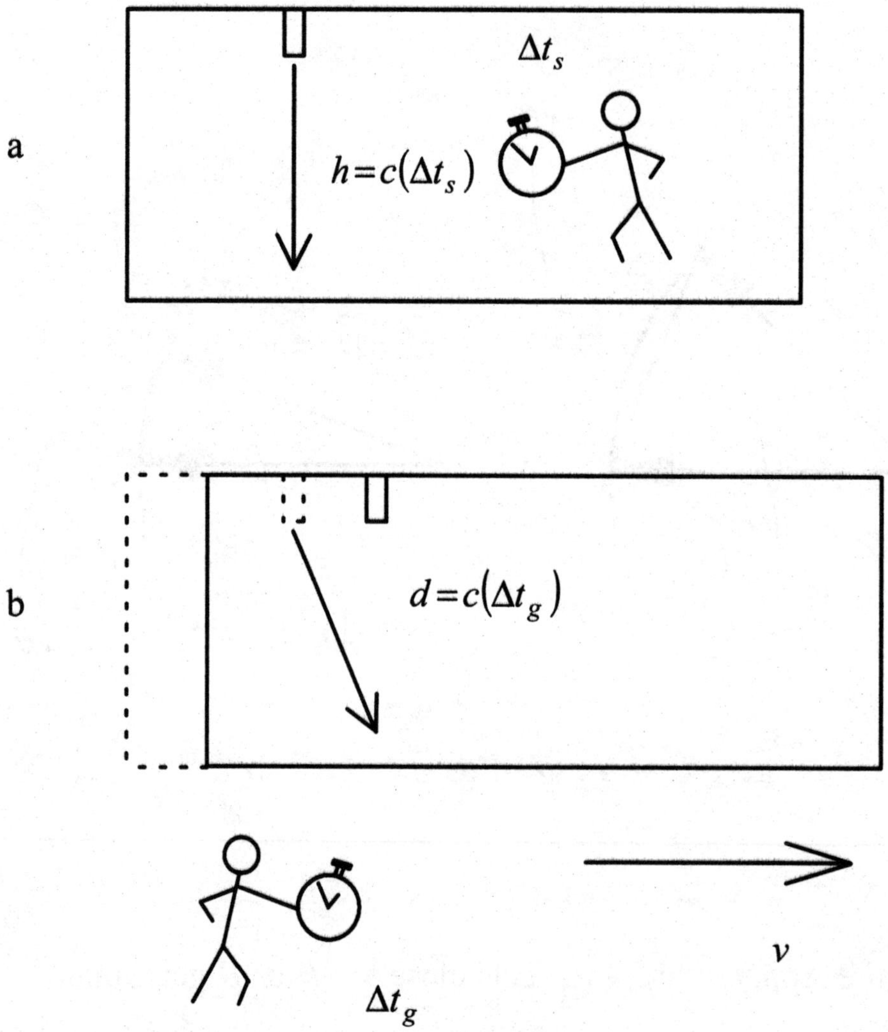

Figure App.10   Laser beam seen from a) inside the ship, and b) outside the ship.

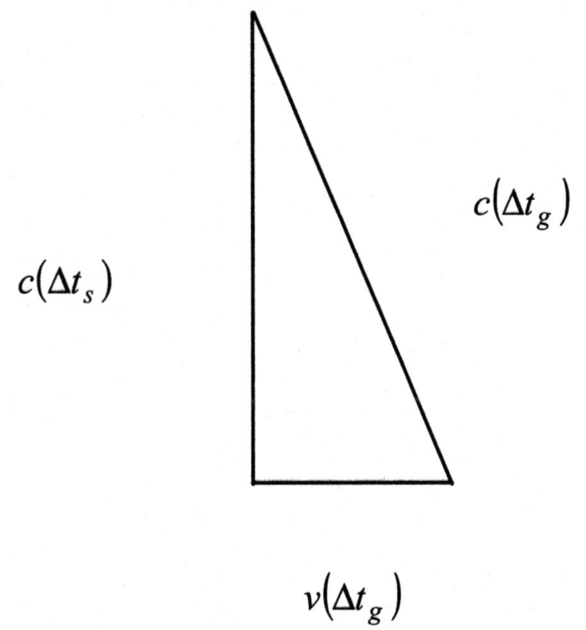

Figure App.11 Pythagorean triangle from Figure App.10

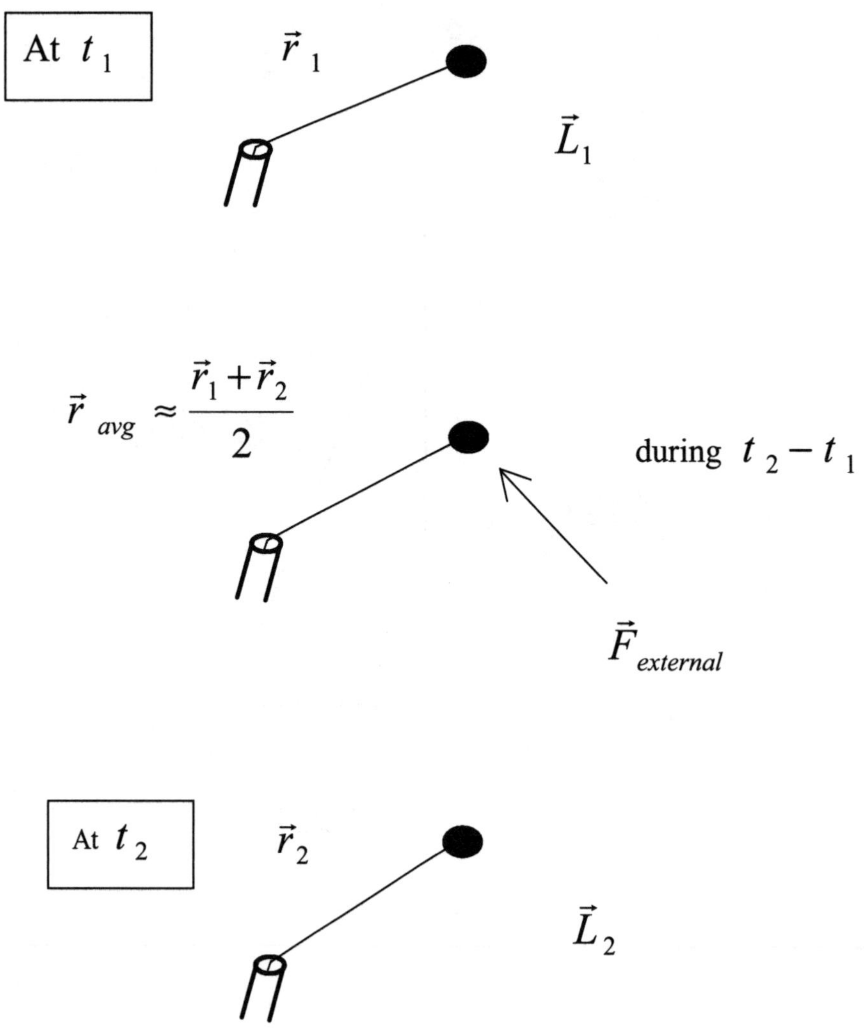

Figure App.12 Conservation of Angular Momentum

Quiz Solutions

Quiz 1.1

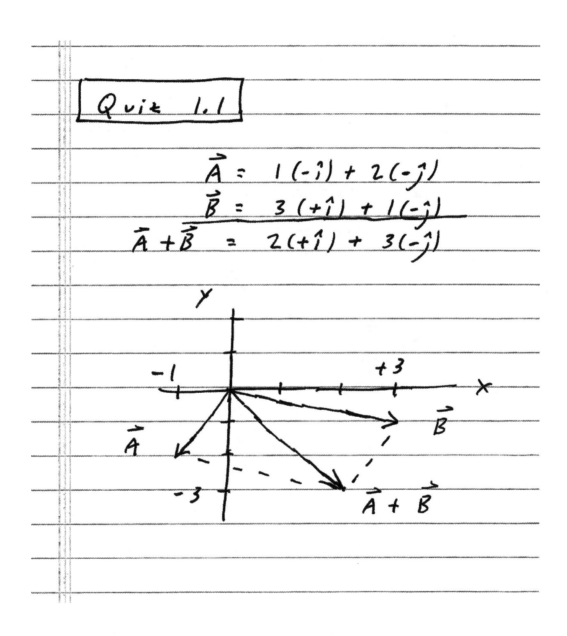

$$\vec{A} = 1(-\hat{i}) + 2(-\hat{j})$$
$$\vec{B} = 3(+\hat{i}) + 1(-\hat{j})$$
$$\vec{A} + \vec{B} = 2(+\hat{i}) + 3(-\hat{j})$$

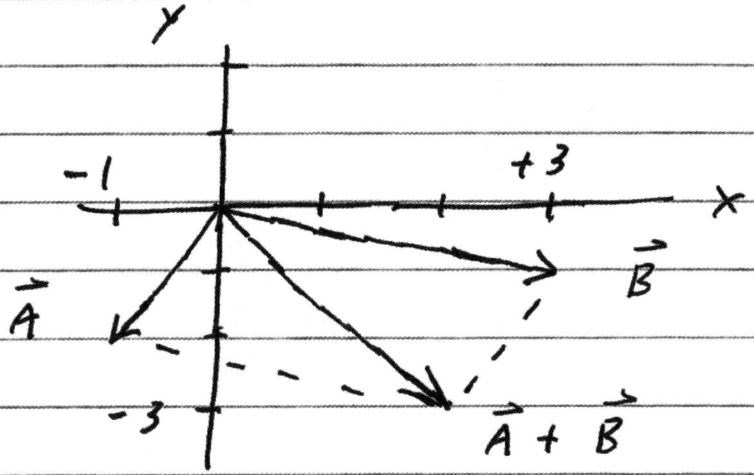

Quiz 1.2

TO − FROM

$(2,-1) - (-1,3) \Rightarrow (3,-4)$

$$\vec{r} = 3(+\hat{i}) + 4(-\hat{j})$$

$$|\vec{r}| = \sqrt{(3)^2 + (4)^2} = \sqrt{9+16} = \sqrt{25}$$

$$|\vec{r}| = 5$$

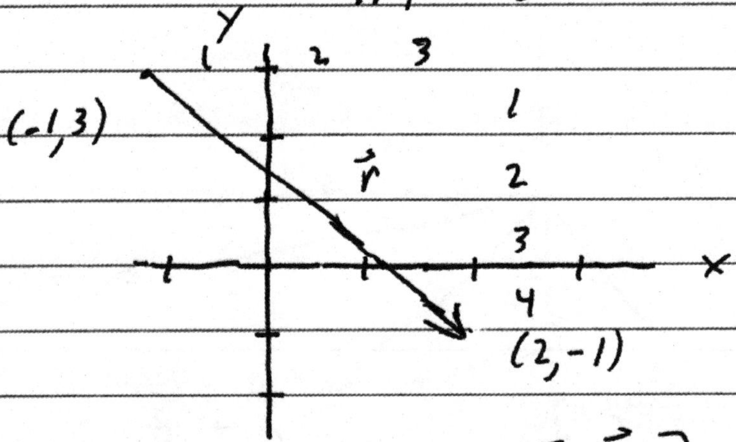

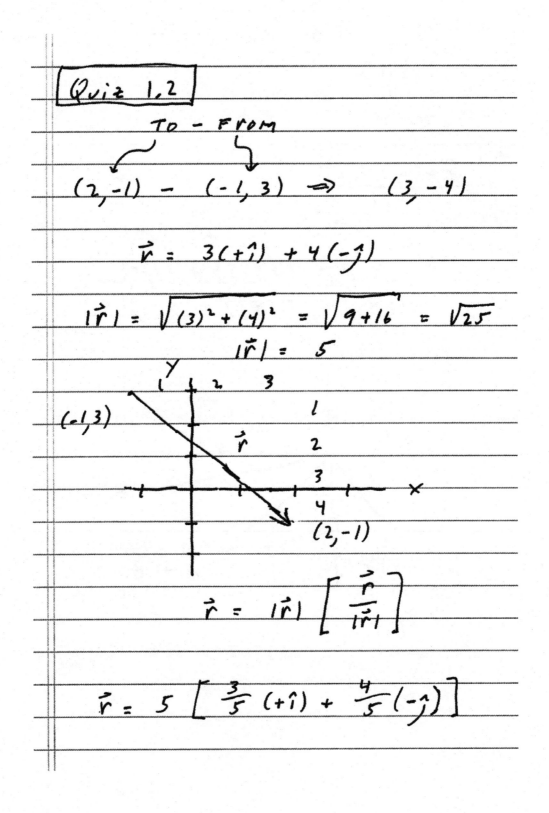

$$\vec{r} = |\vec{r}| \left[\frac{\vec{r}}{|\vec{r}|} \right]$$

$$\vec{r} = 5 \left[\frac{3}{5}(+\hat{i}) + \frac{4}{5}(-\hat{j}) \right]$$

Quiz 1.3

$$\vec{L} = 1.4(-\hat{i}) + 2(+\hat{j})$$
$$\vec{C} = .5(-\hat{i}) + 3(+\hat{j})$$

$$\vec{L}\cdot\vec{C} = [1.4(-\hat{i}) + 2(+\hat{j})]\cdot[.5(-\hat{i}) + 3(+\hat{j})]$$
$$= (-1.4)(-.5) + (+2)(+3)$$
$$= (+.7) + (+6)$$
$$\vec{L}\cdot\vec{C} = 6.7$$

$$\vec{L}\cdot\vec{L} = [1.4(-\hat{i}) + 2(+\hat{j})]\cdot[1.4(-\hat{i}) + 2(+\hat{j})]$$
$$= (-1.4)(-1.4) + (2)(2) = 1.96 + 4$$
$$\vec{L}\cdot\vec{L} = 5.96$$

$$|\vec{L}| = \sqrt{\vec{L}\cdot\vec{L}} = \sqrt{5.96}$$

$$\vec{L} = 1.4(-\hat{i}) + 2(+\hat{j})$$

$$|\vec{L}| = \sqrt{(1.4)^2 + (2)^2} = \sqrt{1.96+4}$$

$$|\vec{L}| = \sqrt{5.96}$$ ✓

Quiz 1.4

$$\phi^2 - 4\phi + 20 = 0$$

$$\phi = \frac{-(-4) \pm \sqrt{(-4)^2 - 4(1)(20)}}{2(1)} = \frac{4 \pm \sqrt{16-80}}{2}$$

$$= \frac{4 \pm \sqrt{-64}}{2} = \frac{4 \pm \sqrt{64(-1)}}{2} = \frac{4 \pm 8\sqrt{-1}}{2}$$

$$= 2 \pm 4i$$

$$\phi_1 = 2+4i \qquad \phi_2 = 2-4i$$

$$\phi_2^* = 2-4(-i) = 2+4i$$

$$\phi_2^*\phi_2 \Longrightarrow \begin{array}{r} 2+4i \\ \underline{2-4i} \\ 4+8i \\ \underline{\quad -8i + 4i(-4i)} \\ 4+0-16i^2 \end{array} \qquad i^2 = -1$$

$$\phi_2^*\phi_2 = 4 - 16(-1) = 4 + 16 = 20$$

$$|\phi_2| = \sqrt{\phi_2^*\phi_2} = \sqrt{20}$$

Quiz 1.5

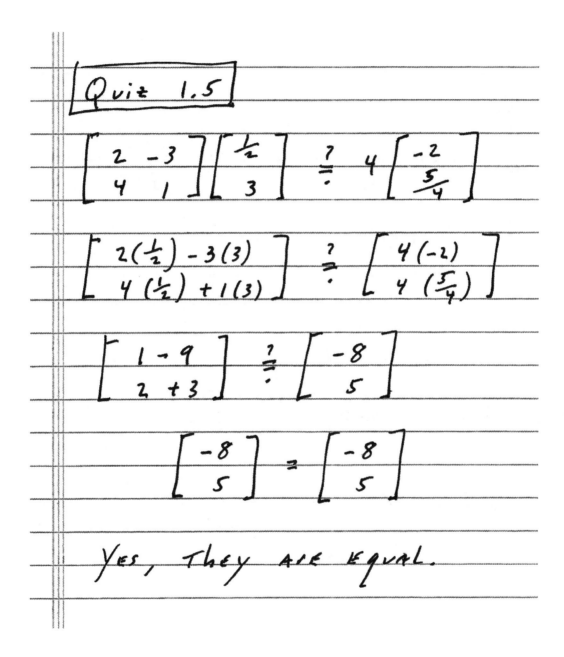

$$\begin{bmatrix} 2 & -3 \\ 4 & 1 \end{bmatrix} \begin{bmatrix} \frac{1}{2} \\ 3 \end{bmatrix} \stackrel{?}{=} 4 \begin{bmatrix} -2 \\ \frac{5}{4} \end{bmatrix}$$

$$\begin{bmatrix} 2(\frac{1}{2}) - 3(3) \\ 4(\frac{1}{2}) + 1(3) \end{bmatrix} \stackrel{?}{=} \begin{bmatrix} 4(-2) \\ 4(\frac{5}{4}) \end{bmatrix}$$

$$\begin{bmatrix} 1 - 9 \\ 2 + 3 \end{bmatrix} \stackrel{?}{=} \begin{bmatrix} -8 \\ 5 \end{bmatrix}$$

$$\begin{bmatrix} -8 \\ 5 \end{bmatrix} = \begin{bmatrix} -8 \\ 5 \end{bmatrix}$$

Yes, they are equal.

Quiz 1.6

$$\det \begin{bmatrix} 2 & 3 \\ x & 5 \end{bmatrix} = \begin{bmatrix} 6 & 2 \end{bmatrix} \begin{bmatrix} 1 \\ -4 \end{bmatrix}$$

$$2(5) - x(3) = 6(1) + 2(-4)$$
$$10 - 3x = 6 - 8$$
$$-3x = -2 - 10$$
$$3x = 12$$
$$x = 4$$

check: $$\det \begin{bmatrix} 2 & 3 \\ 4 & 5 \end{bmatrix} \stackrel{?}{=} \begin{bmatrix} 6 & 2 \end{bmatrix} \begin{bmatrix} 1 \\ -4 \end{bmatrix}$$

$$2(5) - 4(3) \stackrel{?}{=} 6(1) + 2(-4)$$
$$10 - 12 \stackrel{?}{=} 6 - 8$$
$$-2 = -2 \quad \checkmark$$

Quiz 1.7

$$3\ \text{ft} = ?\ \text{m}$$

$$\left(\frac{3\ \cancel{\text{ft}}}{1}\right)\left(\frac{12\ \cancel{\text{in}}}{\cancel{\text{ft}}}\right)\left(\frac{2.54\ \cancel{\text{cm}}}{\cancel{\text{in}}}\right)\left(\frac{1\ \text{m}}{100\ \cancel{\text{cm}}}\right)$$

$$= \frac{(3)(12)(2.54)(1)}{(1)(1)(1)(100)}\ \text{m}$$

$$= .9144\ \text{m}$$

$$3\ \text{ft} \approx .91\ \text{m}$$

Quiz 1.8

$\sin(0) = 0$

$\sin\left(\frac{\pi}{8}\right) \approx .38$

$\sin\left(\frac{2\pi}{8}\right) \approx .71$

$\sin\left(\frac{3\pi}{8}\right) \approx .92$

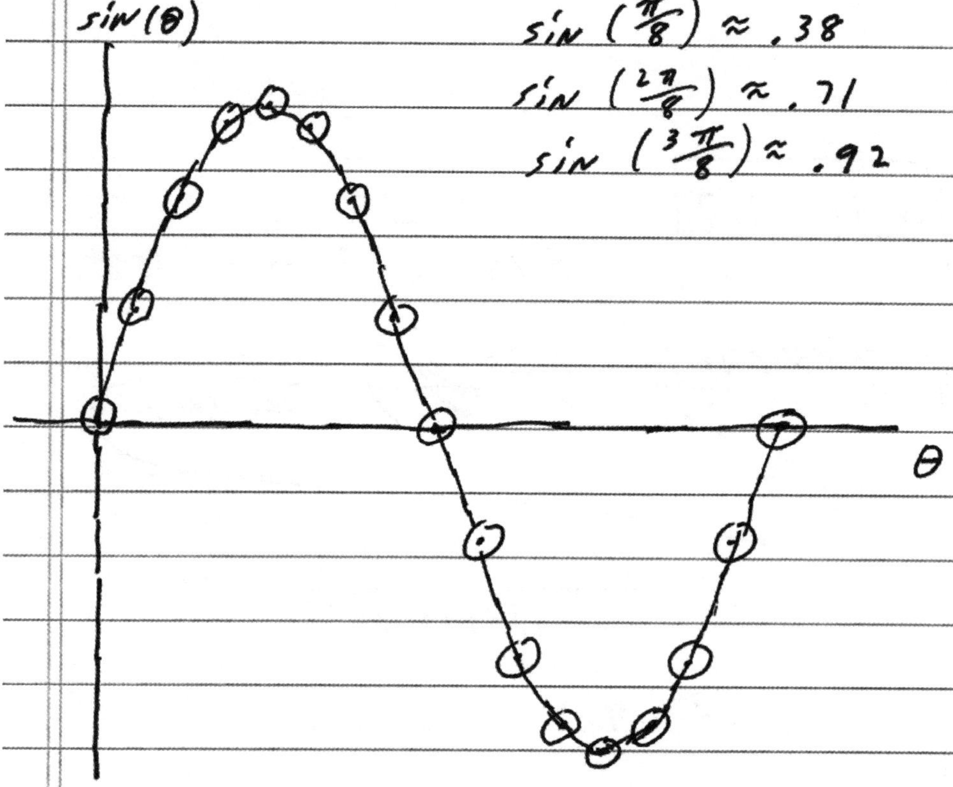

$\sin\left(\frac{4\pi}{8}\right) \approx 1$

$\sin\left(\frac{5\pi}{8}\right) \approx .92$

$\sin\left(\frac{6\pi}{8}\right) \approx .71$

$\sin\left(\frac{7\pi}{8}\right) \approx .38$

$\sin\left(\frac{8\pi}{8}\right) = 0$

$\sin\left(\frac{9\pi}{8}\right) \approx -.38$

$\sin\left(\frac{10\pi}{8}\right) \approx -.71$

$\sin\left(\frac{11\pi}{8}\right) \approx -.92$

$\sin\left(\frac{12\pi}{8}\right) = -1$

$\sin\left(\frac{13\pi}{8}\right) \approx -.92$

$\sin\left(\frac{14\pi}{8}\right) \approx -.71$

$\sin\left(\frac{15\pi}{8}\right) \approx -.38$

$\sin\left(\frac{16\pi}{8}\right) = 0$

Quiz 2.1

$$\sum \vec{F} = m\vec{a} = m(0) = 0$$

$$\vec{F}_1 + \vec{F}_2 + \vec{F}_3 = 0$$

$$[4(-\hat{\imath}) + 3(+\hat{\jmath})]\text{N} + \vec{F}_2 + [1(+\hat{\imath}) + 4(-\hat{\jmath})]\text{N} = 0$$

$$\vec{F}_2 + [3(-\hat{\imath}) + 1(-\hat{\jmath})]\text{N} = 0$$

$$\vec{F}_2 = -[3(-\hat{\imath}) + 1(-\hat{\jmath})]\text{N}$$

$$\vec{F}_2 = [3(+\hat{\imath}) + 1(+\hat{\jmath})]\text{N}$$

check: $\sum \vec{F} \overset{?}{=} 0$

$$[4(-\hat{\imath}) + 3(+\hat{\jmath})]\text{N}$$
$$[3(+\hat{\imath}) + 1(+\hat{\jmath})]\text{N}$$
$$[1(+\hat{\imath}) + 4(-\hat{\jmath})]\text{N}$$

$$\sum \vec{F} = [0(+\hat{\imath}) + 0(+\hat{\jmath})]\text{N} = 0 \quad ✓$$

Quiz 2.2

$$\sum \vec{F} = m\vec{a}$$

$$m\vec{a} = [1(-\hat{i}) + 4(+\hat{j})]\,N$$
$$+ [2(+\hat{i}) + 3(+\hat{j})]\,N$$
$$+ [1(+\hat{i}) + 2(-\hat{j})]\,N$$

$$m\vec{a} = [2(+\hat{i}) + 5(+\hat{j})]\,N = \sum \vec{F}$$

$$|\sum \vec{F}| = \sqrt{(2)^2 + (5)^2}\,N = \sqrt{4 + 25}\,N$$
$$|\sum \vec{F}| = \sqrt{29}\,N$$

$$\sum \vec{F} = \sqrt{29}\,N \left[\frac{2}{\sqrt{29}}(+\hat{i}) + \frac{5}{\sqrt{29}}(+\hat{j}) \right]$$

$$m\vec{a} = \sum \vec{F}$$

$$(1.2\,\text{kg})\,\vec{a} = \sqrt{29}\,\frac{\text{kg}\,\text{m}}{\text{s}^2} \left[\frac{2}{\sqrt{29}}(+\hat{i}) + \frac{5}{\sqrt{29}}(+\hat{j}) \right]$$

$$\vec{a} \approx 4.49\,\frac{\text{m}}{\text{s}^2} \left[\frac{2}{\sqrt{29}}(+\hat{i}) + \frac{5}{\sqrt{29}}(+\hat{j}) \right]$$

Quiz 2.3

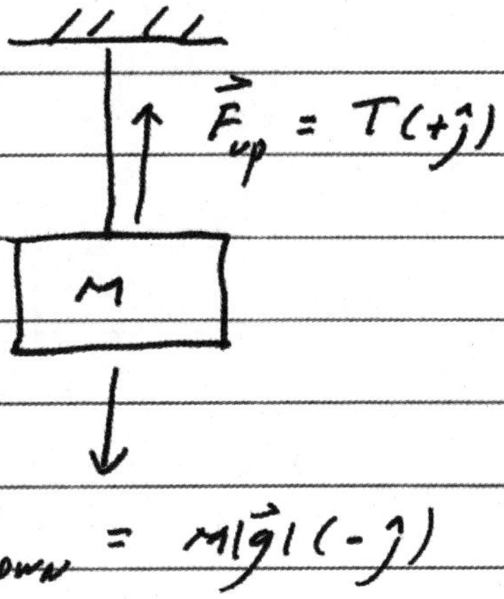

$$\Sigma \vec{F} = m\vec{a}$$
$$= m(0)$$
$$= 0$$

$$\vec{F}_{up} + \vec{F}_{DOWN} = 0$$
$$T(+\hat{j}) + M|\vec{g}|(-\hat{j}) = 0$$
$$T(+\hat{j}) = M|\vec{g}|(+\hat{j})$$

$$T = M|\vec{g}| \Rightarrow M = \frac{T}{|\vec{g}|}$$

$$M = \frac{49\,N}{9.8\,\frac{m}{s^2}} = \frac{49\,\frac{kg\,m}{s^2}}{9.8\,\frac{m}{s^2}}$$

$$M = \frac{49}{9.8}\left(\frac{kg\,m}{s^2}\right)\left(\frac{s^2}{m}\right)$$

$$M = 5\,kg$$

Quiz 2.4

$$\left(\frac{770\ \text{Lbs}}{1}\right)\left(\frac{9.8\ N}{2.2\ \text{Lbs}}\right) = 3430\ N = \text{weight}$$

$$\text{weight} = m|\vec{g}| \implies m = \frac{\text{weight}}{|\vec{g}|}$$

$$m = \frac{3430\ \frac{kg\,m}{s^2}}{9.8\ \frac{m}{s^2}} = 350\ kg$$

$$\vec{F}_{up} = T(+\hat{j})$$

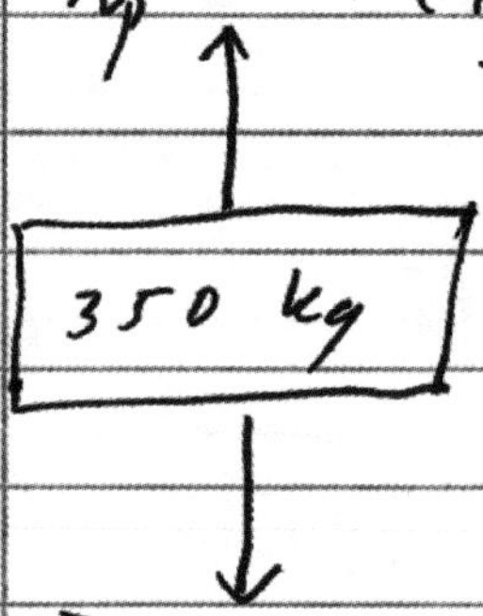

$$\Sigma \vec{F} = m\vec{a}$$

$$\vec{F}_{up} + \vec{F}_{down} = m\vec{a}$$

$$T(+\hat{j}) + m|\vec{g}|(-\hat{j}) = m\vec{a}$$

$$\vec{F}_{down} = m|\vec{g}|(-\hat{j})$$

since $\vec{a}$ is up

$$T(+\hat{j}) + (350\,kg)(9.8\,\tfrac{m}{s^2})(-\hat{j}) = (350\,kg)(2.4\,\tfrac{m}{s^2})(+\hat{j})$$

$$T(+\hat{j}) + (3430\,\tfrac{kg\,m}{s^2})(-\hat{j}) = 840\,\tfrac{kg\,m}{s^2}(+\hat{j})$$

$$T(+\hat{j}) = 3430\,N(+\hat{j}) + 840\,N(+\hat{j})$$

$$T(+\hat{j}) = 4270\,N(+\hat{j})$$

$$T = 4270\ N$$

Quiz 2.5

$$\vec{F}_{\text{Applied}} = 141N(+\hat{\imath}) + 84N(-\hat{\imath}) = 57N(+\hat{\imath})$$

$$|\vec{F}_{fr}|_{\text{STATIC MAX}} = \mu_s M|\vec{g}| = (.32)(8kg)(9.8\,\tfrac{m}{s^2})$$
$$= 25.088\,\tfrac{kg\,m}{s^2}$$

$$|\vec{F}_{fr}|_{\text{STATIC MAX}} \approx 25N$$

$57N > 25N$ ∴ block will ACCELERATE

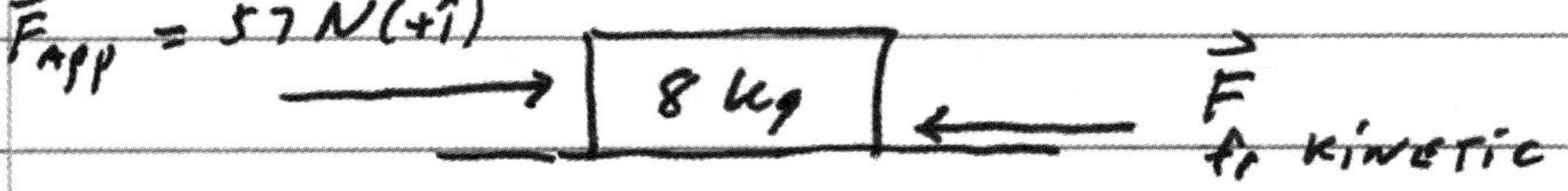

$$\vec{F}_{fr\ \text{KINETIC}} = \mu_K M|\vec{g}|(-\hat{\imath})$$ ← FROM picture
$$= (.28)(8kg)(9.8\,\tfrac{m}{s^2})(-\hat{\imath})$$
$$= 21.952N(-\hat{\imath})$$

$$\Sigma\vec{F} = M\vec{a}$$

$$M\vec{a} = \vec{F}_{App} + \vec{F}_{fr\ \text{KINETIC}}$$
$$(8kg)\vec{a} = 57N(+\hat{\imath}) + 21.952N(-\hat{\imath})$$
$$(8kg)\vec{a} = 35.048\,\tfrac{kg\,m}{s^2}(+\hat{\imath})$$

$$\vec{a} = \frac{35.048\,\tfrac{kg\,m}{s^2}}{8\,kg}(+\hat{\imath})$$

$$\vec{a} = 4.381\,\tfrac{m}{s^2}(+\hat{\imath})$$

Quiz 3.1

$\vec{v}_{1b} = 4\,\frac{m}{s}\,(+\hat{i})$ $\quad \vec{v}_{2b} = 3\,\frac{m}{s}\,(-\hat{i})$

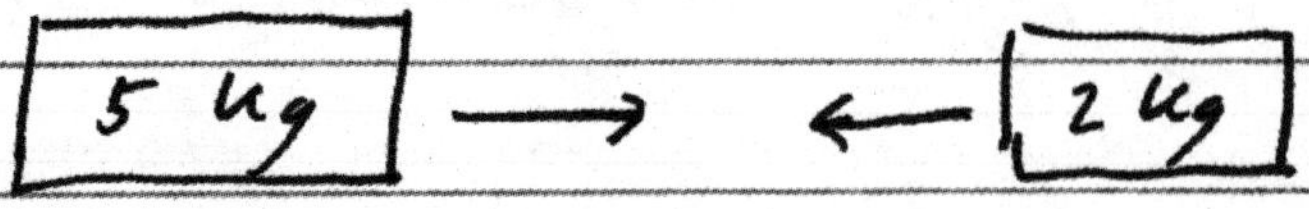

$\vec{v}_{1A} = ?$ $\quad \vec{v}_{2A} = 4.5\,\frac{m}{s}\,(+\hat{i})$

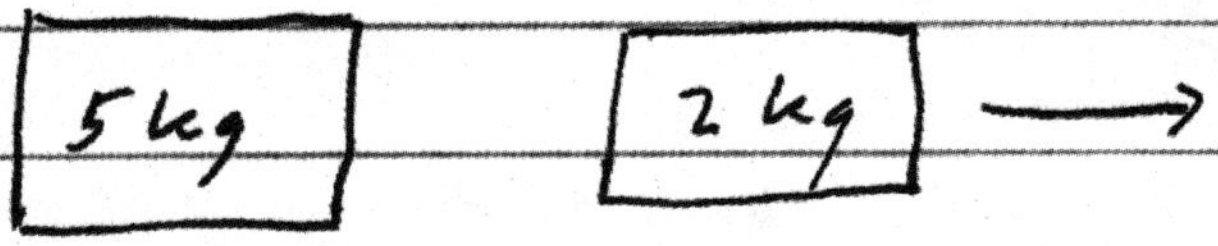

$$m_1\vec{v}_{1b} + m_2\vec{v}_{2b} = m_1\vec{v}_{1A} + m_2\vec{v}_{2A}$$

$$(5\,kg)(4\,\tfrac{m}{s})(+\hat{i}) + (2\,kg)(3\,\tfrac{m}{s})(-\hat{i})$$

$$= (5\,kg)\,\vec{v}_{1A} + (2\,kg)(4.5\,\tfrac{m}{s})(+\hat{i})$$

$$20\,\tfrac{kg\,m}{s}(+\hat{i}) + 6\,\tfrac{kg\,m}{s}(-\hat{i}) = (5\,kg)\,\vec{v}_{1A} + 9\,\tfrac{kg\,m}{s}(+\hat{i})$$

$$14\,\tfrac{kg\,m}{s}(+\hat{i}) + 9\,\tfrac{kg\,m}{s}(-\hat{i}) = (5\,kg)\,\vec{v}_{1A}$$

$$\vec{v}_{1A} = \frac{5\,\cancel{kg}\,\frac{m}{s}}{5\,\cancel{kg}}\,(+\hat{i})$$

$$\vec{v}_{1A} = 1\,\frac{m}{s}\,(+\hat{i})$$

Quiz 3.2

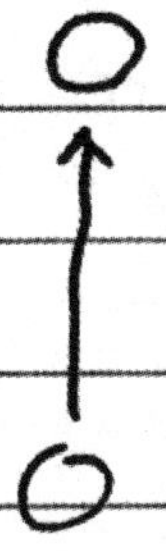

$PE_2 = mgh_2$

$KE_2 = 0$

$PE_1 = 0$

$KE_1 = \frac{1}{2} m v_1^2$

$$KE_2 = \frac{1}{2} m v_2^2 = \frac{1}{2} m (0)^2 = 0$$

$$PE_1 + KE_1 = PE_2 + KE_2 + \cancel{Loss}^{\,0}$$

$$0 + \frac{1}{2} m v_1^2 = mgh_2 + 0$$

$$\cancel{m} v_1^2 = 2 \cancel{m} g h_2$$

$$h_2 = \frac{v_1^2}{2g}$$

Units

$$\frac{\left(\frac{m}{s}\right)^2}{\frac{m}{s^2}} \rightarrow \left(\frac{m^2}{\cancel{s^2}}\right)\left(\frac{\cancel{s^2}}{\cancel{m}}\right) \rightarrow m \checkmark$$

$$h_2 = \left[\frac{(7.92)^2}{2(9.81)}\right] m$$

$$h_2 \approx 3.2 \text{ m}$$

Quiz 3.3

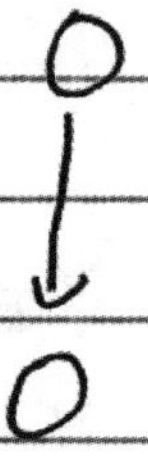

$PE_1 = mgh_1$

$KE_1 = 0$

$PE_2 = mgh_2$

$KE_2 = \frac{1}{2}mv_2^2$

$$PE_1 + KE_1 = PE_2 + KE_2 + \cancel{Loss} \rightarrow 0$$

$$mgh_1 + 0 = mgh_2 + \frac{1}{2}mv_2^2$$

$$2mgh_1 - mv_2^2 = 2mgh_2$$

$$h_2 = \frac{\cancel{m}(2gh_1 - v_2^2)}{2\cancel{m}g} = \frac{\cancel{2g}h_1}{\cancel{2g}} - \frac{v_2^2}{2g}$$

$$h_2 = h_1 - \frac{v_2^2}{2g}$$

<u>UNITS</u>

$$m - \frac{\left(\frac{m}{s}\right)^2}{\frac{m}{s^2}}$$

$$h_2 = \left[20 - \frac{(14)^2}{2(9.8)}\right]m$$

$$m - \left(\frac{m^{\cancel{2}}}{\cancel{s^2}}\right)\left(\frac{\cancel{s^2}}{\cancel{m}}\right)$$

$$m - m \rightarrow m \checkmark$$

$$h_2 = 10\,m$$

Quiz 3.4

$PE_1 = 0$ $\qquad$ $PE_2 = 0$

$KE_1 = \frac{1}{2} m v_1^2$ $\qquad$ $KE_2 = \frac{1}{2} m v_2^2$

.02 kg ⟶ .02 kg

$$PE_1 + KE_1 = PE_2 + KE_2 + Loss$$

$$0 + \frac{1}{2} m v_1^2 = 0 + \frac{1}{2} m v_2^2 + Loss$$

$$m v_1^2 = m v_2^2 + 2(Loss)$$

$$m v_2^2 = m v_1^2 - 2(Loss)$$

$$v_2^2 = v_1^2 - \frac{2(Loss)}{m}$$

$$v_2 = \sqrt{v_1^2 - \frac{2(Loss)}{m}}$$

$$v_2 = \sqrt{(18)^2 - \frac{2(2.1)}{.02}} \ \frac{m}{s}$$

$$v_2 \approx 10.68 \ \frac{m}{s}$$

UNITS

$$\sqrt{\left(\frac{m}{s}\right)^2 - \frac{J}{kg}}$$

$$J = Nm = \left(\frac{kg\,m}{s^2}\right) m$$

$$\sqrt{\frac{m^2}{s^2} - \frac{Nm}{kg}}$$

$$\sqrt{\frac{m^2}{s^2} - \left(\frac{kg\,m}{s^2}\right) m \left(\frac{1}{kg}\right)}$$

$$\sqrt{\frac{m^2}{s^2} - \frac{m^2}{s^2}}$$

$$\sqrt{\frac{m^2}{s^2}} \rightarrow \frac{m}{s} \checkmark$$

Quiz 3.5

$$\left(\frac{12 \text{ cm}}{1}\right)\left(\frac{1 \text{ m}}{100 \text{ cm}}\right) = .12 \text{ m}$$

$$\vec{d} = .12 \text{ m} (+\hat{j})$$

$$W = \vec{F} \cdot \vec{d}$$

$$= 420 \text{N} \left[\frac{2}{\sqrt{20}}(+\hat{i}) + \frac{4}{\sqrt{20}}(+\hat{j}) \right] \cdot \left[0(+\hat{i}) + .12(+\hat{j}) \right] \text{m}$$

$$= \left[420 \left(\frac{2}{\sqrt{20}}\right)(0) + 420\left(\frac{4}{\sqrt{20}}\right)(.12) \right] \text{Nm}$$

$$W \approx 45.08 \text{ J}$$

Quiz 4.1

$$T_{°F} = \frac{9}{5} T_{°C} + 32$$

$$\frac{9}{5} T_{°C} = T_{°F} - 32$$

$$T_{°C} = \frac{5}{9} (T_{°F} - 32)$$

$$T_K = T_{°C} + 273.15 = \frac{5}{9}(T_{°F} - 32) + 273.15$$

$$= \frac{5}{9}(-74 - 32) + 273.15$$

$$= -58.8\bar{8} + 273.15$$

$$\approx 214.26$$

$$T \approx 214.26 \text{ K}$$

Quiz 4.2

$$\frac{P_1 V_1}{T_1} = \frac{P_2 V_2}{T_2}$$

$$\frac{(101300\ P_A)(.001\ m^3)}{300K} = \frac{(303900\ P_A)(.0005\ m^3)}{T_2}$$

$$\frac{101.3\ \cancel{P_A m^3}}{300K} = \frac{151.95\ \cancel{P_A m^3}}{T_2}$$

$$(101.3)\ T_2 = (151.95)(300K)$$

$$T_2 = 450K$$

Quiz 4.3

$$T_{K\ H_2O} = T_{^oC\ H_2O} + 273.15$$
$$= 68 + 273.15$$

$$T_{H_2O} = 341.15\ K$$

$$T_{K\ ALCOHOL} = T_{^oC\ ALCOHOL} + 273.15$$
$$= 32 + 273.15$$

$$T_{ALCOHOL} = 305.15\ K$$

$$\left(\frac{230\ g}{1}\right)\left(\frac{1\ kg}{1000\ g}\right) = .23\ kg$$

$$\left(\frac{360\ g}{1}\right)\left(\frac{1\ kg}{1000\ g}\right) = .36\ kg$$

$$Q_{LOST\ by\ H_2O} + Q_{gained\ by\ ALCOHOL} = 0$$

$$M_{H_2O}\, C_{H_2O}\, (T_f - T_{0\ H_2O})$$
$$+ M_{ALCOHOL}\, C_{ALCOHOL}\, (T_f - T_{0\ ALCOHOL}) = 0$$

$$.23\ kg \left(4190\ \frac{J}{kg\ K}\right)(T_f - 341.15\ K)$$

$$+ .36\ kg \left(2440\ \frac{J}{kg\ K}\right)(T_f - 305.15\ K) = 0$$

Quiz 4.3 continued

$(963.7\,\frac{J}{K})\,T_f - (963.7\,\frac{J}{K})(341.15\,K)$
$+ (878.4\,\frac{J}{K})\,T_f - (878.4\,\frac{J}{K})(305.15\,K) = 0$

$(963.7\,\frac{J}{K})\,T_f - 328766.26\,J$
$+ (878.4\,\frac{J}{K})\,T_f - 268043.76\,J = 0$

$(1842.1\,\frac{J}{K})\,T_f = 596810.02\,J$

units

$\frac{J}{\frac{J}{K}} \rightarrow \left(\frac{J}{1}\right)\left(\frac{K}{J}\right)$

$\rightarrow K$ ✓

$T_f \approx 323.98\,K$

$T_K = T_{°C} + 273.15$

$T_{°C} = T_K - 273.15$

$T_{°C} \approx 323.98 - 273.15$

$T \approx 50.83\,°C$

Quiz 4.4

$$W = W_{AB} + \cancel{W_{BC}}^{\,0} + W_{CD} + \cancel{W_{DA}}^{\,0}$$

$$W = W_{AB} + W_{CD}$$

$$W = P_{AB}(V_B - V_A) + P_{CD}(V_D - V_A)$$

$$120.4\,J = 238000\,P_A\,(V_2 - .004\,m^3) + 152000\,P_A\,(.004\,m^3 - V_2)$$

$$120.4\,J = (238000\,\tfrac{N}{m^2})V_2 - (238000\,\tfrac{N}{m^2})(.004\,m^3) + (152000\,\tfrac{N}{m^2})(.004\,m^3) - (152000\,\tfrac{N}{m^2})V_2$$

$$120.4\,J = (86000\,\tfrac{N}{m^2})V_2 - 952\,\underbrace{Nm}_{J} + 608\,\underbrace{Nm}_{J}$$

$$120.4\,J = (86000\,\tfrac{N}{m^2})V_2 - 344\,J$$

$$V_2 = \frac{464.4\,J}{86000\,\frac{N}{m^2}}$$

Units

$$\frac{J}{\frac{N}{m^2}} \rightarrow \left(\frac{Nm}{1}\right)\left(\frac{m^2}{N}\right) \rightarrow m^3 \checkmark$$

$$V_2 = .0054\,m^3$$

Quiz 4.5

$$\Delta U = (\pm Q) - (\pm W)$$

$$\Delta U = (-Q) - (-W)$$
$$= (-240\,J) - (-400\,J)$$

$$\Delta U = 160\,J$$

Quiz 5.1

TO − FROM

$(-2, 3) - (2, -5) \Rightarrow (-4, 8)$

$\vec{d} = [\,4(-\hat{\imath}) + 8(+\hat{\jmath})\,]\ \text{m}$

$|\vec{d}| = \sqrt{(4)^2 + (8)^2}\ \text{m} = \sqrt{16 + 64}\ \text{m}$

$|\vec{d}| = \sqrt{80}\ \text{m}$

$\vec{d} = \sqrt{80}\ \text{m}\left[\frac{4}{\sqrt{80}}(-\hat{\imath}) + \frac{8}{\sqrt{80}}(+\hat{\jmath})\right]$

$\vec{v} = \frac{\vec{d}}{\Delta t} = \frac{\sqrt{80}\ \text{m}}{3.4\ \text{s}}\left[\frac{4}{\sqrt{80}}(-\hat{\imath}) + \frac{8}{\sqrt{80}}(+\hat{\jmath})\right]$

$\vec{v} \approx 2.63\ \frac{\text{m}}{\text{s}}\left[\frac{4}{\sqrt{80}}(-\hat{\imath}) + \frac{8}{\sqrt{80}}(+\hat{\jmath})\right]$

Quiz 5.2

$$\vec{v}_1 = 10\,\tfrac{m}{s}\left[\tfrac{4}{5}(-\hat{\imath}) + \tfrac{3}{5}(-\hat{\jmath})\right]$$

$$= \left[8(-\hat{\imath}) + 6(-\hat{\jmath})\right]\tfrac{m}{s}$$

$$\vec{v}_2 = \sqrt{82}\,\tfrac{m}{s}\left[\tfrac{1}{\sqrt{82}}(+\hat{\imath}) + \tfrac{9}{\sqrt{82}}(+\hat{\jmath})\right]$$

$$= \left[1(+\hat{\imath}) + 9(+\hat{\jmath})\right]\tfrac{m}{s}$$

$$\vec{a} = \frac{\vec{v}_2 - \vec{v}_1}{\Delta t} \qquad \Delta t = 3\,s$$

$$\vec{a} = \frac{\left[1(+\hat{\imath}) + 9(+\hat{\jmath})\right]\tfrac{m}{s} - \left[8(-\hat{\imath}) + 6(-\hat{\jmath})\right]\tfrac{m}{s}}{3\,s}$$

$$\vec{a} = \frac{\left[9(+\hat{\imath}) + 15(+\hat{\jmath})\right]\tfrac{m}{s}}{3s}$$

$$= \left[3(+\hat{\imath}) + 5(+\hat{\jmath})\right]\tfrac{m}{s^2}$$

$$|\vec{a}| = \sqrt{(3)^2 + (5)^2}\,\tfrac{m}{s^2} = \sqrt{9+25}\,\tfrac{m}{s^2}$$

$$|\vec{a}| = \sqrt{34}\,\tfrac{m}{s^2}$$

$$\vec{a} = \sqrt{34}\,\tfrac{m}{s^2}\left[\tfrac{3}{\sqrt{34}}(+\hat{\imath}) + \tfrac{5}{\sqrt{34}}(+\hat{\jmath})\right]$$

Quiz 5.3

$$|\vec{F}_c| = m|\vec{a}_c|$$

$$m = \frac{|\vec{F}_c|}{|\vec{a}_c|} = \frac{|\vec{F}_c|}{\frac{v^2}{r}} = \frac{r|\vec{F}_c|}{v^2}$$

units

$$\frac{mN}{(\frac{m}{s})^2} \to \frac{m(\frac{kg\,m}{s^2})}{(\frac{m}{s})^2} \to \left(\frac{kg\,m^2}{s^2}\right)\left(\frac{s^2}{m^2}\right)$$

$$\to kg \checkmark$$

$$m = \left[\frac{.4\,(312)}{(26)^2}\right] kg$$

$$m \approx .185 \text{ kg}$$

Quiz 5.4

$$y = .038 \sin[(8\pi)x - (260\pi)t]\ m$$

$$k = \frac{2\pi}{\lambda} \rightarrow \lambda k = 2\pi$$

$$\lambda = \frac{2\pi}{k}$$

$$\lambda = \frac{2\pi}{k} = \frac{2\pi\ rad}{8\pi\ \frac{rad}{m}} = \frac{1}{4}\left(\frac{rad}{1}\right)\left(\frac{m}{rad}\right)$$

$$= \frac{1}{4}\ m$$

$$w = 2\pi f$$

$$f = \frac{w}{2\pi} = \frac{260\pi\ \frac{rad}{s}}{2\pi\ rad} = 130\left(\frac{rad}{s}\right)\left(\frac{1}{rad}\right)$$

$$f = 130\ \frac{1}{s}$$

$$v = \lambda f = \left(\frac{1}{4}\ m\right)\left(130\ \frac{1}{s}\right)$$

$$v = 32.5\ \frac{m}{s}$$

Quiz 5.5

$$w = 2\pi f = (2\pi \text{ rad})\left(\frac{250}{\pi}\frac{1}{s}\right) = 500 \frac{\text{rad}}{s}$$

$$k = \frac{2\pi}{\lambda} = \frac{2\pi \text{ rad}}{\frac{\pi}{8} m} = \left(\frac{2\pi}{1}\right)\left(\frac{8}{\pi}\right)\frac{\text{rad}}{m} = 16 \frac{\text{rad}}{m}$$

$$y = y_0 \sin(kx - wt)$$
$$y = (.035m)\sin(16x - 500t)$$

$$y\Big|_{\substack{x=16m\\t=.7s}} = .035m \sin[16(16) - 500(.7)] = .035m \sin(-94) \approx .035m(.245252)$$

$$y \approx .0086m$$

straight line means "evaluated at"

Quiz 6.1

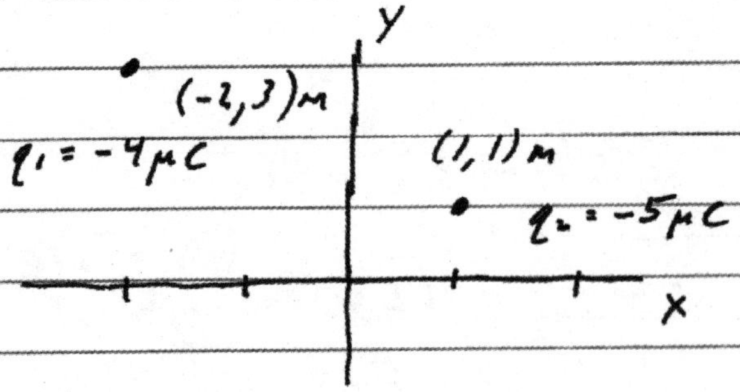

TO − FROM

$(1,1) - (-2,3) \Rightarrow (3,-2)$

$$\vec{r}_{12} = [3(+\hat{i}) + 2(-\hat{j})]\ m$$

$$|\vec{r}_{12}| = \sqrt{(3)^2 + (2)^2}\ m = \sqrt{9+4}\ m = \sqrt{13}\ m$$

$$\frac{\vec{r}_{12}}{|\vec{r}_{12}|} = \left[\frac{3}{\sqrt{13}}(+\hat{i}) + \frac{2}{\sqrt{13}}(-\hat{j})\right] \frac{\cancel{m}}{\cancel{m}}$$

$$\vec{F}_{12} = \frac{1}{4\pi\varepsilon_0}\left[\frac{q_1 q_2}{|\vec{r}_{12}|^2}\right]\frac{\vec{r}_{12}}{|\vec{r}_{12}|}$$

$$= \frac{1}{4\pi(8.85\times10^{-12})}\left[\frac{(-4\times10^{-6})(-5\times10^{-6})}{(\sqrt{13})^2}\right]\frac{\vec{r}_{12}}{|\vec{r}_{12}|}\ N$$

$$\vec{F}_{12} \approx .014\ N\left[\frac{3}{\sqrt{13}}(+\hat{i}) + \frac{2}{\sqrt{13}}(-\hat{j})\right]$$

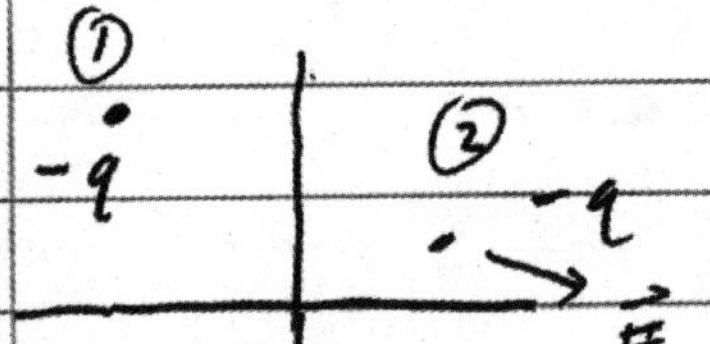

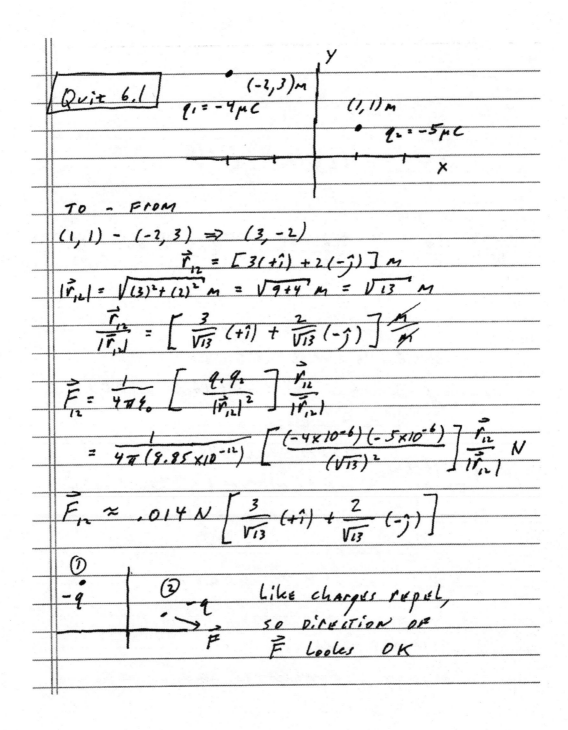

Like charges repel, so direction of $\vec{F}$ looks OK

Quiz 6.2

TO − FROM

$(2,-1) - (3,2) \Rightarrow (-1,-3)$

$\vec{r} = [1(-\hat{i}) + 3(-\hat{j})]\ m$

$|\vec{r}| = \sqrt{(1)^2 + (3)^2}\ m$

$= \sqrt{10}\ m$

$\frac{\vec{r}}{|\vec{r}|} = \left[\frac{1}{\sqrt{10}}(-\hat{i}) + \frac{3}{\sqrt{10}}(-\hat{j})\right] \frac{\cancel{m}}{\cancel{m}}$

$\vec{E} = \frac{1}{4\pi\epsilon_0}\left[\frac{q}{|\vec{r}|}\right]\frac{\vec{r}}{|\vec{r}|}$

$= \frac{1}{4\pi(8.85\times10^{-12})}\left[\frac{-64\times10^{-9}}{(\sqrt{10})^2}\right]\frac{\vec{r}}{|\vec{r}|}\ \frac{N}{C}$

$\approx -57.55\ \frac{N}{C}\left[\frac{1}{\sqrt{10}}(-\hat{i}) + \frac{3}{\sqrt{10}}(-\hat{j})\right]$

$\vec{E} \approx 57.55\ \frac{N}{C}\left[\frac{1}{\sqrt{10}}(+\hat{i}) + \frac{3}{\sqrt{10}}(+\hat{j})\right]$

Quiz 6.3

$$\vec{E}_{TOTAL} = \vec{E}_a + \vec{E}_b$$

$$\vec{E}_a = 141.62 \; \frac{N}{C} \; (+\hat{i})$$

TO - FROM

$(1,2) - (1,0) \Rightarrow (0,2)$ $\quad \vec{r} = 2(+\hat{j}) \; m$

$$|\vec{r}| = 2m$$

$$\frac{\vec{r}}{|\vec{r}|} = \frac{2m}{2m}(+\hat{j}) = (+\hat{j})$$

$$\vec{E}_b = \frac{1}{4\pi\epsilon_0}\left[\frac{q_b}{|\vec{r}|^2}\right]\frac{\vec{r}}{|\vec{r}|}$$

$$= \frac{1}{4\pi(8.85\times10^{-12})}\left[\frac{63\times10^{-9}}{(2)^2}\right]\frac{N}{C}(+\hat{j})$$

$$\vec{E}_b \approx 141.62 \; \frac{N}{C} \; (+\hat{j})$$

$$\vec{E}_{TOTAL} = \left[141.62\,(+\hat{i}) + 141.62\,(+\hat{j})\right]\frac{N}{C}$$

Quiz 6.4

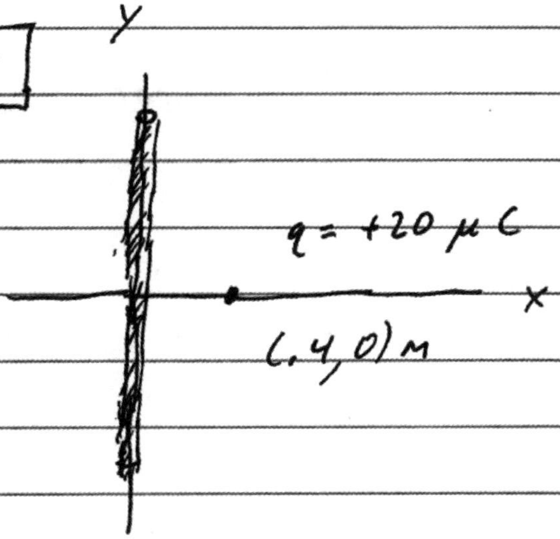

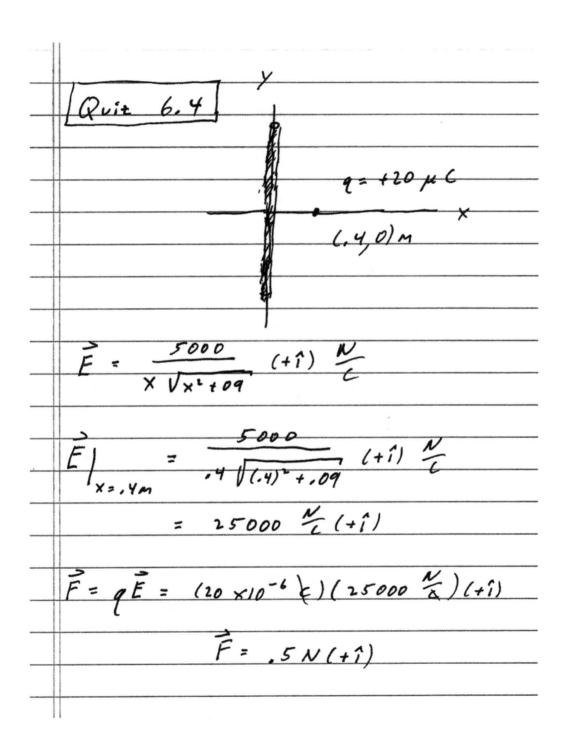

$$\vec{E} = \frac{5000}{x\sqrt{x^2+.09}} \, (+\hat{\imath}) \ \frac{N}{C}$$

$$\vec{E}\Big|_{x=.4m} = \frac{5000}{.4\sqrt{(.4)^2+.09}} \, (+\hat{\imath}) \ \frac{N}{C}$$

$$= 25000 \ \frac{N}{C} \, (+\hat{\imath})$$

$$\vec{F} = q\vec{E} = (20 \times 10^{-6} \, C)\left(25000 \ \frac{N}{C}\right)(+\hat{\imath})$$

$$\vec{F} = .5 \, N \, (+\hat{\imath})$$

Quiz 6.5 $\vec{E} = [600(+\hat{i}) + 300(-\hat{j})]\ \frac{N}{C}$

OVER 6, DOWN 3

TO - FROM

$(.03, .02) - (0, .01) \Rightarrow (.03, .01)$

$\vec{d} = [.03(+\hat{i}) + .01(+\hat{j})]\ M$

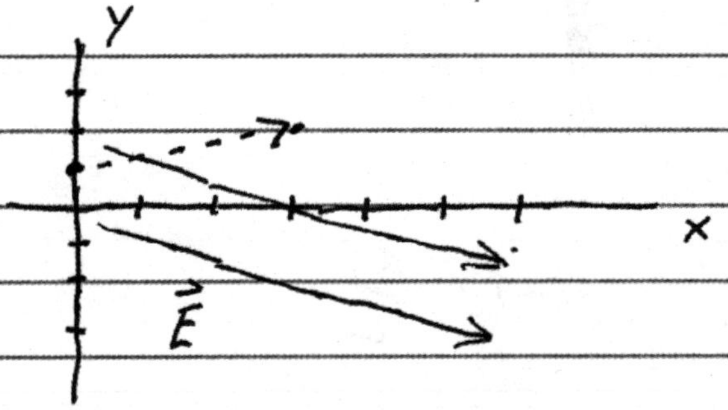

$\vec{d}$ goes "with" $\vec{E}$ so voltage should be NEGATIVE

$V = -\vec{E} \cdot \vec{d}$

$= -[600(+\hat{i}) + 300(-\hat{j})]\ \frac{N}{C} \cdot [.03(+\hat{i}) + .01(+\hat{j})]\ M$

$= -[(+600)(+.03) + (-300)(+.01)]\ \frac{Nm}{C}$

$= -[18 - 3]\ \frac{J}{C}$

$V = -15\ V$

Quiz 7.1

$$v_1' = \frac{v_1 \pm v_2}{1 \pm \frac{v_1 v_2}{c^2}}$$

$v_1 = .9c$ → ← $v_2 = .76c$

$$v_1' = \frac{v_1 + v_2}{1 + \frac{v_1 v_2}{c^2}}$$

$$= \frac{.9c + .76c}{1 + \frac{(.9c)(.76c)}{c^2}}$$

$$= \frac{1.66c}{1 + \frac{.684c^2}{c^2}} = \frac{1.66c}{1.684}$$

$$v_1' \approx .986c$$

Quiz 7.2

$$\Delta\tau_s = \Delta\tau_g \sqrt{1 - \frac{v^2}{c^2}}$$

$$\Delta\tau_g = \frac{\Delta\tau_s}{\sqrt{1 - \frac{v^2}{c^2}}}$$

$$= \frac{100 \text{ sec}}{\sqrt{1 - \frac{(.4c)^2}{c^2}}}$$

$$= \frac{100 \text{ sec}}{\sqrt{1 - \frac{.16\cancel{c^2}}{\cancel{c^2}}}} = \frac{100 \text{ sec}}{\sqrt{.84}}$$

$$\Delta\tau_g \approx 109.1 \text{ sec}$$

Quiz 7.3

$$L = L_0\sqrt{1-\frac{v^2}{c^2}}$$

$$\frac{L}{L_0} = \sqrt{1-\frac{v^2}{c^2}} \Rightarrow \left(\frac{L}{L_0}\right)^2 = 1-\frac{v^2}{c^2}$$

$$\frac{v^2}{c^2} = 1-\left(\frac{L}{L_0}\right)^2$$

$$v^2 = c^2\left[1-\left(\frac{L}{L_0}\right)^2\right]$$

$$v = c\sqrt{1-\left(\frac{L}{L_0}\right)^2} \qquad L_0 = 1\,m$$

$$v = c\sqrt{1-\left(\frac{.8\,m}{1\,m}\right)^2}$$

$$= c\sqrt{1-.64}$$

$$v = .6c$$

Quiz 7.4

$$\left(\frac{2.5\,g}{1}\right)\left(\frac{1\,kg}{1000\,g}\right) = .0025\,kg$$

$$E = M_0 c^2$$
$$= (.0025\,kg)(3\times 10^8\ \tfrac{m}{s})^2$$
$$= (.0025)(9\times 10^{16})\left(\frac{kg\,m}{s^2}\right)m$$
$$= 2.25\times 10^{14}\ Nm$$
$$E = 2.25\times 10^{14}\ J$$

$$\text{USAGE} \Rightarrow \left(\frac{3.42\times 10^9\ J}{mth}\right)\left(\frac{12\ mth}{year}\right)$$
$$= 4.104\times 10^{10}\ \frac{J}{year}$$

$$\frac{2.25\times 10^{14}\ J}{4.104\times 10^{10}\ \frac{J}{year}} \approx 5482.5\left(\frac{J}{1}\right)\left(\frac{year}{J}\right)$$

$$\#\ \text{years} \approx 5482.5\ \text{years}$$

Quiz 7.5 (a) ground FRAME

$\Delta x = 9m - (-3m) = 12\,m, \quad \Delta y = 0$

$\Delta t = 160 \times 10^{-9} s$

$(\Delta S_t)^2 = c^2(\Delta t)^2 - (\Delta x)^2 - (\Delta y)^2$

$= (3\times 10^8 \tfrac{m}{s})^2 (160\times 10^{-9} s)^2 - (12m)^2 - (0)^2$

$= (9\times 10^{16} \tfrac{m^2}{s^2})(2.56\times 10^{-14} s^2) - 144 m^2$

$(\Delta S_t)^2 = 2160\ m^2$

(b) particle FRAME

$\Delta x' = 0, \quad \Delta y' = 0, \quad \Delta t' = \Delta t\sqrt{1-\frac{v^2}{c^2}}$

$v = \dfrac{12\,m}{160\times 10^{-9} s} = 7.5 \times 10^7 \tfrac{m}{s}$

$\Delta t' = 160\times 10^{-9} s \sqrt{1 - \left(\dfrac{7.5\times 10^7 \frac{m}{s}}{3\times 10^8 \frac{m}{s}}\right)^2}$

$\Delta t' = 1.5492 \times 10^{-7}\ \text{SEC}$

$(\Delta S_t')^2 = c^2(\Delta t')^2 - (\Delta x')^2 - (\Delta y')^2$

$= (3\times 10^8 \tfrac{m}{s})^2 (1.5492\times 10^{-7} s)^2 - (0)^2 - (0)^2$

$= (9\times 10^{16} \tfrac{m^2}{s^2})(2.4\times 10^{-14} s^2)$

$(\Delta S_t')^2 = 2160\ m^2$

Quiz 8.1

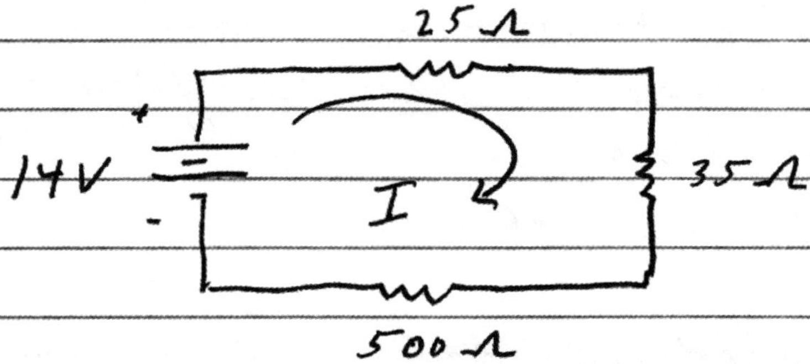

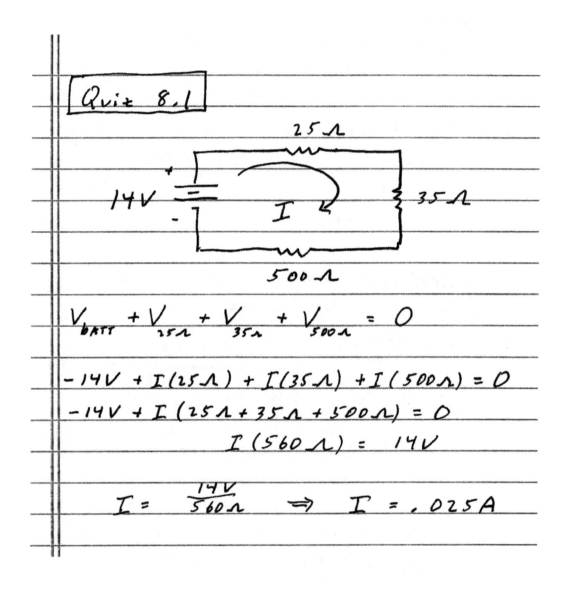

$$V_{BATT} + V_{25\Omega} + V_{35\Omega} + V_{500\Omega} = 0$$

$$-14V + I(25\Omega) + I(35\Omega) + I(500\Omega) = 0$$

$$-14V + I(25\Omega + 35\Omega + 500\Omega) = 0$$

$$I(560\Omega) = 14V$$

$$I = \frac{14V}{560\Omega} \Rightarrow I = .025A$$

Quiz 8.2

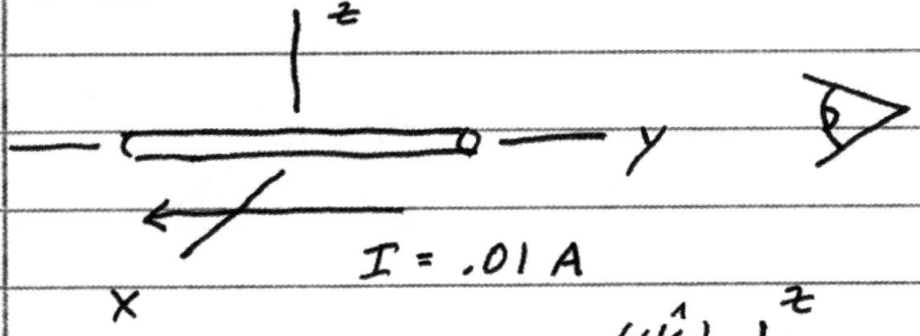

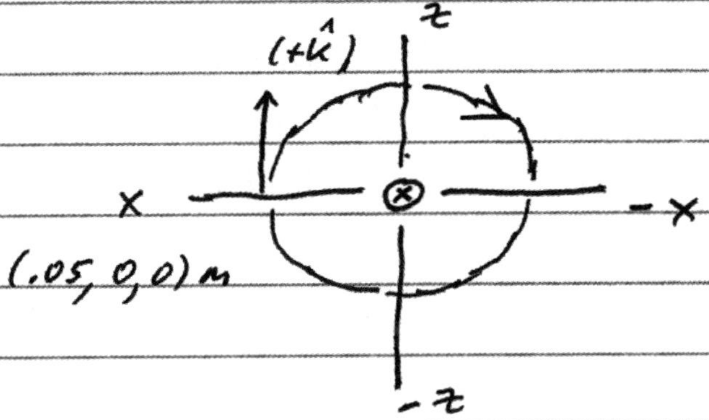

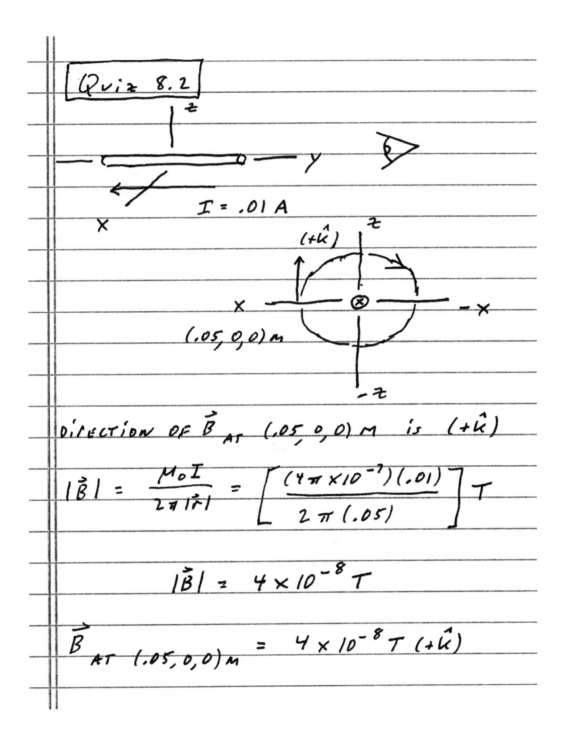

Direction of $\vec{B}$ at (.05, 0, 0) m is $(+\hat{k})$

$$|\vec{B}| = \frac{\mu_0 I}{2\pi |\vec{r}|} = \left[\frac{(4\pi \times 10^{-7})(.01)}{2\pi(.05)} \right] T$$

$$|\vec{B}| = 4 \times 10^{-8}\ T$$

$$\vec{B}_{\text{at } (.05,0,0)\,m} = 4 \times 10^{-8}\ T\ (+\hat{k})$$

Quiz 8.3

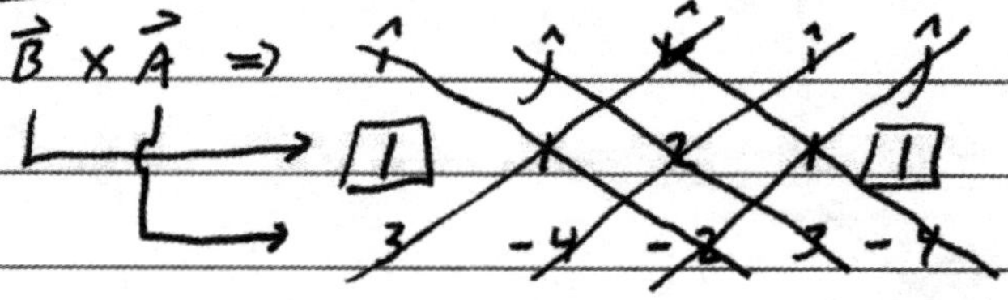

$$\vec{B} \times \vec{A} = [(1)(-2) - (2)(-4)]\,\hat{\imath} + [(2)(3) - (1)(-2)]\,\hat{\jmath} + [(1)(-4) - (1)(3)]\,\hat{k}$$

$$= [-2 - (-8)]\,\hat{\imath} + [6 - (-2)]\,\hat{\jmath} + [-4 - (3)]\,\hat{k}$$

$$\vec{B} \times \vec{A} = 6(+\hat{\imath}) + 8(+\hat{\jmath}) + 7(-\hat{k})$$

check: ① $\vec{B} \cdot (\vec{B} \times \vec{A}) \stackrel{?}{=} 0$

$$[1(+\hat{\imath}) + 1(+\hat{\jmath}) + 2(+\hat{k})] \cdot [6(+\hat{\imath}) + 8(+\hat{\jmath}) + 7(-\hat{k})] \stackrel{?}{=} 0$$

$$(1)(6) + (1)(8) + (2)(-7) \stackrel{?}{=} 0$$

$$6 + 8 - 14 \stackrel{?}{=} 0 \quad \Rightarrow \quad 0 = 0 \checkmark$$

② $\vec{A} \cdot (\vec{B} \times \vec{A}) \stackrel{?}{=} 0$

$$[3(+\hat{\imath}) + 4(-\hat{\jmath}) + 2(-\hat{k})] \cdot [6(+\hat{\imath}) + 8(+\hat{\jmath}) + 7(-\hat{k})] \stackrel{?}{=} 0$$

$$(3)(6) + (-4)(8) + (-2)(-7) \stackrel{?}{=} 0$$

$$18 - 32 + 14 \stackrel{?}{=} 0 \quad \Rightarrow \quad 0 = 0 \checkmark$$

Quit 8, 4

$$\vec{v} \times \vec{B} \Rightarrow \begin{matrix} \hat{i} & \hat{j} & \hat{k} & \hat{i} & \hat{j} \\ 0 & -1800 & 2400 & 0 & -1800 \\ .2 & 0 & 0 & .2 & 0 \end{matrix}$$

$$\vec{v} \times \vec{B} = [0 - 0]\hat{i} + [(2400)(.2) - 0]\hat{j} + [0 - (-1800)(.2)]\hat{k}$$

$$\vec{v} \times \vec{B} = 480(+\hat{j}) + 360(+\hat{k})$$

$$|\vec{v} \times \vec{B}| = \sqrt{(480)^2 + (360)^2} = 600$$

$$\vec{v} \times \vec{B} = 600\left[\frac{480}{600}(+\hat{j}) + \frac{360}{600}(+\hat{k})\right] = 600[.8(+\hat{j}) + .6(+\hat{k})]$$

$$\vec{F}_{mag} = q(\vec{v} \times \vec{B}) = (+4 \times 10^{-6})(600)[.8(+\hat{j}) + .6(+\hat{k})]\ N$$

$$\vec{F}_{mag} = .0024\ N\ [.8(+\hat{j}) + .6(+\hat{k})]$$

Quiz 8.5

A

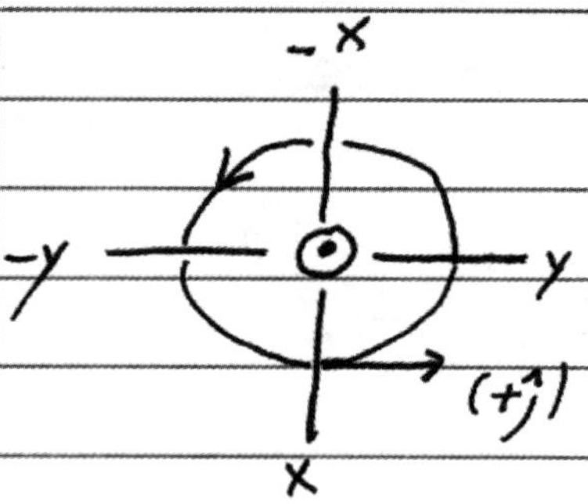

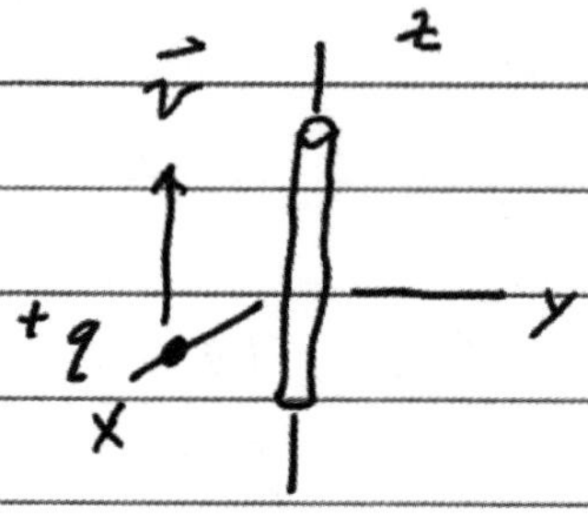

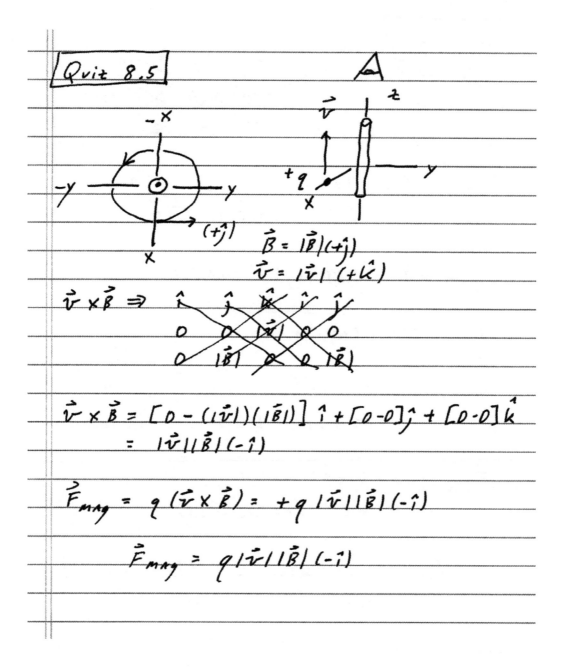

$\vec{B} = |\vec{B}|(+\hat{j})$

$\vec{v} = |\vec{v}|\,(+\hat{k})$

$$\vec{v} \times \vec{B} \Rightarrow \begin{array}{ccccc} \hat{i} & \hat{j} & \hat{k} & \hat{i} & \hat{j} \\ 0 & 0 & |\vec{v}| & 0 & 0 \\ 0 & |\vec{B}| & 0 & 0 & |\vec{B}| \end{array}$$

$$\vec{v} \times \vec{B} = [0 - (|\vec{v}|)(|\vec{B}|)]\,\hat{i} + [0-0]\,\hat{j} + [0-0]\,\hat{k}$$
$$= |\vec{v}||\vec{B}|(-\hat{i})$$

$$\vec{F}_{mag} = q\,(\vec{v} \times \vec{B}) = +q\,|\vec{v}||\vec{B}|(-\hat{i})$$

$$\vec{F}_{mag} = q|\vec{v}||\vec{B}|\,(-\hat{i})$$

Quiz 8.5 continued

q is moving with the +'s and against the −'s

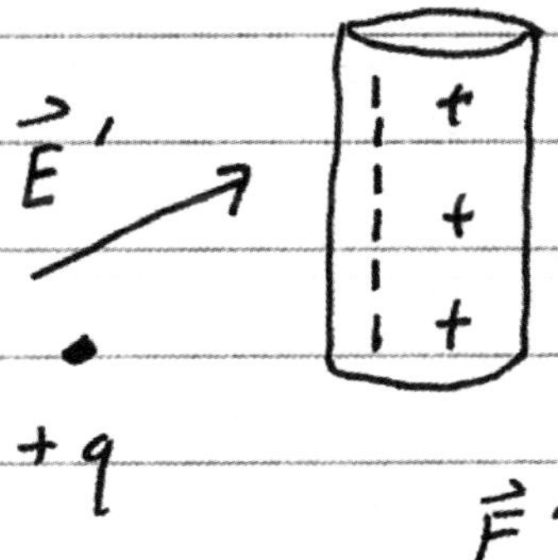

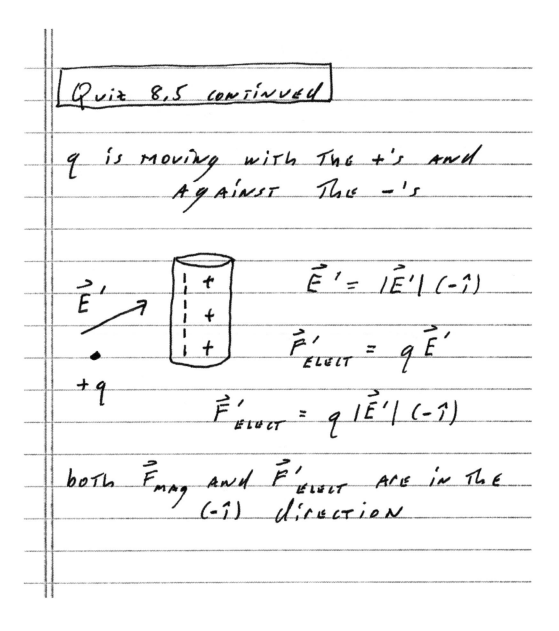

$$\vec{E}' = |\vec{E}'|(-\hat{\imath})$$

$$\vec{F}'_{ELECT} = q\vec{E}'$$

$$\vec{F}'_{ELECT} = q|\vec{E}'|(-\hat{\imath})$$

both $\vec{F}_{MAG}$ and $\vec{F}'_{ELECT}$ are in the $(-\hat{\imath})$ direction

Quiz 9.1 $|\vec{F}| = G\left(\frac{M_1 M_2}{r^2}\right)$

$$|\vec{F}| = 6.673 \times 10^{-11}\left[\frac{(9.11\times10^{-31})(9.11\times10^{-31})}{(1\times10^{-9})^2}\right] N$$

$$|\vec{F}|_{grav} \approx 5.5381 \times 10^{-53}\ N$$

$$|\vec{F}|_{ELECT} = \frac{1}{4\pi\epsilon_0}\left[\frac{q_1 q_2}{|\vec{r}|^2}\right]$$

$$= \frac{1}{4\pi(8.85\times10^{-12})}\left[\frac{(-1.6\times10^{-19})(-1.6\times10^{-19})}{(1\times10^{-9})^2}\right] N$$

$$|\vec{F}|_{ELECT} \approx 2.3019\times10^{-10}\ N$$

$$x\,|\vec{F}|_{grav} = |\vec{F}|_{ELECT} \Rightarrow x = \frac{|\vec{F}|_{ELECT}}{|\vec{F}|_{grav}}$$

$$x \approx \frac{2.3019\times10^{-10}\ N}{5.5381\times10^{-53}\ N}$$

$$x \approx 4.1565\times10^{42}$$

The electric force is about 4×10^{42} times stronger than the gravitational force!

Quiz 9.2

$$\vec{g}_{earth} = G\left(\frac{M_{earth}}{r_{earth}^2}\right)(-\hat{r})$$

$$\approx 6.673\times10^{-11}\left[\frac{5.974\times10^{24}}{(6.37\times10^{6})^2}\right](-\hat{r})$$

$$\vec{g}_{earth} \approx 9.82\ \frac{m}{s^2}(-\hat{r})$$

UNITS

$$\frac{\left(\frac{Nm^2}{kg^2}\right)(kg)}{m^2}$$

$$\left(\frac{Nm^2}{kg^2}\right)\left(\frac{kg}{m^2}\right) \Rightarrow \frac{N}{kg}$$

$$\left(\frac{kg\,m}{s^2}\right)\left(\frac{1}{kg}\right) \Rightarrow \frac{m}{s^2}$$ ✓

Quiz 9.3

$$X_{big} = 4x$$

$$\Delta X_{big} = X_{big\,2} - X_{big\,1}$$

$$= 4x_2 - 4x_1 = 4(x_2 - x_1)$$

$$\Delta X_{big} = 4(\Delta x)$$

$$y_{big} = 3y$$

$$\Delta y_{big} = y_{big\,2} - y_{big\,1}$$

$$= 3y_2 - 3y_1 = 3(y_2 - y_1)$$

$$\Delta y_{big} = 3(\Delta y)$$

$$(\Delta L_{big})^2 = (\Delta X_{big})^2 + (\Delta y_{big})^2$$

$$= [4(\Delta x)]^2 + [3(\Delta y)]^2$$

$$(\Delta L_{big})^2 = 16(\Delta x)^2 + 9(\Delta y)^2$$

Quiz 9.4

$$d\tau_{Jupiter} = d\tau\sqrt{1 - \frac{2GM_{Jup}}{(r_{Jup})c^2}}$$

$$\frac{2GM_{Jup}}{(r_{Jup})c^2} \approx \frac{2(6.673\times10^{-11})(1.9\times10^{27})}{(7.1\times10^{7})(3\times10^{8})^2}$$

UNITS

$$\frac{\left(\frac{Nm^2}{kg^2}\right)(kg)}{m\left(\frac{m}{s}\right)^2} \Rightarrow \left(\frac{Nm^2}{kg}\right)\left(\frac{s^2}{m^3}\right)$$

$$\Rightarrow \left(\frac{kg\,m}{s^2}\right)\left(\frac{1}{kg}\right)\left(\frac{s^2}{m}\right)$$

$\Rightarrow$ NO UNITS

$$d\tau_{Jup} \approx d\tau\sqrt{1 - 3.968\times10^{-8}}$$
$$\approx d\tau\,(1 - 3.968\times10^{-8})^{\frac{1}{2}}$$
$$\approx d\tau\left[1 - \tfrac{1}{2}(3.968\times10^{-8})\right]$$
$$\approx d\tau\left[1 - 1.98\times10^{-8}\right]$$

$$d\tau_{Jup} \approx 86{,}400\text{ s}\left[1 - 1.98\times10^{-8}\right]$$
$$\approx 86{,}400\text{ secs} - .0017\text{ sec}$$

About .0017 seconds slow per DAY

Quiz 9.5

$$C = 2\pi r_{sch}$$

$$C = 2\pi \left(\frac{2GM}{c^2}\right)$$

$$= 2\pi \left[\frac{2(6.673\times10^{-11})(6\times10^{30})}{(3\times10^{8})^2}\right] m$$

$$C \approx 5.59 \times 10^{4}\ m$$

UNITS

$$\frac{\left(\frac{Nm^2}{kg^2}\right)(kg)}{\left(\frac{m}{s}\right)^2} \Rightarrow \left(\frac{Nm^2}{kg}\right)\left(\frac{s^2}{m^2}\right)$$

$$\Rightarrow \left(\frac{kg\,m}{s^2}\right)\left(\frac{1}{kg}\right)\left(\frac{s^2}{1}\right)$$

$$\Rightarrow m \checkmark$$

Note: A balloon with $C \approx 5.59\times10^{4}\ m$ would be about 11 miles in diameter.

Quiz 10.1

$$E_{photon} = hf$$

$$f = \frac{E_{photon}}{h} = \frac{4.32 \times 10^{-19} \text{ J}}{6.626 \times 10^{-34} \text{ J} \cdot \text{s}}$$

$$\approx 6.5198 \times 10^{14} \frac{1}{s}$$

$$v = \lambda f = c \quad \Rightarrow \quad \lambda = \frac{c}{f}$$

$$\lambda = \frac{3 \times 10^{8} \frac{m}{s}}{6.5198 \times 10^{14} \frac{1}{s}}$$

$$\lambda \approx 4.60 \times 10^{-7} \left(\frac{m}{s}\right)\left(\frac{s}{1}\right)$$

$$\lambda \approx 460 \text{ nm}$$

Quiz 10.2

$$E = nhf$$

$$E = (2 \times 10^{32})(6.626 \times 10^{-34}\ \text{J} \cdot \cancel{\text{s}})(20\ \tfrac{1}{\cancel{\text{s}}})$$

$$E \approx 2.65\ \text{J}$$

Quiz 10.3

$$\bar{\Lambda}_{mom} = \begin{bmatrix} \frac{nh}{2L} & 0 \\ 0 & -\frac{nh}{2L} \end{bmatrix}$$

$$\begin{bmatrix} \frac{nh}{2L} - \lambda & 0 \\ 0 & -\frac{nh}{2L} - \lambda \end{bmatrix}$$

$$\left(\frac{nh}{2L} - \lambda\right)\left(-\frac{nh}{2L} - \lambda\right) - (0)(0) = 0$$

$$\begin{array}{l} \frac{nh}{2L} - \lambda \\ -\frac{nh}{2L} - \lambda \\ \hline -\left(\frac{nh}{2L}\right)^2 + \left(\frac{nh}{2L}\right)\lambda \\ \qquad\qquad - \left(\frac{nh}{2L}\right)\lambda + \lambda^2 \\ \hline -\left(\frac{nh}{2L}\right)^2 + \lambda^2 \end{array}$$

$$-\left(\frac{nh}{2L}\right)^2 + \lambda^2 = 0$$

$$\lambda^2 = \left(\frac{nh}{2L}\right)^2$$

$$\lambda = \pm \left(\frac{nh}{2L}\right)$$

$$\lambda_1 = p_1 = \frac{nh}{2L}$$

$$\lambda_2 = p_2 = -\frac{nh}{2L}$$

Quiz 10.4

For $\lambda_1 = \frac{nh}{2L} = p_1$

$$\begin{bmatrix} \frac{nh}{2L} & 0 \\ 0 & -\frac{nh}{2L} \end{bmatrix} \begin{bmatrix} A \\ B \end{bmatrix} = \frac{nh}{2L} \begin{bmatrix} A \\ B \end{bmatrix}$$

$$\left(\frac{nh}{2L}\right) A + (0) B = \left(\frac{nh}{2L}\right) A$$

$$\left(\frac{nh}{2L}\right) A = \left(\frac{nh}{2L}\right) A$$

$$A = A \quad \Rightarrow \quad A = 1$$

$$(0) A + \left(-\frac{nh}{2L}\right) B = \left(\frac{nh}{2L}\right) B$$

$$\left(-\frac{nh}{2L}\right) B = \left(\frac{nh}{2L}\right) B$$

$$-B = B \Rightarrow B = 0$$

$$\phi_1 = \begin{bmatrix} 1 \\ 0 \end{bmatrix} \qquad |\phi_1| = \sqrt{(1)^2 + (0)^2} = 1$$

$$\hat{\phi}_1 = \begin{bmatrix} 1 \\ 0 \end{bmatrix}$$

For $\lambda_2 = -\frac{nh}{2L} = p_2$

$$\begin{bmatrix} \frac{nh}{2L} & 0 \\ 0 & -\frac{nh}{2L} \end{bmatrix} \begin{bmatrix} A \\ B \end{bmatrix} = -\frac{nh}{2L} \begin{bmatrix} A \\ B \end{bmatrix}$$

Quiz 10.4 continued

$$\left(\frac{nh}{2L}\right)A + (0)B = \left(-\frac{nh}{2L}\right)A$$

$$A = -A \implies A = 0$$

$$(0)A + \left(-\frac{nh}{2L}\right)B = \left(-\frac{nh}{2L}\right)B$$

$$B = B \implies B = 1$$

$$\phi_2 = \begin{bmatrix} 0 \\ 1 \end{bmatrix} \qquad |\phi_2| = 1 \qquad \hat{\phi}_2 = \begin{bmatrix} 0 \\ 1 \end{bmatrix}$$

check for orthogonality

$$\hat{\phi}_1 \cdot \hat{\phi}_2 \stackrel{?}{=} 0$$

$$\begin{bmatrix} 1 & 0 \end{bmatrix} \begin{bmatrix} 0 \\ 1 \end{bmatrix} = 0 + 0 = 0 \checkmark$$

For $p_1 = \frac{nh}{2L}$ $\qquad \hat{\phi}_1 = \begin{bmatrix} 1 \\ 0 \end{bmatrix}$

For $p_2 = -\frac{nh}{2L}$ $\qquad \hat{\phi}_2 = \begin{bmatrix} 0 \\ 1 \end{bmatrix}$

Quiz 10.5

$$c_1 = \hat{\phi}_1 \cdot \psi = \begin{bmatrix} 1 & 0 \end{bmatrix} \begin{bmatrix} -\frac{i}{\sqrt{2}} \\ \frac{i}{\sqrt{2}} \end{bmatrix} = -\frac{i}{\sqrt{2}}$$

$$c_2 = \hat{\phi}_2 \cdot \psi = \begin{bmatrix} 0 & 1 \end{bmatrix} \begin{bmatrix} -\frac{i}{\sqrt{2}} \\ \frac{i}{\sqrt{2}} \end{bmatrix} = \frac{i}{\sqrt{2}}$$

$$\psi = \begin{bmatrix} -\frac{i}{\sqrt{2}} \\ \frac{i}{\sqrt{2}} \end{bmatrix} = -\frac{i}{\sqrt{2}} \begin{bmatrix} 1 \\ 0 \end{bmatrix} + \frac{i}{\sqrt{2}} \begin{bmatrix} 0 \\ 1 \end{bmatrix}$$

$$|c_1|^2 = c_1^* c_1 = \left[-\frac{(-i)}{\sqrt{2}} \right] \left(-\frac{i}{\sqrt{2}} \right) = \frac{-i^2}{2} = \frac{-(-1)}{2} = \frac{1}{2}$$

$$|c_2|^2 = c_2^* c_2 = \left(\frac{-i}{\sqrt{2}} \right) \left(\frac{i}{\sqrt{2}} \right) = \frac{-i^2}{2} = \frac{1}{2}$$

$$P\left(p_1 = \frac{nh}{2L}\right) = \frac{1}{2}$$

$$P\left(p_2 = -\frac{nh}{2L}\right) = \frac{1}{2}$$

so it is 50-50 that the particle is moving to the right or to the left

Quiz 11.1

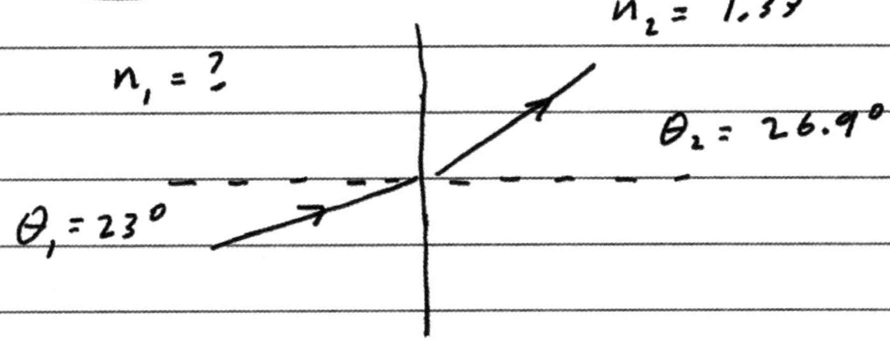

$$n_1 \sin\theta_1 = n_2 \sin\theta_2$$

$$n_1 = n_2 \left[\frac{\sin\theta_2}{\sin\theta_1}\right]$$

$$n_1 = 1.33 \left[\frac{\sin(26.9^\circ)}{\sin(23^\circ)}\right]$$

$$n_1 \approx 1.54$$

$$v = \frac{c}{n} = \frac{3\times10^8 \ \frac{m}{s}}{1.54}$$

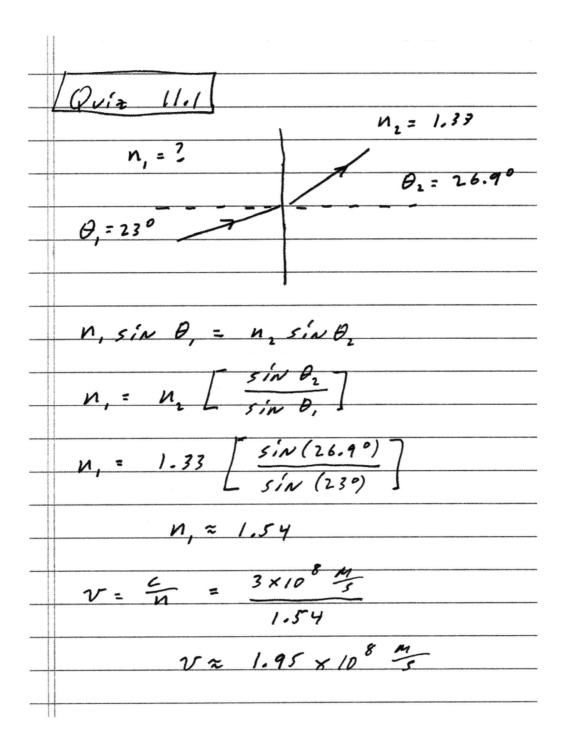

$$v \approx 1.95\times10^8 \ \frac{m}{s}$$

Quiz 11.2

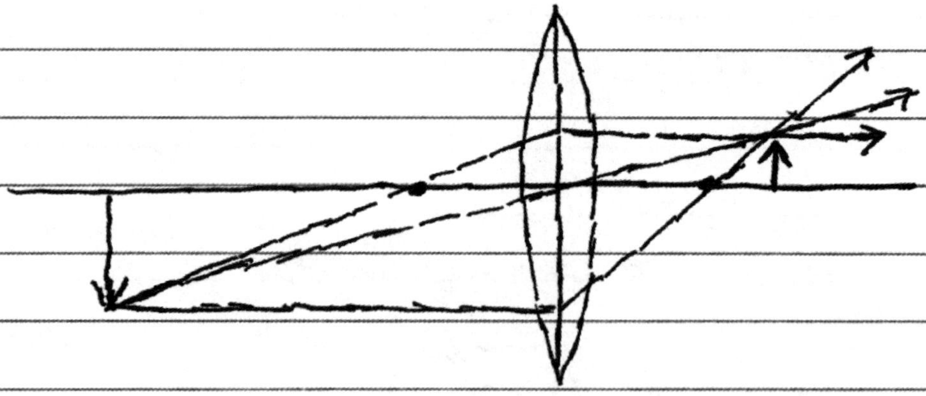

The image is smaller
inverted

Quiz 11.3

$$I = \frac{c}{2\mu_0} |\vec{B}_{MAX}|^2$$

$$2\mu_0 I = c\,|\vec{B}_{MAX}|^2$$

$$|\vec{B}_{MAX}| = \sqrt{\frac{2\mu_0 I}{c}}$$

UNITS

$$\sqrt{\frac{\left(\frac{N}{A^2}\right)\left(\frac{W}{m^2}\right)}{\frac{m}{s}}} \Rightarrow \sqrt{\left(\frac{\cancel{s}}{m}\right)\left(\frac{N}{A^2}\right)\left(\frac{J}{\cancel{s}\,m^2}\right)}$$

$$\sqrt{\left(\frac{N}{\cancel{m}A^2}\right)\left(\frac{N\cancel{m}}{m^2}\right)} \rightarrow \sqrt{\frac{N^2}{A^2 m^2}}$$

$$\frac{N}{Am} \rightarrow T \checkmark$$

Quiz 11.4

$$\left(1.4\ \frac{kW}{m^2}\right)\left(\frac{1000\ W}{kW}\right) = 1400\ \frac{W}{m^2}$$

$$I = \frac{1}{2}\varepsilon_0 c\,|\vec{E}_{MAX}|^2$$

$$|\vec{E}_{MAX}| = \sqrt{\frac{2I}{\varepsilon_0 c}}$$

<u>UNITS</u>

$$\sqrt{\frac{\frac{W}{m^2}}{\left(\frac{C^2}{Nm^2}\right)\left(\frac{m}{s}\right)}} \Rightarrow \sqrt{\frac{N\cancel{m^2}sW}{\cancel{m^2}C^2 m}}$$

$$\sqrt{\frac{N\cancel{s}\left(\frac{J}{\cancel{s}}\right)}{C^2 m}} \Rightarrow \sqrt{\frac{N(N\cancel{m})}{C^2\cancel{m}}} \Rightarrow \sqrt{\frac{N^2}{C^2}}$$

$$|\vec{E}_{MAX}| = \sqrt{\frac{2(1400)}{(8.85\times10^{-12})(3\times10^8)}}\ \frac{N}{C}$$

$$|\vec{E}_{MAX}| \approx 1027\ N/C$$

yellow light $\approx$ 575 nm

Quiz 11.4 continued

$v = \lambda f \qquad 2\pi f = \omega \qquad v = \lambda \left(\frac{\omega}{2\pi}\right)$

$2\pi v = \lambda \omega$

$\omega = \frac{2\pi v}{\lambda}$

Units

$\frac{\text{rad}\left(\frac{m}{s}\right)}{m} \Rightarrow \frac{\text{rad}}{s}$ ✓

$\omega = \frac{(2\pi)(3\times10^{8})}{575\times10^{-9}}\ \frac{\text{rad}}{s} \approx 3.28\times10^{15}\ \frac{\text{rad}}{s}$

$k = \frac{2\pi}{\lambda} = \frac{2\pi}{575\times10^{-9}}\ \frac{\text{rad}}{m} \approx 1.09\times10^{7}\ \frac{\text{rad}}{m}$

$|\vec{E}| = \left|\, |\vec{E}_{max}| \sin(kx - \omega t) \right|$

$|\vec{E}| \approx \left| \left(1027\ \frac{N}{C}\right) \sin\left[(1.09\times10^{7})x - (3.28\times10^{15})t\right] \right|$

Quiz 11.5

$$(KE)_{MAX} = hf - \phi$$

$$0 = hf_{\substack{CUT\\OFF}} - \phi \Rightarrow \phi = hf_{\substack{CUT\\OFF}}$$

$$f_{\substack{CUT\\OFF}} = \frac{\phi}{h}$$

$$\phi = \left(\frac{1.91\,eV}{1}\right)\left(\frac{1.6\times10^{-19}\,J}{eV}\right) = 3.056\times10^{-19}\,J$$

$$f_{\substack{CUT\\OFF}} = \frac{3.056\times10^{-19}\,J}{6.626\times10^{-34}\,J\cdot s} \approx 4.61\times10^{14}\,\frac{1}{s}$$

$$f_{\substack{CUT\\OFF}} \approx 4.61\times10^{14}\,Hz$$

Quiz 12.1

$$\sum \tau_{ccw} = \sum \tau_{cw}$$

$$F_1 d_1 = F_2 d_2$$

$$F_1 d_1 = m g d_2$$

$$F(.4\,m) = (.8\,kg)(9.8\,\tfrac{m}{s^2})(.7\,m)$$

$$F = \frac{(.8)(9.8)(.7)}{(.4)}\ \frac{kg\,m}{s^2}$$

$$F = 13.72\ N$$

Quiz 12.2

$$\vec{r} = [\,.3(+\hat{j}) + .4(+\hat{k})\,]\ \text{m}$$

$$\vec{F} = [\,35(-\hat{j}) + 7(+\hat{k})\,]\ \text{N}$$

$$\vec{r} \times \vec{F} \implies \begin{matrix} \hat{i} & \hat{j} & \hat{k} & \hat{i} & \hat{j} \\ 0 & .3 & .4 & 0 & .3 \\ 0 & -35 & 7 & 0 & -35 \end{matrix}$$

$$\vec{r} \times \vec{F} = [\,(.3)(7) - (.4)(-35)\,]\,\hat{i} + [0 - 0]\,\hat{j} + [0 - 0]\,\hat{k}$$

$$= [\,2.1 - (-14)\,]\,\hat{i}$$

$$\vec{\tau} = 16.1\ \text{mN}\ (+\hat{i})$$

Quiz 12.3

$$|\vec{v}| = \sqrt{(4)^2 + (3)^2}\ \tfrac{m}{s} = 5\ \tfrac{m}{s}$$

$$|\vec{r}| = \sqrt{(.3)^2 + (.4)^2}\ m = .5\ m$$

From Figure 12.8 $\Rightarrow$ $\vec{r} = .5\ m\ (+\hat{i})$

$\vec{v} = 5\ \tfrac{m}{s}\ (+\hat{j})$

$$\vec{p} = m\vec{v}$$

$$= (.38\ kg)(5\ \tfrac{m}{s})(+\hat{j})$$

$$\vec{p} = 1.9\ \tfrac{kg\,m}{s}\ (+\hat{j})$$

$$\vec{L} = \vec{r} \times \vec{p}$$

$$\vec{r} \times \vec{p} \Rightarrow \begin{array}{ccccc} \hat{i} & \hat{j} & \hat{k} & \hat{i} & \hat{j} \\ .5 & 0 & 0 & .5 & 0 \\ 0 & 1.9 & 0 & 0 & 1.9 \end{array}$$

$$\vec{r} \times \vec{p} = [0 - 0]\hat{i} + [0 - 0]\hat{j} + [(.5)(1.9) - 0]\hat{k}$$

$$\vec{L} = .95\ \tfrac{kg\,m^2}{s}\ (+\hat{k})$$

Quiz 12.4

$$r_1 v_1 = r_2 v_2$$

$$(.18\,m)(21\,\tfrac{m}{s}) = r_2\,(14\,\tfrac{m}{s})$$

$$r_2 = \frac{(.18\,m)(21\,\tfrac{m}{s})}{14\,\tfrac{m}{s}}$$

$$r_2 = .27\,m$$

check: $(.18)(21) \stackrel{?}{=} (.27)(14)$

$$3.78 = 3.78\ \checkmark$$

Quiz 12.5

$$v = v$$

$$\sqrt{\frac{e^2}{m_e (4\pi \varepsilon_0) r}} = \frac{n\hbar}{m_e r}$$

$$\frac{e^2}{m_e (4\pi \varepsilon_0) r} = \frac{n^2 \hbar^2}{m_e^2 r^2}$$

$$e^2 m_e r = n^2 \hbar^2 (4\pi \varepsilon_0)$$

$$r = \frac{n^2 \hbar^2 (4\pi \varepsilon_0)}{e^2 m_e}$$

Answers to odd numbered Homework Problems

1.1

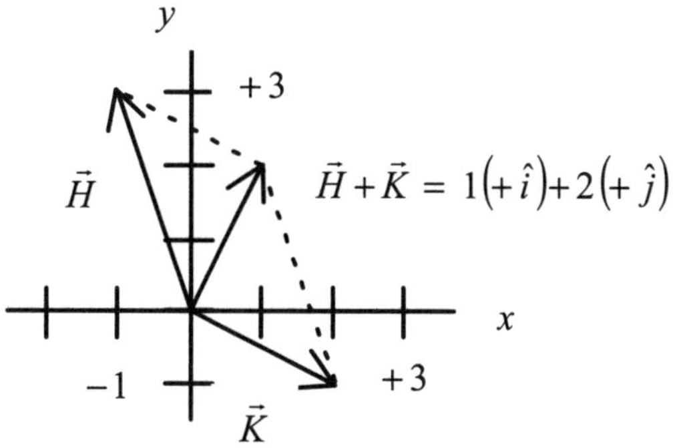

1.3 $\dfrac{\vec{r}}{|\vec{r}|} = \dfrac{9}{\sqrt{85}}(+\hat{i}) + \dfrac{2}{\sqrt{85}}(-\hat{j})$

1.5 $\vec{B} \bullet \vec{A} = -12, \quad \vec{A} \bullet \vec{B} = -12, \quad |\vec{B}|^2 = 5$

1.7 $\Psi_1 = 3+i, \quad \Psi_2 = 3-i, \quad |\Psi_1| = \sqrt{10}$

1.9 $x = 8$

1.11 $10 = 10$; Yes

1.13 $1000m \approx .621mi$

1.15 $1\ rad \approx 57.29578^o \Rightarrow 57.30^o$
$\sin(1\ rad) \approx .84147, \qquad \sin(57.30^o) \approx .84151$
The answers are different because the angle in degrees was rounded to 2 decimal places.

2.1 $\vec{F}_3 = [8(-\hat{i})+5(-\hat{j})]N$

2.3 $\vec{a} \approx 4.52\dfrac{m}{s^2}\left[\dfrac{6}{\sqrt{40}}(+\hat{i}) + \dfrac{2}{\sqrt{40}}(+\hat{j})\right]$

2.5 $|\vec{g}| = 8.8\ \dfrac{m}{s^2} \quad \therefore\ Venus$

2.7 T = 1935 N

2.9 $\vec{a} \approx .63 \frac{m}{s^2} \left(-\hat{i}\right)$

3.1 $m_2 = 4.5\ kg$

3.3 $g_m \approx 1.62\ \frac{m}{s^2}$

3.5 $v_2 \approx 24.41\ \frac{m}{s}$

3.7 $h_2 = 1.5\ m$

3.9 $Work = 512\ J$

4.1 $\text{T} = -459.67\ ^oF$

4.3 $P_{new} = 2.5 P_{old}$

4.5 $m_{Silver} \approx .344\ kg$

4.7 $\text{W} = 720\ J$ (since 2 cycles)

4.9 $\Delta U = -50\ J$, so internal energy goes down

5.1 $\Delta t \approx 2$ sec

5.3 $\Delta t = 3$ sec

5.5 $r = .25\ m$

5.7 $y = .04 \sin\left[(10\pi)x - (120\pi)\,t\right]\ m$

5.9 $y\ \Big|_{\substack{x=4.6\ m \\ t=24\ s}} \approx .018\ m$

6.1 $\vec{F}_{12} \approx .270\ N \left[\frac{4}{\sqrt{17}}\left(+\hat{i}\right) + \frac{1}{\sqrt{17}}\left(+\hat{j}\right)\right]$

6.3 $\vec{E} = \frac{1}{4\pi\varepsilon_o}\left[\frac{+|q|}{\left(\sqrt{x^2+y^2}\right)^2}\right]\left[\frac{x}{\sqrt{x^2+y^2}}(+\hat{i}) + \frac{y}{\sqrt{x^2+y^2}}(+\hat{j})\right]$

6.5 $\vec{E}_{total} \approx 1611.36\,\frac{N}{C}\,(+\hat{j})$

6.7 $\vec{F} \approx .0013\ N\,(+\hat{j})$

6.9 a) $V = 10\ V$ b) $V = 10\ V$ These answers are the same because the voltage from point 1 to point 2 does not depend on the path that you take to get from 1 to 2.

7.1 a) Galileo: $v_1^{'} = 1.98\ c$

b) Einstein: $v_1^{'} \approx .99995\ c$

7.3 $\Delta t_s = 36$ sec

7.5 $L_o \approx 83.14\ m$

7.7 a) $E \approx 3.28 \times 10^{18}\ J$

b) $E = 2.34 \times 10^{18}\ J$

7.9 particle frame: $(S_t^{'})^2 = 576\ m^2$

rest frame: $(S_t)^2 = 576\ m^2$

8.1 $R = 90\ \Omega$

8.3 $\vec{B} = 1 \times 10^{-6}\,(-\hat{k})\ T$

8.5 $\vec{H} \times \vec{K} = 6(-\hat{i}) + 1(+\hat{j}) + 15(-\hat{k})$

8.7 $\vec{F}_{mag} = .00288\ N\,(-\hat{k})$

8.9 Both $\vec{F}_{mag}$ and $\vec{F}^{'}_{elect}$ are in the $(+\hat{j})$ direction.

9.1 $|\vec{F}| \approx 3.6 \times 10^{22}\ N$

9.3 $\vec{g}_{Mars} \approx 3.64 \frac{m}{s^2}(-\hat{r})$

9.5 $\Delta L_{sq} \approx 16.43$

9.7 $dt_{star} \approx 7.78\ days$

9.9 $m \approx 8.37 \times 10^{25}\ kg$

10.1 $E \approx 3.82 \times 10^{-19}\ J$

10.3 $n \approx 2.14 \times 10^{32}$

10.5 $\lambda_1 = 6 \qquad \lambda_2 = -7$

10.7 $\hat{\Phi}_1 = \begin{bmatrix} 3/\sqrt{13} \\ 2/\sqrt{13} \end{bmatrix} \qquad \hat{\Phi}_2 = \begin{bmatrix} 2/\sqrt{13} \\ -3/\sqrt{13} \end{bmatrix}$

10.8 $\hat{\Phi}_1 = \begin{bmatrix} 1/\sqrt{2} \\ i/\sqrt{2} \end{bmatrix} \qquad \hat{\Phi}_2 = \begin{bmatrix} 1/\sqrt{2} \\ -i/\sqrt{2} \end{bmatrix}$

10.9 $P(\lambda = 6) = \frac{4}{13} \qquad P(\lambda = -7) = \frac{9}{13}$

11.1 $\theta_2 \approx 36.2^o$

11.3

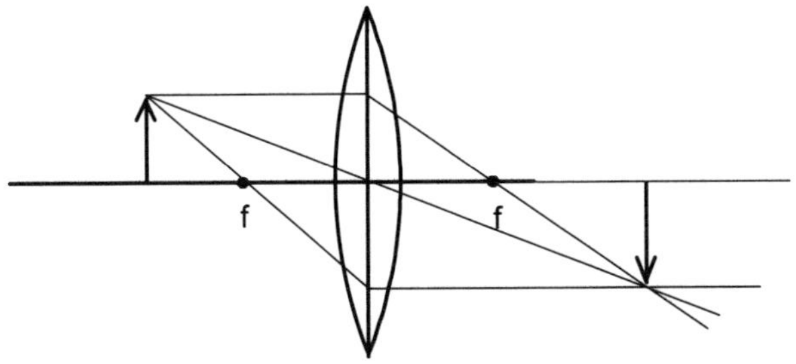

The image is inverted and larger.

11.5 $\quad I = I \quad \rightarrow \quad \frac{1}{2}\varepsilon_o c\left|\vec{E}_{\max}\right|^2 = \frac{1}{2}\frac{c}{\mu_o}\left|\vec{B}_{\max}\right|^2$

$$\varepsilon_o\left[c\left|\vec{B}_{\max}\right|\right]^2 = \frac{1}{\mu_o}\left|\vec{B}_{\max}\right|^2$$

$$c = \frac{1}{\sqrt{\varepsilon_o \mu_o}}$$

11.7 $\quad \left|\vec{B}\right| = \left|1.94{\times}10^{-6}\, T\left\{\sin\left[\left(1.21\times 10^{7}\right)x - \left(3.62\times 10^{15}\right)t\right]\right\}\right|$

11.9 $\quad v_{\max} \approx 1.43\times 10^{5}\,\frac{m}{s}$

12.1 $\quad m = .8\ kg$

12.3 $\quad \vec{\tau} = 8\sqrt{2}\ m N\left[\frac{1}{\sqrt{2}}\left(-\hat{i}\right) + \frac{1}{\sqrt{2}}\left(+\hat{j}\right)\right]$

12.5 $\quad \vec{L} = .95\,\frac{kg\, m^2}{s}\left(+\hat{k}\right)$

12.7 $\quad v_2 = 10\,\frac{m}{s}$

12.9 $$\frac{(J\,s)^2\left(\dfrac{C^2}{N\,m^2}\right)}{kg\,C^2} \rightarrow \left[\frac{(N\,m\,s)^2\,C^2}{N\,m^2}\right]\left(\frac{1}{kg\,C^2}\right)$$

$$\rightarrow \frac{N^2 m^2 s^2}{kg\,N\,m^2} \rightarrow \frac{N\,s^2}{kg} \rightarrow \left(\frac{kg\,m}{s^2}\right)\left(\frac{s^2}{kg}\right)$$

$$\rightarrow m$$

Main Occurrence Text Index

Units

Acceleration $\rightarrow \frac{m}{s^2}$

Angular momentum $\rightarrow \frac{kg\, m^2}{s}$

Charge $\rightarrow C$

Coefficient kinetic friction $\rightarrow$ *no units*

Coefficient static friction $\rightarrow$ *no units*

Current $\rightarrow A = \frac{C}{s}$

Electric field $\rightarrow \frac{N}{C}$

Electric potential difference $\rightarrow V = \frac{J}{C}$

Energy $\rightarrow J = N\, m$

Force $\rightarrow N = \frac{kg\, m}{s^2}$

Frequency $\rightarrow H_z = \frac{1}{s}$

Heat $\rightarrow J = N\, m$

Intensity $\rightarrow \frac{W}{m^2}$

Internal energy $\rightarrow J = N\, m$

Kinetic Energy $\rightarrow J = N\, m$

Magnetic Field $\rightarrow T = \frac{N}{A\, m}$

Mass $\rightarrow kg$

Momentum $\rightarrow \frac{kg\, m}{s}$

Period $\rightarrow s$

Permeability $\rightarrow \frac{N}{A^2}$

Permittivity $\rightarrow \frac{C^2}{N\, m^2}$

Planck's constant $\rightarrow J \cdot s$

Power $\rightarrow W = \frac{J}{s}$

Pressure $\rightarrow Pa = \frac{N}{m^2}$

Radian frequency $\rightarrow \frac{rad}{s}$

Resistance $\rightarrow \Omega = \frac{V}{A}$

Spacetime interval $\rightarrow m$

Specific heat $\rightarrow \frac{J}{kg\, K}$

Speed $\rightarrow \frac{m}{s}$

Temperature $\rightarrow K$

Tension $\rightarrow N$

Torque $\rightarrow m\, N$

Universal Gravitation Constant $\rightarrow \frac{N\, m^2}{kg^2}$

Velocity $\rightarrow \frac{m}{s}$

Voltage $\rightarrow V = \frac{J}{C}$

Weight $\rightarrow N$

Work $\rightarrow J$

Work function $\rightarrow J$